# BARBECUING & SAUSAGE-MAKING
# SECRETS

By Charlie & Ruthie Knote

Dedicated to "food-panicked" Americans
and to the remaining
disgusted, confused Americans
who'll appreciate its
"FOOD TRUTHS".
_SECRETS'_ safe, delicious barbecue,
lean sausages and 300 easy, flavorful
recipes make eating food fun again!

Published by
The Culinary Institute of Smoke-Cooking
2323 Brookwood • Box 163 • Cape Girardeau, MO 63702-0163

Published by
## The Culinary Institute of Smoke-Cooking
## 2323 Brookwood • Box 163
## Cape Girardeau, MO 62702-0163

Additional copies may be obtained from the publisher at the cost of $14.95 per book, plus $2.50 postage and handling. Missouri residents add 6.125% sales tax.

This cookbook is available at special quantity discounts for bulk purchases for sales promotion, premiums, fund raising or educational use. Special excerpts can also be created. Write the publisher.

This book includes the finest plastic ring binders available, BUT, like most plastics, the BINDERS CAN BE DAMAGED BY EXCESSIVE HEAT. Avoid exposing them to the direct rays of the SUN or excessive heat such as IN A CAR on a hot day, on top of the kitchen STOVE or next to a BABECUE GRILL.

Library of Congress Cataloging in Publication Data
Knote, Charles E.; Knote, Ruth R.
    "Barbecuing & Sausage-Making Secrets"

Includes index
1. Barbecuing  2. Sausage-making  3. Buying meat, poultry, fish

Library of Congress No. 92-070046
ISBN No. 0-9632082-0-9

Cover and food design by Teresa Hampton
Cover photo by Robertson's Creative Photography
Illustrations by Teresa Hampton

# WE AUTHORS THANK:

NANCY WIBBENMEYER FENWICK: Our lady and friend behind our MAC Computer for 100's of hours of faithful help.

TERESA HAMPTON: Who stretched our imaginations and produced excellent illustrations.

DR. MAX JUDGE, CAROLYN WELLS, and MIKE MILLS: Who's technical guidance and inspiration gave us more confidence.

JOHN BLUE: Whose editing raised the level of our writing.

PAT ZELLMER: Who encouraged and helped us get "things" done.

TECHNICAL EDITORS; THREE SPECIAL ONES: Wynn Bellerjeau, Bill Miller, Hugh Walker, Jr, PLUS: Ernie Beutenmiller, Sr., Karen Boillot, Dave Combelle, Robin Ganse, Don Gillis, Ann Goodnight, Mary Johnson, Paul Kirk, Robin Kline, Danny Lewis, Pat Murphy, Kay Mogusar, Susie Oberdahloff, Kneibert Stillman, Jim Tabb, Wei Chan Tan, John Willingham, and Jim Wulfers.

WRITING EDITORS: Dr. Jake Gaskins, Susan Hekmat, Ken Heischmidt, Ruthie Knote, Jr., Charlotte Malahy, Beth Meyer, Barbara Barklage, Mary Blue, Lela Boldrey.

TYPISTS: Beth Meyer, Jackie Tan, Bill Zellmer, Jr., Shelly Barks.

SPECIAL HELP WITH RECIPES: Miriam Bechtol, Mary Blue, Lela Boldry, Ricki Brasington, Nita Endicott, Nancy Knote Evenden, Robert Evenden, Teresa Hampton, Barbara Knote Head, John Head, Alice Hecht, Cindy Heischmidt, Edna Herron, Ann Lamkin Kinder, Miriam Klimstra, Elizabeth Ann Knote, Margaret Hill Knote, Mary Coble Knote, Patricia Jane Knote, Richard Charles Knote, Ruth Whipple Knote, Charlotte Malahy, Sue McHaney, Dottie Osmun, Judy Rueseler, Hugh Walker, Jr., John Walker, III.

# WARNING — DISCLAIMER

This cookbook is designed to provide information regarding the subject matter covered. It is sold with the understanding that the publisher and authors are not rendering professional cooking or sausage making advice and service. If expert assistance is needed, the services of a competent professional should be sought.

The reader is urged to learn as much as possible about barbecuing, smoke cooking, sausage making and home cooking to fit his/her individual needs.

The use of these recipes and techniques does not guarantee success. Every effort has been made to make this cookbook as accurate as possible. However, there may be mistakes, both typographical and in contents. This cookbook is not the ultimate source on barbecuing and sausage making procedures, techniques, and systems.

The Culinary Institute of Smoke Cooking and the authors shall have neither liability nor responsibility for failure of the recipes nor injury while preparing them.

If you do not wish to be bound by the above, you may return this book to the publisher for full refund.

# Table of Contents

# "Food Panicked" Americans

### You needn't be one!

## "FOOD-PANICKED" AMERICANS

This unusual cookbook has been written because we found a big American food need. People like more flavorful, zestful, and tastier foods. However, thousands of Americans are "food-panicked" and millions are now afraid of America's food!

"Food-panicked" Americans? — Yes! The Institute of Food Technologists, 25,000 food scientists, tell us that one American in twelve either no longer eats chicken or has greatly reduced the amount they eat. Why? Fear of salmonella! Millions of Americans have stopped eating beef. Why? Fear of cholesterol and saturated fats. Millions of Americans don't eat pork — fear of saturated fats, cholesterol, calories, and trichinosis! One "healthy heart" cookbook writer and lecturer even recommended, "Eat chicken white meat only. Throw away the legs and thighs — too high in fat!"

### Food Truths Don't Support "Panic"

America's FOOD TRUTHS don't support this food panic! To share America's real FOOD TRUTHS easily, we created three fictitious characters: John, a sensible self-trained and self-educated outdoor cook whose wife is "J.J.," a "food-panicked" American. Blossom Do-Rite is J.J.'s close friend who shares her continuous fears about America's foods. They help us keep our food truths alive rather than let them become dry as "old toast."

Many times J.J. and Blossom would tell you, "America's meats will hurt or eventually kill you because they're so unhealthy. If you want to live a longer and happier life, you'd better eat only a little fish, maybe a tiny bit of chicken or turkey. You can eat "tons" of oat bran, plus complex carbohydrates, soluble and insoluble fiber. But you shouldn't eat any red meats with their fats and cholesterol problems." In this cookbook we uncover many food myths and discover America's FOOD TRUTHS.

The authors, not being Einsteins with habits of masterful thinking, nor being skilled in the art of grand composition, nor even able to pronounce the names of some fancy French foods, still felt qualified to write this "down-home" cookbook. We named it *Barbecuing & Sausage Making SECRETS* — SECRETS for short. Barbecue and sausages, good ole American foods, are totally forbidden by some "experts." <u>SECRETS</u> shows people how to unchain themselves safely and eliminate confusion. Besides, eating food should be fun again.

We wrote this cookbook for outdoor cooks, their families and friends who appreciate more zestful meat flavors and having fun together. These people feel that eating tasty, healthy foods is still important — one of the requirements of the good life for Americans.

## Cook-Out's Cooking Problems

In addition to the "food panic," nearly everyone questions what they're buying at the supermarket's meat and fish counters. How tender? How good? How clean? How safe? Many want to know, "How do I cook it outdoors?" "When is it done and not overdone and dried out?" "What outstanding barbecued flavor changes *can* take place?" "How do I successfully create them?"

We can truthfully say, "What we recommend we have tested or created from scratch, and it works and it's tasty! And it's part of today's real food world, and very probably tomorrow's — all of this without fancy nearly-impossible-to-find expensive seasonings. Certainly, <u>SECRETS</u> does not use those "neat" tiny add-on's of the trendy, faddish, "new" cuisines. Maybe this cookbook is a bit old-fashioned, but with a low fat and low calorie approach, it will make eating food fun.

Finally a sign hangs over our desk. "Our writing must eliminate big $10 words and reduce stress for our readers." <u>SECRETS</u> is fun and easy to read without technical jargon. We guarantee <u>SECRETS</u> will help you, the cook-out cook at your house, create flavorful, grilled, smoke-cooked, and barbecued foods. You'll produce cook-out masterpieces that you'll be proud to serve to your family, and friends, and relish yourself.

Dec. 1992: Johns Hopkins Medical News Letter "Health After 50" warns: Keep your cholesterol above 160. Medical research shows that low cholesterol has been associated with increased death rate from cerebral hemorrhage (strokes), lung, liver, and pancreatic cancer. For the best heart disease control, no higher than 200.

THE WIZARD OF ID—By Brant Parker and Johnny Hart

By permission of Johnny Hart and NAS, Inc.

# Why Eat Meats?

They make staying healthy
much easier

## WHY EAT MEATS?

J.J., John's continuously "food-panicked" wife, walked from the kitchen to the TV room where John sat. He was reading the editorial page, not watching TV — it was boring. She said, "John, did you see that story in the weekly news magazine about some folks who have stopped eating meat? Blossom Do-Rite said she has nearly quit eating red meats.

"She said her 14-year-old niece had stopped eating all meats and anything that contained cholesterol. Her niece told her that saturated fats and cholesterol will absolutely kill you! She said her niece occasionally eats yogurt, drinks a little milk, but eats nearly all veggies and fruits, and a little cereal. John, what do you think about that cholesterol and vegetarian stuff?"

John answered, "I don't really know too much about cholesterol. But don't all dairy products have some cholesterol and saturated fat? On the other hand, three big servings of meat every day aren't healthy either."

John, you're right on track. "Overdosing" with meats isn't healthy. Certainly, Blossom's niece is mixed up eating nearly all vegetables. She's not taking good care of herself, and she needs to understand that she's still a growing young woman. She's not a mature 40-year-old Hollywood type trying to stay "thin-as-a-board." Her young body still needs the benefits of meat's easily assimilated iron, calcium, zinc, and B-complex vitamins.

She just heard and saw this slim, very curvy Hollywood star talk about eating nearly all vegetables. It sounded so simple and easy to stay thin. What she didn't see: (1) how hard the Hollywood star exercises, (2) how she uses other special dietetic foods, (3) how she spends most of her time trying to stay thin because she gets paid megabucks to stay thin, and (4) doesn't know that younger women miss their menstrual periods or damage their babies because they eat only vegetables and no meat.

Vegetarians called "vegans" absolutely avoid all meat but are relatively few in number. Most so-called vegetarians still eat animal products, such as the "in-foods" like yogurt and skim milk. Vegetarians spend time finding their special foods. They need trained food nutritionists to help them carefully balance out their diet. People who eat meat or meat products don't need this special training.

Most people are not dedicated to studying foods as thoroughly as a nutritionist. They have other things to do. Therefore, they eat some meats to balance out their diets easily. Nutrients from meats are five times easier for our bodies to absorb than vegetable and cereal nutrients. Also, meats have proven they will *help* all vegetables' nutrients become more usable by our bodies.

## Our Forefathers Told Us

Since the beginning of recorded time, meat has been a symbol of healthy living. The Bible says, "I was hungry and You gave me meat." (Matthew 25:35) The Ancients have written, "A human without meat is a sorry creature." The Apicius' Cookbook, started about 70 B.C. in Ancient Rome, said "A nobleman felt like a social outcast if he didn't offer his guests pork cutlets, pigs' feet and sausages."

Even in the 1980s, the Polish people rioted and chanted, "Give us meat." They had grains, such as bread, and rice, and enough calories to supply their bodies' needs. Why did they riot for meats? They satisfy our appetites better and longer. Regardless of how grains are "flavored-up" to give them a "meaty" taste, they still don't taste exactly like MEAT. Meats add more variety to our diets than any other food group. Many Americans tire quickly of milk-soaked breakfast cereal flakes seven mornings per week.

Even a very large continuously "food-panicked" consumer group admitted, "Bacon for breakfast once a week *might* be alright"! SECRETS recommends common-sense balancing of our diets with the meats, grains (wheat, corn, rice, pasta), vegetables, fruits, and dairy products.

## How Much?

With all the anti-meat furor by the media and some government agencies, you ask how much meat is healthy? The American Heart Association working with food scientists say to fat-trim your meat before cooking. Eat 6 ounces of deboned cooked lean meat, poultry, or fish per day. To help you visualize this — one 3-ounce serving of cooked meat equals the size of a deck of cards or an average-sized woman's hand.

Americans should become aware of their fat consumption. A small woman who sits nearly all day can consume up to 40 grams of fat per day safely. A man doing heavy physical labor or exercises can consume 83 grams of fat per day safely. Today's concern: Americans should not eat a double cheeseburger with "fries" for 2 meals per day 7 days per week.

## Other Food Fats

All our fats in foods don't come from meats despite what some food writers infer. For example: One tablespoon of peanut butter has 8.1 grams; a small slice of pizza has 8 grams; one tablespoon of standard salad dressing 6 up to 9 grams. Compare this with 3 ounces of cooked pork loin only 6.4 grams, and 3 ounces of chuck roast 16.0 grams.

Also, calories come from lots of places including breads, pasta, carbohydrates, sugars, etc. You can be sure that excess calories of any kind "will-still-a-belly-make"!

You should eat meat on a regular basis to stay healthy easier. For that special treat, eating a 12-ounce grilled T-bone steak or grilled lamb chops or two ¾-inch thick pork chops, all fat trimmed, 3 to 4 times per year will not kill you.

Two thoughts ladies may want to remember about meats — "meats reawaken a man's love" and "however fickle a man's heart, his stomach remains constant." Honest, that's what some old timers wrote — probably written by men! However, when we think about some of the girls and women we've known we're positive they had "constant stomachs" also.

By permission of Food Safety Note Book, Eric Isaccsen, and Lydra Associates, Inc.

# Master BBQing & Cooking Temperature Chart in °F and °C

Courtesy of CISC Master BBQ Cook's School, Pages 281-282

| | Farenheit | Centrigrade |
|---|---|---|
| Good home freezer temperature | 0° | -18° |
| Water freezes | 32° | 0° |
| Better refrigerator temperature and lower | 40° | 5° |
| Comfortable room temperature | 65° to 78° | 18° to 25° |
| Cold smoking temperature for flavoring | 85° to 120° | 30° to 49° |
| Warm comfortable water | 115° to 120° | 46° to 49° |
| Meat contracts and begins losing juices | 120° | 49° |
| Very rare beef* and lamb; red, cool center | 130° | 54° |
| Fish turns opaque, flakes | 130° to 135° | 54° to 57° |
| Pork's trichinosis killed | 137° | 58° |
| Rare, but more tender beef* and lamb | 140° | 60° |
| Meat's connective tissues changing to gelatin | 140° | 60° |
| Cooked foods holding temperature | 140° | 60° |
| Protein hardening begins | 145° | 63° |
| E. coli controlled in beef steaks | 145° | 63° |
| Medium rare beef and lamb (pink centers) | 145° to 150° | 63° to 66° |
| Pork cooked done (home barbecuers) | 155° to 160° | 68° to 71° |
| E. coli controlled in hamburgers | 160° | 71° |
| Juices run clear (brown centers) | 160° | 71° |
| Heavy protein hardening | 160° | 71° |
| Medium done meats | 160° | 71° |
| Leftover foods' safe temperature | 165° | 74° |
| Medium well-done meats | 165° | 74° |
| Salmonella controlled | 165° | 74° |
| Poultry cooked done | 165° to 170° | 74° |
| Proteins hardened and shrunken | 170° | 77° |
| Crumbly meats start | 170° | 77° |
| Meat cooked well-done | 170° | 77° |
| Pork cooked done (Barbecue cook-offs) | 170° to 180° | 77 to 82° |
| Overcooked dry, hardened stringy meats | 180° to 185° | 82° to 85° |
| Simmering water -- little bubbles | 190° to 200° | 88 to 93° |
| Meats brown (caramelize) slowly | 200° to 225° | 93° to 107° |
| Boil -- small rolling waves, big bubbles | 212° | 100° |
| Water in juices boil off | 212° | 100° |
| Smoke-cooking and professional barbecuing temperatures | 300° down to 175° | 149° down to 79° |
| Slow grilling or slow oven temperature | 300° | 149° |
| Meats brown (caramelize) rapidly | 315° | 158° |
| Oven temperature for roasting meats | 325° | 163° |
| Moderate grilling or moderate oven temperature | 350° to 375° | 177° to 191° |
| Oven temperatures for baking cakes, vegetables | 350° | 177° |
| Barbecue sauces blacken quickly | 400° | 205° |
| Medium hot oven | 400° to 450° | 205° to 232° |
| Medium hot grilling temperature | 450° to 500° | 232° to 260° |
| Hot grilling temperature | 500° to 550° | 260° to 288° |
| Oven broiler (electric) rack 3" from heat | 550° | 288° |
| Blackening fish temperature of skillet | 800° to 900° | 427° to 482° |

*Beef Steaks: USDA's new safe minimum steak grilling temperature: 145°F.

# Basics of Barbecuing
### Dry Heat Cooking's effects on meat & Meat, Poultry & Fish Doneness Tests

## CREATING COOK-OUT MASTERPIECES

J.J., John's continuously "food-panicked" wife, came home early and mad. She'd been out to her monthly card party this evening. She "hit" the back door and shook John back to reality from his TV baseball game.

Then she started real serious, "John, I've never been so humiliated in my life. Tonight, that Blossom Do-Rite took me to task about my saying you are very good at barbecuing. And do you know how she started? Well, she called the grill at their house her husband's burger crematory. She said, "Regardless of how I want my burger done, it's always black — well-done black and bitter. Everything he grills — well, it's always black'."

"Then she stood there and blowed around about how her daddy was the only real barbecue expert she ever knew. Why? Well, he cooked over a hardwood fire and smoked his meats for a long time at low temperatures."

### Change To Flavorful Barbecue

"And then she had the guts to say to me, 'Your sweet John — why, all he does is grill that meat, not barbecue it.' Now, John, I know what you barbecue for us is really good. I don't care if she's right, honey, I like what you do for me! And then I told her, if she's so smart, why didn't she help her husband change his blackened bitter meat to flavorful barbecue?"

J.J. and John, before we start talking about producing flavorful barbecue or grilled meats, we need to know how meats are "put together" and how dry heat cooking affects them.

### Lean Meat is Muscle

The lean of any meat is the muscles of that animal — and muscle contains many individual fibers, some over one foot long in beef. These fibers are called the "grain" of the meat. You carve meat across the grain of these fibers, *not with* the grain if you want more tender meat.

A "sack-like" very thin membrane covers each muscle fiber. Inside this sack along with the lean meat are sugars, minerals, and salts (one is common table salt) acids, vitamins, enzymes, 40% to 60% water, and a little fat. All of these make up the juices of meats. These sacks of muscle fibers are separated from each other by juices with some marbled fats. These individual fibers are tied together by tough connective tissues which hold the muscles in place so they work efficiently. If the connective tissues are totally removed by overcooking, the meat crumbles when you carve it. Thousands of these sacks make up a lean cut of meat. Cook-out masterpieces are lean meats cooked so they'll be (1) juicy, (2) tender, and (3) flavorful. How you cook meats determines how tasty your masterpiece will be.

## Grilling/Smoke-Cooking

When you grill, you use dry very hot air at 500°F. down to 300°F. When you barbecue (smoke-cook) thick or tougher cuts of meat, you use dry hot air at 175°F. up to 275°F. Heating meat causes its muscle fibers to contract and the sacks covering them to break. The more you heat the meat, the more these contracting fibers squeeze out the meat's juices. When you grill and sear meats, you seal its outside some, but not completely. Searing's high heat evaporates the water in the juices on the meat's surface. Smoke-cooking's low temperature is a blessing for keeping meats juicy.

When your cooking bursts the sacks covering the meat fibers, it allows their liquid contents to mix together with the contents of other muscle fibers. This helps to make meat juicier and gives meat part of its elegant delicious cooked flavor. This "freed-juice," 90% water, dissolves meat's water-soluble proteins, sugars, salts, vitamins, etc. All together, these, along with the melted fats, become meat's center juices. Most of these juices can be squeezed out during long, hot, dry heat cooking. Your goal: You want to retain all of the natural juices you can. It's important to remember: *The longer and hotter you cook meats, the more juices you squeeze out.*

## Lose Juice at 120°F

Cooked meats start to lose juices when they reach only 120°F. center temperature. Then pro barbecuers say, "The meat starts to sweat." Why? Because the muscle fibers have started to contract and droplets of juice form on the surfaces. When these fibers reach 130°F. to 140°F., they draw together and thicken the meat. Then, red juices may appear on the edges and on the tops of uncooked burgers, steaks, or chops.

These red oozing juices change to pink at 145°F. to 150°F. and to a brown/gray or clear at 160°F. At this temperature, if you cut the meat, its center juices will be clear or pale yellow. At 140°F. cooked temperature, the meat's tough connective tissues (collagen) have shrunk and started to change to easy-to-chew gelatine. At 145°F., the protein starts to harden and becomes somewhat more difficult to chew. This protein hardening grows as the meat's cooked temperature increases. Protein hardening is easily recognized as the slightly-toughened surface of seared meats.

## No Longer Raw

Meats are actually cooked done at 160°F. They're no longer raw. People cook chicken and turkey to 165°F. to control potentially harmful bacteria. At 165°F. the center of the meat has changed color completely to a grayish brown for beef, lamb, chicken and turkey legs/thighs, and pork shoulder. The center has changed to white for a pork loin and the poultry breast meat. At 170°F., meat's fibers have shrunk completely. Beyond this 170°F. they all start to break and toughen; they dry out rapidly unless covered with foil.

Stop cooking (heating and drying) foods when they reach your desired doneness for maximum juiciness. Please don't delay reaching this stage! For example: When you smoke-cook turkeys done to 165°F., you can use either 5 hours or 9 hours to reach this temperature, depending upon your smoker's cooking temperature and the size of the turkey. The turkey may reach 150°F. in 4 to 5 hours, but it needs 15 more degrees to be cooked done. If you're using a 175°F. charcoal fire, you may use 4 to 5 more hours cooking time. This 175°F. and 4 hours severely dries out the turkey's lean breast meat. It would be better to add enough lighted charcoal briquettes to raise the cooking temperature to 220°F. Then, complete the cooking in 2 hours or finish it wrapped in aluminum foil in the oven.

## Overcooked, Dried-Out

Many of meat's juices and its natural water-soluble chemicals have been cooked out and dripped away if the meat's temperature reaches 185°F. Then, much of the meat's remaining juiciness comes from the melted fats. Fats have not been squeezed out, dripped away, or evaporated at this higher cooked temperature. Red meats (beef, pork, lamb) and turkey/chicken reach the over-done dried-out stage at 185°F., well past the standard well-done 170°F. Many fish reach their over-done stage at 145°F. grilled temperature.

When cooked to 170°F., your hopefully elegant, juicy grilled steak suffers terribly! It was a naturally tender cut of meat before you started to grill it. At this temperature, most of its juices have been cooked out. This means cooking a steak no more than a medium 160°F., barely past the pale pink center stage; then, you'll save more of its natural juices. Lean pork, and lamb also benefit from this gentle treatment.

## Barbecuing for Juiciness

Here's where some people's grilling technique fails easily. Some juice loss occurs despite every cookbook's very standard directions, "You sear the meat to seal in the juices." Meat's juices contain over 90% water, and water boils away rapidly at 212°F. cooking temperature, and above. Water evaporates even at 120°F. At 150°F., not only do you continue to squeeze out meat's juices, but you also evaporate more water from the juice itself. A cook-out "masterpiece" starts with retaining meat's natural juices, including the water in the juices. Research proves that 14% of the meat's total moisture is lost when its cooked temperature is raised from 145°F. to 175°F. — this can be the difference between very juicy and dry meats. As long as the bacteria is controlled at lower temperatures, you may need to rethink desired doneness temperatures.

Some cuts of meat have considerable fats marbled in the lean. And some of meat's natural juiciness comes from the melting of these flecks of fat at lower temperatures. However, very lean meat has little marbling. Because of the higher temperatures (350°F. to 550°F.) used when grilling, lean meat can be very dry with little flavor. Therefore, you baste very lean meat with a liquid marinade containing some vegetable oil. Smoke-cooking lean meat in a water smoker with its small amount of vapors, and stopping at a lower done temperature will also help to keep it juicy.

## Barbecued and Grilled Flavors and Aromas

When you grill, smoke-cook, or barbecue you want to produce a flavorful smoked, browned, and caramelized outside crust with a great aroma. It still needs to have a tender juicy center. If you don't produce this delicious browned crust, you might as well cook all meats in a microwave oven. Your microwave's quicker and easier, but your meat tastes "blah" when compared to a great barbecue flavor. Why? Microwaving cooks meat in its own steam — the moist-cooking method. A microwave oven's cool outside air surrounds the cooking meat. It does not produce the high surface temperature required for browning.

## Raw vs Cooked Flavor

Some people love steak tartare as an appetizer. This is twice fine ground <u>raw</u> beef tenderloin or raw beef top round, or even very carefully fat trimmed but still raw beef chuck (lean content — over 95%). You then add spices and flavorings or serve them separately. Some people rave about steak tartare's flavor. Others, however, must be dared to eat it and it tastes "blah" to other folks, even with all of its extra elegant seasonings.

If you mix this lean meat and seasonings with a small amount of good beef fat, you can develop a totally new group of much more intense delicious flavors. It becomes a <u>superb grilled hamburger</u> — all from this "blah" seasoned meat only because you browned, lightly smoked, and lightly charred it. Heating also melts the fats mixed in with the lean particles. These fats add flavor, great mouth feel, and lubrication which helps us chew the meat. Smoke-cooking's long cooking time and its seasonings plus its low temperature produce the browned, juicy BBQed flavor.

## Caramelized Flavors

Barbecuing, grilling, and smoke-cooking with the seasonings can increase your meat's flavor intensity — three to five times over meat that is stewed in water or microwaved. These methods all use dry heat cooking which gives meats flavor advantages. These dry heat cooking methods cause two of meat's natural products to react with each other. A portion of meat's proteins (amino acids) reacts with meat's natural sugars (glucose, etc.) when dry heated. This chemical reaction is called the Browning Reaction. Combined, they create a browned, caramelized glaze which eventually becomes part of the tasty, desirable, safe barbecued crust or "outside" meat. (Compare the increased flavor intensities of a lightly-roasted browned caramelized marshmallow with a non-roasted one.)

Only forms of dry heat cooking produce this Browning Reaction. This occurs when the dry heat evaporates water from meat's own juices on its surfaces. These concentrated, dried brown juices or crust contain a big <u>part</u> of the "meaty" flavor of outstanding barbecue. A thin beginning dried crust continues to thicken by drawing more juices from the meat's moist interior like a blotter, creating a thicker outside crust.

## Meaty BBQed Flavor

You taste this elegant meaty BBQed flavor — this outside crust of meat — when it's: (1) seared and grilled at 450°F. to 550°F., (2) smoke-cooked at home, or barbecued in a contest, with dry hot air from 300°F. down to 175°F., or (3) browned like a sausage in the skillet. Prove this increased flavor to yourself; just taste the browned juices oozing from the browned seared burger or the smoke-cooked chicken on the serving platter. This Browning Reaction occurs slowly and naturally when the surface of meat is dry heat cooked using 175°F. air temperature. It occurs very rapidly at 315°F. air temperature and above.

What are your problems with developing this outside crust? Many times the meat's crust dries out into stringy, dry, tough fibers because: (1) it's grilled too long, (2) grilled too hot without applying a complimentary baste, or (3) exposed to too much wood smoke when smoke-cooked too long. Another problem occurs when the meat is cut too thin (½" thick or less) and you overcook the center trying to brown the outside. Also, meat can be cooked to a blackened bitter burned flavor because of long heavy smoke, or a grill's long hot grease fire or an 800°F. blackening fire.

Your grilling goal: to develop the full-flavored tender outside browned crust and with a juicy, tender, red rare to a medium rare pink center, or a browned medium cooked center. You choose how you like your meat grilled or smoke-cooked. You may want to increase the outside crust by using "browning" aids, such as: (1) a meat "rub" containing paprika or sugar, or a baste of honey, fruit juices, barbecue sauces, vegetable oil, (2) higher momentary cooking temperatures, (3) intermittent flame searing, and (4) smoke-cooking or barbecuing a little longer.

Professional food technologists do not know exactly what takes place chemically when you brown and caramelize foods with this Browning Reaction. But everyone enjoys its safety and excellent flavor. However, great flavor, aroma, and juiciness themselves do not produce barbecued masterpieces. You must be able to chew and swallow the meat with ease.

## Tough vs Tender Meat

We're sure that you have eaten some cuts of meat which are less tender and you may have mentally commented, "This meat must have come from a tough old cow."

Even a seven-year-old Holstein cow has two muscles which can be tender even when grilled or smoke-cooked — two whole beef tenderloins or filets. Why? They're the back muscles inside the body cavity which receive very little exercise. The other cuts coming from this animal have been exercised heavily, as she fed and walked, and can be very tough if grilled. However, these tough cuts make tasty, tender ground meat. Grinding cuts tough meat's many connective tissues and its coarse muscle fibers into very small pieces — 35,000/lb. — called ground-beef, pork, chicken, turkey, lamb, or venison.

To understand muscle toughness in meats, imagine playing "Steer." You get down on all "fours." Your arms become your new front legs. As you use your head to graze grass, your neck muscles get lots of exercise. When you walk out in the pasture, you use your shoulder and arm muscles to pull yourself forward (beef's chuck or shoulder cuts). You push your body forward with your hind "legs" (beef's round, rump, and arm cuts). The longer and older these muscles, the coarser they become with more and tougher connective tissues.

So, you want to buy cuts from a younger steer whose back muscles get nearly a free ride. These muscles will be much more tender. Here's where you'll find tender steaks — the rib, ribeye, T-bone, porterhouse, and the sirloin steaks (see Index: Beef).

But there's good tenderizing news. Younger steers and heifers are confined to feed lots for 90 up to 150 days and fed highly nutritious feed, all with little exercise. This allows small flecks of fat (marbling) to grow in between the bundles of muscle fibers. When cooked, these flecks of fat melt and protect the lean fibers during cooking to prevent their drying out.

Marbling increases the juiciness of the cut of meat and makes it more flavorful and elegant with a great aroma. The improved juiciness also makes the meat seem more tender. It also increases that cut's calories. However, U.S. *Choice* grades of meat have only 5% to 7% fat within the muscle. Most people would rather eat a smaller piece of tender elegant tasting meat — we know we would. Beef may be tenderized during one stage of processing. Beef carcasses are stimulated with a high electrical charge to produce massive muscle contractions which tenderize leaner meats. As a result, USDA *Select* grade beef becomes as tender as *Choice* grade, but without the marbling.

A juicy tender piece of meat makes the difference between a cook-out masterpiece and a big disappointment. A very tender beef filet becomes a dried-out, inferior tasting, maybe blackened piece of meat easily when it's overcooked. However, undercooking presents problems also, even with a tender cut of meat. You can grill a very rare steak to only 130°F. (blood red center). With this temperature, the tough collagen has not started to change to tender gelatin. It will change some when the steak is cooked to 145°F, the new safe E. coli temperature for steak.

Please become aware of all very lean meat before you start to grill or barbecue it. It'll be dry and tough without basting it with some oil in your baste in addition to juices and other liquids. Use a marinade with either vegetable oil for lower cholesterol, or an animal fat for higher flavor intensities. Outstanding animal fat is melted beef kidney or rind fat.

## Dry Heat and Tenderness

When you heat muscle fibers, they start to contract, shorten in length, grow together as low as 120°F. internal cooked temperature. The more you heat these fibers, the more they contract, and the denser, firmer, and less tender they become. With tender cuts of meat (steaks and chops), these fibers begin to toughen when grilled beyond 160°F. When you barbecue tough cuts of meat (beef brisket, etc.), they should be held at 160°F. to allow time for tenderizing. Higher temperatures toughen and dry them out. If you cook beyond this temperature, use a baste or liquid marinade or wrap in foil to keep the meats from drying out. Overcooked muscle fibers become hardened and stringy at the 175°F. to 180°F. temperature or crumbly if wrapped in foil.

Muscle fibers are held together in "bundles" by tough connective tissues (collagen). The lean in red meats contain 3% collagen, plus other connective tissues. You successfully tenderize some of the collagen in tougher meats by cooking them even to just 150°F. You change much of the collagen into easy-to-chew gelatine (equal to an unflavored gelatine) by moist-cooking to medium internal temperature of 160°F. and holding this temperature for some hours.

## Liquid and Dry Tenderizers

Marinating with a liquid which contains an acid-based marinade helps to tenderize tougher cuts of meat somewhat. Dry red or white wine, beer, lemon, orange or lime juice, soy sauce and Worcestershire sauce, vinegars, and apple cider and juice are all acids. Combine them with other dry seasonings for marinades. They certainly will flavor the meats, and will tenderize some portions of the meats which they penetrate.

Beer makes a good marinade. Since it loses its bitterness and changes to a slightly sweet flavor as the alcohol cooks out, it's a good baste for juiciness on ground meat patties if you like the very small flavor change.

Commercial powdered tenderizers contain papain from the papaya plant or bromelain (bromelin) from pineapples. These powdered plant enzymes pre-digest meat's connective tissues and muscle fibers. They "soften" the meat which makes the meat fibers easier to chew. But, they reduce your meat's juice-holding capacity which allows the meat to dry out as it cooks. Tenderized meat should be cooked only up to 150°F. or a pale pink doneness to keep the meat juicy.

Tenderizers start to work at 140°F. and work rapidly at 149°F. Papain tenderizers plus moisture are normally forked into the meat for better penetration. Excessive tenderizer turns meats mushy and slick, leaving a poor mouth feel. Be careful not to overuse them.

TENDERIZING PHYSICALLY means scoring very lightly across the grain of the meat, or pounding which tenderizes less tender cuts of meat. We tested a hand-held tenderizing gadget having 36 needles. We had little success using this gadget. Commercial use of similar systems have not been very successful either. Physically tenderized meat does not grill well because it no longer can hold the meat's juices. Cube steaks and other tenderized meats are much better pan grilled. The pan collects their excess juice loss. These delicious juices and browned crumbs make outstanding sauces for your meats. When pounding meats to tenderize, use ½" thick cuts or less; they are easier to work with.

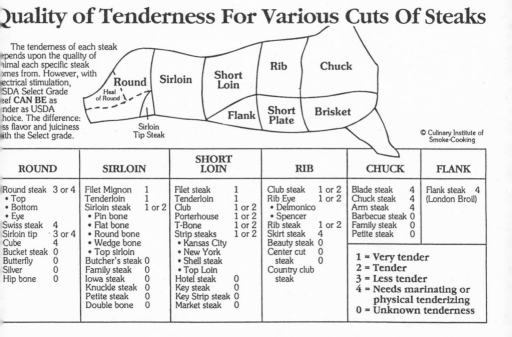

# Quality of Tenderness For Various Cuts Of Steaks

The tenderness of each steak depends upon the quality of animal each specific steak comes from. However, with electrical stimulation, USDA Select Grade beef CAN BE as tender as USDA choice. The difference: less flavor and juiciness with the Select grade.

© Culinary Institute of Smoke-Cooking

| ROUND | SIRLOIN | SHORT LOIN | RIB | CHUCK | FLANK |
|---|---|---|---|---|---|
| Round steak  3 or 4 | Filet Mignon  1 | Filet steak  1 | Club steak  1 or 2 | Blade steak  4 | Flank steak  4 |
| • Top | Tenderloin  1 | Tenderloin  1 | Rib Eye  1 or 2 | Chuck steak  4 | (London Broil) |
| • Bottom | Sirloin steak  1 or 2 | Club  1 or 2 | • Delmonico | Arm steak  4 | |
| • Eye | • Pin bone | Porterhouse  1 or 2 | • Spencer | Barbecue steak 0 | |
| Swiss steak  4 | • Flat bone | T-Bone  1 or 2 | Rib steak  1 or 2 | Family steak  0 | |
| Sirloin tip  · 3 or 4 | • Round bone | Strip steaks  1 or 2 | Skirt steak  4 | Petite steak  0 | |
| Cube  4 | • Wedge bone | • Kansas City | Beauty steak 0 | | |
| Bucket steak 0 | • Top sirloin | • New York | Center cut  0 | | 1 = Very tender |
| Butterfly  0 | Butcher's steak 0 | • Shell steak | steak  0 | | 2 = Tender |
| Silver  0 | Family steak  0 | • Top Loin | Country club | | 3 = Less tender |
| Hip bone  0 | Iowa steak  0 | Hotel steak  0 | steak | | 4 = Needs marinating or |
| | Knuckle steak  0 | Key steak  0 | | | physical tenderizing |
| | Petite steak  0 | Key Strip steak 0 | | | 0 = Unknown tenderness |
| | Double bone  0 | Market steak  0 | | | |

# MEAT, POULTRY, AND FISH DONENESS GUIDES

J J., John's continuously "food-panicked" wife, touched him less than gently • this Sunday evening and said, "John, I do want my pork chops cooked well-done. I want my pork to be absolutely white. I'm deathly afraid of that trichinosis." And John only nodded a "yes" and did that with little enthusiasm.

John had read some USDA information on trichinosis and pork. This information said that trichinosis is killed at 137°F., the rare-doneness temperature for a steak. It'll have a rare red center color. He had grilled pork for a few years and liked it juicy. He knew that if he grilled pork white done that their pork chops could be dry, tough, and certainly not very tasty. He also knew that J.J. would complain bitterly about this.

He had been caught in the middle before. Grilling ½-inch thick pork chops with a browned, delicious, tasty crust while keeping the center juicy was difficult. Ordinarily to produce a grilled browned crust, their centers are overcooked — they're dried out. Maybe he'd sear them and cook their center to a very light pink but safe-from-trichinosis pink — 155°F. doneness temperature. He finally adopted CHARLIE'S kNOTE-WORTHY "Dim-Candlelight" law for picky family members and guests — *"Always serve browned, crusty pork chops with juicy, pale, light pink/white centers by very dim candlelight."* This time John served his chops with a delicious brown sauce.

The next morning, J.J. called Blossom Do-Rite to report on her exciting evening. "John was such a dear; he sparkled like a big diamond ring, and it even got more romantic with the dim candlelight. His pork chops were excellent, and his sauce was superb. And would you believe, this is our second candlelight dinner this month? He cooked out that night too, and both nights the pork chops have been just delicious — so juicy and tender."

John, you are a good man! You know what's tasty and juicy and how to satisfy women. Also, many Americans have discovered full juiciness means more tender, flavorful, and elegant meat. Many people now finish cooking meat at a lower temperature — all meat — beef, pork, lamb, chicken, turkey, and fish.

## Daring Outdoor Cook

One sign of a daring outdoor cook: he/she cooks out regardless of the weather. However, even a daring cook may have some anxious moments about when-to-take-the-meat-off. Knowing when to stop cooking makes a big difference in how confident we feel about our outdoor cooking, and a very big difference in the flavor, juiciness, tenderness, and elegance of meat.

When you grill, barbecue, or smoke-cook meats, their doneness can range from very rare (a quick "hello-to-the-fire") to well-done — and even to a dried-out over-done. With very lean cuts of meat only ½-inch thick, using a medium hot searing fire, at some point grilled meat can go from medium rare to *well-done* in 60 seconds. And it can cook to a dried-out *overdone* in 90 seconds.

With America's big push to eliminate fats from food, let's look at CHARLIE kNOTE-WORTHY "Shoe-Leather" Cook-Out law — *"The longer and hotter you cook tender low fat meats — the more they'll be like shoe leather, tough, dry and tasteless."* Therefore, we all could use some reliable doneness tests when cooking. Testing for doneness using the "fork-tender" system, punctures the meat and causes it to lose its juices.

## Changed Meat Doneness

Some people recommend that you grill beef to a very rare 125°F. Meat scientists have measured the tenderness of beef at 125°F. and at 145°F. rare doneness. The 145°F. doneness wins because it converts more tough connective tissues to tender gelatin. It also controls E. coli.

In addition to beef's lower doneness temperature, pork's doneness has dropped from 185°F. to 155°F. to 160°F. Lamb's old 185°F. doneness has dropped to 140°F. to 155°F. Why? Americans have discovered juicier, more flavorful meats with these new lower doneness temperatures. The 185°F. temperature dries out meats, hardens proteins, and causes meats to crumble easily when carved.

## Meats, Poultry, and Fish Doneness Tests

SECRETS has devised simple easy tests for checking the doneness of various meats.

## Center Temperature Test

MEATS: Use ⅛" diameter stemmed thermometer with a glass dial (it works even on only ¾-inch thick steaks, chops, etc.) to measure meat's center temperatures. A standard ¼" stemmed thermometer is okay for thicker cuts. Insert the stem into the center of the meat not touching the bone or fat. The temperature of the center of the meat changes from a cold 40°F. *raw* to a *very rare* at 130°F., to *rare* at 140°F., to *medium rare* at 145°F. to 150°F. through *medium done* at 160°F., to *well-done* at 170°F., to *overdone* at 185°F. and above.

POULTRY: Cook to only 165°F. to control salmonella, and stop. Insert the thermometer deep into the skin cavity between the thigh and the breast and measure the temperature there. This is the last place for poultry to get cooked done. Do not touch the thigh bone.

FISH: Fish is cooked when it flakes deep into the meat next to the backbone and becomes opaque. With many fish, this happens at 135°F. Catfish needs 165°F. to flake along its backbone.

## Juice Color Test

MEAT: Barbecuing and grilling squeezes out meat's juices. They ooze out the edges and the tops of meats. These juices start as a cherry red for *very rare*, and go into rosy red to rosy to pale pink or pale yellow or clear for *medium well* and *well-done*, and finally to a dried-out *overdone* with little juice. You may need to press the cooking meat's center gently to make its juices appear when grilling or smoke-cooking.

POULTRY: Use a small, sharp, pointed knife for checking the juice color coming from the skin cavity between the thigh and the breast meat. Cook until the juices run clear or yellow with no pink color at 165°F.

FISH: Juices change from clear to white when done at 130°F. to 135°F.

## Touch Test

Start this test by gently pressing on the *raw* meat before cooking for a comparative standard. Meat's edges and center range from very "soft" for *raw* or *very rare*, and progress through "spongy" to "springy," to "firm" for *well-done*, and finally to "hard" for *overdone*. The edges firm up before the center, so always touch-test the meat's top and its center. Meats can be hot, so protect your finger with a cloth.

## Hand/Finger Test Number

You use both of your hands. The muscle between your left hand's thumb and first finger becomes the "meat" (this is for right-handed people). Hold the left hand very relaxed with its first finger and thumb drooped and parallel to each other. Use the first finger of your right hand for your "doneness tester." Push against the "loose" muscle (not the loose skin) between your thumb and finger on your left hand. This soft feel compares to the center of your meat if it is *raw* up to *rare* for a rating of 1.0. Next, straighten your thumb and finger out straight, push against the same muscle. This springy feel equals meat cooked *medium* for a rating of 2.0. Next, make a tight fist; test the same muscle area. This firmness equals meat cooked *well-done* for a rating of 3.0. Test knuckle for a rating of 4.0 or *overdone*.

## Meat's Center Color

MEAT COLOR: Use a sharp knife and cut to the center of the meat or next to a bone. The meat's center color ranges from a cherry red for *rare* — to pink for *medium rare* — to brown/gray for *medium and well-done*. As the meat cooks, its edges, top and bottom turn brown. The longer you cook it, the more its browned edges grow toward its center. When the top and bottom are brown/gray and meet in the center, the meat is *medium or well-done*.

CHICKEN BONE COLOR: Chicken pieces are done when the juices run clear or light yellow despite the fact that some of the bone may have a pink color.

FISH COLOR: The meat fibers change from a transparent to an opaque color when it's done.

NOTE: Resting time will increase the center temperature momentarily and its color and touch may change toward *well-done* during any delay in serving.

## Pork Rib Doneness

Cooking shrinks the meat surrounding the rib bones. It exposes the end of the rib bones ⅛" to ¼" when ribs are done. When two rib bones are pulled apart, the meat separates easily. A complete "slab" or side of ribs can be doubled back over itself easily. Ribs are done when the temperature is 170°F. or the meat comes loose around the rib bones easily. The meat may be red or pink due to wood smoke penetration.

## Meat Doneness Guide
### (Beef, Pork or Lamb, Steaks, Burgers, Chops, Fresh Sausage, Poultry & Fish)

| Cooked Description | Meat Types (1) | Temp. of Cooked Center | Juice Test: Amount Oozing/Purging | Juice Test: Color | Touch Test: Edges | Touch Test: Center | Hand/Finger Number (2) | Edges: Color | Edges: Color Change Size | Center: Color | Center: Percent Still Red/Pink |
|---|---|---|---|---|---|---|---|---|---|---|---|
| Uncooked or Raw | All Meats | 34°F. to 100°F. | none to little | cherry red | very soft | very soft | 1.0 | cherry red | 100% | cherry red | 100% |
| Very Rare | L. | 130°F. | some | cherry red | 1/32 inch firm | soft | 1.0 | pale brown | 1/32 inch thick | red | 90% |
| Rare | L. | 140°F. | much | rosy red | 1/16 inch firm | spongy | 1.0 | brown | 1/16 inch thick | red | 85% |
| Medium Rare | B.,L. | 145°F. to 150°F. | much | rosy | 1/4 inch firm | very center spongy | 2.0 | brown | 1/8 inch thick | pink | 40% to 60% |
| Medium | B.,L.,P. | 155°F. to 160°F. | much | rosy-clear | 1/2 inch firmed | center springy | 2.0 | brown | 3/16 inch | pink in center | 10% |
| Medium Well | B.,L.,P. | 165°F. | some | clear yellow | 100% firm | 100% | 2.5 | brown | 100% brown | light | 0.0% |
| Well Done | B.,L.,P. | 170°F. | some | clear or yellow | stiff no spring | stiff, little spring | 3.0 | brown/gray | 100% | brown/gray | 0.0% |
| Over Done | None | 185°F. | little-none | clear or yellow | hard dense | hard dense | 4.0 | brown/gray | 100% | brown/gray | 0.0% |

1) B is the abbreviation for Beef, L for Lamb, P for Pork (see Index: Pork and Ribs), C for Chicken, T for Turkey, D for Duck, G for Goose.

2) Hand/Finger Number Test (See Index)

## Poultry Doneness Test

| Cooked Description | Meat Types (1) | Temp. of Cooked Center | Juice Test: Amount Oozing/Purging | Juice Test: Color | Touch Test: Edges | Touch Test: Center | Hand/Finger Number (2) | Meat Cross Sectional Color Cut Tests: Edges Color | Edges Color Change Size | Center Color | Center Percent Red/Pink |
|---|---|---|---|---|---|---|---|---|---|---|---|
| Well Done | C.,T.,G.,D. | 165°F. to 170°F. | little | clear or yellow | stiff no spring | stiff no spring | 3.0 | brown/ gray | 100% | brown/ gray | 0.0% |
| Over Done | None | 185°F. | little-none | clear or yellow | hard dense | hard dense | 3.5 | brown/ gray | 100% | brown/ gray | 0.0% |

## Fish Doneness Test

| Cooked Description | Meat Types (1) | Temp. of Cooked Center | Juice Test: Amount Oozing/Purging | Juice Test: Color | Touch Test: Edges | Touch Test: Center | Hand/Finger Number (2) | Meat Cross Sectional Color Cut Tests: Edges Color | Edges Color Change Size | Center Color | Center Percent Red/Pink |
|---|---|---|---|---|---|---|---|---|---|---|---|
| Uncooked or Raw | All Fish | 29°F. to 100°F. | little | clear | very soft | very soft | 1.0 | transparent white/pink | 100% | transparent white/pink | 0.0% |
| Well Done | All Fish | 130°F. to 135°F. | none | white | stiff | stiff | 3.0 | opaque white/pink | 100% | opaque white/pink | 0.0% |
| Over Done | None | 145°F. to 150°F. | none | white | stiff | stiff | 3.5 | opaque white/pink | 100% | opaque white/pink | 0.0% |

1) B is the abbreviation for Beef, L for Lamb, P for Pork (see Index: Pork and Ribs), C for Chicken, T for Turkey, D for Duck, G for Goose.

2) Hand/Finger Number Test (See Index)

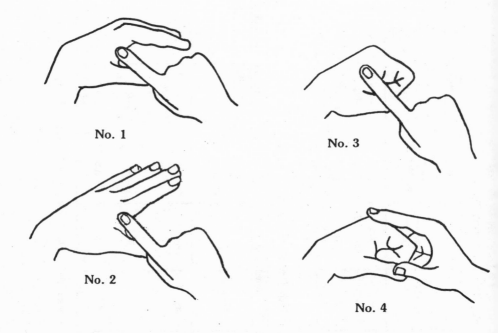

No. 1

No. 3

No. 2

No. 4

**Hand/Finger Doneness Test Numbers
Page 17, 18, 19**

# NEW RUBS, MARINADES, BASTES, AND SAUCES

Seasonings are an important part of your cook-out masterpiece. They can make it into something "big time." BBQed meats mean spiced meats — but not limited to hot, spicy meats and not always seasoned with a tomato flavor. However, for most BBQ cook-offs, BBQed means some tomato flavor.

Many times learning to season BBQ has meant learning "secret" spices and herbs. Here we hope to open up some of the mystery that surrounds BBQ flavorings and seasonings. With over 50 common spices, herbs, and other ingredients, you'll be able to create many exciting seasonings with SECRETS' basic ideas and recipes.

Spice specialists use their own language and terms to describe spices and herbs. To be able to use and know these materials, a person needs to know some of their terms and meanings. Generally spices come from seeds of trees, bushes, etc. Herbs come from the leaves of annual plants. To reduce confusion, we'll use "spices" as a general term describing all seasonings unless we need to refer to herbs.

## BBQ Seasonings

DRY RUBS: (Sprinkle seasonings or a dry seasoning salt.) A rub usually consists of a mixture of ground spices, probably some salt and maybe some sugar. Rubs are sprinkled on the meat before and during cooking and season better if applied one hour ahead. They may be applied up to 72 hours ahead if refrigerated. Thin filets of fish need only 45 minutes. The rub is actually rubbed into the meat.

Dry rubs season difficult meats easier — such as whole chickens, turkeys, or bony irregular pieces of meat. Also, they are ready-to-use and easier than marinades for small quantities of meat. Meats need to be turned over for more equal penetration. Rubs are used for seasoning meats in barbecue cook-offs. They can serve as a browning aid for meats that are *quick grilled* for only a few minutes.

LIQUID RUBS: Mixtures of liquid seasonings that are brushed or rubbed onto the meat's exterior before cooking. Example: Worcestershire sauce mixed with prepared mustard.

MARINADES: Mixtures of 2 to 20 different liquid and dry seasonings. Meats are soaked in a marinade from 30 minutes up to 2 hours at room temperature or up to 7 days in a refrigerator. The length of time depends upon the thickness of the meats and the fullness of flavor of the seasonings you desire. Long-term liquid marinating may give some meats a gamy flavor.

Marinades allow the mixing of liquid seasonings and dry seasonings. Examples: lemon, lime, or orange juices; barbecue, soy, or Worcestershire sauces; catsup, honey, maple syrup, maple flavoring; sherries, red and white wines, vermouths, brandies, beers; salad dressings, vegetable oil, and water. Various dry and fresh herbs and spices are then added.

You soak meats, poultry, or fish separately in a liquid marinade in a plastic "curing" bag, glass dish, or stainless steel pan (not aluminum or cast iron). Marinades may contain a small amount of tenderizers to tenderize tougher meats.

BASTES: Thinner liquids containing a food acid such as vinegar, wine, beer, etc., applied while the meat is barbecued or grilled. Many dry-heat-cooked meats must be kept moist to be juicy when cooked for longer periods. Some bastes contain vegetable oil to protect the leaner meats even with short cooking times.

These bastes add juiciness and help keep meats from sticking to the grill's grid. Many marinades double as bastes.

SAUCES: Usually thicker mixtures of liquid seasonings and many times are sweet tasting. These sauces are partially made of jellies, marmalades, fruit juices, catsup, sugars, wines, spices, and herbs. Many sauces contain a small amount of a fat such as butter, margarine, or oil to give them spreading and sticking qualities and good "mouth feel." Most sauces burn and blacken easily.

Sauces serve two distinct functions: (1) As a finishing sauce for dry cooked meats, these are applied in the last 10 to 30 minutes before the meat is cooked done. Then they dry to an appetizing glaze; and (2) As a serving sauce, which is applied to the cooked meat just before serving.

It's been estimated that over 95% of Americans think of a BBQ sauce as being tomato-based or tomato flavored. Americans choose barbecue sauce 77% of the time as a meat topping or sauce.

For cook-out cooking, we feel that Americans may prefer flavors other than tomato. Therefore, SECRETS contains recipes for sauces using lemon, lime, apple, pineapple, and orange juices; wines and beer; Worcestershire, soy, and other meat sauces. They'll add extra sparkle and zip to your cook-out foods. However, SECRETS contains several tasty tomato-based BBQ sauce recipes.

GLAZES: Some BBQers apply a tomato- or fruit-based sauce to the meat. Then, they cook the meat until the sauce dries down to a shiny glaze.

DRY CURES: Used for curing meats such as bacon and ham. They are dry mixtures containing salt, sugar, probably a curing mixture (such as sodium nitrate/nitrite) or saltpeter (potassium nitrate) and some spices.

BRINES: Water mixtures containing salt, sugar, curing compound and maybe some spices for curing meats. Brines normally contain heavier salt concentrations than marinades. Small fish are brined for 1 to 2 hours and fish filets for 30 minutes.

## Spices and Different Flavors

For ease in understanding their flavors and actions on meats and foods, we have subdivided common spices into 11 groups. Some individual spices may belong to 2 different groups, and will produce 2 different basic flavors.

AROMATIC SPICES: Strong, penetrating, pleasant smell (aroma) and taste. *Spices:* Allspice, basil, caraway, cardamom, celery seed, chervil, chili powder blend, cinnamon, cloves, coriander, curry powder blend, dill weed, ginger, mace, marjoram, nutmeg, pickling spice blend, sage, saffron, tarragon, and thyme.

BITTER TASTE: Disagreeable puckering taste when too much of any one spice is used. *Spices:* Allspice, celery seed, clove, mace, marjoram, nutmeg, oregano, rosemary, savory, turmeric, saffron, sage, excessive smoke flavor, and excessive liquid smoke. Basil, chili peppers, fennel, ginger, pepper, rosemary, thyme, and various sugars are suggested for decreasing bitterness.

PEPPERY: Sharp, stinging, biting, pungent, or piquant taste. *Spices:* Capsicum pepper (chili peppers, jalapenos, etc.), ginger, horseradish, mustard, black and white pepper.

PEPPERY: Sweet and woody. *Spices:* Cloves and cinnamon.

ONIONY TASTE: Taste like onions — strong or mild. *Spices:* Chives, garlic, onions, shallots, scallions (green onions).

LICORICE TASTE: Tastes like licorice candy. *Spices:* Anise, chervil, fennel, star anise, sweet basil, tarragon.

WARM, COOLING TASTE: *Spices:* Basil, oregano, peppermint, spearmint.
SWEET, WARM, FRUITY TASTE: *Spices:* Anise, bay leaf, caraway, cardamom, cumin, fennel, rosemary, and savory.
HERBY TASTE: *Spices:* Dill weed, parsley, rosemary, sage, and thyme.
FRAGRANT AND LIGHT TASTE: Sweet taste and aroma. *Spice:* Sweet basil.
HEAVY EARTHY TASTE: High aroma, warm. *Spice:* Cumin.
MONOSODIUM GLUTAMATE: Is this a good or bad seasoning? It has little flavor, and supposedly, it can cause health problems.
J.J., John's continuously "food-panicked" wife, called to him from the kitchen, "John, I'm afraid to use that MSG anymore. I watched a TV show, and they said it would cause all kinds of trouble. In fact, Blossom Do-Rite told me that she suffers terribly even when she just gets near it."
John, forget about Blossom. You'd better get J.J. back on track. She needs more information. The TV broadcast did not present scientific data, only the opinion of one emergency-room doctor. Nor did the TV broadcast present any data from recognized toxicologists who have researched MSG thoroughly. The U.S. Food and Drug Administration said using it was safe.
The Institute of Food Technologists — a non-profit group of 25,000 food scientists from universities, federal government agencies and industry — has researched MSG very carefully. Their expert panel on Food Safety and Nutrition published a complete report. Here's a quick summary: MSG means Mono-Sodium-Glutamate. It's the sodium salt of the amino acid — glutamic acid. This amino acid is one of the most important protein building blocks for our bodies. It occurs naturally in protein-containing foods — meat, fish, milk, and many vegetables. All of us produce it naturally because it's so important to our bodies.
Our body does not distinguish between its own produced glutamate and glutamate-treated foods. The human body produces about 50 grams (1⅔ ounces) of free glutamate daily to keep itself healthy. The amount of glutamate we consume from all foods is about 10 grams of bound glutamate and 1 gram of free glutamate per day. The University of Washington tested people who said they were "very allergic" to MSG. In a series of blindfold tests, these volunteers alternated eating foods treated with MSG and others plain. Only one person out of the 13 "very allergic" people developed any signs of MSG reaction. Only one person was able to identify the MSG treated foods.
For people who have any allergic reaction to MSG, SECRETS recommends that they not eat it; however, it's not a chemical killer as we've been led to believe. For the remainder of us, it's safe to eat. It enhances flavor and makes it taste better.
John, some people's response to MSG could be one of the lessons of our "food-panicked" times. If it even sounds like a chemical, even though it's a natural one, it's bad. We sometimes wonder how "panicked" people would react to that important chemical, dihydrogen oxide, if it was not called "water", which is its common name.

## Spice and Food Flavor Intensities

Carl Reitz, author of A Guide to the Selection, Combination and Cooking of Foods, (AVI Publishing Co., Vol. I, 1961), spent 30 years studying flavor intensities of spices and foods. Many qualified people helped with the evaluations.
He rated distilled water as 1.0 because it was flat with no flavor intensity. Cayenne pepper had the highest flavor intensity and was rated about 1000. All

other spices, seasonings, and foods were rated between 1.0 and 1000. These ratings are useful to anyone who wishes to create his own new BBQ sauces, rubs, bastes, etc.

For example, A barbecue sauce recipe calls for one quart of tomato catsup, which has a flavor rating of 175. Then you add ½ teaspoon of basil rated at 65. Conclusion: your new sauce will still taste exactly like tomato catsup.

But if you add one teaspoon of powdered cinnamon, rated 450, and ½ cup of vinegar, rated 600, you change its flavor. You may have given your new sauce too high a flavor. You may need to calm it down with brown sugar, rated 125. Flavor rating numbers are helpful guides when creating new seasonings.

## Food Flavor Intensities and Ratings

Researchers steamed all meats for a uniform rating of cooked foods. Then they tested them for flavor and averaged each meat's flavor ratings together.

STEAMED MEATS average ratings: Veal rated 20; chicken and rabbit 30; pork and quail 35; domestic duck 40; beef 45; lamb and turkey 50; goose 55; game meats 60; wild goose and duck 80; fish rated a 25 for trout and perch, a 70 for catfish, and 90 for tuna. Shellfish averaged 75 to 80. Smoking raised chicken and turkey to an estimated 200 and BBQed pork, beef, and lamb to 225. In general, smoking meats increased its flavor intensity 3 to 4 times.

FRESH TOMATOES AND ONION POWDER: Rated 60; tomato juice 125.

FATS: Vegetable oils rated 25; butter and margarine 40; lard, beef tallow 45.

DRIED LEAFY HERBS: Anise, dill weed, marjoram, oregano, rosemary, sage, thyme rated 80 to 95; tarragon rated 110; dill seed 160.

SUGARS: White sugar (sucrose) rated 100; brown sugar, molasses, honey 125; corn syrup (glucose) 50.

LIQUIDS USED IN MARINADES: Meat broths rated 40; cider 75; beer, catsup, soy sauce, vermouth, Worcestershire sauce rated 150 up to 225; lemon juice 275; lime juice 350; rum 400.

SPICY SEEDS: Mustard seed, coriander, cumin, fennel rated 225 to 300.

EVERYDAY SEASONINGS: Salt rated 300; black pepper 450; white pepper 400.

ONIONS: Yellow, white, or red dry onions, green onions (scallions), shallots 400.

SEEDS AND BARKS WITH "SPARKLE": Celery seed, cinnamon, nutmeg, and star anise rated 400 to 500.

POTENT SEASONINGS: Bay leaf, cloves, garlic, ginger, ground mustard, vinegar rated from 500 to 800.

POWERFUL SEASONINGS: Horseradish, cayenne and red pepper rated 850 to 1000.

Mr. Reitz's book is very worthwhile owning for other more detailed information about food preparation.

## Basic Guidelines for Using Spices

(1) MANKIND'S CARDINAL TASTES are: SWEET equals sugar, SOUR (acid) equals vinegar or lemon juice, SALTY equals table salt, and BITTER equals burned or heavily smoked food.

(2) The full flavor of any spice consists of over 50% for aroma and remainder is its taste. To taste any food, you need to inhale its aroma deeply.

(3) Our tasting ability starts to diminish after continuing to taste a food for a few minutes because "flavor fatigue" sets in.

(4) Dried herbs usually have 3 to 5 times more flavor intensity than the fresh herbs of the same weight. Fresh herbs contain lots of water.

(5) Spices and herbs contain aromatic oils (aroma-type chemicals) which give each one its unique aroma and flavor. These oils can be strong or weak.

(6) The art of seasoning is blending down heavy flavors to a pleasing taste. If you taste any spice strongly in a food, that spice has been over-used.

(7) Heating (cooking) releases spice flavors. Barbecuing's low-temperature dry-heat cooking causes spices' oils to evaporate. This causes an estimated 2 to 3 times the loss of spice intensity when compared with food cooked in a covered stew pot. This means you may need to reapply spices in the last 30 to 45 minutes before serving. The high heat of grilling and broiling rapidly destroys spices. When you season grilled meats, marinate them ahead or make heavier applications of rubs before grilling or apply them lightly during grilling.

(8) Finely ground spices lose their flavor faster than coarse ground spices. Coarse spices take more time or higher heat to release their flavors.

(9) Adding mixtures of spices to other spiced foods may produce "wild" flavors. It's best to add a single spice to boost flavors, using only ⅛ to ¼ teaspoon per pound or per pint of food. Taste after each addition.

(10) Some spices increase (multiply) the flavors of another. A little garlic strengthens onion flavor. However, other spices may decrease the flavor of each other such as basil's reported affect on tarragon.

## Off Flavor Masking

(1) Off-flavors may be masked partly by using an acid, a sugar, raw vegetables, or strong spices, then cooking the food.

(2) When cooking down to concentrate a BBQ sauce, you increase its spiciness and potential for a bitter flavor. Compensate with sugar.

(3) Tomato-based BBQ sauces with their millions of tiny tomato particles cover up many spice flavorings easily.

(4) Add volatile seasonings such as liquid smoke after the BBQ sauce simmering step is completed and the sauce is cooled. Otherwise the smoke flavor may be lost.

(5) Powdered spices do not penetrate through skin of meats, poultry, or fish rapidly. Therefore, rubs sprinkled on meat surfaces need time. Marinate the meats for 2 hours at room temperature and 72 hours in a refrigerator, if possible. You can score the skin, then apply the rub to the exposed meat.

(6) Meat from younger animals has less flavor than more mature animals. Example: veal has a rating of only 20 and a mature steer 45. Pork shoulders have more flavor than fresh ham, and beef chuck more flavor than beef rounds. Why? Heavily exercised animal muscles develop more flavor. The exercised chicken legs and thighs have more flavor than breast, which is exercised little.

(7) All meats, poultry, and most fish have mild flavors rating 50 and below when braised or stewed. Spices in addition to salt and black pepper add zip to meat's flavors. Also, meat's own flavor intensities increase drastically from a refrigerator temperature (45°F.) to a heated 125°F. Lamb moves from 40 to 60 simply by heating to 120°F.

(8) Adding small quantities of high quality bouillon with the same flavor strengthens each meat's flavor.

## Using Salt

J.J., John's "food-panicked" wife, sat at the supper table and watched John sprinkle his meat lightly with salt and then said, "John, you know they are really talking about eating lots less salt. They say it raises your blood pressure, and can cause a heart attack or a stroke." John replied, "J.J., I like the taste of salt. That little bit of salt is not going to hurt me."

John, you're right; that is, if you're not salt sensitive. Good research studies show reducing salt consumption will not help 90% of the U.S. population. It would reduce people's blood pressure only 1/10 of one point. The other 10% of the people are salt sensitive. Salt reduction helps reduce their blood pressure. Many nutritionists still feel that losing weight and exercising are much more effective for reducing blood pressure for everyone.

Let's be fair about salt. Our bodies need some salt to function efficiently. However, Americans could reduce their salt consumption 50% to 90% and still eat enough to preserve the body's proper balance. On the other hand, let's not let a very few vocal people ban the use of salt for everyone who enjoys it.

This brings us to our most popular seasonings — salt and pepper. Because salt was the major preservation method of meats before refrigeration, nearly everyone has been taught to use excess salt. Some countries still preserve their foods with large quantities of salt and continue to teach their people to use lots of salt. They season all their foods with excess salt. Generally, foods become repellent when their salt content exceeds 3.0%. Normally, people like foods with only 1.0% to 1.3% salt. Country-cured ham can contain 4.0%, and most people must soak it in water to reduce its salt content.

Finally, we come to that ever-popular spice — pepper. Pepper of all kinds adds sparkle to most meats. With good-tasting BBQ, we must still balance the amount of pepper to produce food that is not repellent.

## Creating A Rub

SECRETS presents two general ideas for rubs. We have listed several ready-to-use recipes for making your own rubs. We have suggestions for creating your own special rubs. Here you start with a simple basic seasoning mixture that you buy off the shelf in your supermarket — lemon-pepper. It's used to season many BBQed foods. Most lemon-pepper mixtures use some salt (non-iodized), coarse ground black pepper, citric acid crystals (the acid from lemons, called "sour salt"), lemon peel, lemon oil, and "flavorings." Using a little lemon-pepper mixture adds a peppery bite and a light lemony-sour flavor to meats. The citric acid supports the lemony flavor of this seasoning mixture.

To make a new rub, let's start with 3 tablespoons of lemon pepper as a base. Then add 1 tablespoon of ground thyme and mix together with a large spoon. Thyme is recognized as a good spice for many different kinds of meats. Now, we can stop here and call this Rub No. 1, or a "meat sprinkle."

## Paprika Browns

If we want the meat to brown easily, we add one tablespoon of paprika. It adds red color, but no peppery HEAT. Garlic goes well with beef and most other meats. So we add ½ teaspoon of granular garlic (it does not cake and can be called powdered garlic) and mix everything together. It would be good on meat, and we call this Rub No. 2.

Next, add ¼ teaspoon of MSG (monosodium glutamate) to enhance the overall flavor. Then, add ⅛ teaspoon of ground coriander and ¹/₁₆ teaspoon of cumin (very strong); it brings out meat flavors. Then we add a touch of "HEAT" by using ¹/₁₆ teaspoon of cayenne pepper and mixing with the other spices. We taste it and it lacks something. So we add ½ teaspoon of sugar, and increase the garlic by ½ teaspoon, for Rub No. 3, we think.

We'll brush our top sirloin steak lightly with oil and sprinkle it with the new rub. We grilled the steaks. It has a nice steak flavor — none of the spices dominated, they blended — but it needed a touch of salt for Rub No. 3.

## Making More Rubs Easily

PORK: You use the same system to create a special pork rub, by substituting sage for cumin and adjusting it to your taste.

LAMB: Substitute ground marjoram or oregano and ground rosemary for the thyme and cumin.

POULTRY: Substitute ground celery seed for the cumin.

## A Different Way

One of our most unusual and successful original rub creations is named El Greco. It has a distinct Greek flavor, which is a stronger herb flavor than a commercially-made national Greek seasoning. It does great things for grilling lamb, and it's rated better than "good" for beef, pork, poultry, and fish.

## EL GRECO RUB

| | |
|---|---|
| 2 Tablespoons sugar | 1 Tablespoon ground marjoram |
| 1½ Tablespoons non-iodized salt | 1 Tablespoon ground rosemary |
| (canning or sea salt) | ½ teaspoon garlic powder  . |
| 1½ teaspoons black pepper | ½ teaspoon MSG (monosodium |
| 1½ teaspoons paprika | glutamate), optional |
| 1 Tablespoon ground thyme | |

Using a large spoon, mix together, crushing any ingredient lumps.

The thyme, marjoram, rosemary, and garlic powder give El Greco its special flavor. All the remaining ingredients from the sugar to MSG can be your basic rub mixture. You can change to other spices. SECRETS has many new rub recipes. See index for Rubs, Sauces, etc.

## MARINADES AND BASTES

Good liquid marinades can help you produce more elegant cook-out masterpieces. They can: (1) tenderize a tougher cut of meat somewhat, (2) change the meat's flavor a little or greatly, (3) help overcome the gaminess or off-flavor of meats, (4) add juice and a little fat to very lean meat, (5) help prevent meats from sticking to the grids while grilling, (6) help brown meats, and (7) help prevent spoilage.

Food acids (vinegar, lemon juice, etc.) will tenderize somewhat, change flavor, help with gaminess, add juiciness, and help control drying out. If you use any fats (vegetable oil, butter, etc.) with lean meats, you help control sticking, add juiciness, help with drying out and give meat a better mouth feel.

If you add sugars (honey, molasses, fruit juices, etc.) you change flavors, help with gaminess and browning, and increase grill sticking and blackening potential. If you use spices with high flavor ratings, you change flavors and help with gaminess. If you use enzyme tenderizers (papain, etc.), you tenderize tough meat, but reduce its juice-holding ability. If you use part water, you reduce the meat's flavor but add moisture.

## Marinades Tenderize?

Some cookbooks imply that marinades will tenderize tough meats greatly. One reliable cookbook recommends reducing cooking time by ⅓ (you should still use the thermometer to check for doneness). Food acids (vinegar, lemon juice, etc.) do tenderize meat's tough connective fibers some. But they must penetrate the meat's muscles to contact these fibers.

The lean of any meat is not constructed like a sponge with easy channels for marinades to follow. Lean meats are solid and need deep penetration to be tenderized. For deep tenderizing action, the marinade's ingredients themselves must have the ability to penetrate deeply. Common table salt penetrates meats deeply in 40 days in a brine cure for hams. Long marinating can give some meats a gamy flavor.

Marinating at room temperature beyond 2 hours brings spoilage problems unless the marinade is primarily oil, food acids, and sugars. Forking the marinade into the meat causes some of the meat's own juices to escape easily while it is being cooked. These escaped juices usually cannot be collected and used as a sauce when cooking out.

## Food Acids and Flavor

Food acids play an important part in most marinade recipes for flavor. They all have an acidity rating for their sourness. SECRETS has broken the common, naturally occurring food acids into four groups — (1) mild food acids that are agreeably tart-tasting: tomato and pineapple juices, and beer; (2) medium strength acids: orange juice, Worcestershire sauce, and soy sauce; (3) strong food acids: dry wines, cider, grapefruit juice; and (4) very strong acids: vinegar and lemon and lime juices.

Marinades are normally a combination of a sweet/sour or a mild/sour, or tangy taste. When you create a marinade, you first find your own preferred sweet/sour ratio and taste. Next, you add salt and taste again. Then, add spices.

Meat scientists recommend using papain as a tenderizer at a concentration of 0.0002% (200 parts per million) of the weight of the meat. This is very technical. Therefore, ask your spice dealer to contact the spice company for specific directions on the use of its papain.

## Marinades and Marinating

Marinades are not the answer to all seasoning problems.

QUICK GRILLED TENDER MEAT AND ODD-SHAPED FOODS (WHOLE CHICKENS, ETC.): Use dry rubs or sprinkle seasonings unless the liquid ingredient contains your desired flavors. Light basting with vegetable oil helps to stop sticking of meats to the grid. Rubs save time and mess. However, with *Quick Grilling's* high heat, more dry seasoning may be needed late in the grilling.

USE ENOUGH MARINADE: Cover over one-half of the thickness of the meat. Then turn the meat every 2 to 12 hours depending upon the total marinating time, the kind of marinade, and the desired flavor.

A GENERAL RULE: Use ½ cup of marinade per pound of thick meat cuts. Thin cuts may need more because of more surface area.

MARINATING CONTAINERS: Use glass, plastic ware, plastic bags, or stainless steel. Aluminum and cast iron containers react with acids in marinades, causing meat discoloration and flavor changes.

CRUSH OR GRIND SPICES: Whole spice seeds need to be ground to release their flavors quickly. Tie them in a cloth for easy removal, if necessary. For leafy herbs, rub between the palms of your hands for faster release.

AVOID FLAVOR LOSS: When using chopped fresh seasonings, such as onions and garlic, immediately add them to the marinade. Much of their flavor is volatile.

VEGETABLE OILS: Some anti-fat people recommend avoiding oils in marinades. Vegetable oils help greatly when grilling chicken and lean meats to avoid grid-sticking problems. Marinating and basting recipes vary from zero up to 4 parts oil to 1 part seasoning liquids. A good low-fat level, mix 1 part oil to 1 part, or 2 or 3 parts seasoning liquids.

SUGARS: Any marinade containing lots of sugar, syrups, preserves, jellies, or sauces which contain sugar can cause blackening. If sugar-based marinades are used, the meats must be cooked over a low fire. Marinades containing sugar can be used as a finishing sauce or as a glaze during the last few minutes of cooking time.

MEAT BROTHS: These are good flavoring ingredients for longer marination of meats. Add a food acid (vinegar, etc.) to control fermentation.

WILD GAME: May need marinade ingredients with high flavor intensities to overcome unwanted gamy flavor.

## SECRETS Recipe Research

All of the chicken marinade ingredients listed in this one marinade recipe sounded good. The recipe called for many garlic cloves, vegetable oil, and lemon juice at a ratio of 1 to 1, and prepared mustard and spices. Mustards, dry or prepared, cause the oil and lemon juice to stay mixed together and to thicken. When we added the suggested cloves of fresh garlic, this mixture became too thick to spread easily on chicken pieces. It could not penetrate the chicken easily.

We added more lemon juice and oil to thin the marinade to a semi-brushing consistency. We liked the flavor combination, but it charred the chicken heavily and too quickly. We remedied the recipe by using granular garlic and increasing the oil and lemon juice; it worked nicely.

### Other Research Findings

We found lean, low-fat beef, pork, and lamb need a little fat to keep them from sticking to the grid. The latest heart information recommends canola and olive oil, because they have the least saturated fats. Butter and margarine have more flavor, but both have some saturated fat problems.

When *Slow Grilling* chicken and turkey pieces, use marinades that have added vegetable oil. Poultry's skin sticks easily to the grill unless lubricated with some oil. If the skin is removed before grilling, it needs basting with some fats to keep these pieces from drying out. However, you can use an extremely low fire and baste often with a non-oil marinade.

The ratio of oil to other liquids can be as low as 1 part oil and 3 parts other liquids. However, we produce juicier chicken pieces when our ratio is ¾ part oil to 1 part other liquids. The other successful flavorings have been lemon and lime juices (lemon is better), orange juice, pineapple juice, cider, wines, vermouths, beer, Worcestershire and soy sauces.

## Creating New Marinades

We grilled chicken for over 200 people each year for our Agape Sunday celebration. This marinade/baste has been very successful. We have reduced the recipe down to home BBQ size.

½ cup lemon juice
⅜ cup canola oil
1 Tablespoon non-iodized salt
1 teaspoon paprika
½ teaspoon onion, granular or powder
½ teaspoon garlic, granular or powder
½ teaspoon ground thyme
1 Tablespoon lemon peel (zest)
2 teaspoons basil leaves

You mix all of the ingredients together. Basil is the accent flavor. The salt, paprika, onion, garlic, thyme are support flavor ingredients.

This basil marinade worked well, so we researched it further. When experimenting with seasonings, it is best to follow one master research rule: *Change only one ingredient at a time; then test your results. Keep all other ingredients exactly the same.* When we checked the flavor rating of basil, we found marjoram, rosemary, and tarragon have a similar flavor intensity. Therefore, each one could be substituted and each one compliments chicken. We made the exact recipe of the dry support ingredients of salt, paprika, onion, garlic, and thyme. We made 3 new recipes using rosemary, tarragon, and marjoram. Then we tasted each one. We felt the marjoram marinade needed more flavor, so we added ¼ teaspoon more marjoram. We basted one chicken leg and thigh with each of the three new marinades, then gas-grilled them. The tarragon gave us the most flavor, which was excellent. The rosemary was very good and the marjoram had the lightest flavor. We readily concluded that we could change accent flavors. We could adjust the amount of spice used in this recipe based on its flavor intensity. Using flavor intensities of various spices can be very helpful in creating new bastes.

## BBQ and Finishing Sauces

A recent survey of sauces used by Americans as toppings for cooked meat revealed that BBQ sauce was chosen 76% of the time, catsup 71%, Worcestershire sauce 54%, prepared mustard 53%, steak sauce 50%, and soy sauce 46%. We have listed several excellent barbecue sauce recipes. (See Index.)

## Important

Your BBQed meat already has flavor and character. Your BBQ sauce (whether homemade or store bought) should compliment, not overwhelm the meat. The sauce should not be bland so that it lies there like a gob of bland "gravy" on meat. It should add zip and life to your cooked meat.

## Tomato-Based BBQ Sauces

There are many choices for providing the tomato flavor of a traditional BBQ sauce. Tomato taste can come from tomato paste, which is the thickest and most concentrated, then tomato puree, tomato sauce, chili sauce, canned tomato soup, canned tomatoes, and finally catsup.

The easiest, lowest cost, and probably the best starting point, is a good brand of catsup.

However, with any BBQ sauce, you probably want to build a reputation as an outstanding cook-out cook. Catsup can be bland or spicy, have a thick or thin consistency. You choose which one you want to start testing.

In addition to the catsup, most tomato-based BBQ sauces contain vinegar. Vinegars have a higher flavor rating and cost less than lemon juice. Distilled vinegar (white vinegar) contains 5.0% acetic acid, the same natural food acid in cider vinegar, but it has more sour flavor. The white and red wine and tarragon vinegars have distinct flavors. Malt vinegar has a distinct flavor for fish and might be an unusual addition to a BBQ sauce. Many flavored vinegars are made by soaking herbs and spices in standard vinegars. Some recipes use balsamic vinegar, which is produced in Italy and is quite expensive. Some BBQ sauces do contain lemon and lime juices in place of the vinegars or in addition to vinegars.

## Sugars in BBQ Sauce

Tomato-based BBQ sauces contain some type of sugar, which is one reason why they burn easily when heated unless handled carefully. With sugars, there are several choices: white granulated sugar (sucrose), molasses, light or dark brown sugars (molasses sprayed on white sugars), standard corn syrups (white and dark), high fructose corn syrup (sweeter than granulated sugar, used in commercial BBQ sauce and soda pop), maple syrup, and maple-flavored syrups. Finally a saccharin concentrate is used to make diet BBQ sauce. It withstands heat when cooked. Aspartame ("NutraSweet®") does not.

## Other Seasonings

Worcestershire is a major flavoring ingredient in many BBQ sauces. A small amount of the combination of medium to highly flavored spices is also added to make a BBQ sauce. The following spices can be used: Allspice, cayenne pepper, chili powder blend, cumin, ginger, prepared or dry mustard, nutmeg, powdered chili peppers, black pepper, and onion. Finally, some people add liquid smoke.

Dry spices and seasonings give up their flavorings to the sauce very slowly when they are whole. When spices are finely ground in a blender or small coffee grinder and heated, they release their flavors more quickly.

Many spices in BBQ sauces grow stronger after setting for 2 weeks. They have more of a peppery taste or may turn bitter. BBQ sauces store very well for months when kept sealed and covered.

## Creating a BBQ Sauce

If you want to use raw onions or garlic, you saute them in a little canola oil. You add vinegar, Worcestershire sauce, sugar, and catsup. Mix, heat, and taste for the sweet/sour ratio. You may need to adjust the ratio for flavor, then add salt and taste again. Start adding spices one or two at a time or try one of SECRETS' BBQ spice and rub mixtures. Use it very gently; then mix and blend. Finally, bring the mixture to a boil and simmer for at least 5 minutes to activate the spices and blend other ingredients, then taste. Wait 7 days and taste; then wait 7 more days and taste. If it's too thick, then add water.

SECRETS contains over 8 BBQ sauce recipes, each of them with somewhat different flavors. BBQ sauces can have several different tastes: (1) sweet, (2) sour, (3) salty, (4) bitter, (5) tangy (somewhat sour), (6) spicy, (7) peppery, (8) tomato taste, (9) smoky, (10) fruity, and (11) mustardy. You choose what you want your sauce to taste like. This is your personal creation.

Also, you can start with a commercial tomato-based BBQ sauce and modify it. SECRETS has included one such recipe.

## Meat and Finishing Sauces

One important part of being a good cook-out cook is being adventuresome. Tomato-based BBQ sauces taste much alike — spicy tomato, sweet tomato, etc.

Our food world is blessed with many outstanding flavors. Look forward to testing fruit jellies (plum, currant, grape, apple), fruit marmalades (orange, pineapple, lime), fruit butters (apricot, peach, and apple), whole fruits (pineapples, cherries, cranberries, raisins, even rhubarb), and finally chutney.

Generally, mix 3 parts of the fruit base with 1 part of food acid (vinegar, lemon juice, lime juice, etc.). Now, make your sweet/sour taste test. Adjust the flavor, then add higher flavor-rated spices to taste, such as one of SECRETS BBQ spice mixtures. After you have found a pleasing food acid-spice mixture, you create others from it.

## Meat Sauces

SECRETS has found that aged, spicy BBQ sauces have a smoother and more peppery taste. They are good with meats and are considerably less expensive than small bottles of other meat sauces. There are several commercial meat sauces. One brand appears to combine a tomato-based BBQ sauce with boiled raisins, orange juice concentrate, and caramelized color (which is deeply browned sugar and not necessarily an important flavor ingredient), plus additional spices, such as a barbecue spice mixture with a touch of cayenne. Experimenting can be frustrating at times, but finally quite rewarding.

## Marinating Game for Smoking or Grilling

Some people are very fond of wild game. They relish its gamy flavor. Other people prefer this gamy flavor reduced considerably. This gamy flavor occurs primarily in the fat of the animals. This fat's flavor intensity rates higher than domestic meat's fats.

You can reduce gamy flavor 3 ways: (1) trim out the fats; grind the meat and make burgers or sausage; (2) trim out the fat and blend it down with domestic animal meats to make sausage; and (3) mask the gamy flavors with marinades or rubs. This method works with whole birds and roasts.

When you mask gamy flavors, you use seasonings which have higher flavor intensities. Raw vegetables such as carrots, celery leaves, garlic, onions, parsley, sage, tarragon, or thyme work well. Many times these vegetables are left with the game until it's ¾ cooked, then removed. They act like a sponge and take out gamy flavor. Liquid seasonings such as buttermilk, vinegar, soy sauce, Worcestershire sauce, lime, lemon, orange, and pineapple juices, white wine for white meats and red wine for red meats help create tasty game.

Sometimes marinades are used as blotters. The game is cooked ⅔ to ¾ done in the marinade. Then the marinade is completely replaced with fresh. The first marinade removes much of the gaminess. Marinades for game should contain some oil because game is lean or you have trimmed its fat.

Olive oil has a distinct flavor. Canola and other vegetable oils can be seasoned with spices. You soak crushed leaves or berries in oil for 2 to 3 weeks.

Finally, there are special herbs that help game — juniper berries and barbecue spice combinations (see recipes). Don't forget sugar and salt's benefits. A small amount of either can change people's taste perceptions. Combined, they change game's taste greatly.

When marinating, cover over ½ the thickness of the meat with marinade and turn the meat for 100% coverage 2 or 3 times. Thin cuts of meat need 2 to 3 hours, thick roasts 24 to 48 hours of marinating time.

## GRILLING GUIDE
### For Charcoal or Gas or Electric Grills

Medium Hot Fire = 450° to 500°F.
Medium Fire = 350° to 400°F.

| Type of Food | Meat Cut or Portion | Meat Thickness | Fire Temp. | APPROXIMATE Total Grilling Time in Minutes | | |
|---|---|---|---|---|---|---|
| | | | | Rare 145°F. | Medium 155°F. - 160°F. | Well Done 165°F. - 170°F. |
| Burgers | Beef**, Pork, Lamb, or Chicken | ½ inch | Med. Hot | | 9 - 11 | 11 - 14 |
| | | ¾ inch | Med. Hot | | 11 - 13 | 11 - 17 |
| Beef Steak | Porterhouse, T-Bone, Top Sirloin | ¾ inch | Med. Hot | 9 - 12 | 12 - 13 | 15 - 18 |
| | | 1 inch | Med. Hot | 9 - 12 | 12 - 16 | 16 - 20 |
| | | 1½ inches | Med. Hot/ drop to Med. | 15 - 18 | 19 - 24 | 12 - 26 |
| Pork | Loin & Rib Chops Pork Steak or Blade | 1 inch | Med. | XXXX | 14 - 18 | 19 - 24* |
| | | 1¼ inches | Med. | XXXX | 16 - 20 | 22 - 27* |
| | | ¾ inch | Med. | XXXX | 12 - 16 | 15 - 20* |
| Lamb | Rib Chops | 1 inch | Med. Hot | 9 - 12 | 12 - 16 | 16 - 20 |
| | | 1½ inches | Med. Hot | 15 - 18 | 19 - 24 | 21 - 26 |
| | Leg Steaks or Chops | 1 inch | Med. Hot | 9 - 12 | 12 - 16 | 16 - 20 |
| | Shoulder Chops | 1 inch | Med. Hot | 9 - 12 | 12 - 16 | 16 - 20 |
| Chicken | Fryer Pieces, Larger Legs, Thighs, Breasts-Bone in | | Med. | XXXX | XXXX | 30 - 50 |
| | Breasts Deboned Skin Off | 5-8 oz. each | Med. Hot. | XXXX | XXXX | 8 - 12 |
| Fish and Seafood | | | | | | |
| Fish | Whole Dressed | 1 inch | Med. Hot | 135°-155°F. 8 - 10 | | |
| | Whole Dressed | 1½ inches | Med. Hot | 11 - 15 | | |
| | Fillets | ½ inch | Med. Hot | 5 - 7 | | |
| | | 1 inch | Med. Hot | 7 - 9 | | |
| Seafood | Shrimp, Shell on | Med. | Med. Hot | 4 - 7 | | |
| | Scallops | Sea 1-1½ inches | Med. Hot | 7 - 10 | | |
| | | Bay ½ inch | Med. Hot | 5 - 8 | | |

* Cooked Done
** See index E. coli for Beef Burgers

# Comparative Cook-Out Methods

## Grilling • Smoke-Cooking • Barbecuing

# Comparative "Cook-Out" Methods

| Raw Meat Types | Meat Thickness | Cooking Method | Grill/Smoker Temperatures | Cooking Time | Equipment Ease of Use Rating (1) | COVER: Use Open or Closed | Smoke Wood Flavoring Ability (2) | Special Instructions |
|---|---|---|---|---|---|---|---|---|
| Fish Fillets<br>Hamburger<br>2-inch Steaks | ¼ inch<br>to<br>2 inches | Quick Grilling | 600°F.<br>down to<br>300°F. | 3 min.<br>to<br>25 min. | GRILL<br>1. Gas<br>2. Charcoal<br>3. Electric | Open and/or Closed | None to Very Light | Intermittent flame & sear "outside" on HIGH; then cook center on LOW. |
| Turkey Breast<br>Brisket, Chicken<br>Pork Roast | 2 inches<br>to<br>5 inches | Slow Grilling (Rotisserie) | 400°F.<br>down to<br>200°F. | 30 min.<br>to<br>6 hr. | 1. Gas<br>2. Charcoal<br>3. Electric | Open and/or Closed | Light to Heavy | Direct Heat: Indirect low heat. Use drip pan. Add smoke wood system. |
| Smoked<br>Cornish Hens<br>16 lb. Shoulder<br>20 lb. Turkey | 1 inch<br>to<br>5 inches | Water Smoker Cooking | 300°F.<br>down to<br>175°F. | 2 hr.<br>to<br>12 hr. | WATER SMOKER<br>1. Electric<br>2. Gas<br>3. Charcoal | Closed | Light to Very Heavy | Use water smoker or kettle grill with water pan. |
| Smoked<br>Fish Filets<br>Sausages<br>Pork Loin | ½ inch<br>to<br>5 inches | Dry Smoke-Cooking | 300°F.<br>down to<br>175°F. | 30 min.<br>to<br>1½ hr. | WATER SMOKER<br>1. With dry water pan | Closed | Light to Very Heavy | Use sawdust in smoker's dry water pan. |
| Smoked<br>Pork Ribs<br>Whole Hogs<br>Brisket | ½" inch<br>to<br>6 inches | Contest Barbecuing (The Pro's) | 275°F.<br>down to<br>175°F. | 5 hr.<br>to<br>24 hr. | CUSTOM BUILT COOKER<br>1. Charcoal<br>2. Wood | Closed | Light to Very Heavy | Professional BBQ Contests. See Index. |
| Smoking Cured<br>Bacon<br>Sausage<br>Ham<br>Whole Fish | ½ inch<br>to<br>6 inches | Cold Smoking | 85°F.<br>up to<br>120°F. | 1 hr.<br>to<br>24 hr. | WATER SMOKER<br>Charcoal or Electric<br>(Limit Briquette Numbers) | Closed | Light to Heavy | Smoke flavoring only; doesn't cook food. Brine foods to stop bacterial growth. |

(1) Ease of Use Rating Consists of: (A) Getting the equipment ready to cook, (B) Cleaning up after cooking, (C) Cooking in cold or hot weather.

(2) Smoke Wood Flavor Ability: Smoke wood flavoring takes more than 10 to 30 minutes exposure time. *Quick Grilled* foods' smoke flavor comes from fat droplets that vaporize from the juice dripping onto the hot "rocks" in the grill's fire box.

# GREAT GRILLINGS

## GRILLING BASICS

The last word in eating is a nice thick grilled steak! People receive a satisfied feeling of great dining with a steak's mouth-watering aroma, plus its outstanding flavor, tenderness and juiciness.

How people should like a steak cooked is a point people debate. A delightful book, *The First Really Important Survey of American Habits* gives us some insights into America's steak-eating habits. Its authors found that 59% of Americans like their steaks cooked medium, 26% liked them rare, and only 15% wanted them well-done.

Regardless of how people like the center of their steak, burger, or chop, they prefer seared meats with lightly charred crusts. Why? These meats have a more intense caramelized flavor with greater aroma. People may want them cooked well-done, but they still want them juicy. This presents a problem to the cook-out cook. Before we move on to grilling a steak, burger, or a chop, let's have a look at some basic grilling ideas.

### Grilling's Effect On Flavor

Grilling's hot dry air (400°F. up to 550°F.) sears meat and evaporates the water from its juices. This leaves a browned caramelized outside crust. Using these higher temperatures, meat needs only 3 to 4 minutes of searing on its serving side to produce this attractive flavorful crust. This develops grilled foods' superb aromas. These temperatures and time brown meat to a depth of $1/32$ to $1/16$" below meat's surfaces. You lower the heat to finish grilling after searing thicker pieces.

To produce this browned crust when grilling thinner cuts ($1/2$" thick or less) of meat and fish presents a problem. If you want a browned outside, you overcook the meat's center easily. These searing temperatures destroy much of the coating of herbs and seasonings (dry rubs or marinades) on the meat's surfaces. So you need to apply extra seasonings if you want flavors to come through. With bone-in chicken, use 350°F. up to 400°F. and grill for a longer time to develop its crust and cook it to the desired doneness.

### Grilling's Effect On Juiciness

You need to retain all of your meat's natural juices! You may want to add to their juices by using a tasty baste or marinade. You need a baste which contains some vegetable oil for lean cuts of meat to help them retain juiciness. You grill meat only until the center is just barely done to your liking. For the best juicy centers, meat's cooked centers range from 130°F. to 160°F. for beef and lamb, 150°F. to 160°F. for pork, 165°F. for poultry, and 135°F. to 140°F. for most fish. Beyond these temperatures, you dry out foods unnecessarily. When you grill poultry or even fatter red meat cuts to 165°F. and beyond you should baste them to keep them juicy.

### Grilling's Effect On Tenderness

Grilling toughens tender meat if it is cooked too long. You want to retain all of the meat's natural tenderness. With grilling, you can start with (1) a natural tender cut of meat, (2) a tenderized tougher cut, or (3) ground meats. When you grill slightly tougher cuts of meat above a rare 140°F., their tougher connective tissues (collagen) start to convert to tender gelatin. However, the best interior doneness temperature of very tender cuts of red meats is 140°F., but the meats will be rare and red. Your best doneness temperature is 145°F. to 150°F. (a pink color) for slightly tougher cuts of meat.

## Rethink Grilling

With the "Healthy Heart" push to eat less meat, thinner meat cuts may work better for some people. Grilling a steak or chop with (1) full-flavored browned crusty outside, (2) juicy rare, or medium rare or medium center — may take some rethinking of grilling techniques. Few people praise dried-out, tough grilled meats.

## Solutions For Grilling Problems

(1) Start with a hot grill fire 450°F. to 550°F. for *Quick Grilling*. Paint the hot grid with cold vegetable oil to reduce sticking of the meat to the grid. Then grill immediately.

(2) Use intermittent flame-ups for the first 3 to 4 minutes on each side to sear and lightly char meats for a fuller flavor.

(3) Blot meat free of moisture or liquids just before you start to grill, if you can. Moisture slows down the browning effect. If part of your seasoning is a liquid (Worcestershire sauce, etc.), you can't blot it.

(4) Use a Browning Rub if needed. (See Index.)

The weight of a cut of meat does not determine the grilling time — a 2 pound top sirloin steak may be 2" thick or 1" thick. The grilling time for a 1-inch-thick cut of meat will be about 60% of the time compared with 2-inch-thick cut of meat. *One Big Grilling Rule: Generally, meat 1" thick will cook to 140°F. (rare beef or lamb) in 8 to 10 minutes using a medium hot fire.*

With all direct grilling the top of the food grid or rack will have hot and cool spots. You move thin foods to the outside edges of the fire. Place longer-grilled foods in the center of the grid.

## Different Thicknesses

(1) For ½-inch-thick meats grilled to a rare or medium rare center, apply the Browning Rub first. Then freeze the meats on a cookie sheet and grill them nearly frozen.

(2) For ¾-inch-thick meats, start with semi-thawed meats using the Browning Rub.

(3) For 1-inch-thick meats, start with cold meats from the refrigerator, then grill.

(4) For 1½-inch to 2-inch-thick meats, bring to room temperature.

(5) Grill all thicker meats with a medium hot fire until seared, then grill on low to cook the center.

Some cookbooks give recommendations for you to place meat and chicken 6 inches above the heat source and fish 4 to 6 inches. This distance could be 3 inches on a very slow fire for chicken or 3 inches for a hot fire when searing a steak. Whatever the meat's distance from the fire, you need to know the grid's cooking temperature.

## Measuring Grilling Temperatures

FOR GAS, CHARCOAL, AND ELECTRIC GRILLS: The best method for knowing grilling temperatures is an inexpensive oven thermometer which measures up to 600°F. SECRETS' Hand/Palm heat-sensing method substitutes accurately enough for a thermometer when grilling at higher temperatures. Use an oven or candy thermometer when your cooking temperatures need to be below 300°F.

## Hand/Palm Heat-Sensing System

This system consists of holding your palm, at its normal body temperature, one inch above the cooking grid level and saying "1001" up to "1006." You hold this position and count before the fire forces your hand away. Each one of these "1001s" through "1006" equals one second.

**Measuring Grill Temperature**

You'll receive a false reading if your hand has been holding a cold drink — or if you've just checked the fire. You'll count to "1006" with the heated palm and "1002" with the cold drink palm, both with the same 350°F. LOW fire.

SPECIFIC     READINGS:    Saying "1001" up to "1002" equals a very high **Hand/Palm Heat Sensing System** (550°F. to 700°F.) fire; saying "1001" up to "1003" equals a medium hot or "high" (500°F.) fire; saying "1001" up to "1004" equals a medium (400°F.) fire; saying "1001" up to "1005" equals a low (350°F.) fire; "1006" equals a very low and slow (300°F.) grilling fire.

## Safe Grilling; Using Charcoal, Gas, or Electric

(1) Always keep a fire extinguisher handy.

(2) Keep all types of grills uncovered while starting the fire. Don't cover a charcoal fire until all the lighter fluid has been burned off.

(3) Do not wear loose-hanging clothes, or use clothing or hot pads with a fringe when working over the fire.

(4) Use long-handled tools for basting and turning foods.

(5) Keep children away from hot grills.

(6) Keep grill 5 feet away from the building's wooden overhang.

(7) Use the grill's cover (hood, lid) to put out fat fires of charcoal grills, or help control them (gas grills).

(8) Keep a water bottle (clean detergent bottle with a pouring cap) next to the grill for pouring a quick short stream of water on a fat fire. Water spritzers can chase fat fires. However, intermittent flame-ups produce the lightly-charred flavor of excellent grilled foods.

(9) If you grill indoors, use the fireplace for ventilating smoke.

(10) To clean the grid, heat for five minutes and brush with a brass wire brush or nylon pad to reduce meat sticking.

(11) Use tongs to turn meats. Use a wide-tined fork to gently lift under ground meat patties after grilling 2 to 3 minutes, which helps with sticking.

(12) Heat the grid hot to produce grill marks. Then brush with cold vegetable oil. Then place the meat on the grill.

## Grilling's Two Types

Grilling is divided into two types: indirect and direct. Direct grilling places food directly over the "fire", which may be gas, charcoal, or electric. The "fire's" dry heat cooks the food above it on the grill's grid. This direct grilling method works best when cooking meats with nearly equal thickness and which lay flat on the grid. You use direct grilling to cook steaks, burgers, chops, chicken, turkey or rabbit pieces, whole fish, fish fillets, and sausages. It caramelizes, lightly smokes and lightly chars the food, and gives it a browned grill-marked appearance. With direct grilling, the grill's cover may be closed or open or a combination of the two.

Meats lying on the grids receive the results of the fire's direct heat with the cover closed. The top of the meat is heated by indirect hot air flowing over it and will be 100°F. up to 150°F. cooler. Direct-grilled meats can be *Quick Grilled* — cooked in 5 up to 20 minutes, or *Slow Grilled* in 30 to 60 minutes using lower temperatures. You do most home grilling with the grill's cover closed. This increases the grid's temperature as much as 75°F. to 150°F.

## Skewering and Direct Grilling

Meat cubes, ¾" up to 2" in size, are pushed onto metal, bamboo, or wood skewers 6 to 14 inches long. Be sure the metal skewers are rectangular or "V" shaped, not round. A single round metal skewer will not "turn" meat cubes when it's turned; you'll need to use two round ones to hold the meats as the skewers are turned. If skewers are bamboo or wood, soak them in water for 30 minutes to prevent burning.

Skewered meats are *Quick Grilled* usually. Meat and raw vegetables' cooking times vary greatly. Therefore, you parboil slow-cooking vegetables a few minutes to cook them partially done before skewering them between meat cubes. You can grill the meat leaving lots of space between the cubes. Toward the end of cooking, scoot the meat cubes closer together and place any fast-cooking vegetables on the end of the skewers.

The Grill Topper is one of the new important tools for grilling. It is a porcelain-coated steel plate with ¼" holes, sides, and a back. The Grill Topper is ideal for grilling smaller pieces of meat, fish fillets and other more difficult-to-turn or handle foods. Other manufacturers make a similar device. Buy one that has the ¼" holes. Wire mesh toppers are very difficult to clean after grilling fish and other foods.

## Rotisserie and Direct Grilling

This is a spectacular showy way to grill meat. It eliminates flame-ups if the rotisserie is set up correctly with none of the meat fats dripping onto the open fire. It works well when the cooking temperature must be higher or direct grilling must be used. Otherwise, our choice is to use low temperatures, and slow cook with fat drippage shields or water pans covering the fire. Then turn the meat occasionally. Rotisserie is not necessary when you indirect grill and use a drip pan.

## Indirect Grilling

With indirect grilling, the grill's fire produces hot air which circulates under and over meats in the center of the grid. A drip pan sits directly under the meat. This type of indirect grilling is used with a charcoal grill and with a three burner gas grill (only the 2 outside burners are lit). With indirect grilling the fires are on the sides of the drip pan and the meat. With other gas grills, the drip pan and meat are placed on the end without a fire. Indirect grilling's cooking temperatures (the heated air) range from 150°F. up to 425°F.

Indirect grilling systems work nicely for cooking whole chickens, turkeys, pork loins, chops and shoulders, a "slab" (side), or rack of ribs, beef briskets, legs of lamb, rabbits, and sausages.

Because of its lower temperatures, people smoke-cook meat by adding wet smoke wood. Indirect grilled meat is cooked from 4 up to 12 hours. Meat higher in fat or a tougher cut respond well to lower temperatures used in indirect grilling. For smoke-cooking turkeys, chickens, and pork shoulders, a water smoker is easier to use than a kettle or square grill.

## Master Grilling Steps
## For Grilling All Meats, Poultry, Fish,
## Sausages, and Kabobs

PREPARE THE GRILL: Charcoal grill, light the fire — Gas grill, preheat and burn off fat deposits on the briquettes or rock. This will help prevent big fat fires. See Gas Grilling, which follows.

STEP 1: Use meats ½" thick up to 2" thick; 3½ to 4½-pound chicken pieces.

STEP 2: Trim excess rind fats (outside fats) to ⅛" or less thick. Remove large deposits of fat between layers of lean. Pin lean layers back with wet wooden picks if necessary.

STEP 3: Score the skin membrane and fat edges only (not the meat) every 1½" to prevent curling.

STEP 4: Pick out each meat cut's best side for your serving side.

STEP 5: Season meat. See Index for recipes for grilling various meats and marinades.

STEP 6: Marinate for 30 minutes up to 2 hours at room temperature or for up to 24 hours or longer covered in a refrigerator. If 1" thick or over, bring to room temperature before grilling.

STEP 7: Clean grill's cooking grid (rack) of previous cooked-on food deposits to prevent sticking and off flavors.

STEP 8: Heat the cooking grid to searing temperature if grill marks are desired. Then apply cold vegetable oil to the grid to help prevent foods from sticking, using a long-handled brush. Watch for flame-ups coming from oil dripping onto the fire.

STEP 9: *QUICK GRILLING:* Grill with MEDIUM HIGH heat with Cover Closed; Steaks, Chops: 1" thick or over, room temperature; Burgers: ¾" thick, refrigerated; Steaks, Chops: ½" thick, semi-frozen. Regardless of the food, place serving side down to develop grill marks. Use intermittent flame-ups to sear and brown the meat. This develops a delicious browned caramelized lightly charred crust.

Two minutes after starting to grill, using a long-handled, wide-spaced two-pronged fork, straddle the grid wire directly under the meat. Gently lift meat up only ⅛" to help prevent sticking. This is particularly important with all types of burgers. At three minutes for steaks, use long-handled tongs or a pancake turner for burgers to turn the meat 90° and grill for 1 to 2 minutes if needed. This develops cross-hatched grill marks. You can turn meats over completely depending upon how much they're cooked. Grill meat on MEDIUM to MEDIUM HIGH for 2 to 5 minutes to cook the second side. Total cooking time: 6 to 15 minutes, depending upon meat's thickness and whether you want it cooked Rare, Medium, or Well Done. If the meat is over 1" thick or fully frozen thinner meats, turn to LOW or use indirect heat to cook seared meat until done. You may need to move meat to a cooler portion of the grill if the meats are extremely thin. (See Index: Doneness of Meats.)

SAUCING: If you are using tomato-based barbecue or sugar-based sauces when *Quick Grilling,* apply them before you start grilling if you want them to become a glaze. Serve immediately with the serving side up when done to your liking.

STEP 10: *SLOW GRILLING* for chicken pieces and thick meats using MEDIUM heat: Place legs, thighs, breast meat on the hotter areas in the center of the grid. Then place the wings and backs on the grill's edges. Place bone and meat side down with skin side up. Maintain MEDIUM to LOW heat, depending upon your grill's ability to generate heat, with Cover Closed.

Turn and baste chicken every 6 to 8 minutes with a thin marinade containing some vegetable oil. Apply any sauce containing tomato or sugar during the last 10 to 15 minutes of cooking. Total cooking time from 30 to 60 minutes depending upon your grill's temperature. Check for doneness 5 to 10 minutes before the meat is supposed to be done. Serve immediately when done. Keep warm until served. (See Index: Doneness of Meats.)

## Skewer Grilling Steps
## For Meats, Poultry, Seafoods,
## Sausages, and Ground Meats

This is a dramatic fast and flavorful way to present combinations of meats and colorful vegetables.

(1) Cook meat cubes separately if possible.

(2) Match sizes and cooking times of meats and vegetables. Beef, lamb and seafoods, and some sausages require less time. Pork and poultry require more time. Parboil or precook potatoes, cauliflower, onions to the almost tender stage, then skewer. Tomatoes need very little grilling time.

(3) Use more tender cuts of meat (beef top sirloin rather than round steak).

(4) Leave space between meat cubes for heat to penetrate, particularly pork and poultry. Meats cooked to rare or medium rare may be pushed together.

## Grilling Skewered Ground Meatballs

(1) Mix the meats together with salt, water, and egg. After forming into meatballs, chill for easier handling before skewering. Avoid combining vegetables and meatballs on the same skewer.

(2) Heat grid hot, then brush with cold oil. Baste the meatballs with an oil or oily marinade.

(3) Leave space for rolling a skewer-full of meatballs. You can't lift them without tearing them up, so you roll them across the grid to turn them.

(4) Lift meatballs ¹/₁₆", however, with a two-tined fork straddling the grid wire underneath each meatball after 2 to 3 minutes to prevent sticking. When the bottoms of the meatballs set up, turn by gently rolling ¹/₄ to ¹/₂ turn, then baste with a marinade.

# EASY, QUICK, FLAVORFUL GAS GRILLING

J.J., John's continuously "food-panicked" wife, was in an easy spring mood. She gazed out the window looking over their backyard and said, "John, it's spring, the grass has greened up. I've got to work late tomorrow night. Why don't you give the kids and me a big thrill with your first cook-out?"

John grunted — he mentally went over all of a cook-out's complications. His charcoal grill took 40 to 50 minutes to set up, light the fire, and get it to grilling temperature. Then it took only 8 to 10 minutes to grill burgers. After his charcoal grill finally cooled, he'd spend 10 minutes then or later emptying the ashes and cleaning the grill. And tomorrow night he had a big complication — he wanted to watch his favorite baseball team on TV. John's a good daddy and husband, but this was to be a very special game. Finally, he "came-around" and replied, "J.J., Honey, you know I'd like to, but the time it takes to get a charcoal fire started, then cook and clean up the mess, well, I'd just rather not tomorrow night."

With that, J.J. got "big steam" up, "If it's such a problem to charcoal grill, then why don't you settle for a gas grill, like I've been suggesting?" John replied sharply, "Hamburgers can't get much charcoal smoke flavor from a gas grill."

## Charcoal's Smoke Flavor?

J.J. came right back with, "Boy, you pick on me for being way-out on foods. How about you being so fussy about that charcoal smoke flavor? I heard my brother say that charcoal by itself doesn't give much smoked flavor. The charcoal manufacturers burn out 98.0% of the smoke flavor when they kiln cook hard woods to make lump charcoal. Then, they grind this lump charcoal to make those charcoal briquettes. Yes, they do add raw sawdust or particles of wood to the ground charcoal, and it smokes a little. But, he says you use charcoal briquettes only to produce grilling or barbecuing heat. To give any food a good smoke wood flavor, you need 40 to 60 minutes of heavy smoking. You need smoke wood, like hickory or oak, and more than just a few shavings."

J.J. forcefully continued, "I know how much you like our microwave's easy use and speed. Well, my brother says his gas grill gives him close to a microwave's speed and convenience when he's cooking out. John, while we're on the subject, please, I'd like more than your usual three big cook-outs this year — Memorial Day, 4th of July, and Labor Day. With a gas grill, you could cook once a week for the kids and me very easily. Please, John, think about it."

## Gas Grills? — It's a YES

Now, John, if you'll get your gas grill to "grillin' right", there may be a tiny difference in flavor between a charcoal or gas-grilled hamburger. This is true of other *Quick Grilled* meats (cooked in 5 to 15 minutes). The smoky flavor of *Quick Grilled* foods comes from the smoke you create when the melted fat droplets and meat juices hit the hot fire box below. This is true, regardless of whether it's a gas or charcoal grill.

Many charcoal grillers have switched to gas grills. Gas grilling lets us create a cook-out's smoked flavor and aroma with close to a microwave oven's convenience. Many folks do grill on gas more than once a week, summer or winter. Compared to charcoal grilling, gas grills save 80% of the preparation and clean up time. You can easily grill after work. They save 85% of the fuel cost and 98% of the mess of charcoal. Their constant grilling temperature winter or summer and rapid heat recovery is an advantage. You can easily adjust their heat from 600°F. down to 150°F. by merely turning the controls or opening or cracking the cover to adjust the grill's heat. You grill 1½-inch to 2-inch-thick meats on MEDIUM HIGH for maximum browned "outside" crust using intermittent flame-ups. Then, you *Slow Grill* 2-inch-thick meats on LOW or even bake cornbread sticks, etc., because of their even heat.

## Fat Fires — A No No!

Gas grills are wonderful except for blackening fat fires. Meat's melting fat deposits drip onto the "rock," metal plate, or metal bars in the grill's fire box. Vegetable oil bastes add their fat drippings also. If these fats are not turned into smoke immediately, they soak in and build up. They'll build up on any kind of "rock" whether it's lava rocks, pumice briquettes, ceramic pyramids, metal plates, or metal bars in grills where metal has been used to replace the rock in the fire box. All this accumulated fat becomes fuel for hot, long burning, blackening fat fires.

We have researched the fat fire problem for some time. We found that you can prevent 95% of the long-burning fat fires. You keep the dripping fats from building up directly on or next to open flames. You control these few fires by pouring water on them. You utilize the occasional intermittent flame-up to lightly char foods.

## Charlie's DUO-FIRE-BOX

Charlie's DUO-FIRE-BOX helps control fat fires. With this system of gas grilling: (1) You fill one half of your fire box 3 inches thick with large and small lava rock. This reduces flame-ups greatly from foods such as chicken pieces or pork steaks which have melting fats or oil drippings from marinades; (2) In the other half of the fire box, you use one thickness of compressed pumice briquettes or larger lava rocks for searing steaks, burgers, and chops.

The grill's thin side allows you to *Quick Grill* meat so you can develop a light charred flavor. You can turn pumice briquettes or large lava rocks for easy access to your high preheated fire and you burn off the fat deposits. This heat burns off accumulated fat deposits which greatly reduce flame-ups. It's important when you're grilling fat meat or if using a marinade which contains some vegetable oil.

With the 3-inch-thick side, you cover the live flame holes with small lava rocks to prevent the fat from hitting the open flame. Fat drippings are absorbed onto the top layer of the 3-inch-thick rock, turning it black.

On this 3-inch-thick side, you'll be able to control 95% of the flame-ups, by pouring 1 or 2 ounces of water directly on any big flame-ups that may develop. Do not use a water spritzer to spray water. You'll spread the fire and not put it out easily.

Chicken pieces, turkey pieces, beef and pork roasts, and pork steaks are grilled over the thick 3-inch side of lava rock. Many of these foods must be basted with a marinade containing some vegetable fat to keep them juicy. With this DUO-FIRE-BOX System, you move chicken and pork steak from the 1-inch side to the 3-inch side after it has been seared. The 3-inch side takes 4 minutes longer to come to a 450°F. grilling temperature with a 60°F. air temperature, or about 12 total minutes.

## Research Using DUO-FIRE-BOX

Both the right and left gas controls were set on HIGH, Cover Closed. After 3 minutes, the thick (left) side measured 150°F., the 1-inch thin (right) side 400°F. After 8 minutes the thick side was 275°F. and the thin side — 550°F. At 10 minutes, the gas controls were turned to MEDIUM. The grid wires were oiled and started to grill chicken pieces which had been marinated in a 50/50 lemon juice/oil/dry spice marinade. The thin side cooled to 400°F. and the thick side to 450°F. The opening and closing of any grill cools it rather quickly.

The chicken was turned and basted with the marinade about every 6 to 8 minutes. After about 20 minutes, during one basting, the cover was opened and flames immediately covered ⅔ of the surface of the grill's 3-inch-thick side. It had very little flame-up before this. This complete flame-up was stopped by pouring about two ounces of water in the flame's center. When grilling other times, the grill's fire on the 3-inch side needed water poured in two places.

We grilled chicken easily with a light desirable char, browning it elegantly. With the amount of fat deposits in the chicken plus the oil in this marinade, we found grilling chicken on a gas grill to be much easier. We controlled fat fires using the DUO-FIRE-BOX system.

However, you should still check for big, long-burning fat fires! You recognize big fat fires by increased heavy smoke rolling out of the grill sides and ends, and cover's exhaust slot. You can hear the heavy crackling and popping of a big fat fire. Fat fires develop a burned off-odor, which is different than the standard barbecue smoke odor.

When large fires develop, pour a little water directly on them to prevent burning and blackening. Short intermittent flame-ups, however, help develop a delicious browned outside crust and light char. Fat fires occur most frequently just when the cover is raised for basting or turning. Much of the time, the grill's cover keeps the oxygen low enough that small fires are the desirable intermittent flame-ups.

## Gas Grilling Basics

First: *Please re-read your gas grill Manufacturer's User's Guide.* Important basics: *SAFETY FOR LIGHTING THE FIRE: (1) Every grill's cover (lid, hood) MUST BE OPEN for safe lighting of fire; (2) Keep your head and clothing away from open grill while lighting and cooking; and (3) If fire does not light within 5 seconds, turn off gas and wait for 5 minutes with Cover Open for gas to clear out. Then try lighting again. KEEP SMALL CHILDREN AWAY FROM ANY HOT GRILL.*

IMPORTANT: Yearly service will help your gas grill cook more efficiently. Remove its burner, then (1) clean and reopen the small burner holes using a wire brush, toothpick, or ice pick; and (2) clean venturi tubes of spider webs, etc., using a long flexible venturi brush, or long pipe cleaners through the venturi's adjustment ports. Replace cleaned burner completely covering the grill's gas jets.

Check for any gas leaks before lighting, using soapy water. See Manufacturer's User's Guide.

KNOW YOUR GRILL: Your gas grill's cooking temperatures can range from 800°F. down to 150°F., depending upon how you regulate it. You can (1) Grill, using *Direct Heat*. Food sets directly over the fire with the gas controls set on HIGH, MEDIUM, or LOW; (2) Grill, using *Indirect Heat* with food on the unlit side of a two-burner grill (or cover one side of a single burner with heavy aluminum foil) with gas controls set on HIGH, MEDIUM, or LOW. With the three-burner gas grill, you will cook over the unlit center burner; (3) Grill, *Direct* or *Indirect* by propping the cover open one or two inches to produce smoke flavor for slow-cooking foods.

Windy weather can cool your grill up to 50°F. When grilling Cover Open, turn the grill away from the wind, allowing the cover to shield the cooking grid. Opening and closing the cover to baste or to inspect food cools your grill considerably, but most gas grills regain heat rapidly.

TEST YOUR GRILL'S TEMPERATURES: Use an oven thermometer to test the cooking grid's temperature. Preheat, using each of the major control settings of HIGH, MEDIUM, or LOW — Cover Closed — just one time. Also test for hot spots and cooler spots. grilling temperatures used for *Quick Grilling* (meat cooked done in 5 to 15 total minutes) will match a kitchen oven's broiling temperatures. (One oven broiler tested 550°F. within 3 inches of the heat.)

BURN OFF: You burn off your previous cook-out's fat deposits on briquettes or rocks on the one-inch thin side of a DUO-FIRE-BOX grill or overall over the briquettes or rocks if you do not have a thick side. You'll save gas by turning them over for a burn-off during your 5 to 10 minutes preheat on HIGH — Cover Closed. Ceramic blocks (pyramids) work best with their base down. Therefore, you'll burn them off using 15 minutes on HIGH without turning — Cover Closed, cover them with heavy aluminum foil. Next, you light the fire and set on HIGH for your preheat and wait 5 to 7 minutes in summer, and 10 to 14 minutes in winter, depending upon whether you are grilling on the 1-inch thin side or the 3-inch thick side of your grill. Then, you adjust from MEDIUM HIGH down to LOW, depending on the food you're grilling.

Heat-radiating surfaces are the key to gas grilling's ability to produce a desirable outside browned crust with a juicy center. These radiating surfaces must be preheated for 5 to 7 minutes in the summer to 10 minutes in the winter before they reach searing temperatures and will burn meat drippings.

These heat-radiating surfaces which rest on the coal grate above the burner in the fire box can be: (1) compressed pumice stone briquettes, (2) ceramic clay pyramids, (3) pieces of lava rock, (4) porcelain-covered steel box, (5) ceramic-covered sheet steel "V"-shaped bars.

## GAS GRILLS

SUMMARY: Gas grills will grill foods with nearly equal flavor to a charcoal grill if operated correctly using the *Quick Grill* method. They have a short preheat and preparation time, 5 to 10 minutes before cooking. They develop nearly constant cooking temperatures--easily adjustable from 600°F. down to 150°F. You direct grill with the Cover Closed or Open. You can indirect grill over the left burner which is not lit with the Cover Closed. With the Cover Closed, you'll develop nearly even temperatures over the cooking grids.

Gas grills have enough heating ability for year round grilling even in zero weather. They are somewhat more difficult to add smoke wood flavor when *Slow Grilling* foods than with charcoal grills. They have very little clean up time. If you're thinking about buying a gas grill, read on.

## How Grills Are Constructed

Nearly all good gas grills consist of: (1) cast iron, aluminum or sheet metal box with air holes in the bottom and a hinged cover (hood or lid); (2) double or triple gas burners, only a few have a single burner; (3) heat radiating surfaces which spread out the gas flame's heat and keep fat drippings from falling directly onto the gas burner's open flame. The gas burners and these heat radiating surfaces together are called the "fire box," (4) a food cooking grid (rack), (5) gas controls for HIGH (may be called "preheat"), MEDIUM and LOW, (6) a built-in gas lighter, (7) a gas supply of bottled propane or can be hooked to natural gas, (8) many are on wheels, (9) many have warming racks inside the grill plus attached outside front and side shelves.

Gas grills come in three general sizes and heat: (1) a portable 12,000 B.T.U. single burner with about 144 square inches (9" x 16") of cooking grid surface, (2) 24,000 to 32,000 B.T.U.'s with about 290 square inches (14" x 21") of cooking grid surface with a single or double burner, (3) 35,000 to 46,000 B.T.U. with 300 to 400 square inches (approximately 15½" x 24") of cooking grid surface with duo burners or with triple burners.

Efficient gas grills average producing 85 to 120 B.T.U.'s per square inch of cooking grid surface when set on HIGH. You should be able to heat the cooking grid surface to 600°F. with Cover Closed on HIGH in 5 to 10 minutes. For example: A 32,000 B.T.U. grill uses a 290 square inch grid. This equals 110 B.T.U.'s per square inch of grid surface. This grill measured 600°F. HIGH in 5 minutes in the summertime.

The heat radiating surfaces: (1) spread out and even out the heat from the central gas burner's flames to cook your foods. Therefore, the cooking grid is heated fairly evenly, (2) burn and vaporize fat drippings from the meat which creates smoke. These surfaces must be hot. This smoke gives a smoked flavor to *Quick Grilled* foods, (3) keeps fats from dripping directly onto gas flames and help to minimize fat fires by absorbing unburned fat drippings, (4) maximize searing, browning, and light charring with their intermittent flame-ups. These surfaces are the key to gas grilling's ability to produce a desirable outside browned crust with a juicy center.

## Temperatures Developed

A gas grill's flame equals 3,000°F. at its tip. With the radiating surfaces, your gas grill will develop many different grilling heats quickly. In one of our tests, a 32,000 B.T.U. capacity grill, with Cover Closed, set on HIGH heated to 700°F., in 15 minutes in 30°F. weather. It quickly dropped to 270°F. over the left burner (not lit), with right burner set on LOW, Cover Closed for indirect grilling. With its Cover Open, both burners on LOW, it produced 250°F.

We found that we could lower the heat about 40°F. by opening the cover for one minute, or by propping the cover open 1 inch. When we propped the cover open 2 inches, the temperature dropped considerably more. High winds will drop the temperature 50 degrees when you open the cover or 25 degrees without opening the cover. Some gas grills can have "hot" spots just like baking ovens in kitchen stoves. Use an oven thermometer to test your grill for hot and cold areas. The exterior weather's temperature and wind will vary the cooking temperatures but they have enough heat to overcome this problem. Cover Closed grilling helps to stabilize these temperatures after preheating.

Based upon our research, we prefer compressed round-shaped white pumice rock briquettes for *Quick Grilling*. They produce intermittent flame-ups for searing and light charring for maximum flavor easily. These briquettes radiate heat, absorb fats, and are easily turned over for cleaning before your next grilling while preheating. The pumice briquettes' white color turns brownish black when they need to be turned. Large pieces of lava rock can be used also, but pumice is better.

## Pumice Briquettes

One other change will improve a standard lava rock gas grill. Replace the lava rock with inexpensive uniform-sized compressed pumice stone briquettes only one layer thick on the searing side of your DUO-FIRE-BOX grill. They are permanent, and are white colored. With pumice briquettes, any unburned fat droplets stay on the white surface. They turn black or brown giving you a warning of too much fat deposit which encourages flame-up. You turn the briquettes over during Preheat and burn off any built-up deposits. It will help reduce long-burning or fat fires.

Gas grilling works well. You'll cook-out more easily and probably more frequently. You'll feel comfortable using your gas grill. They're not hard to master.

## Direct and Indirect Grilling

Most lower cost and medium and large sized gas grills have two heat control knobs. Each one controls the fire and the heat for half of the grid. Using these controls, you vary the grill's temperature for direct or indirect cooking.

Direct grilling's temperatures can range from 700°F., both controls on HIGH, Cover Closed after 15 minutes, down to 250°F. with Cover Open with both controls set on LOW. It will produce 150°F. on the unlit side with the other burner set on LOW and the Cover Open.

For indirect grilling, place the food on the left side with no fire and over a drip pan with Cover Closed. You control its temperature from a HIGH of 450°F. down to 150°F. with the cover propped open 1 inch and only one burner lit.

# ELECTRIC GRILLING

Electric grills are convenient and easy. You plug them in and turn the switch. Their electric element cooks the food placed above it on the cooking grid. These grills have metal reflector pans which must get very hot to generate a small amount of smoke when the meat's drippings fall on it. When the grills are covered, this traps the smoke which gives a tiny smoked flavor. Some electric grills have hinged covers. Other electric grills have open electric elements mounted in thick ceramic or plastic bowls.

## 1670 Watt Test

We tested a 1670 watt electric grill with a hinged cover with a sloping grid. The weather was 40°F. with a slight wind. With its Cover Closed, the control set on HIGH, the grill needed 25 minutes to reach the searing temperature of about 500°F. It maintained 350°F. when the controls were set on MEDIUM. We grilled whole catfish on it.

At the same time, we grilled whole catfish on a 30,000 BTU gas grill. With its Cover Closed, and the controls set on HIGH, it reached a searing temperature of 500°F. in 8 minutes. We preferred the gas grill's positive grilling action and the catfish's browned crust and full grilled flavor.

This electric grill would serve fairly well for grilling inside the home, if used in a fireplace which can handle a little smoke. It did not have the ability to do indirect grilling.

We tested one of the inexpensive open table top electric grill. The grilling principle would be the same with any electric grill without a cover. Our unit used 1,000 watts to heat the ⅜-inch-thick ceramic, 4½-inch-tall shaped bowl which was the holder for the electric element. It had a metal reflector in the bottom. It's food rack measured 10" wide x 15" long. However, the effective cooking areas was only 9" x 13 ¾". This was large enough for 4 to 6 burgers or chops or small steaks.

## Still 350°F.

We plugged the grill in and used an oven thermometer to check temperatures. In 7 minutes our temperature stood at 350°F. on the cooking surface. At 10 minutes it still remained at 350°F. When grilling thinner cuts or patties of meat ¾ inches thick and less, you need 450°F. to 500°F. to sear and brown them quickly. Long cooking dries out the meat before it can develop a delicious browned crust. Finally, we put an aluminum foil tent over the grill and in 2 minutes raised its temperature to 500°F. This type of grill develops little smoke because the drippings must hit the red electric element before any smoke develops. This is an advantage for grilling indoors. It's a disadvantage if you like lightly smoked and lightly charred flavors from gas or charcoal grills.

We grilled sausage patties. They were seared and browned particularly over the red hot electric element, but 1½ inches to the side, the patties did not brown. The grilled patties were tasty — but not as good as gas or charcoal grilled ones. Electric grills give us a health advantage. Some of meat's fat particles melt and drop into the bottom of the grill. When you compare this with frying, these grills help us control fat calorie intake and give us the delicious browned flavor of frying.

CHARCOAL

# CHARCOAL GRILLING DOES ITS STUFF

So many people love a cook-out. Why? They anticipate, they sniff the mouth-watering aroma, they see the delicious browned lightly-charred coating, and finally they taste the grilled results — and their juices flow. Here are some basics for producing excellent flavors using charcoal grills.

The most popular grills are the covered kettle and square charcoal grills which produce tasty, smoked meats. Their cover also allows you to control flame-ups easily. These grills started the big revolution toward much more and better cook-out cooking. (See Index: TRUE BLUE BARBECUE.)

All charcoal grills can produce tasty grilled foods when used correctly. The hibachi and the brazier, both open charcoal grills, cook their foods without the covered grill's smoking ability. Some people use hibachis in their fireplaces. Braziers are used for picnics. In general, charcoal briquettes work best and are the most convenient fuels.

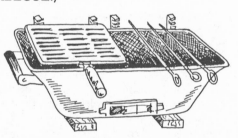

## Starting Charcoal Fires

ELECTRIC STARTERS: Clean, fast, but may leave some briquettes unlit. You must remove the starter 10 minutes after the fire starts. The concentrated charcoal heat melts the starter's heating element (we lost two). You must have an electrical connection close by, which eliminates its use on many picnics.

CHIMNEY FIRE STARTER: You can purchase a ready made large one which uses newspapers to start the briquettes. You can make your own using an empty No. 10 vegetable or fruit can. Use a beer can opener to make 6 to 8 triangular cuts for breathers on the side at the can's bottom. Then, remove the can's bottom. Bend the metal triangles down to make legs. This starter will hold about 40 to 50 charcoal briquettes.

LIGHTING A FIRE WITHOUT A CHIMNEY: Make a mound of charcoal in the center of the grill's fire grate. Use adequate starter fluid to wet all briquettes for an even fire. Let the fluid soak in for 2 minutes then light the fire and wait until all the starter's odor is burned off before you start grilling food.

## Charcoal Fire Pointers

(1) Do not use gasoline or alcohol to start a charcoal fire.

(2) Do not add charcoal starter fluid to burning charcoal — after 8 hours the charcoal may still be alive with fire. Don't dump live coals on grass or wood.

(3) Always burn all charcoal starter fluid out of the fire before grilling. It causes off-flavors to foods. Starter fluid has a distinct odor and can be detected by smelling the fire gently. Self-starting charcoal briquettes should be used only to start fires. Never add them to a fire where foods are cooking. They give food a "starter" flavor.

(4) Your charcoal grill cover works like magic for snuffing out food-burning, blackening fat fires. Just cover your grill. This problem stops in 30 seconds.

## Know Grill's Temperatures

Knowing your grill's ability to produce a fairly accurate cooking temperature is important. Your grill works like a broiler in a kitchen stove. All oven cooking uses (1) a specified temperature, (2) a definite length of cooking time, and (3) a thickness or weight of meat. With your grill, you need to know the temperature to match it with the cooking time and the meat thickness.

The following are the results of our direct and indirect charcoal grilling tests which should serve only as guides. Please test your grill and charcoal for a better idea of more efficient use and better grilling results.

## Direct Kettle Grilling Research

A 22-inch-diameter kettle grill was used in 50°F. windy weather. We tested temperatures with standard oven thermometers which lay directly on the grill's grid (food rack). All temperatures were read after the lighted charcoal briquettes were spread out one briquette thick and laid tightly together. All briquettes were covered with a thin coating of gray ash. The grill was covered and all breathers were 100% open. No food was added during these direct and indirect grilling tests. The addition of refrigerated food will drop these temperatures a few degrees.

Knowing the temperatures of different numbers of briquettes would help the user direct-grill foods better. Forty standard briquettes covered a 12-inch diameter of the coal grate; 50 briquettes covered 14 inches; and 70 briquettes covered its complete 18-inch diameter.

## 70 Briquette Test

Temperatures were taken in the center and on two sides of the grid. There was a big difference in temperatures even with the 70 briquettes from the grid's center to the outer edge of the 22-inch diameter grid. They ranged from 25°F. to 110°F. difference between the two sides. The cooler temperatures were always on the windy side. The cover was removed for 2 minutes to imitate basting and turning the meats. This cooled the grid's cooking temperatures about 150°F. It took 17 minutes to regain its original temperatures. With 70 briquettes our grill was always in the sear range of 600°F. down to 485°F. for the first hour. This was true over the center and at the grid's edges.

We placed a standard oven thermometer directly on top of a hole in the breather of the grill's cover. It read 270°F. when inside temperature on the grid reached 550°F. Then, we started using a 4-inch metal stem glass-faced candy thermometer which was easier to use and more reliable.

## 50 and 40 Briquette Test

This direct grilling test with 50 briquettes produced temperatures nearly in the searing range for about 1 hour also. These temperatures ranged up to 600°F. 10 minutes after the grills was covered and after the charcoal briquettes spread out to a 14-inch diameter. The temperature next to the outside wall was 450°F. The cover was removed for the 2 minute basting test and the temperature dropped 140°F. This fire needed 19 minutes to regain close to its original temperatures. The 40 briquette test reached 500°F. in the center and 450°F. on the sides after 20 minutes. At 1 hour, the center temperature was 450°F. and 350°F. on the side. At 2 hours, the center temperature was 250°F. and the sides — 175°F. The 2 minute turning and basting test dropped temperatures 75°F.

## Searing Tests

Cook-out masterpieces should be seared and grill marked for superior appearance and flavor. This means a higher but even temperature under the meat. With 40 briquettes, you need to cover the grill and wait 10 minutes after spreading the briquettes for searing. You need 3 minutes for 50 briquettes and only 2 minutes for 70 briquettes for a 500°F. searing temperature.

With 50 or 70 briquettes you'll have 600°F. heat if you don't open the grill to turn and baste during the first 5 to 7 minutes. This is too hot for good grilling.

## Indirect Kettle Grilling

This grilling method has been researched and used much less than direct grilling. Indirect grilling's most important cooking temperature is at the grid's center over a drip pan. The two fires on the sides control this center temperature. Three oven thermometers were used for our testing — one over each of the side fires, and the third one in the grid's center. The testing was done on a 40°F. windy fall day. No food was cooked in this test.

The manufacturer of the 22-inch diameter kettle grills gives the following general directions: (1) use 50 total briquettes (25 per side), (2) place the meat over a drip pan between the two fires, and (3) add 6 to 8 briquettes per side about every hour if cooking longer than 1½ hours. Then, add smoke wood to the fire if you want smoke wood-flavored meats.

## Split 25 and 15 Tests

We placed 25 briquettes, 2 to 3 briquettes thick, behind charcoal fences on each side of the covered grill. In these tests, the briquettes were all lighted and just started to gray with ash before the tests started. We quickly closed the cover after each reading of the thermometer.

The first reading, 15 minutes after the test started, the center measured 320°F., the sides averaged 450°F. The center went up to 425°F. and back down to 350°F. during the first hour. With indirect grilling, the basting of the meat is not as frequent. The grill lost 75°F. when uncovered for 2 minutes.

We tested 30 total briquettes 15 per side. At 15 minutes, center reading was 295°F. and the side reading 500°F. The center reached 325°F. at the one hour reading. After 2 hours, the center reading was 300°F. and the side 460°F. without adding charcoal or wood. Our basting loss was 50°F.

## 12 Total Briquettes

Finally, we tested 12 total briquettes, using 6 per side in a pile. At 15 minutes the center reading was 125°F. and the sides were 250°F. At 30 minutes, the center was 160°F. and the sides — 350°F. At one hour, the center was 200°F. and the sides — 275°F. At 2 hours, 125°F. center, and a 200°F. side.

## "Cook It Low"

Nearly all "pro" barbecuers who cook in contests quote a famous guideline, "Cook it low and cook it slow, if you want tougher cuts of meat to be tender." Generally, they try to maintain 250°F. down to 190°F. cooking temperatures.

After reviewing our 12 briquette kettle grill tests, an important barbecuing fact was very apparent. Any grill's low temperature barbecuing, using a kettle grill will need easy and frequent temperature monitoring. A metal-stemmed, glass-faced candy thermometer will help you "watch" the inside of this grill nicely. Many "pro" barbecuers use this kind of thermometer.

When you use a candy thermometer, you must run a test to know the cooking temperature on the center of the grid compared to that temperature on the candy thermometer. The candy thermometer read 165°F. with the grid's center temperature at 300°F. Also, it read 130°F. when the grid's center temperature was 220°F.

We regulated the internal temperature of our kettle grill using the top breather. The top breather's 4 holes were closed down to only a 1/16" crack compared to its normal 3/4-inch diameter holes. This reduced the grill's cooking temperatures up to 125°F.

## Smoking With A Kettle Grill

We smoke-cooked a 4½ pound whole chicken using the indirect method. A small water pan was placed over one of the fires. We used 50 briquettes and 30-minute-water-soaked smoke wood, and added more briquettes and smoke wood on 2 different occasions. Our chicken reached 163°F. doneness in the thigh/-breast skin pocket area in 3 hours and 40 minutes. One pint of water was evaporated. We spent much more time tending the grill than a charcoal water smoker. A water smoker gives a more intense smoked flavor also.

## Indirect Cooking With A Kettle Grill

CONCLUSIONS: (1) Covered kettle and square grills can be used as modified water smokers but required more tending than a standard charcoal water smoker and much more tending than an electric water smoker. (2) Covered grills with 50 briquettes, split 25 on each side, can vary in temperature over the first hour of cooking from 320°F. up to 425°F. and down to 350°F. in the center, but will continue to produce 200°F. heat even at the 3 hour mark. (3) Covered grills can produce juicy smoked-cooked meats. (4) Covered grills which evaporate moisture helps keep food moist.

## Charcoal Grilling Conclusions

Charcoal kettle and square grills will continue as a major piece of barbecuing equipment. They produce good food. In today's "hurried-precious-time-world," gas grilling will grow. People have discovered that they can produce nearly equal flavor to charcoal using much less time and expensive fuel. They can grill after work, in cold weather, and do it much easier.

# CHARCOAL'S HEAT

The amount of heat produced by charcoal can be very high — 2,000°F. at the flame's tip. The amount of smoke wood flavor you'll produce from burning charcoal briquettes only will be very small.

Charcoal briquette's can contain two up to six basic ingredients: (1) coarse ground lump hardwood charcoal which is nearly pure carbon, (2) raw hardwood sawdust or raw wood particles, (3) white specks of sodium nitrate for quicker lighting, (4) anthracite coal which adds to charcoal's heat-producing ability (it burns without smoking), (5) powdered limestone for its whitening effect to produce a gray ash, and (6) liquid cornstarch paste which glues these powdered and granular products together. None of these products contain raw materials which produce much smoke or smoke flavor.

Many standard brands of briquettes contain all six ingredients. The ingredients are mixed together, then compressed into briquette-sized pellets. The briquettes are dried over a gas fire and are then ready to be bagged.

Anthracite coal briquettes produce light tan ash rather than the white gray ash, and when burned will hold their briquette shapes if not disturbed. This is one way to identify this ingredient if it bothers you.

We researched briquettes for their heating ability. We found several brands of standard 2"x2"x1" charcoal briquettes. They do not all have the same size and density. Brand A, which contained anthracite coal weighed 10% more than Brand B, which weighed 15% more than Brand C. Brand A weighed 25% more than C.

TEMPERATURE TESTS: Brand A averaged 16% to 20% hotter fire with the same number of briquettes as Brand B. This difference occurred at all times over the 1½ hour of tests.

CONCLUSIONS: (1) Charcoal with a portion of anthracite coal will burn longer and somewhat hotter. (2) After the liquid starter has completely burned off of all three brands of charcoal, no detectable off-odor was present in any of these three brands.

## Charcoal's Wood Smoke Flavoring?

What about the smoke flavoring ability of hardwood charcoal? The briquette processor "burns" hardwood boards and chunks from oak, hickory, and other hardwood trees in kilns. These kilns use reduced oxygen atmosphere which causes the wood to only smolder. The wood does not catch fire and burn to a gray ash. However, the heat cooks out nearly 100% of the smoke flavoring, leaving only charred black wood lump charcoal or nearly pure carbon. The briquette manufacturer coarsely grinds the lump charcoal and adds other ingredients to make briquette-shaped pellets. Any smoke wood flavor comes from the raw hardwood sawdust or wood particles in the charcoal. The smoke flavor you taste in a charcoal-grilled steak comes from the burning of melted fats and meat juices dripping onto the charcoal fire.

To cook foods with a good smoke wood flavor using charcoal, you must add raw wood pieces, shavings, or sawdust. Secondly, you must expose the meat to heavy wood smoke for one hour to develop a good smoked flavor. However, you can add tantalizing aromas and atmosphere to your cook-out by using some smoke wood or sawdust on the fire. You'll develop this great aroma even if you grill the burgers only 6 to 10 minutes. Many people will admire your technique but the foods' smoky flavor comes from their fats dripping onto the burning charcoal. Special brands of briquettes contain only coarse ground lump charcoal and cornstarch paste.

Finally, minute contaminating flavors can come from the various ingredients in the charcoal as it burns. They are probably not recognizable except by those persons who have very sensitive or trained taste buds. If all charcoal lighter fluid has been burned off, most standard charcoal will not cause off-flavors.

# SMOKE COOKING AND BARBECUING

When most Americans cook-out, they say "Let's have a barbecue!"
Most true barbecuers divide American cook-outs into two groups of people: (1) the "Grillers" who cook thinner, more tender cuts of meat over a "hotter" fire for a shorter time, (2) "Smokers," the true barbecuers who smoke and cook thicker, less tender cuts of meat over a "cooler," smokier fire for a longer period of time. True barbecuers add aromatic smoke-wood, such as hickory, apple, mesquite, etc. to their fire to develop maximum smoked flavor. However, both grillers and true barbecuers hold their cook-out with great emphasis on a true party "attitude."

## Where Did Barbecue Come From?

Most BBQers don't get hysterical about historical BBQ. They just want to barbecue it, eat it, and party with people who are fun to be with.

However, for the record, we think that SECRETS' needs to lightly touch true BBQ history while it's being made. BBQ cook-offs are the newest and fastest growing participating sport in the U.S. They are a family affair — wives and husbands and their kids rally around the ole BBQ pit. In 1992, the International American Royal BBQ contest drew 212 participating BBQ teams from over the U.S., Canada, and Ireland. This contest started with only 6 teams in 1979.

Memphis-in-May's International BBQ contest grew from 17 backyard BBQers into 176 teams by 1992. And the Texans will not be outdone, their BBQ started with cowboys and chuckwagons way back. Now, they hold "hundreds" of BBQ cook-offs.

Some BBQ folks predict that the 1990s will be the BBQ decade and it will be the new food rage. We predict that it will not fall by the wayside like "blackened" foods did after the 1980s. BBQ's are too much fun to be had by both the cooks and the eaters of the good food.

## BBQ Fiction

Charles Lamb, a delightful English story teller, infers that the ancient Chinese were into BBQ big time hundreds of years ago.

In his tale, "A Dissertation Upon Roast Pig," he tells about a small not-too-bright Chinese "country" boy, Bo-bo, playing with fire in his papa's absence. He "fired" their wooden shack which also housed a litter of pigs (Poland China breed, we'd bet). Bo-bo burned their shack to the ground leaving smoke-cooked pigs which naturally laid very still. He tried to revive them and finally pushed one, using a finger as a prod.

Naturally, Bo-bo burned his finger. For relief like every child bright or not, he stuck his burning finger into his mouth and discovered, "Wow, what a good taste." Just then, his raging papa appeared. Bo-bo hustled him over to the smoked pig for his special taste. Immediately Bo-bo and papa "pigged-out" on pig. Then papa and Bo-bo came forth with a regular routine of roasting pigs: building and burning wooden shacks. Mr. Lamb concludes his tale: Bo-bo's BBQing "secret" was "pulled" from him by the Chinese FEDs in Peking, who leaked-it-to-the-press. With that, thousands of Chinese regularly torched wooden shacks.

## BBQing Facts?

Authentic BBQing history is not all that clear. Like any good food, the French claimed to have originated BBQ with their term - *barbe-a-quene...* meaning cooking from beard to tail. Some say they used bearded billy goats, not pigs, always covered with a fancy sauce to make it truly French. Some say the French sailors were supposed to have invaded the Caribbean islands to learn the French BBQ technique.

The Real Truth: Arawak Indians from the Caribbean Islands taught the Spanish sailors the art of BBQing (Columbus' boats made several round trips before the French even sailed by). The Arawaks cooked meat over a frame of green wooden sticks over a wood fire... outdoors... some say it was a spit suspended from 2 forked branches driven in the ground. Anyhow, these Indians called it "barbacoa" for the wooden sticks. The Spanish took it back to Europe where it laid dormant for a couple hundred years except for cooking on the spit in fireplaces... indoors.

Finally, BBQ came back to the U.S. early in the 1700s for cooking whole animals primarily for political and other big gatherings. General George Washington tells about going to a BBQ in his memoirs. Finally, BBQ received the blessings of our Southern folks. The Southerners found the lowly pig to be an ideal meat to be given the royal smoked, sauced treatment. They created "Southern BBQ" using the whole hog. Finally, some smart Southerners found out that BBQed pork shoulders and pork ribs taste more flavorful than whole hog meat.

Now, lots of U.S. restaurants sell "Southern BBQ." The New York folks can go to a "Dallas BBQ" restaurant and hold their heads high for the prestige of its name — "Dallas." But knowing True Barbecuers point with pride to Kansas City and Memphis BBQ. Californians flock to restaurants for a helping of good ole "Southern BBQ." Even a chain of London restaurants featured meat grilled over a metal grate with mesquite wood (costing $2 per 2 foot long for imported U.S. chunks), and called it BBQ.

But for the remaining millions of fun-loving Americans, it's "Let's roll out the smoker or smoker grill and BBQ." Today, many don't wait until summer anymore. They know that if they want tasty meat, they BBQ it in the dead of winter. And they're living BBQ history because they're creating lots of great entertainment and good times for their family and friends.

Thousands of Americans barbecuing in their backyard find water pan smokers to be ideal for creating superb smoke-cooked foods — foods that are tender and juicy, with a fine gourmet taste. Water smokers require little cooking effort and tending by the cook-out cook.

SECRETS' has divided smoke-cooking into two major segments — the Pro Barbecuers in the chapter on True Blue Barbecue (page 72) and those people who want to be successful backyard barbecuers using inexpensive water pan smokers.

## Water Pan Smokers

J.J., John's continuously "food-panicked" wife, looked at John across their breakfast table. She smiled, leaned back, and said, "John, honey, I certainly liked that smoked chicken you did for our guests last night. Even Blossom said so many nice things. She used words like mouth watering, tender, tasty, elegant, and juicy. You should be very proud — satisfying two of us picky women with one food."

You could see John nearly explode with pride. He was surprised. Normally, J.J. was fairly reasonable, but that other "sister" — well, you couldn't please her.

He knew his water smoking technique was good, but he wondered why its produced such outstanding, woman-satisfying chicken. So, John, here for the record, we'll look at how smokers can consistently produce elegant foods.

## How They Work

The smoker's heat sources, electricity, gas, or charcoal, causes the smoke wood to smolder and produce tiny smoke particles. The smoker's water pan is heated to slowly produce some steam vapors.

As the steam vapors rise from the water pan, they unite with the smoke particles from the smoldering aromatic smoke wood. Together they become tiny exquisite "flavor droplets." These nearly invisible droplets continuously baste and gently poach the food, then drip back into the water pan.

With a water smoker, you'll entertain with new food discoveries — juicy, tender, less expensive cuts of meat. Smoking enhances the flavor of the meat, and you'll spend far less time turning and basting it. You use much longer cooking times — 2 to 4 hours for smoked chicken compared to 30 to 50 minutes for grilled chicken.

Some "food-panicked" Americans fear the alleged threat of cancer from smoked foods. Natives of some undeveloped countries do have more digestive tract cancers. They eat smoked foods nearly every meal. The remainder of the world does not eat smoked foods nearly as frequently. Reliable toxicologists conclude that smoked foods do not present a problem.

## Water Smoker Advantages

Foods slowly cook at 300°F. down to 175°F. for a tenderizing effect. Compare the tender white of a poached egg (it contains protein like meat) with a fried egg cooked at 400°F. with its toughened white. Smoke-cooked meats at low temperatures (1) tenderize the meat's tough connective tissues (collagen) changing them into tender gelatin, and (2) kill all surface bacteria and 99. + % of any hidden bacteria down inside the meat.

The water pan smoker cooks foods juicier, healthier, and more flavorful six ways: (1) It carries smoke flavor deep into meat. (2) It catches the condensed vapor droplets of the meat's own juices and dissolved seasonings. It uses them to automatically self-baste the meat again and again. (3) Its moist vapors reduce the evaporation rate of the food's natural juices compared to a grill's or oven broiler's totally dry heat. This reduces the shrinkage of the meat and retains juiciness. (4) It vaporizes some liquid at low temperatures, which is a more tenderizing heat. (5) It allows meat to brown with a elegant tasty caramelized "outside." (6) It catches the cooked-out inlaid fats, cholesterol, and calories into the water pan for easy disposal. *(SMOKING RESEARCH: 3 ounces of fat in the water pan came from two 3½ pound chickens.)* You can smoke combinations of chicken, pork, beef, or sausage all at the same time.

## Types of Water Smoking

HOT SMOKING: You smoke-color, then cooks foods to produce an elegant flavor and aroma. The smoker's interior temperatures are normally kept at 210°F. - 250°F. Use an oven thermometer to know your temperatures.

COLD SMOKING: Smoke colors foods giving them an elegant smoky flavor and aroma. It does not cook foods. The air temperature inside the smoker will range from 85°F. to 120°F. You use a standard weather thermometer to check the temperature.

Cold smoking's potential problems: Bacteria multiply about 10,000 times faster at 85°F. to 120°F. than at 40°F. refrigerator temperature, or above a 140°F. cooking temperature. After the meat "takes" some smoke, the smoke acts as a protector. For long cold-smoking, 4 to 6 hours, you may want to start with dry-cured or brined meat with its higher salt content. With cold smoking, first you should dry all meats with a paper towel or an electric hair dryer or by refrigerating. This will save smoking time. Use the water pan without water to catch any drippings.

In a standard charcoal water smoker, you reduce charcoal from 100 down to 5 briquettes in the charcoal pan. Then you add smoke wood. This reduces the smoker's temperature to 85°F. to 120°F. With an electric water smoker, you remove its electric heating element. Then use 4 to 5 fully-lighted charcoal briquettes and smoke wood pieces in the loaf pan for cold smoking. You must replace them every 1 to 2 hours to reach the desired smoke color.

Old-fashioned bacon is brined or dry cured, then cold smoked for hours. You can create "old time bacon" using commercially cured slab bacon and your added seasonings. Then cold smoke for 3 to 4 hours.

WET SMOKING: This is the normal way to use a standard water pan smoker. You can use a supplemental pan with water in a covered kettle or square type charcoal grill. Either way, when the water is heated, it produces water vapors which help to keep long-smoked foods from drying out. Wet smoking is the first step for smoke-cooking thin meats (less than 2 inches thick) to an internal temperature of 130°F. Then you finishing cooking by dry smoking.

DRY SMOKING: You use a water pan smoker without water in the water pan. Place a thin coating of wood granules in this water pan to absorb fats and juice drippings from the meat. This type smoking raises the cooking temperature 25°F. to 40°F. from 260°F. to 300°F. unless you compensate for it.

Dry smoke-cooking helps create the delicious, smoked brown barbecued outside flavors. It helps keep the juicy center for outstanding barbecued meats. You create the great barbecue flavor like the "Pros" who barbecue in contests. Dry smoking is essential when smoking thin, less then 2 inches thick, meats, poultry, fish, and seafood. Why? With some water smokers you can cook thin meats and fish to the overdone stage — long before you can create the desirable, browned outside smoky crust.

Dry smoke-cooking using water smokers has been researched in depth by the CULINARY INSTITUTE OF SMOKE-COOKING and is a major innovation for producing elegant smoked foods that are thin and quickly cooked done. You can add some smoke flavoring to nearly any food using dry smoking.

Using the water smoker's Basic Master Steps, you stop water smoking when the thin meats or poultry (except fish) have reached 130°F. internal temperature. At this point you recharge the smoker with smoke wood. Lift out the grids with food resting on them as well as the water pan, using hot pads or gloves. You empty the water pan and spread wood granules thinly on the pan's bottom. Be extremely careful with these hot foods and hot water, they can burn. Eliminate any pools of liquid on the meat's top surface by blotting with paper towels for maximum smoke "take" quickly. Meat can cool up to 30 minutes until your smoker has started to generate heavy smoke.

Even the water pan's wood granules need to generate smoke for smoking thin foods. Let the smoker generate smoke for 15 to 20 minutes. Then replace the grids with the meat and the dome. Dry smoke-cook for 40 to 60 minutes to correct doneness temperature for that cut of meat. You can dry smoke foods using a closed kettle or a square type grill with smoke wood and low temperature indirect grilling.

## Smoking Basics — Electric, Charcoal, Gas Smokers

Make a 30" drip circle by spreading aluminum foil underneath the smoker. This will catch any condensation which may develop on the walls of the smoker and drip to stain wood or concrete. Be sure you move your smoker away from the wooden overhang of the building 6 feet. Smoke can discolor paints.

Any food will "take" a smoke color and flavor only when its exterior surfaces are reasonably dry and does not touch other foods. Remove thicker meats over 2 inches from the refrigerator to come to room temperature 60 minutes or longer before starting to smoke if you're in a hurry. Uncover foods so that their surfaces can dry. Place foods with the shorter cooking time on the top grid for easy removal. Always thaw frozen meats completely before starting to smoke them.

When you start smoking, you should smell the wood smoke coming from a charcoal or gas smoker immediately, or in a few minutes from an electric smoker. Your smoker's temperature gauge gives you only a general idea of the smoker's internal air temperature. (Many gauges are not accurate — use a standard oven thermometer to check temperatures.) The bottom grid cooks slower than the top grid.

Smoke-cooking time varies with each smoker's ability to generate heat. The amount of time also depends upon: (1) how cold the air temperature, (2) how much wind, (3) how thick and big the pieces of meat are, (4) how cold the pieces of meat when you started, and (5) are you cooking in the mountains?

For example: Two 20-pound turkeys coming from the refrigerator will need nearly double the smoke-cooking time compared with two 4-pound frying chickens from the refrigerator. You can reduce a smoker's temperature 30°F. to 40°F. by opening the inspection door 1½ inches, or moving it's dome to the side 1 inch to 1½ inches to uncover the smoker body.

## Smoke Flavoring and Smoke Woods

The smoke wood flavor of the meats depends upon the darkness of the smoked color. Smoke woods flavor foods somewhat differently and are a matter of preference. Hickory flavor has been the old stand-by with dry or wet wood chunks, shavings, or sawdust. Oak, apple, peach, alder, cherry, mesquite, pecan, maple, or combinations are preferred by some. Too much smoke from any wood can turn meat bitter. Smoke wood flavor ratings: Alder: (from the West Coast) sweet, mild; Apple: mild, fruity; Hickory: sweet to strong; Maple: sweet and light; Mesquite: sweet to strong; Oak: medium to heavy. DO NOT use sassafras, pine, spruce, or any evergreen type wood. Sawdust from a lumber yard normally contains softwoods. It can be contaminated and not safe, or its flavor is poor. Use hardwoods only.

You control the meat's finished smoked color by: (1) the length of smoking time, (2) the amount of smoke wood granules, wood pieces or chips used, (3) the dryness of the outside surface of the meat at the beginning of smoking, and (4) the amount of liquid in the water pan during the complete smoking time. If you want more smoke color, you eliminate the water in the water pan. Then substitute wood granules for an electric smoker or add more wood to a charcoal smoker, but retain a dry water pan to catch meat drippings.

Smoke-color controls your smoke flavor: (1) deep brown for a country ham flavor, (2) medium to deep brown for barbecued ribs, or (3) very light brown delicate smoke for fish. You want a smoked crusted coating on the outside surface of meat and the inside should remain juicy, tender, and flavorful.

For medium brown smoked color and good flavor, use the amount of smoke wood and smoking time suggested in SECRETS' smoke-cooking guides.

## Smoke-Cooking Time

Absolute to-the-minute cooking times are impossible for smoke-cooking. Winds and high altitude will increase smoking time 25% to 30%. Very cold weather will increase cooking time 50% or more; 90°F. temperatures and direct sunshine reduce smoking time 25% to 33%.

The thickness of a piece of meat also controls cooking time. Oysters and thin fish fillets smoke-cook to their done stage in 20 to 45 minutes. If cooked longer, they dry out. Therefore, their surfaces need to be free of moisture before you start smoking for maximum "take" of smoke.

Smoking hardens the outside skin of poultry and fish unless they are brushed with vegetable oil. Removing this skin makes carving easier. Medium smoked poultry becomes lightly smoke-flavored chicken when the skin is removed. (See Index: Smoke-Cooking Guides: Electric or Charcoal.)

## Simple "Curing" For More Flavor

SECRETS' plastic bag "curing" system uses dry rubs which gives your smoked and grilled foods added flavor and zest. Use a white or clear strong 4 to 8 gallon food grade plastic bag as a curing bag. This holds the meat and doesn't leak the liquid which a dry rub generates. Dry rubs or wet marinades which contain a small amount of salt help to carry seasonings into the meat. Dry rubs, liquid marinades, or other seasonings can overwhelm the meats. They should only complement the meat.

DRY RUBS: Sprinkle one of SECRETS' dry rubs very generously over all surfaces and cavities of meat, poultry, or fish and rub in. Place food in a plastic curing bag in refrigerator for up to 72 hours or at room temperature below 75°F. for 2 hours before smoking. Thin pieces of fish or meat need marinating only for 45 minutes at room temperature. Longer marinating (72 hours) gives better flavor to thick meats. Turn every 12 to 24 hours for seasonings to penetrate all surfaces. Use dry rubs when you marinate small quantities or difficult pieces such as whole chickens, turkeys, big bony irregular pieces or when you want to save time. (See Index: Dry Rub Recipes.)

LIQUID MARINATING: Marinades allow you to mix liquid seasonings: lemon juice, soy or Worcestershire sauces, honey, maple flavoring, vinegar — wines, sherries, beers — salad dressings, dry and fresh herbs and spices.

Soak meat, poultry or fish separately in a liquid marinade in a plastic curing bag, glass dish, or stainless steel pan. The length of time depends upon the thickness of the food and the fullness of flavor of the seasonings you desire. (See Index: Marinades recipes.)

## Basic Master Smoke-Cooking Steps

You will follow these BASIC MASTER SMOKE-COOKING STEPS regardless of the type of smoker. However, each type of smoker may have different cooking times.

STEP (1): Produce heat to cook and generate smoke.

(a) Electric Smoker: Uses a small electric element like an electric stove. This heats the slightly wet wood granules (sawdust) or slightly water-soaked wood chips so that they smolder and smoke. You just plug it in.

(b) Charcoal Smoker: Uses charcoal briquettes which cause wet pieces of smoke wood to smolder and smoke. You start the charcoal with an electric starter or light with the charcoal lighter and wait to burn off the charcoal starter odor — usually 25 to 40 minutes. Then you start smoking.

(c) Gas Smoker: Uses propane or natural gas to heat the wet wood which smolders and smokes; a gas water smoker's fire is blown out easily by high winds. Protect it with a screen.

STEP (2): Place smoke wood on the fire or in pans on the electric heating element to generate smoke. Use a drip pan under the smoker to protect walks, patios, decks, etc., against smoker drippage.

STEP (3): Place water pan on its holders inside the smoker. Use 1 to 8 quarts of liquid depending upon the amount of food you are smoking and your type of smoker.

STEP (4): Spray food grids (racks) with a food release agent (PAM, etc.) or brushed with vegetable oil for easier clean up after smoking.

STEP (5) PREPARE MEAT: Trim fats, season with rubs, etc. This may be done 2 up to 72 hours ahead. Keep meats from touching each other or the side of the smoker.

STEP (6): Place dome or cover on smoker. It should fit somewhat loosely. Smoke needs to circulate over the meat. Stale smoke gives meat a bitter taste.

STEP (7): The temperature gauge or thermometer mounted in the smoker's dome measures the approximate air temperature only, not the food temperature. Sometimes these thermometers are not accurate. Use an oven thermometer for measuring the air temperature inside the smoker one time. Then you'll know how to estimate the smoker's temperature based upon its gauge's reading. Your oven thermometer should run between 175°F. and 300°F.

STEP (8): Testing for doneness. Check the meat's temperature using a meat thermometer before the end of the minimum suggested smoking time. Then leave the thermometer in the meat until you take it off. (See Index: Doneness Chart for specific foods.)

STEP (9): Smoking time — See Index for Smoking Guides, Electric or Charcoal. See manufacturer's instructions for gas, electric or charcoal smokers.

## CHARCOAL SMOKE COOKING GUIDE

| Meat Type Surface Fat Trimmed | Weight or Thickness | Amount of Charcoal in Fire Pan | Amount of Wood Chunks | Timing/Hours | Doneness Test Best Temp. for Juiciness (3) |
|---|---|---|---|---|---|
| **BEEF** | | | | | |
| (1) Roast, Rib or Sirloin Tip | 3-5 lb. (3-4 inches) | level full | 1-2 | 4½-6 | 145° for medium rare and up |
| (2) Top Round Roast | 3-5 lb. (2½-4 inches) | level full | 1-2 | 3½-4½ | 145° for medium rare and up |
| (3) Brisket | 3-4 lb. 8-16 lbs. | Moist cook before dry smoking (approximately 3-4 hours) | | 160° 6-8 hours | 160° |
| **FISH** | | | | | |
| Whole Dressed | 10-12 ounces (1¼ inches) 1 lb. 4 lb. | level level rounded | 1-2 1-2 1-2 | 1¾ - 2¾ 1-3 | 135°* 135°** 135°** |
| Fillets | | | | | |
| Fillets & Steaks | ½ inch thick 1-1¼ inch thick | level level | 1-2 1-2 | 1-2 1½-3 | 135° 135° |
| **PORK** | | | | | |
| Pork Shoulder Roast (Boston Butt) - boneless | 3-6 lb. (3 inches-) | rounded | 1-2 | 5-7 | 155°-160°F. |
| Pork Loin, boneless Pork Loin, bone in | 3-6 lb. (2 - 3 inches) 3-6 lb. (3 - 4 inches) | heaping | 2-3 | 3½-5 3½-7 | 155° - 160° 155° - 160° |
| Country Style Ribs | 3-6 lb. (1½ inches) | | | 3-4½ | 155°-160° |
| Spare Ribs | 3½ lb. (1 inch) 2 sides | heaping | 1-2 | 3½-5½ | meat releases from bone |
| Loin Back Ribs Baby Back | 2-6 lb. (1 inch) | rounded | 1-2 | 3-5 | meat releases from bone |
| Pork Chops | 3-6 lb. (1 inch) 4-8 chops | rounded | 1-2 | 3-4 | 155°-160° |
| Pork Shoulder, whole deboned, skinned or fresh ham (green) | 8-12 lb. | heaping | 2-3 | 7-10 | 155°-160° |
| Sausage, (linked, pork, Italian, Cajun, or rope) | 1 inch -1¼ inches | level to rounded | 1-2 | 2-3 | 160° juice runs clear |

| | | | | | |
|---|---|---|---|---|---|
| Sausage, cured | 3 inches diameter | rounded | 1-2 | 4½-6 | 150° |
| ½ Ham fully cooked skinned, defatted, bone-in | 5-8 lb. 4 inches thick | level | 1-2 | 3-5 | 130° |
| POULTRY | | | | | |
| Chickens 2 whole | 3½-4½ lb./ea. | rounded | 1-2 | 4-6 | 165° |
| 4 whole | 3½-4½ lb/ea. | | 2 | 5-7 | 165° |
| Turkey Wild or Tame | 8-10 lb. | heaping | 2 | 5-7 | 165° |
| | 11-13 lb. | heaping | 2-3 | 6-8 | 165° |
| | 18-20 lb. | | | 10-12 | 165° |
| Turkey Breast bone-in | 4-7 lb. | rounded | 1-2 | 4-6 | 165° |
| Rock Cornish Game Hens - (4) | 1-1½ lb./ea. | level | 1-2 | 2½-3½ | 165° |

* Catfish will not separate from its backbone until it reaches 160°F. It flakes at 135°F.

## CHARCOAL SMOKING GUIDE
## For a Standard Two Grid Water Smoker

1. A smoker placed in bright sunshine, no wind 90°F.: reduce smoking time 10% to 20%.

2. A charcoal water smoker cooks food easily when the outside temperature is above 70°F.

3. Unless additional lighted charcoal is added, a charcoal smoker's fire dies down rapidly after 4 hours. After 6 hours, the fire does not produce enough heat to cook foods.

4. With 50°F. temperatures, be prepared to add lighted charcoal.

5. With 20°-30°F. temperatures and below, smoke-flavor larger meats (7 lb. turkey breast, 12 lb. turkey, 14 lb. shoulder) then cook the meat done in the oven unless you want to feed the smoker for 12 hours.

6. Windy weather increase smoking time 25%. Mountains add 20% to cooking time.

7. A charcoal pan filled with charcoal level full equals about 6 lb., a rounded pan—8 lb., a heaping pan—9 lb.

8. Smoke wood can be fresh cut or water soaked for 30 minutes to produce longer smoke. A chunk equals 4 inch squares x 1 inch thick. Use the equivalent in smaller pieces.

9. Use 4 quarts of water for most smokings. Refill for long smoking.

## ELECTRIC SMOKE-COOKING GUIDE
## 1650 Watt (1) Water Smoker

| Meat Type / Surface Fat / Trimmed | Weight or Thickness | 60° or less; or Windy; or In-A-Hurry; Use Blanket(s) or Smoke Box (2) (Time in hours) | Summer-70° plus, No Wind (3) (Time in hours) | Best "Temp" for Juiciness or Doneness Test (4) |
|---|---|---|---|---|
| BEEF | | | | |
| Brisket | 3-4 lb. / 8-12 lb. (See text.) | 3 to 5 / 6 to 10 | 3 to 5 / 6 to 10 | 160° (5) / 160° (4) |
| Roast, Rib or Sirloin Tip | 4-5 lb. (3-4 inches) | 3½ to 5 | 4 to 6 | 140° for rare and up |
| FISH | | | | |
| Fillets | ½ inch thick | 1 to 1½ | Don't blanket dry smoke only | 135° (6) |
| Fillets & steaks | 1 to 1½ inch thick | 1½ to 2½ | 2-3 | 135° (6) |
| Whole, Dressed | 10-12 ounces (1¼ inches) / 1 lb. (1½ inches) / 4 lb. (2½ inches) | 1½ to 2½ / ¾ to 2¾ / 3 to 5 | 1¾ to 2¾ / 2 to 3½ / 4 to 6 | 135° (6) / 135° (6) / 135° (6) |
| PORK | | | | |
| ½ HAM fully cooked, skinned, defatted, bone-in | 5-8 lb. (4 inches) | 2 to 3 | 2½ to 3½ | 130°-140° |
| Pork Chops | 3-6 lb. (1 inch) (6-8 chops) | 1½ to 2¼ | 2 to 3 | 155°-160° |
| Pork loin, bone-in | 3-6 lb. (3-4 inches) | 3 to 3½ | 3½ to 5 | 155°-160° |
| Pork loin, boneless | 3-6 lb. (2-3 inches) | 2 to 3 | 2½ to 4 | 155°-160° |
| Pork shoulder Roast (Boston Butt) - boneless | 3-6 lb. (3-4 inches) | 3 to 3½ | 3½ to 4½ | 160° |

| | | | | |
|---|---|---|---|---|
| Pork shoulder, whole deboned, skinned or fresh ham (green) | 8-12 lb. (3-5 inches) | 3½ to 4½ | 4 to 5½ | 160° |
| Ribs, Country Style | 3-6 lb. (1½ inches) | 1¾ to 2¼ | 2¼ to 2¾ | 155°-160° |
| Ribs, Loin Back (baby back) | 2-6 lb. (1 inch) | 2½ to 3½ | 3 to 4 | meat releases from bones |
| Ribs, Spare | 3½ lb. (1 inch) | 3-4 | 3½-4½ | meat releases from bones |
| Sausage, cured, linked | 3 inches diameter | 2½ to 3½ | 3 to 4 | 150°-155° |
| Sausage, cured without casing | 2 inches diameter | 2½ to 3½ | 3 to 4 | 150°-155° |
| Sausage, fresh linked, rope, pork, Italian | 1-1½ inches diameter | 1¼ to 1¾ | 1½ to 2 | 160° juice runs clear |
| POULTRY Chicken 2 Whole 4 Whole | 3½-4½ lb./ea. 3½-4½ lb./ea. | 2½ to 3¼ 3 to 4 | 2½ to 3½ 3 to 4½ | 165° 165° |
| Turkey Breast, bone-in | 4-7 lb. | 2 to 3 | 2½ to 4 | 165° |
| Whole, Wild or Tame | 8-10 lb./ea. 11-13 lb./ea. 18-20 lb./ea. | 3 to 4 3½ to 4½ 4½ to 5½ | 3½ to 4½ 4 to 5 5 to 6 | 165° 165° 165° |
| Rock Cornish Game Hens | 1-1½ lb./ea. | 1½ to 1¾ | 1½ to 2½ | 165° |

(1) Use 2 quarts of water for most smokings; 3 quarts for extra long smoking.
(2) Use two blankets for 20°F. or colder temperatures.
(3) Smoker placed in bright sunshine, no wind 90°F. reduces smoking time 10% to 20%.
(4) See Doneness Chart.
(5) See index: Brisket Cooking.
(6) Cook until the fish flakes or becomes free of backbone.

## Smoking Different Foods

*We like smoked chicken best. It is juicier and more flavorful than smoked turkey. You can entertain 12 to 16 people beautifully and inexpensively with four 3½ to 4½ pound frying chickens. Leftover smoked chicken is great for "reruns."*

### Smoking Chicken

(1) Buy two big whole frying chickens — 3½ to 4½ pounds each.

(2) Rinse the abdominal and neck cavities and the exterior thoroughly with water.

(3) Season the neck and abdominal cavities and the exterior with a rub (see Index for recipes); sprinkle approximately 1½ to 2 tablespoons per chicken.

(4) Place chickens in a plastic bag, and marinate at room temperature (below 75°F.) up to 2 hours or up to 72 hours in the refrigerator. Rotate for better coverage.

(5) Remove and let the skin surfaces dry for 30 minutes, if you have time.

(6) Place chickens breast side up, using top grid for only two chickens. You can smoke 4 chickens using both grids. The top 2 chickens will be 10 degrees higher than the bottom and cook done sooner.

SMOKING: Follow Master Smoke-Cooking Steps, the Smoke Cooking Guide for Electric or Charcoal Smokers, and the Doneness Guides.

### Smoking Turkey

Buy a 12 to 20 pound turkey. Leftovers freeze beautifully for exciting re-runs, OR buy a 5 to 7 pound frozen or fresh turkey breast. Thaw frozen whole turkey completely. Turkey breast: Thaw in refrigerator or microwave. (See Index: Specific turkey preparation.)

WHOLE TURKEYS: Remove excess moisture from the tail cavity with a paper towel. Sprinkle a rub (See Index) into the cavities and heavily all over the exterior using 3 to 4 tablespoons per whole bird (rub the seasoning in). Cook any stuffing separately.

TURKEY BREAST: Use 1½ to 2 tablespoons of a rub for bone-in turkey breast. Marinate either the whole turkey or turkey breast at room temperature, ·75°F. and below for two hours or place in plastic bag and marinate up to 72 hours in the refrigerator.

SMOKING: Follow Basic Smoke-cooking Steps, the Smoke-cooking Guide for Electric and Charcoal Smokers, and the Doneness Guides.

For doneness: Above all don't rely on the little built-in button "thermometer" which comes with every frozen turkey which supposedly tells you when the turkey is done. They have never been reliable at 165°F. cooking temperature. Anything above 165°F. overcooks turkey and is not needed to control bacteria.

*Smoking Research: Two 19-pound turkeys smoke-cooked to 185°F. were significantly drier, less tasty, and had crumbly slices than did the four 19-pound turkeys smoke-cooked to 170°F. — these turkeys were very juicy. Later, 165°F. doneness proved even better.*

*Take the turkey off the smoker when done and let it rest for 20 minutes. Set your oven on 140°F. or on warm with the door open slightly to keep it warm if you need to hold it. Cover the turkey with aluminum foil to keep it from drying out.*

## Smoking Pork

Pork smokes nicely and develops excellent flavor. One of the best cuts is the pork loin. See Pork Chapter.

When smoking a Boston butt or a pork shoulder, you may butterfly it to give you more smoke-cooked "outside" meat. Sprinkle meat with a rub (See Index) generously. Rub in the rub; place meat in a plastic bag and "cure" 2 hours at room temperature (below 75°F.) or in the refrigerator up to 72 hours. NOTE: When smoking thin pieces of pork (2 inches or less, such as: loins, butterflied Boston butts, or other foods which smoke-cook done too fast before they take on a good smoke color and flavor) — use two steps: (1) wet smoking, (2) dry smoking. (See Index.)

SMOKING: Follow Basic Master Smoke-cooking Steps in this chapter, the Smoke-cooking Guide for Electric and Charcoal Smokers, and the Doneness Guides. You can still smoke-cook pork to 185°F. if you wish, but you'll dry it out. Try eating smoked pork without any extra wet tomato-based barbecue sauce. Taste the browned "outside" meat. It's delicious with its smoke-cooked flavor, plus the addition of the rubs or dried BBQ sauce.

Carving Pork: When done, remove the meat; let it set for about 10 to 20 minutes so the meat's juices can be reabsorbed and the meat "sets up" for better slicing and less purging (juice loss).

## Smoking Ribs

See Index: True Blue BBQ chapter for preparation. Apply rub generously to both sides of spare ribs or baby back ribs. Marinate in a plastic bag for 2 hours at room temperature (below 75°F.) or in refrigerator up to 72 hours. Bring to room temperature when refrigerated, if you have time. Follow BASIC MASTER SMOKE-COOKING STEPS.

Doneness Test: Ribs are done when $\frac{1}{8}$ to $\frac{1}{4}$ inch of bone end shows and the ribs separate easily. Try eating them without a wet tomato-based barbecue sauce. They're called "dry ribs" and are delicious. Country Ribs: Follow BASIC MASTER SMOKE-COOKING STEPS to 130°F. and then dry-smoke to 155°F. and quit; they dry out easily after 155°F.

## Smoking Beef Brisket

The beef brisket cut comes from the chest muscle meat directly between and behind the front legs of cattle. Even a USDA *Choice* grade brisket contains lots of over-exercised tough connective tissue (collagen). This means slow moist low temperature cooking to 160°F. for maximum tenderness, and holding this temperature for several hours.

Based upon good animal science and cooking research, brisket and other tough meats need prolonged cooking at the internal temperature of 160°F. to become tender. Long cooking dries out these meats easily because they are lean. For the backyard BBQer, SECRETS recommends cooking them in foil at 160°F. for 1 to 3 hours. Then unwrap and smoke-cook for flavor still at the 160°F. temperature until tender, following Basic Master Smoking Steps.

Start with a 4 to 6 pound brisket. Do not trim the brisket's fat; you trim it later. You will need to marinate it. (See Index: Brisket Marinade.) Cover brisket with marinade in a plastic bag and marinate for up to 72 hours.

VERY IMPORTANT: Brisket and "Chewy" Meats: Slice ⅛-inch-thick 45°-angle slices across the grain with the knife held close to parallel with the meat itself.

## Smoking Lamb

Use a leg of lamb or a lamb shoulder roast, rolled, debone, remove outside fat and thick layers of fat. Apply olive oil or canola oil to the surfaces, then sprinkle with 2 to 3 tablespoons El Greco Rub (See Index) over all surfaces. Then roll and tie in 2 or 3 places with butcher's twine. Place in a plastic bag and "cure" at room temperature (below 75°F.) for 2 hours or in a refrigerator up to 72 hours. Smoke to 140°F. to 160°F.

## Sausage Without A Casing

(See Index: Recipes and Meat Preparations for Pork/Beef, Chicken or Turkey, Deer or Elk Mettwurst, and Smoking Sausage Without a Casing see page 104, 105. For Linked sausages see page 97.)

# JUST PLUG IT IN (Electric Water Smoke-Cooking)

We have used as our standard an electric water smoker that is approximately 31" to 33" tall, 16" to 18" in diameter, mounted on legs with a dome (cover or lid), a sliding or hinged inspection door on its side, a 1650 watt electric cooking element, two cooking grids (racks), 5 to 8 quart capacity water pan, temperature indicator in the dome. This general design allows you to control smoke-cooking and smoke flavor easier and safer — much better than other designs.

Other electric units have 1100, 500, and 300 watt heating elements. The 300 watt unit functions best as a "cold smoker" for flavoring only, or for smoke-cooking fish for many hours. The 1650 watt units smoke and cook foods at the same time. Check your manufacturer's instructions for their specific recommendations.

## Electric Smoking Steps

Setting up Wood Pans: Electric smokers work better with extra smoke wood pans. They help you produce good smoke color and flavor. With the 1650 watt unit, we suggest using a 9-inch diameter cake pan and an 8½" x 4½" x 2½" loaf pan with extended lips. (Check with your manufacturer for safety.) If you need to use an extension, use one with a No. 12 or 14 size wire. Watch out for blowing fuses or tripping circuit breakers if several other appliances are in use on the same circuit. NOTE: You can lift the dome and inspect the food and lose very little heat with a 1650 watt electric smoker because it recovers heat quickly.

STEP (1): With smoke wood granules (raw hardwood sawdust), add 1½ cups to the cake pan. Add 3 cups to the loaf pan, plus ¼ cup of water to these granules to extend their smoking ability. This amount of wood granules adds a mahogany smoked color and good smoked flavor. (NOTE: Use fewer granules in the loaf pan if you want lighter smoked color and flavor.

STEP (2): Place the filled wood pans directly on the electric heating coil just as you would place pans on an electric stove's heating element. Check your smoker's manufacturer for safety. If smoker has an inspection door, place loaf pan for easy removal during smoking, using a pair of pliers. You may want to replace the nearly burned granules with fresh wood granules. Or remove to stop adding more smoke to the food. This pan will still contain live fire; soak with water to extinguish the burning particles. This pan will be very hot, so be careful.

STEP (3): Place water pan on its holders inside the smoker, then pour only 2 quarts of hot water or 1 quart of water plus one-fifth bottle of wine or two cans of beer into the water pan. This amount of liquid will smoke-cook for 3 to 4 hours using a 1650 watt electric smoker. By reducing the amount of water in the electric units, the water pan liquid (see Water Pan Sauce) becomes more concentrated and flavorful.

STEP (4): Follow Basic Master Smoking Steps for all types of water smokers.

STEP (5): See Index: Electric Smoking Guide and Doneness Temperature's Guide for each food.

A GENERAL RULE OF THUMB for an electric smoker producing 250°F. to 270°F. temperatures: MEAT ROASTS of 3 or more pounds, or over 3 inches thick, need 50 to 80 minutes per pound for 160°F. doneness.

## Electric Dry Smoking

Dry smoking is essential when smoking thin, less than 2 inches thick, fast smoked-cooked meats, poultry, fish, and seafood. Why? The 1650 watt electric water smokers can cook thin meats and fish "to-a-dry-overdone" quickly — long before you create a desirable, delicious "outside" browned smoky crust.

When the wet smoked meats, poultry, and sausage without casings (except fish) have reached 130°F. internal temperature, using the Basic Master steps, unplug the smoker. With an electric smoker, the meat can cool up to 20 minutes while your smoker is generating heavy smoke again. You'll use dry wood granules in the 9-inch cake pan, the loaf pan, and in the dry water pan. (You may want to save the water pan liquid for basting food or for water pan sauce. See Index.)

Rinse out coagulated materials in water pan, then add (1) one cup of wood granules to the dry water pan, spreading out thinly and evenly on the bottom; (2) use one cup of dry wood granules in the 9-inch round cake pan; and (3) check the loaf pan. It needs to contain enough unburned wood granules to generate smoke for 1½ hours. Replace with fresh wood granules, if needed. Run water over any burning wood granules before disposing of them, when recharging the loaf pan. Replace all wood granule pans on electric heating element. Then replace the water pan with its wood granules. The water pan's granules need to generate smoke for fast dry smoking. Plug smoker into the electricity. Let the smoker generate smoke for 15 to 20 minutes. Then replace the meat and the dome. Dry smoke-cook for 40 to 60 minutes to correct doneness temperature.

EASY CLEAN UP: Burned wood granules in the pans are safe to place in your garbage or in your garden after they are no longer burning. Most people do not clean the interior of their smoker. However, you can clean the smoke off its exterior by using a very fine steel wool, plus a grease-reducing detergent (Dawn or equivalent) mixed with a little water. If particles of food stick to the grid wires, soak the grid in a plastic bag with soap and water for 10 to 30 minutes. Then brush lightly with a brass grill brush. The water pan collects some difficult to remove hard crusty spots. Soften with hot water, then use a stainless steel - steel wool scouring pad, soap, and water to clean it.

## Shortening Smoking Time

This is a useful procedure, but you must be very careful. If the weather is cool or cold or wind blowing hard, or you are rushed to get the food cooked, cover with an old blanket, or non-flammable type cover. DO NOT USE A COVER WITH A CHARCOAL SMOKER BECAUSE OF THE FIRE HAZARD. In cold winter weather, place the electric (not charcoal) smoker on 6 to 8 thicknesses of newspaper to insulate it from the cold surface. When covered with a blanket, check the smoker's temperature in 20 minutes; it may move into the "HOT" area. (If your smoker's thermometer runs in the "HOT" area without a cover blanket, its thermometer is very inaccurate.) Check with an oven thermometer on the top grid (food rack). It should read between 175°F. and 300°F. for safe and good smoking temperature. If it is still hot, remove some of the blanket and check the temperature again after 20 minutes. Do not smoke but a few minutes above the "HOT" 300°F. area; you'll dry out the food and could catch the inside of the smoker on fire if left for too long a time. When covering with a blanket, be careful of the handles on the inspection doors; they get extremely hot and may burn holes in the blanket or catch the blanket on fire. See Electric Smoke-Cooking Guide on pages 64-65.

# CHARCOAL WATER SMOKING

Charcoal water smokers are a unique low-cost barbecuing tool for smoke-cooking elegant, tasty, juicy foods.

Many charcoal water smokers look like two 5-gallon metal buckets welded together. They are 15" to 17" in diameter by 18" to 20" tall, and tube shaped. Manufacturers give this tube a big dome (cover) and mount it on legs.

Inside this vertical tube you'll find a charcoal pan with a breather hole in its bottom, which may hold up to 10 pounds of charcoal. You add wet smoke wood to lighted charcoal for smoke flavoring and aroma. A 5 to 8 quart water pan sits above the charcoal pan to give some steam vapors. Directly above this water pan are usually 2 food grids (racks) 8" to 10" apart. Finally the 8" deep dome fits loosely over the top food rack.

This cooking tool needs a patient operator — charcoal smoke-cooking takes time. You spend little time basting the meat, but considerable cooking time — 2 to 10 hours depending upon the thickness of the food and how cold and windy the weather.

Charcoal water smokers have two problems compared to electric water smokers: (1) producing consistent long-term heat when smoke-cooking a 12 to 20 pound turkey or 8 to 10 pound pork shoulder, fresh ham, leg of lamb — any food which is 3 to 5 inches thick. These foods take a long time to cook done in fall and winter temperatures; (2) Charcoal smoker fires start out at 250°F. to 270°F. but dwindle down to 175°F. over long smoking hours. Electric smokers have consistent heat over these long hours.

We researched a two-rack standard charcoal smoker. The air temperature was 80°F., with no wind. The charcoal pan was rounded up with 120 standard-sized briquettes (8½ pounds) and the fire lit with charcoal starter which was spread completely over the surface of the charcoal. We used no smoke wood. At the end of 45 minutes, the briquettes had no starter fluid odor and the charcoal was completely gray on top.

We used 9 pounds of ice and 7 pounds of ice water in a pan sitting on the top rack. This paralleled cooking an 18 to 20 pound refrigerated turkey. This cooled the smoker immediately just as a refrigerated turkey does. Over the first 4 hours, our highest air temperature was 280°F. and it finally dropped to 240°F.

After 4 hours, the mock turkey (cold water) had been raised to 160°F. and never exceeded this temperature. At the end of 9 hours, the air temperature had dropped to 150°F. on the top grid.

Even at this 80°F. summertime temperature we would need to add lighted charcoal to raise the temperature for a big turkey to be cooked done. Charcoal smokers do not smoke-cook foods in colder weather (40°F. and down) without adding freshly lighted charcoal more than one time. If the food has smoked enough, it can be wrapped in aluminum foil and finished cooking in an oven or buy an electrical conversion unit.

## Charcoal Smoking Master Steps

Before your light any charcoal, place a 10" to 14" diameter metal pan or any kind of a square pan directly under the smoker on a wooden deck. This will catch any pieces of burning charcoal which may sift through the charcoal pan's breather hole. Place empty water pan on the smoker supports. Then, carefully fill with 5 to 6 quarts of hot tap water for faster smoking. Add juices, herbs, spices, and wine to water if you wish, reducing amount of water to compensate. Follow Master Smoke-Cooking Steps 3 through 9. Check doneness (See Index: Doneness Chart) for specific foods. (See Charcoal Smoke-Cooking Guide on pages 62-63.)

# TRUE BLUE BARBECUE

J. J., John's continuously "food-panicked" wife came home from church this
. Sunday. She had just talked with Blossom Do-Rite and was shaking her
head. Blossom's daddy, a true barbecuer, had taken Blossom to a barbecue
contest yesterday.

"Now, John, get this. Blossom told me that one of those 'cooker guys' there
told her that his team only cooked the hogs' right shoulders in any barbecue cook-
off. Then, he told her some story about the hogs always rubbing their left shoulder
when they scratched themselves, and they scratched lots. This continuous rubbing
made their left shoulders tough. He said that's the reason his barbecue team only
used right shoulder meat — because it was so much more tender than a barbecued
left shoulder. Now, John, you know lots about barbecuing. Honest, is this right
shoulder stuff true?"

John is a true city boy — from the big city suburbs. And he'd never been
around any pigs, shoats, hogs, gilts, barrows, sows, boars, nor stags and watched
them rub and scratch. His closest "call" to hogs was watching them in a petting
pen on a children's TV show when he was a kid. But he did have a good hint
about where Blossom's "cooker guys" were comin' from. In fact, John had read
about one barbecue team really telling-it-like-it-was.

## Their Secrets Revealed

This team said they'd finally reveal their greatest BBQ cooking secret. They
wrote, "Our barbecue team has a full-time crew of pig shepherds. One time each
day, our shepherds 'pole-our-pigs.' They hold each pig on a pole so it gets its full
fill of green acorns, plus what they can eat off the ground. Along with this poling,
the shepherd moves our pedigreed razorback hogs very slowly counter clockwise
around the hills on our acorn farm to fatten them more. This exercise causes their
right side to toughen, but their left sides get very little exercise and stay tender.
Now, our team only cooks shoulders and ribs from the left side of these pedigreed,
razorback hogs.

"But, you know, we like right-side home-cured bacon best. This counter
clockwise exercise gives these hogs and their right side bellies just the exact
amount of exercise for delicious lean bacons. Then we give these bellies our special dry cure and long hickory/apple wood smoke. Why, our bacon is so tender
and delicious, it melts right in your mouth!"

Blossom and J.J. were the recipients of good-natured big story-telling by
"talented" members of a barbecue team. These tall tales are typical of a good
barbecue contest. Some of the teams' unusual names range from Great Boars of
Fire to Trichinosis Terry and Her Borderline Swine and finally to the Baron of
Barbecue and His Pit Masters. These tall-tales and "piggy and boarish" names are
part of the charm and atmosphere of true blue barbecue.

Barbecue contests' tall tales are part of their exciting atmosphere — just like
wood smoke! They are told for effect on the judges and anybody else who'll listen.
True blue barbecuers' reputations for story spinning go back to Apicius' time, 70
B.C. His book, Cooking and Dining in Imperial Rome, was written in Latin and
finally it was translated in the eighth century.

This is one of his recipes: TO COOK A PORK SHOULDER. "Simply cook
in water with figs usually dressed on a baking pan, sprinkled with crumbs and
reduced wine or better still, with spiced wine and is glazed under the open flame

or with a shovel containing red hot embers." (This is no tall tale, but could be "modernized" with a little imagination by a barbecue team.)

## Backyard Barbecue

Back in the 1930s, Americans cooked hot dogs over a wood fire. People called it a "wiener roast." But it could have been called a "wiener barbecue." Everything was done exactly as it should for the old time definition of 1930s barbecue. "Roast meat over an open fire using some spicy seasoning."

Through barbecue, today's working wives found that husbands could share part of the cooking load. In their very MANLY way, men could put on their custom designed aprons and "do-their-own-thing" at the BBQ grill.

Many women also found barbecuing was not just a man's "big-deal," but ladies could light the charcoal or gas grill fire. They could cook-out even better than the man or men of their lives and win BBQ cook-offs. Many working women found that barbecuing helped them care for their family and entertain friends easier. Their darling "ole man" did the cooking and didn't feel like his manhood was challenged. Instead, he found that he became important.

## How Barbecue Cook-Offs Started

America's whole cook-out revolution started after WW II. People tasted backyard grilled or smoked meats for the first time and they returned for seconds. Americans discovered how charcoal briquettes helped them create tasty foods — well beyond the flavor of stewed or pot-roasted meats.

Backyard barbecue went "big-time" when the Weber charcoal grill appeared. Open braziers (24-inch diameter open pans) with an adjustable height cooking rack could not hold their own when compared with the closed Weber kettle grill. Finally, people tasted seared, browned, lightly charred, and smoked steaks, chops, and burgers. They liked them because they weren't blackened — most of the time.

Other people smoke-cook and smoke-flavor meats with a covered Weber. This grill set the pace for backyard barbecuers. It came with three air breathers in its bottom and one in the cover. By adjusting these breathers carefully and counting the number of charcoal briquettes, people controlled its cooking temperature. The Weber could produce a hot or slow fire for cooking different foods. One more advantage, it was affordable. Other manufacturers followed with square or rectangular metal boxes with hinged covers. Some made their grill's housings out of cast aluminum which reflected the heat better for more even cooking than the porcelain-covered steel Weber.

## 55-Gallon Custom Grill and Smoker

Many do-it-yourself guys cut 55-gallon steel drums in half, then hinge the top half for a cover. The bottom half was mounted on legs and it became the fire box. They installed a metal rack above the fire to hold the meat. Some prize-winning BBQers still use them. Other teams built bigger custom rigs; others still use factory-built charcoal water smokers or Weber grills.

These 55-gallon drums can burn aromatic firewoods, such as hickory, oak, etc., or charcoal, or a combination. Their heat would stay reasonably constant for 1 to 1½ hours before they needed more lighted charcoal. Weber's covered grill idea and the 55-gallon barrel grills allowed for experimentation to see who could produce the best barbecue. And that's how barbecue cook-offs started.

## Custom-Built Cookers or Pits

From this, a sport was born. Barbecue cook-offs and contests blossomed. Why do teams compete in contests? They know how to cook better and want to prove it, and maybe want to talk about their winnings. However, many teams compete just for the fun of it.

Today's typical custom-built cooker or barbecue "pit" consists of a 200- to 300-gallon metal tank mounted on a trailer. It has a hinged lid with a meat grid (inside meat-holding rack), a fire box, and small doors to tend the smoke wood and fire. The team may use charcoal for the heat and various woods for smoke flavoring.

Some successful BBQ cooks have designed and commercially manufactured large and small barbecue units. Their customers have won major BBQ cook-offs and contests. As with any primarily male sport, the complexity, the size and price of the "toys" has risen. Today, however, it has become a family sport. All kinds of rigs from a tall bottle-shaped one to a converted 1900s commercial washing machine with a fire box in the bottom — compete. Then, you'll see 200- to 1,500-gallon tanks all with ingenious special equipment. They all have covers, breathers, and smoke stacks.

## True Barbecue Flavor

Most BBQ contest winners strive for a seasoned with some spice, brown-colored, caramelize-flavored smoked outside meat. This outside meat (also called "bark") must not be hardened, tough, stringy, blackened, or bitter tasting to win. The meat's center (the "inside" meat) must be cooked done with no red or pink juices nor raw meat next to the bone in many entries. This center meat must be tender, but firm, not mushy or crumbly. It may or may not have a smoke ring. (The meat turns a red or pink color below its surface to a depth of $\frac{1}{8}$" to 1 inch created from long hardwood smoking.) This ring may not add to the meat's smoked flavor, tenderness, or juiciness.

## Barbecue's "Second Skin"

John Willingham's team found a "second skin" had formed on the skinned area on the back of their whole hog. The cell walls holding the back fat contain proteins. Meat's juices naturally contain some sugars. This team had applied their dry rub which contained a little sugar (sucrose) all over the hog. This "second skin" or crust occurs naturally when meat's protein chemically reacts with the meat's natural and the rub's sugars during dry heat cooking. This is called the "browning reaction" or "browning effect." You can see it easily on the delicious browned crust (skin) of a carefully roasted marshmallow. This browning reaction formed the tasty browned "outside second skin" on the back fat and over the remainder of the hog.

When barbecuing meat, you use hot air (dry heat cooking) which dries the meat's juices on its surfaces, leaving dried natural sugars, salts, vitamins, and natural enzymes. The crust or outside meat which forms comes from these juices reacting with each other and drying. This dried outside surface continues to pull more juices from the meat's center and finally builds a concentrated "browned-outside-crust" or bark. If you roast meat in your kitchen, its outside crust has a flavor intensity 2 times higher than its inside meat. This inside meat is basically moist-cooked (stewed) in the water of the meat's own juices.

When you barbecue meats, you can apply a dry or liquid rub without sugar, and smoke-cook it gently. Then you may use a baste or a sauce plus a little unique spice. You automatically build a more flavorful outside crust with flavor intensities 3 to 5 times higher than stewed meats.

Barbecuers want their meat to develop a "second skin" or crust on all of its surfaces. However, too much drying heat produces stringy, dried out, tough, even hardened surfaces on meats. Many "Pro" BBQers use some type of water pan inside their custom-built smokers to add moisture while cooking. They may still baste with a liquid during the 5 to 20 hours used to cook their meat.

## Buying Meats for Contests

You can't afford to enter a contest with meat of poor quality. However, buying better quality meat does not guarantee you'll be THE WINNER, but it gives you a good start. Take time to develop a friendship with a meat company, meat market, or a supermarket that is a major supplier of meats. They'll be able to help you buy quality meats. BBQ contests are great fun but do take some money. If it's a hometown contest, you may entertain many "friends" you didn't know you had. That's when you wish you had a local business as a sponsor. However, many BBQers feel contest cooking is the best recreation they share with their family.

Where do you learn about buying meats? Start out with SECRETS' chapters for buying each kind of meat. Its chapters on pork, beef, lamb, chicken, turkey, fish, and sausage all contain good information. Enroll in the Culinary Institute of Smoke Cooking's Correspondence Course to become a Master Cook-Out Cook. See Index. You'll learn lots more about meats.

The following are the more ideal sizes of meat cuts used in barbecue contests. Also, we have described preliminary preparation before seasoning, which may improve each cut's appearance or tenderness.

## Better Sizes of Meats

SPARE RIBS: Come in "slabs" or sides. Best size — 3 pounds and down. The breast bone and cartilage need to be removed. Large rib bones (1¼" oval shaped) come from larger, older, potentially tougher animals. See removing membrane under loin ribs, below.

LOIN RIBS ("Baby Backs"): Best size is 2¼ pounds down to 1¼ pounds. Preparation for both spare and loin ribs: Remove membrane covering the inside of the ribs. Bend the ribs backward into a "U" shape, stretching the membrane. Then insert a Phillips screwdriver under the membrane covering a center rib. Lift the membrane up to make a pocket. Insert your finger in the pocket and lift. Removal of this makes your ribs easier to chew for a higher tenderness score.

PORK SHOULDER: Sixteen pounds down to 14 pounds; both are better than a 12-pound. Preparation: Trim out all bloody spots. Skin the shoulder, leaving a portion of the skin on the shank for easier handling.

BONE-IN WHOLE PORK LOIN: Twelve pounds and down; deboned 5 to 7 pounds. Preparation: Trim some of the fat from the top layer and remove any chunks of fat and trim up loin of any tag ends.

WHOLE HOG: Complete carcass weighing 85 pounds dressed weight minimum for Memphis-in-May sanctioned contests. Other pro barbecuers in other contests use 75-pound to 125-pound whole hog carcasses. Remove all internal fat and any tag ends of meat to dress up the carcass. "SOURED" WHOLE HOG:

If a whole hog carcass is not processed properly, cooled out completely, and refrigerated until cooked, it grows spoilage bacteria along its bones easily and turns a sour flavor.

BEEF BRISKETS: Range from 4 pounds for the thin end only, which is about 2 inches thick, up to 12 pounds for the complete brisket, which can be 4 inches thick or more. The thick end will have a fat layer about ¼" to ½" thick between the layers of lean, as well as about ¾"-thick fat cover. Preparation: Some of the fat may or may not be removed before starting to cook. Many barbecuers cut it down to only ½" thick. Proper cooking and seasoning transforms this tough cut into moist, tender, delicious meat.

LAMB CHOPS: A 2-rib-bone lamb chop portion of a rack of lamb. Preparation: Trim excess fat deposits from the cut. "French" the presentation. See Lamb Chapter.

LEG OF LAMB: Nine pounds down to 5 pounds. Preparation: Trim excess fat. Remove this cut's fell (parchment-like fiber covering the exterior).

TURKEY BREAST: Seven and one-half pounds and down to 5 pounds. Preparation: If breast comes with ribs still connected to the breast bone, cut away the rib bones, leaving the breast bone and meat. Trim off the fat and excess skin for a good-looking presentation.

CHICKEN: Three and one-half pounds up to 4½ pounds, fryer. Preparation: Remove fat deposits from abdominal cavity. CHICKEN BREASTS: Trim tag ends and fat deposits. One-half deboned breast weighs from 5 to 8 ounces.

RABBITS: Two and one-half pounds down. Preparation: Check for hair and bloody spots.

SAUSAGE: Many people prefer sausages stuffed in 31- to 34-mm (1 ¼" up to 1⅜" diameter) hog casings because they're easier to eat.

## Seasoning Meats

Seasoning barbecue means testing by tasting. This is fun! It means consistency also. We judged a BBQ contest which had 15 total teams. One team had cooked outstanding ribs, but in the preliminary judging, they were placed below the top 4 teams. All other factors considered, their ribs should have scored a first or second in this contest. What happened? Their ribs were too peppery for some blind and on-site judges. They used too much pepper. People judge and rate foods based upon their personal likes and dislikes. They give good scores to foods they like.

When cooking in a contest, you estimate the tastes of the judges. For example, BBQ can taste sweet, sour, salty, bitter, peppery, tangy, burning-cayenne-peppery hot, tomatoy, or smoky. It may be served with a thick or thin sauce or no sauce at all. What are the judges' tastes for barbecue? Your personal taste comes into play because that's what you can sell to the on-site judges. If the contest is totally blind judging, you are at the mercy of their taste. But remember that your preference for barbecue which is very peppery and spicy may not be "appreciated" by the judges.

SEASONING GUIDE NO. 1: Taste some of the winning meats from other BBQ contests by other teams. These meats represent the judges' tastes for that contest. Generally, they would represent the judges' tastes in other contests.

SEASONING GUIDE NO. 2: Combine your seasonings and cooking techniques for your best estimate of the judges' tastes. You ask what will that be like? Their tastes are many of what are called "nots": (1) not too peppery, (2) not too sour or vinegary, (3) not too winey, (4) not too sweet, (5) not too bitter, (6) not too salty, (7) not too smoky, nor too light with wood smoke, (8) not bitter black, and (9) certainly not wet with tomatoy BBQ sauce.

SEASONING GUIDE NO. 3: Plan to gently season your meat entry within 30 to 60 minutes of its being judged. Why? Spices loose their flavor easily. Dry heat cooking for 2 hours up to 20 hours "burns off" spices and herbs. Even a slow-cooking temperature of 175°F. will "boil-off" or volatilize many spice ingredients that have low boiling points like alcohol.

SEASONING GUIDE NO. 4: Regardless of what seasoning you use and at what stage during the cooking of the meat it is applied, do not overwhelm the meat's natural flavor. Any seasonings you apply must compliment the meat. To avoid overseasoning, set up a routine for applying your seasonings. Remember, even slow cooking for 5 to 14 hours allows only a small amount of spice to penetrate the meat. The vast majority is cooked off if the meat is not covered. See SECRETS' chapter on *New Rubs, Marinades, Bastes, and Sauces* for more detailed ideas on what to use.

## Cooking

Winning BBQ contests depends on how the team uses available meat cooking science. Preparing excellent BBQ needs understanding of meat's reactions to dry heat cooking temperatures, marinades and bastes.

Be sure to cook out the fats in the meats. Longer, low-temperature cooking will help you do this. You want your meat to be without a score-lowering greasy taste. See *Cook-Out Masterpieces* chapter for details.

## Thermometers Make Sense

Cooking temperatures need to be measured if you are to benefit from meat science's discoveries. There are many thermometers to choose from: (1) meat thermometer with an 1/8-inch diameter, 6-inch-long metal stem has a 1¾-inch diameter glass dial which gives readings from 130°F. to 190°F. Use this thermometer to measure the internal temperatures of thin or thick meat. It's called an "instant reading" thermometer. Another glass dial thermometer with 1/4-inch diameter stems works well with thicker meat; (2) A candy thermometer, 1/4-inch diameter by 4-inch-long stem with a 2-inch diameter glass dial with readings from 100°F. to 400°F. (some go from 50°F. to 550°F.). Use the candy thermometer to measure the inside cooking temperature by placing it through a hole in your cooker.

Inexpensive oven thermometers have temperatures ranging from 100°F. to 600°F. They can be used to check out grid temperatures in cookers and on grills but the glass face can become smoked over. They are very useful.

## Slow BBQ Cooking

Successful BBQ teams start with their cooker's temperature at 250°F. They let the fires die slowly and drop the temperature as they cook their meat. Other successful teams cook at 225°F. down to 190°F., adding lighted charcoal every 1 to 1¼ hours to maintain their temperature. Some may take advantage of the newly recognized maximum internal meat temperature of 160°F. to produce maximum tenderness with minimum protein hardening and meat crumbling. This system requires long cooking at reduced final cooker temperatures, ranging from 165°F. to 175°F. However, if cooking time is limited for brisquet, raise the cooker's temperature and cook it to 185°F. Otherwise, it may be tough because of its large number of connective tissues. Try not to overcook to a mushy stage.

## Cook By Weight and Thickness

Cooking by meat's thickness and weight are important factors in cook-off BBQing. Teams have preferred weights or thicknesses for cuts of meat. For example, baby back ribs weighing 2¼ pounds down to 1¾ pounds are preferred in one area. Yet 425 miles away, standard baby back ribs weighing only 1½ pounds and down are considered ideal. Both teams win contests with their preferred weights.

The following table shows weights and approximate cooking times for various cuts of meat. You will find that some of the larger weights use the same amount of time as some of the smaller ones. Teams hold the meat for judging, and holding is part of the art of barbecuing in contests.

## BARBECUING TIME TABLE

|  |  | Approximate Cooking Times for "Pro" BBQers. |
| --- | --- | --- |
| Pork Ribs |  |  |
| Baby Back | 1½ lb. and down | 3-5 hours |
| Baby Back | 2¼ lb. to 1¾ lb. | 4-6 hours |
| Spareribs | 3 lb. down | 5-8 hours |
| Pork Shoulder | 12 lb. to 16 lb. | 12-16 hours |
| Pork Loin | 8 lb. to 10 lb. | 7-8 hours |
| Whole Hog | 85 lb. to 135 lb. | 20-24 hours |
|  | 75 lb. to 85 lb. | 18-22 hours |
| Beef Brisket | 5 lb. to 12 lb. | 8-18 hours |
| Chicken | 2½ lb. to 3 lb. | 3-4 hours |
| Chicken | 3½ to 4½ lb. | 4-5 hours |
| Chicken Breast | 5 to 8 ounces | 1-3 hours or grill |
| Lamb Leg | 7-9 lb. to 140°F. | 4-8 hours |
| Sausage | 1¼" to 1½" diameter | 1-3 hours |
| Sausage | 2½" diameter | 1-3 hours |

## Smoking Meats

True barbecued meat must have a wood smoked flavor. The amount of smoke flavor your meat entry develops makes a difference to judges. It must have smoked aroma and flavor; otherwise, judges will give it a lower score.

Too much smoke can give the meat a bitter taste. Successful teams use hickory, oak, mesquite, maple, alder, pecan, apple, or other fruit wood. Use one that tastes good to you and is popular in your area. Alder is popular on the West Coast, mesquite is favored in the Southwest, and hickory, oak, and fruit woods in the remaining sections of the U.S.

Many successful teams cut 3-inch to 6-inch diameter slices ½-inch thick of their preferred wood and water soak them for a period of time to produce more smoke. They use small amounts to develop smoked color and flavor. Some teams cook exclusively with wood. Too much smoke can blacken meat and give it a bad appearance even though it has an excellent taste. Your meat's smoke ring is a nice feature to talk about, but don't oversell that it increases the smoke flavor.

## Barbecuing a Pork Shoulder for a MIM Cook-off

This method won first place in several BBQ contests.

1. Buy 4 to 6 pork shoulders weighing 14 to 16 pounds, with shanks still in place.

2. Skin the shoulders and trim some fat, but leave skin on the shank areas for easier handling.

3. Apply your favorite rub and rub it into the meat all over.

4. Start cooker out at 275°F. temperature.

5. Place shoulders meat side down on the grill rack for 1½ hours to develop good-looking grill marks. This will be part of your presentation.

6. Let your fire start to die down to 225°F. Maintain this 225°F. temperature throughout the cooking time. Be sure to use a thermometer.

7. At 1½ hours turn shoulders fat side down and smoke heavily for 5 to 5½ hours until the blade bone is exposed beyond the meat about ¼ inch.

8. At this point wrap shoulders in heavy aluminum foil and continue to cook for 4 hours. Then stick 3 holes into the aluminum foil about ¾ inches up the side from the bottom of the shoulders. This will let melted fat drain out, but keep the shoulder meat from sticking to the foil.

9. Check again for your best-looking shoulder. Use your best shoulder for the preliminaries. Display only this shoulder. Dispose of all foil.

10. Unwrap this shoulder 15 minutes before your first judge arrives. You must win the preliminaries to get into the finals.

11. Ten minutes before the judge shows up, apply a small amount of wood sawdust to your fire. When you open your cooker, smoke comes floating to the judge's nose. Show your shoulder to its maximum advantage.

12. Keep other shoulders ready for the finals.

## NOW FOR THE CONTEST

This is an exciting time for every BBQ team. You want to meet the challenge. Therefore, you put your best foot forward, but a cook-off still must be fun. You may be cooking because you have community spirit, or you want to boost your company, but you're still there to win. You may be on the barbecue circuit going from contest to contest. Here are some basic ideas which may help you. At least you won't come in last because you have done some preparation.

### On-Site MIM Preparation

YOUR COOKER: A painted, clean cooker leaves a better impression on judges. Many cookers have deposits of old smoky grease on the cooking grid. Remove these because they are not appetizing. Clean the cooker for a fresh look. Judges want to see inside your cooker with the meat in it.

YOUR AREA'S APPEARANCE: Each judge should be treated like a guest in your home, so you should put your best foot forward. You rake the grass, if you don't have a ground cover. Clean up the cigarette butts, empty beer cans and soda cans. Pick up the trash and organize your equipment. If you have spices sitting on a work table, organize these. Have clean work areas and utensils. Dispose of used paper towels and foil.

"DINING TABLE" FOR THE JUDGES: It may be a card table, but use a clean tablecloth with nice dinner-sized paper napkins. Place the silverware and napkins and glasses correctly. How you organize the table is very important. Set the table so that your team's presenter sits directly across from each preliminary judge so he/she can talk "eyeball-to-eyeball" to the judge.

FLIES: With summertime and garbage cans you'll normally draw flies, particularly at dusk. Thirty minutes before your first judge is to arrive, cover the food and dishes with paper toweling, not plastic wrap. Then thoroughly aerosol all posts, braces, ropes, and the top of the tent using a flying-insect bomb labeled for flies, mosquitoes, and wasps. Do not use one that has any residual effect and labeled for killing cockroaches, ants, etc.

OTHER PEOPLE: Please don't try to entertain your friends while you're being judged. Being judged on-site is like selling your home to a stranger; it's difficult to keep your prospect's attention (the judge's attention) while entertaining people. Please ask your cook not to hold hands with his very beautiful young lady while he's trying to talk to the judge. If it's a male judge, he'll be watching her. If it's a female judge, your score just went down and down.

Be ready to be judged on time. Charlie, the author, was the first judge and waited 8 minutes past starting time for the head cook, who was the presenter, to appear. Finally, he came out of his trailer with his girl friend. His girl friend was cute but she did not add to the team's score. You could say, "that old man was just jealous."

PERSONAL APPEARANCE: In 95°F. weather, cooking next to a BBQ cooker brings out the sweat. Towel down sweaty faces before the judge arrives. Wear bright, fresh T-shirts that are tucked in, not faded ones even if they have the team's name on them. Please don't wear caps when sitting at the dining table with your judge — you don't at home. If your kids do, have a little chat with them because they'll carry it over into college classes, a poor impression.

Be sure your hands and fingernails are clean. One judge said, "You're handling my food, and I want it clean." Many teams wear plastic or rubber gloves when handling meat. Gloves tell a judge that you care about your food and his or hers. Trim any beards very neatly when you're handling foods. Hair in food does not appeal to some judges, so wear a chin net and a hair net if you have pigtails and long hair. Excellent food does not overcome poor impressions. Wear clean clothes. Lay off the alcoholic drinks.

MEETING THE JUDGE: Nearly all judges attend cook-offs and contests at their own expense. Nobody pays them, and to date we have never heard of anybody being paid off. Some judges are knowledgeable, others are not. However, you can be sure most are impressed by excellent BBQ and BBQ know-how. Judges may think they know excellent BBQ. Make certain that they know that your BBQ is excellent! Demonstrate your BBQ and show that it exceeds all the requirements of excellent BBQ. Judges are requested by all contest officials to look for and judge tenderness, juiciness, BBQ flavor, and doneness.

## Meat Demonstrations

Your BBQ team may have a presenter and cook who divide up the duties. The presenter meets the judge. Hand him/her a glass of cold water to clean the palate. It is appreciated in hot weather, and helps the judge taste your meat. The presenter introduces the team and asks the judge what he/she cares to drink while eating the BBQ. The presenter invites the judge to come and look at the cooker. Here, a good presenter finds something that is unique to talk about. Most cooks will tell why they designed or use this particular cooker.

Then demonstrate your meat's (1) doneness, (2) tenderness, and (3) juiciness. If it is a whole hog entry, pull some meat from the ham area next to the tail head for doneness. This is the most difficult area to get cooked done on a whole hog. If it's a shoulder, twist out the blade bone. If it's ribs, make the "side" into a "U" to show their tenderness, juiciness, and color.

Be certain the judge understands about the brown caramelized "outside" meat (bark) which you have produced with your entry. Make certain the judge gets a taste of it. This should be your special tasting BBQ. Show your smoke ring if there is one. Cut one small sample of meat across the grain and squeeze the end to show the judge your juiciness. Many judges do not want to eat their meat sliced with a knife. Experienced judges expect whole hog and shoulder meat to be "pulled" in a MIM sanctioned contest.

## Your Presentation

If it is a whole hog entry, ask the judge to watch you collect the meat samples for him/her. An experienced judge will tell you the samples he/she prefers. Serve the judge, and sit directly across from the judge to make your presentation. Develop a believable but charming story about your sauce. If you can, take your whole shoulder to the table to serve it in finals and demonstrate its tenderness there. The table may be where you want to demonstrate your ribs' tenderness by making a "U" out of them. Remember, there are time limits for on-site judges in most contests.

TABLE TALK: Only one team member talks at one time in preliminary judging. The judge is distracted when two team members are talking at the same time. Emphasize the uniqueness of your cooking system and your entry: (1) why and how you chose your particular cut of meat, (2) why its quality is above a standard cut of a same type, and (3) how you cooked it to make it extra great BBQ. Then demonstrate that it's not stringy, or mushy, only tender and juicy. Try to make only three distinct points, because this is all the judge probably will remember.

## Losing "Don't's"

Here are some "don't's" that have been used or heard which did not impress judges.

(1) Don't say: "This is our first contest." (2) Don't make exaggerated claims for your cooker. If your cooker cannot make the meat more tender, juicy, and flavorful, don't say so, but it should if operated correctly. (3) Don't name any commercial ingredient you use. Keep some mystery and "show" about your cooking. XYZ's Commercial Vinegar Sauce becomes your team's vinegar/spice baste or marinade. (4) Don't say, "We changed our sauce from last year." Today's judges don't even know what your sauce tasted like last year. (5) Don't say, "I've got that shoulder too done, it may be dried out." In reality, it wasn't dry; let the judge decide. (6) Don't tell them that you are inexperienced. If your barbecue tastes good and other people like it, tell the judge that. (7) Don't stand over a judge and talk. Sit across from him and make your presentation. (8) Don't ask questions like, "Is our barbecue good?" Just say, "Our BBQ is good because of so-and-so, etc.," and shake your head — yes. (9) Don't say you're nervous. Remember, most judges are somewhat nervous being there as a judge. (10) Don't cover ribs with a thick, wet coating of barbecue sauce. Dry it down to a glaze if you use one. (11) Don't think that charcoal lighter burns off in 10 to 15 minutes. You'd better allow 20 to 25 minutes to get rid of this off-odor. Even the most inexperienced judge

recognizes a charcoal lighter taste. (12) Don't buy spareribs with big rib bones; they came from an older hog which can be tough. Don't cook totally in foil. You miss BBQ's brown smoked flavor. If you do use foil, dispose of it completely before the judge arrives.

## Winning "Do's"

(1) Do ask the judge for information. (2) Always give a full presentation even in the finals and the finals' judges have heard your presentation two times already. It's better to save a little "talk" if you think you're going to make the finals. (3) Serve ribs with the meat side up and with the breast bone, cartilage, and diaphragm muscle removed from spareribs. (4) Remove the membrane that covers the rib bones of spareribs and baby back ribs. (5) Keep your entry moist. (6) Wear plastic or rubber gloves (not the big black rubber work gloves) when touching the meat. (7) Invite the judge to come by and get some of <u>your very good barbecue</u> after the contest is over.

## Suggestions for BBQ Cook-Off Judges

Judging is a very important function in any BBQ contest. It's an honor to be a judge. Judges pay for their own travel and expenses. They have a good time at the contest also, the same as the cooking team. Well-trained judges satisfy the cooking teams better. Teams sometime draw uninformed judges who leave them with a poor taste for that contest.

Most BBQ cooking teams are not sponsored by businesses. They spend their own money, time, and hard work to cook for the judges. They deserve to be judged fairly. Most teams cook delicious BBQed food; therefore, judges should score each entry as accurately as possible compared with others in that contest or to an established rating system. The judges must taste the team's meat to be able to score the team fairly. If the judge can't taste the meat for some reason in any contest, the team and the officials hope that he/she will not judge at all. Organizers should have extra judges so that they can handle this problem.

BBQ contests use two general types of judging. BLIND JUDGING: The teams send their meat in containers to the blind judging room. There the judges taste and score it. The judges use the standard scoring card designed by the contest's sanctioning group or organizers to rate the meat entry. The second type of judging is ON-SITE JUDGING: Here, the judges visit the team's cooking location, hear the team's presentation and taste their food, then score them. The on-site judge should not score the team where members of any team are present. BBQed meats must be tasty, easy, and fun to eat. Therefore, most contests ask the judges to score each entry for tenderness, flavor, and appearance.

TENDERNESS: Consists of: (1) Juiciness — can you squeeze the meat and produce juice without any sauce? (2) Can you chew the meat easily? Is it tough, hard, stringy, dried out or overcooked and mushy?

FLAVOR: The judge tastes the meat alone for a caramelized, smoked, seasoned, barbecued, "outside" flavor. This flavor should be 3 to 5 times more intense than a stewed or microwaved cut of the same meat. Then taste the center of the meat for flavor. Next, taste the sauce and finally the combination of the meat and the sauce. The judge should check for blackened, charred, burned, bitter-flavored meats. These flavors deserve lower scores. A charcoal fluid flavor is not part of a good BBQ flavor. A greasy taste and feel should be scored lower.

BBQ aroma must be considered as part of the flavor factor because over 50% of our ability to taste comes from meat's aroma.

APPEARANCE AND DONENESS: Good BBQ appears evenly smoked, medium to deep brown, moist outside with a juicy center. The judges should score blackened meat lower. A pork entry with bloody juices is not cooked and it should be scored low. However, rare-cooked beef or lamb can have red/pink juices. These are appropriate entries in some BBQ contests.

## BBQ Sanctioning Groups

The BBQ contest circuits have several sanctioning groups: (1) The International Barbecue Cooker's Association (IBCA), Dallas, Texas. (2) The Kansas City Barbecue Society (KCBS), Kansas City, Missouri, and (3) The Memphis-in-May (MIM), Memphis, Tennessee. Each has its distinct scoring systems.

## The International BBQ Cooker's Association (IBCA)

The IBCA sanctions BBQ cook-offs in Texas and the Southwest. They have a distinct system that differs somewhat from other sanctioning groups. Their top scoring is a 10. They use a double blind judging system.

Each team is given two tickets with the same number. One ticket the cooks sign and keeps on his/her person during the contest. All cooked entries are submitted with this number. They run preliminary blind judging. After the finalists are determined, they have a run off. If the contest has a large number of teams, they will have semifinals. They do not have on-site judging.

Their rules eliminate all garnishes. They allow only a sheet of aluminum foil to protect the bottom of the styrofoam container. At the awards ceremony, IBCA announces the 10 top winners in each category, which helps increase the incentive for all contestants.

## Kansas City BBQ Society (KCBS)

KCBS sanctions BBQ contests in the Midwest, East Coast, and in the Midsouth. Their rules are used in West Coast contests also. The American Royal BBQ contest held in the fall of each year uses KCBS rules. Approximately 200 teams cook in this contest. The Royal contestants cook pork ribs, poultry (chicken or turkey), beef brisket, pork other than ribs, lamb, and sausage. The contestant must cook in all six categories to be eligible for the grand championship. Each meat category from ribs through sausage has a champion. The team having the largest total number of points in all six categories wins the grand championship at the Royal. Some smaller contests only cook four meats.

The KCBS uses only blind judging of all meat entries. Their scoring system runs from a 1, which is the lowest, up to a 9, which is the highest. They score the meat for three standard qualities: (1) tenderness, 2) taste, and (3) appearance. The taste score is the most important and is doubled when the team's final score in each category is calculated.

Six judges sit at the same table and score the same six meat entries. The contest officials have devised an innovative, specially-coated, white cardboard "scoring plate" with six designated areas for each team's meat entry to be placed. This scoring plate system helps judges make better comparisons. The society members also sponsor BBQing benefits for the unfortunate at Christmas as well as BBQ-cooking training. It publishes a newspaper called "The Bull Sheet."

## Memphis in May Sanctioned Contests (MIM)

In these contests three specific kinds of pork are cooked: (1) a whole hog with the carcass weighing over 85 pounds, (2) whole pork shoulder or fresh ham, and (3) pork ribs, spare or loin ribs (baby back). Some MIM contests have a category of anything but pork. The scoring systems start out at 10 being the best, and go down to a 5 for the lowest score.

MIM-sanctioned contests use on-site as well as blind preliminary judging. Three on-site judges visit the team individually, staying 10 to 15 minutes, during which he/she hears the team's presentation and tastes the meat. Each team sends their food to the blind judges. Each team receives a combined score of the on-site and blind judges in three pork categories.

In addition to the categories for scoring of the meat, two additional on-site categories are judged: (1) Area and Personal Appearance and (2) Presentation. MIM scoring system also contains a final category of Overall Impression. This last category gives the judge an opportunity to make a final comparison of the team and its meat entry with the other teams.

The three teams having the largest score for each pork category then compete in the finals. Four final judges score the three teams on-site in each category, and taste the meat. From these scores a champion of each pork category is chosen and the team receiving the most points in any one individual pork category becomes the grand champion of the contest.

## BBQers — Dynamic Fun Loving

The United States is very lucky. We have many organized sanctioned BBQ groups and societies, all of which have definite scoring systems. BBQ contests are truly international affairs. Many other countries in the world have BBQ contests, such as Ireland, Thailand, and others. If you ever attend a BBQ cook-off or a contest, you'll find True Blue Barbecuers are dynamic and fun people. They are sincere and they like to cook and eat barbecue. Above all, they need to feel that you, as a judge or a visitor, appreciate their cooking skills and their sincere effort to produce excellent BBQ.

True Blue Barbecuers should be pleased. We have the advantage of three newspapers and a national association which specialize in BBQ contests and cook-offs, equipment, and techniques.

1. Bull Sheet, published by the Kansas City BBQ Society (KCBS), 1151 and Hickman Mills Drive, Kansas City, Missouri 64134.

2. Goat Gap Gazette, published at 5110 Bayard Lane #2, Houston, Texas 77006.

3. National BBQ News, published in Douglas, Georgia 31530, P.O. Box 981.

### Now, a National BBQ Association

National BBQ Association, P.O. Box 29051, Charlotte, North Carolina 28229, which holds national BBQ conventions for suppliers, cooking teams, BBQ restaurants, and interested BBQers.

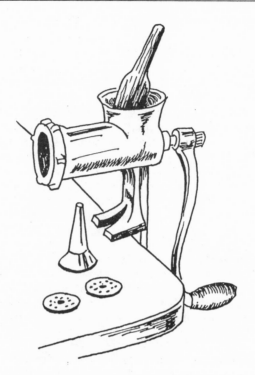

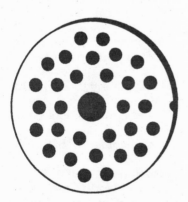

**Sausage Plate**
(³⁄₁₆" diameter holes)

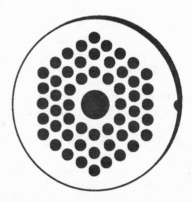

**Hamburger Plate**
(¹⁄₈" diameter holes)

# SAFE DELICIOUS SAUSAGES

J.J., John's continuously "food-panicked" wife, looked up over her oat bran and skimmed milk. They had time to talk a few minutes, and she said, "John, we used to eat pork sausage for breakfast many mornings. I sure did like it and I still get really hungry for it, but Blossom Do-Rite said that all pork sausages contain 50% fat — and worst yet, it's all saturated fat, with lots of that nitrite stuff — that's the stuff that gives you cancer, she says.

"John, I'm scared of eating that pork sausage in the plastic wrapper. When you unwrapped it — it's all white fat, no lean. And yesterday Blossom said, 'Sausage is not at all sanitary. They put just about everything in it'."

Slow J.J. down, John. She's mounting her soapbox again. Some commercially-made pork sausage has 40% fat, but it doesn't need that much and you don't need to buy it. Before we doom sausage, let's have a historic, and current scientific look at all sausages.

Our personal sausage history goes back to the 1920s. Charlie, the author, tells his own experience, "I was raised on a hog farm, and I ate pork sausage at least 2 times a day for months during the year. Now I look back, and consider myself lucky in the 30's to have had lots of good food to eat.

"My daddy was a pork-sausage hound. One morning at breakfast he said, 'I could eat pork sausage three times a day; in fact, I want our next sausage made from our best hogs, using the 'back straps' (pork loins) and fresh hams (momma groaned) plus the shoulders — everything that'll make it good.'

"Our next pork sausage, every bit of four 200-pound hogs was ground and stuffed into Knote family sausage. Daddy let Calvin, a professional butcher, season our complete year's supply of sausage. Calvin hit-the-bottle with gusto and his hand must have gotten shaky with the red pepper. Because that winter, spring, and summer, we all ate Chorizo-style sausage — hot, hot, hot! None of us Indiana country folks knew that such a fancy Spanish/Mexican sausage named Chorizo even existed for hot pork sausage — and momma, well, she suffered, and suffered, not always in silence."

### Sausage Names

What's in a sausage name? Chorizo is a Mexican/Spanish sausage and it's made with cayenne pepper, black pepper, vinegar, cumin, and other spices. Other true sausage names range from Augsburger-wurst to Wurst-chen in Germany. Experts say more than 300 different sausages are manufactured in Germany.

Then there's the Italian Salami sausage which really originated in Salamis, an ancient Greek city on the island of Crete. It was destroyed in 500 B.C. The Italians "borrowed" this salami name because it apparently went along with their bologna (our "baloney") from Bologna, Italy.

### 50,000 Different Sausage Recipes

The Germans and Italians don't leave much room for the Poles, Greeks, French, Chinese, Mexicans, Canadians, Swedes, Scots, English, and us Americans. Nearly everybody makes sausage! This could mean that there are at least 1,000 different sausage names in the world. Potentially there are over 50,000 different high quality sausage recipes and formulas in the world. H.W. Ockerman, in his book *Sausage and Processed Meats*, 1988 2nd Edition, lists 42,000 potential ways to season various combinations of pork meats for our "standard" pork sausage in the United States.

Basic sausage recipes have been modified by many different individual families and professional sausage makers. The availability of local meats and local spices, plus the creativity of the butchers and the people of each country control how sausages are seasoned. They passed down their secret recipes from father to sons, or to Knote daughters and son. Now, we pass them on to you, the readers of this cookbook which features sausage making. Many experts rate Germans as truly the *meister wurstmachers* (master sausage makers) of the world. They do make tasty sausage, but so do our U.S. sausage makers.

## Sausage Types

All sausage starts with ground red meats, turkey, chicken, fish, game, etc. General sausage types are: (1) fresh, (2) fresh smoked, (3) cured (salt, plus "curing" compound), (4) smoked-cured, and (5) dry smoked-cooked or water-cooked cured sausage. Sausage is stuffed into an animal or plastic casing or into a loaf pan. It can be packed in plastic tubes which you slice to make patty sausage. This cookbook teaches you how to make and smoke-cook summer sausages without casings. They're easy, tasty, and healthy. SECRETS contains many different recipes for fresh, cured and smoked sausages.

Sausages the world over contain salt and one or more of 50 different spices, herbs, and other ingredients, plus meat. Some sausage makers add eggs, cereals, fresh vegetables or fruits to (1) enhance the meat's flavors, (2) stretch out their scarce meats, or (3) make a traditional local sausage. Local U.S. sausage makers add many different kinds of liquids, varying from ice water, beer, wine, brandy, and buttermilk.

When you buy USDA-inspected sausages you can expect them to be produced under sanitary conditions. Yes, our present commercial sausages may have too high a fat and/or salt content — but they're clean and sanitary!

## Worst of the Wurst, to the Best Wurst

U.S. commercial sausage problems: (1) Some are very fat sausages. It may be called pork sausage, country sausage, or farmer-style sausages. Some "whole hog" fresh pork sausages contain about 33% fat. (2) Some U.S. sausage may have up to 3.0% salt; and (3) Many people still fear the problem of trichinosis from pork. They intentionally overcook and dry out sausage.

The "Best Wurst" — a juicy/low-fat/low-salt/low-nitrite/no-trichinosis sausage — and you can make it easily. It will have lots of flavor, be juicy and sanitary. It should cost less for the actual protein content you receive if you buy meats wisely.

## Sausage Health Truths

CUTTING DOWN ON FAT CONTENT: Most red meat has veins of fat between the lean as well as marbled-in fats in the lean (little lines or flecks). Poultry's fat is under and in the skin and in solid deposits. Many fish contain oils (fats).

Sausage must contain some fat to be juicy. A fat content of 20% is about right for good taste, tenderness, and juiciness. For a smoked, cured Mettwurst (summer sausage), sausage use a Boston butt (pork shoulder roast) and beef chuck, both trimmed of surface fat for a lean sausage. You make sausage from frozen ground turkey with 15% fat, and it will be somewhat dry. An 18% fat ground chicken will be tastier and juicier. For fresh delicious breakfast sausage, trim a Boston butt of fats or use a picnic (the shank portion of a pork shoulder) and trim it of fat to make a sausage with only 18% to 20% fat. You'll probably see various sausages with fancy names made with only 5% to 10% fat. They'll contain one of the following extenders: carrageenan (a processed but healthy seaweed product), a food gum, or oat bran. One of them is added to water along with hydrolyzed plant proteins (HPP) or meat broth and lean pork meat. Carrageenan-type products absorb the water and jell like a meat gelatin when cooked. The HPP gives this water mixture a meaty flavor. This type of processing is being used to make a low-fat ground beef. A university panel of trained testers in blind tests rated low fat hamburgers equal to standard 20% fat ground beef burgers in flavor, taste, and mouth feel. Low fat sausage is coming.

When you can purchase extenders, you'll be able to make a much lower fat sausage. Some commercial sausage makers already have learned one of CHARLIE'S kNOTE-WORTHY 1990s Food Laws: "EAT WATER! — IT'S 100% FAT FREE." U.S. processors are already making 96.5% fat-free ground beef. They'll be using fresh hams to make 95% fat-free sausage.

## Sodium Nitrite

Sodium nitrite is not used commercially, nor in our fresh sausage recipes. It is not needed because it's only used to protect cured or smoked-cured sausages. Sodium nitrite is not considered a cancer threat in the real-food-world. The USDA scientists division and other food scientists recommend its use at low concentrations. "You Just Can't Eat 100 Pounds of Smoked Sausage Every Day For 30 Years," one of our locals said, referring to the far-out laboratory animal feeding tests for cancer. These tests were used to bring about the ban of cyclamates and now admitted to being safe, and Alar, and an attempted ban on saccharin.

SODIUM NITRITE'S ADVANTAGES: (1) kills botulism disease and other germs to prevent spoiling; (2) lowers the cooking temperature for killing heat-resistant bacterial spores produced by botulism and staph bacteria and other germs; (3) reduces flavor losses in pre-cooked convenience meats by retarding warmed-over flavors; (4) contributes a piquant flavor to cured meats; and (5) acts as a spoilage indicator. IMPORTANT: by adding ascorbic acid (vitamin C, Fruit Fresh, or equivalent) along with the sodium nitrite to your sausage, you can further reduce its effect if you wish. The USDA requires vitamin C be added to cured sausages.

## Non-Iodized or Canning Salt

Some salt is needed to make the sausage taste good. SECRETS' sausage recipes use only 1.0% to 1.3% salt (not 3.0% like many old-time commercial sausages). Cured smoked sausage meats must have some salt to react with the meat's protein. Together, they form a small amount of a light, smooth, sticky paste called an "emulsion." This paste causes ground meats to stick together for making smoked-cooked sausage without casings. It also increases the quality of all the sausages you'll make.

## Trichinosis — A Solved Problem

Trichinosis in sausages is a big bug-a-boo because many sausages contain pork. The USDA says, cooking pork to 137°F. or freezing it to 5°F. for 20 days, kills trichinosis (known since the 1920s; almost everyone, including some graduate home economists, is amazed.) When you cook cured sausages containing pork to only 150°F., you have a 13°F. safety margin. This temperature will not dry out sausages. If you use the 185°F. done temperature suggested on meat thermometers, you'll dry out 10% to 15% fat sausage. Cook fresh sausage until its juices are clear, not rosy colored and you'll be safe.

Processors use freezing to create a product known as "certified pork," which is free of trichinosis. It is used in some non-cooked pork products such as Prosciutto or Parma hams. U.S. meat processors make many good sausages. Some are very conscious of consumers' desires for lower-fat sausages.

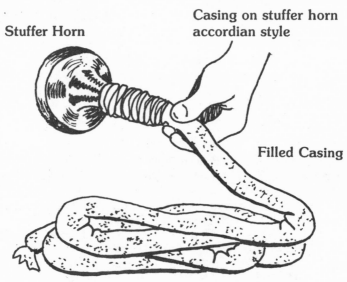

Stuffer Horn

Casing on stuffer horn accordian style

Filled Casing

Rope style sausage

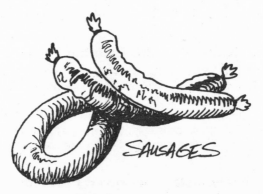

Polish sausage links

# IT'S THE BEST OF THE WURSTS

## Making Your Own Sausages

Some popular food magazines carry articles about making sausage. They tell you "use two parts lean pork (with its normal fat content) plus one part pork fat." This makes "Old Time Sausage," which contains about 40% fat. This recipe comes from a USDA butchering bulletin written about 75 years ago. It tastes good and is juicy with the fat, but my-oh-my, the unnecessary calories, and cholesterol.

The modern do-it-yourself sausage maker and consumer wants a low-fat, low-cholesterol, and low-calorie sausage. However, this sausage must still taste good and be juicy. Our experience proves you can make sausage too lean. A standard 85%-fat-free sausage can be dry — it has little juice.

## You'll be a "Pioneer"

When you take your first bold-stab at making sausage, you'll have joined thousands of other pioneers. They too had great spirit, gusto, and brave bold hearts. Over the last 5,000 years, pioneers from China, Greece, Italy, Germany, and other countries made sausage. Our American founding fathers added their own experience to this outstanding food art form — sausage. You can easily recreate this art form. It's being lost to millions of Americans.

## Mankind's First Convenience Food

You'll be recreating man's first convenience food — sausage. Your smoke-cooked and cured summer sausage can be ready-to-serve in 30 seconds. And everybody talks about fast food. You've already had it for thousands of years.

Learning to make sausage overnight is somewhat like Charlie the author's great-great-grandpa John landing in New York from Germany in the 1820s. They say he expected to "stagecoach-it" completely to Kansas City the next day. Please don't expect to satisfy your true sausage pioneering spirit with your first batch. Your first "sausage" stagecoach might get you to New Jersey, but only Jerseyites stay there!

Today, sausage making can be a big party time with the gathering of your family and friends. It adds fun, joy of living, and a great feeling of accomplishment. Homemade sausages cost less, and you'll know how you made yours — low fat, low salt, and low nitrite. The amazing thing about homemade sausage, you'll receive lots of raves from your friends. "You don't mean you're clever enough to make that good stuff?" Or a syrupy traditional, "Your sausage is so tasty, so divine, so delightful, and etc.!" If you receive this compliment, you're expected to give him/her an extra link — particularly if she's sincere, charming, and pretty, or if he's a hunk! Remember, one of them might just help with sausage making, and that could be exciting.

## Simple to Make

If your mate turns thumbs down on wanting to help you make sausage, please remind her/him, it's as simple as making meat loaf. You mix ground meats with seasonings and place the mixture in a holder (a casing or loaf pan) while it's cooked and "set-up," then smoked or you pack it in plastic bags and freeze to cook as breakfast patties or pizza sausage later.

Very few of you will butcher a hog or a steer, so we have simplified your buying to standard supermarket meat cuts. You'll probably want to control fats, so you buy cuts of meats that have not been ground to make leaner sausages. We recommend that you trim your beef very closely of all surface and seam fats when you combine pork and beef. Pork fat is usually better tasting than beef fat for most sausages. It's younger in age and has a nice flavor which takes seasonings well. Boston butts or pork shoulders work well for sausage.

## Meats For Homemade Sausage

FRESH SAUSAGES are pork, breakfast, farmers, bockwurst, bratwurst, fresh Italian, and chorizo sausage. All use ground pork or mixtures of pork, beef, and sometimes veal. Buying fresh veal in the U.S. is expensive. Therefore, we suggest substituting pork. Its flavor intensity is just a little higher than veal. After you season your sausage, you'll have difficulty telling whether it's made from lean pork or veal. For a lean all-pork sausage, you must trim some fat from the pork.

SMOKED CURED SAUSAGES: PORK AND BEEF SAUSAGE. If you use all beef, it makes a very firm, hard-cured sausage. Pork helps to make more tender smoke-cured sausage. We recommend a combination of 60% pork to 40% beef for smoked sausage.

SMOKED CHICKEN/TURKEY SAUSAGE: Buy one-pound plastic tubes of frozen ground chicken or turkey from your supermarket to make smoke-cured sausage without a casing. Buy chicken with 17% or 18% fat; it will be moist, not dry.

SMOKED DEER AND ELK SAUSAGE: Trim venison or elk of all of its surface and seam fats to reduce the wild, gamy taste. With this fat trimming and wild game's lean meat, you produce a very dry sausage. We have successfully mixed 60% wild meat with 40% Boston butts (pork shoulder roasts) not fat trimmed. This mixture makes a sausage with about 18% to 20% fat content for a very tasty, moist wild game sausage. Some meat markets will sell you pork trimmings containing 50% fat for deer sausage. You'll like the Boston butts much better because of their lower fat content. (See Index: Venison Sausage.)

Pork and beef sausages, and fresh sausages made with SECRETS' recipes, have been frozen successfully for 3 to 6 months. Wrap them in aluminum foil and then put in a plastic bag. The smoke-cured sausage does not go rancid like some cookbooks tell you. However, the spice level may drop slightly.

## Grinders for Homemade Sausage

ELECTRIC GRINDERS: The Hamilton Beach model 226 grinder/stuffer works well for home sausage making. It has coarse and fine grinding plates and a grinder knife, plus the stuffer tube. Two electric food mixers with grinder and stuffer attachments are: The Kitchen Aid, which grinds faster than the Oster unit. Both are equipped with two grinding plates and a grinder knife. These 2 units can be fitted with stuffing tubes. If you don't have access to an electric grinder, get ready for action — cranking a hand-crank grinder.

FOOD PROCESSOR GRINDING; Food processor manufacturers say to use the metal cutting blade in the machine and it will grind raw meats. We tested a large commercial-sized food processor. To an experienced home sausage maker, the food processor did not grind raw meats into high-quality, good-looking sausage. It crushed the meat.

HAND CRANK GRINDERS: You can grind little or lots of meat with one. However, if you are going to make a 50-pound batch of sausage, it would be nice if you had the services of three very strong-armed, eager guys and gals who will trade off.

We'd prefer to borrow or even buy a second-hand Chop-Rite or Universal hand-crank grinder. (The new electric Hamilton Beach costs less than a new Chop-Rite.) You will solve the meats' tough connective tissue problem much easier. You'll grind the meat into acceptable ⅛" diameter by ¼" long ground fresh meat pellets — just like any meat you buy at the supermarket. Some hand-crank grinders are designed to use standard small sized commerical electric grinder's cutting plates and knife. You need both a sausage plate (size ³⁄₁₆" hole or larger), and a hamburger plate (⅛" hole) to be able to grind <u>raw</u> meats efficiently and finely. You <u>don't</u> need to trim out all connective tissues and membranes if your cutting plate and knife are sharp.

If you buy a used grinder at a "swap meet" or a flea market, make sure your grinder is all metal (not made partly of plastic) with a heavy-duty table-top screw clamp (not a suction cup) along with 2 to 3 grinding plates and a grinder knife. Grinder's plates and knife may need sharpening.

SHARPENING GRINDER PLATES AND KNIVES: Use medium grade emery cloth (paper). Lay the paper on a flat level surface, a piece of glass or a plastic table top. Push the grinder plate over the emery paper with some force until it shines all over. Sharpen the grinder knife until its cutting edges are shiny. Store in mineral oil to prevent rusting.

## Other Important Equipment

MIXING PANS: For a 25- up to 50-pound batch of meat, you will need a restaurant-size plastic storage tub (the best) or a cleaned No. 1 or 2 galvanized wash tub; or a large dishpan for 10 pounds; or a plastic or metal bowl, 12 inches or more in diameter for 2 to 4 pounds.

WEIGHING DEVICES: Kitchen scales for weighing meats, plus measuring cups, and spoons for measuring spices, etc.

KNIVES: You need one good 5-inch to 6-inch stiff-bladed boning knife and a good butcher's steel for sharpening knives for easier deboning and cutting.

## Home Sausage Making

It's very much like making a meatloaf — so please relax!

CLEAN EQUIPMENT: You'll need a work table or kitchen counter. Wash down with soap and water, then sanitize with household bleach (3 tablespoons per ½ gallon of water). Let the bleach set for 60 seconds, then flush with water. Scrub all equipment with soap and hot water. If you're super fussy, you can dip it for 30 seconds in a 5.25% chlorine bleach, but it's not necessary. Then flush thoroughly with tap water — you'll be nearly "Public Health" pure and sanitary for <u>that moment</u>.

MEASURING SPICES: Use measuring cups for measuring liquids, and measuring spoons or a postal scales to measure all dry herbs and spices. Please don't guess. Your sausage reputation and your pioneering spirit are on the line. You may need to modify your recipe if you don't like your result, or you'll want to repeat it if it's good to excellent. Either way, you need to know how much and what you used. Keep a written record.

SALT: Please don't try to make sausage without any salt, even if you are on an anti-salt kick. Water plus salt dissolve some proteins, making the meats tacky for a better quality sausage.

ICE WATER: Ice water is a good carrier for the spices and salt. Then mix the mixture thoroughly and completely with the meat. Water makes hand-mixing the sausage easier, and you'll do a more thorough job. The ice water chills the meat and adds moisture, which makes the meat more juicy. It replaces some of the moisture lost in smoking or cooking and makes stuffing the casings easier.

COLD MEAT: When grinding, you'll raise your meat's temperature considerably, and it gets soft. It's best to start with meat at the maximum temperature of 40°F. or lower, even to 30°F. is better, to make sausage. If your meat gets warm, spread it on a cookie sheet and put it in a freezer or you can spread it out in a plastic bag to chill rapidly. When you regrind your spice/sausage meat mixture over the hamburger plate (⅛-inch-diameter holes), it feeds through the grinder much easier when chilled.

## Meat Preparation

Cut meat into 1" to 1½" by 2" to 3" long chunk sizes that will fit into your grinder's throat (opening). Check the opening on your food processor if you use one. Cut out the blood spots and gristle and cut or pull out loose, tough, connective tissues (clear and white membranes) and trim off some thick surface fats. Leave some fat to make sausage tasty and juicy. *Several very precise college students helped us make sausage. They cut out nearly every strand of fat. Result: Our sausage was extremely dry and not tasty.*

## Grinding Raw Meat

Use a meat grinder with a grinder plate and a grinder knife. Coarse grind all meats the first time over the sausage plate (³⁄₁₆-inch-diameter hole) or larger holed plate. Weigh the amounts of each coarse ground meat to be used; place meat in the mixing pan. We recommend that you grind the mixed meat and spices the second time over a hamburger plate (⅛-inch-diameter hole) for a finer textured sausage. On the second grinding you'll need a "pusher" (a large spoon or a "stomper") to push the ground meat down into the grinder.

GRINDER-CAUSED "SMEARING": Some meats come from the grinder looking like tiny strands of meat instead of standard full-size clean-cut bullets or pellets of meat. Causes of "smearing" are (1) grinder plate and knife do not fit "pressure" tight against each other or are dull; (2) plate and knife do not fit the grinder or are not aligned with each other; or (3) meat's tough connective tissues and fibers get lodged in the very tiny space between the knife and the grinder plate. Remedies: Take the grinder apart and clean completely. Sharpen both knife and plate, if necessary, and reassemble free of any fibers. Then tighten the outside locking unit of the grinder to hold the knife firmly against the plate.

## Mixing and Seasoning Meats

Here you mix coarse-ground meat with the spices, seasonings, and water. Some "Nervous Nellie" cookbook writers recommend that you mix the sausage and spices together with two big spoons or forks, not your hands. That's okay for 1 pound of meat — if you must. For a 4-pound to 10-pound batch of meat and spices, those ladies "ain't-never-been-there." Jeff Smith, the nationally recognized Frugal Gourmet TV cook and cookbook writer, recommends using your hands even for one to two pounds of meat. He makes sense! For mixing sausage: Clean all fingernails completely — take off your rings and wrist watch, roll up your shirt or blouse sleeves — scrub your hands, clear up to your elbows, with soap and water — then please watch carefully where and what you scratch and where you put your hands and what you touch. Maybe it would be easier to wear rubber gloves, but you still must be careful about scratching, touching, and patting. However, don't get overly excited about "germs." You will want gloves if the meat is cold.

Now, plunge your hands into the meat. Pull from the bottom, moving up and over to the top side and punch down the center and repeat, always working from the bottom, much like kneading bread dough. After mixing thoroughly one time, check the edges at the bottom and repeat the process for a first class spice/sausage mixture. Remember, you can't hurt the sausage by mixing it thoroughly.

## Stuffing and Linking

You do not need to stuff and link sausage if you make SECRETS' smoked sausage without casing, or sausage for patties, or Italian sausage which is crumbled for a pizza. You package all these in plastic bags and save money and lots of time.

CASINGS FOR STUFFING: Most U.S. sausages are stuffed in natural casings. Many are clear-colored membranes from the cleaned intestines usually from hogs, sometimes from sheep. Natural casings are safe to eat along with the sausage when cooked. However, 4- to 5-inch-diameter plastic casings are used for making bologna and other commercial sausages; these are removed before it is eaten.

Casing diameters are measured in millimeters (mm; 10 mm equals 0.4 inch). Standard supermarket sausages (pork or Italian) are stuffed in 31 mm to 34 mm casings (about 1¼") in diameter and can be 3 to 20 feet long. These sausages are linked into 4-inch to 6-inch long frankfurter-size lengths. Pork or farmer's sausages, bockwurst, bratwurst, cajun, chorizo, and Italian sausages use this size casing. Use what your meat market carries because these should be the least costly. Some people use larger-diameter pork casings 38 mm to 42 mm (about 1.6 inches in diameter) and make 10-inch to 12-inch long links of Polish and braunschweiger sausages.

## Larger Casings

One group of casings looks like plastic, but is regenerated natural collagen. These casings are processed and formed into 2¼-inch to 3-inch diameter dry casings. When soaked in water, they become soft and are efficient, safe sausage casings. You can buy these by mail or your meat dealer can order them for you. These casings are used for making summer sausage. One popular size is 60 mm (2.4 inches) diameter by 18 inches (some 24 inches) long and will hold approximately 2 to 2½ pounds of meat. After loosely filling with the sausage meat, this casing is tied in the center, which makes 2 one-pound sausages. Larger size collagen casing is a 90 mm (3½ inches) diameter by 24 inches long, holds approximately 5 pounds of meat. These types of casings are the easiest to use. Beef "middles" or "straights" are natural beef casings, but take lots more work.

## Stuffing Equipment

STUFFING EQUIPMENT: The Hamilton Beach meat grinder comes with a stuffer tube. We liked how this machine ground meats and stuffed sausages. It is well built and for the price it is a good buy to capitalize on do-it-yourself ground meats and sausages. The Kitchen Aid or Oster Mixer/ Grinder can be equipped with a stuffer tube. They worked well also, but are more expensive. The middle and larger-sized Choprite and old Universal hand meat grinders can be equipped with a stuffer tube. If you don't have access to any of this kind of stuffer equipment, consider using a stuffing funnel. It has a large throat for easier passage of sausage meats. You can buy these funnels at a butcher supply house or by mail.

Older cast iron 1-gallon and 2-gallon stuffers can be made much more efficiently with a large homemade "O" ring. When you crank the stuffer, the pressure on the stuffer plate causes wet finely ground meats to "squish-up-around" and by-pass the plate next to the stuffer's wall. Sometimes you'll lose 25% of the meat you put in the stuffer. It does not get into the casing; it by-passes the plate. This "O" ring fits directly under the stuffer plate and solves the problem. You make the "O" ring out of rubber windshield washer hose. You fasten it in a "ring" shape to fit the stuffer, with a piece of wire which joins the two ends.

You'll be able to buy natural hog casings locally from your meat dealer or a supermarket that makes sausage. If not, special sausage mail-order houses will ship them to you. Casings are shipped safely by mail, without spoiling, because they are very heavily salted. Therefore, they must be washed thoroughly with water to soak out the salt. Be sure to buy wet pork casings not the dry ones for much easier handling. (See Index: Sausage Supplies.)

NATURAL CASINGS ARE CLEAN. Some food magazines and cookbooks would have you believe that these casings must receive a very special sanitizing. They say to use vinegar and water and soak for one hour. This is okay, but not usually necessary. However, if they have a strong odor, soak them in vinegar for 5 minutes. These casings have been turned inside out, cleaned with water pressure, then washed and rinsed three times. Beef casings ("straights" or "middles") use only the center wall of a three-wall intestine. All casings are stored and shipped in heavy salt water. Germs cannot live in heavy salt solutions. However, you can use 8 ounces of vinegar per quart of water and soak casings for one or two minutes, then rinse with plain water.

## Preparing Casings

Find the end of a hog casing and fit it over the water faucet and run warm water completely through its full length. You cut out pieces which have large holes and make two shorter pieces of casings. Place the end of the casing on the side of a storage container with water for easier retrieving when you get ready to stuff.

STUFFER TUBE: Wet the stuffing tube's exterior with water then push the end of the casing (2 feet to 10 feet long) onto the tube — bunch it up like an accordion. Tie a knot in the casing's end and start pushing the meat into the casing. Use an ice pick or sharp pointed knife to prick air pockets which develop in the sausage as you stuff it.

ROPE SAUSAGE: You can stuff one casing 2 feet to 10 feet long with sausage to make a rope. You can "smoke-a-rope" 2 feet long in a circle on your grill. This long length may be difficult to handle in a skillet. Therefore, link it in 4- to 8-inch lengths.

LINK SAUSAGE: Linking is easier after your first trial run of mistakes and successes. Until you get-on-to-it, linking is easier done with a second person's help. Don't stuff the casing too tightly with sausage. The second person pinches it about every 5 to 6 inches. Then you twist the filled casing at these thinner spots to make links. If you "bust-a-gut" (a casing breaks) when stuffing, you pinch it off into a link, then continue stuffing and cut out the broken casing and reuse the meat in the next batch you stuff. The meat does not come out of a twisted casing. Well-linked sausages stay linked unless they're blood sausages. You don't need to tie string around each link except blood sausage. You can store unused casings in heavy salt water in your freezer for years.

## Cooking Cured Sausages

MEAT BROTH OR WATER COOKING: Commercial wieners and frankfurters have no wrinkles in the casing (the meat fits the casing tightly). They have been cooked in broth or water. For homemade sausage, use the bottom of a roasting pan using broth from cooked meats or plain water to cook the sausages. Place loosely-stuffed sausages in the liquid and heat the liquid to only 170°F. Use a thermometer and watch heat carefully. Overheating will bust the casings. Use a meat thermometer and cook the sausage's internal temperature to 150°F. to 155°F. Remove from liquid and cool quickly by flushing with cold water. Store in refrigerator. You can freeze these sausages.

You can cold smoke sausage to a good smoke color before cooking it "done" in the liquid. Polish sausage (Kielbasa, the name for all Polish sausages) and its Austrian, German, and Italian cousins are called Kolbassa or Kobassa are smoked. Brotwurst (not bratwurst), standard bologna, Lebanon bologna, and, sometimes, braunschweiger liver sausage are smoked also. However, many of these sausages can be cooked in water or meat broth only and not smoked. You choose how you want to do yours.

## Smoking Stuffed Sausages

Smoke-cooking at 190°F. to 250°F. or cold smoking at 85°F. to 120°F. improves the flavor of nearly any sausage. You can use any type smoker: (1) a water smoker, (2) a kettle or square grill, (3) a smaller or larger custom smoker, or (4) a barbecue pit. You can smoke ready-to-eat, cured summer-type sausages stuffed into a larger-diameter casing (60 mm). Summer sausages can be stuffed into larger pork casings (38-42 mm) and smoked.

Generally, you smoke sausages until the casings or their exterior reached the "right smoked color." This smoke color determines the amount of smoke flavor. Deep brown coloring means heavily smoked all at one time, or cold smoked slowly for a long time. However, you need to reach only 150°F. to 155°F. internal temperature for any sausages containing pork to be safely cooked if you use sodium nitrite (curing). Measure with a meat thermometer. Don't delay cooking sausage to their proper doneness after they reach your desired smoke color. You will dry them out. Sausages do not need to be tenderized with long cooking.

All casings burn when placed on metal grid wires which transfer heat efficiently and quickly. Watch out for smoker heats above 250°F. Therefore, drape smaller links of sausages over wooden dowels; they look like wooden broom handles. For longer sausages, tie ends with loops of butcher twine or heavy string and hang them.

Keep sausages from touching each other, because they will not take smoke at these points. Move sausages around because those next to the smoker's wall will not cook as fast as those hanging over the fire. Be careful of fats dripping into the fire itself. They cause fires and ruin sausages.

Fuels for fires for smoking can be any kind that will heat, cook, and cause smoke woods to smolder. You can use charcoal, gas, electric, or wood to heat sausage. You add high quality smoke wood for flavoring. (See Index: Smoking.)

## Master Steps for Making Sausages

You use many of these same steps when making: (1) standard bulk sausage,

(2) sausages with a casing, and (3) sausages without a casing. You prepare sausage meats according to one of SECRETS' recipes or use your own recipe. Each kind of sausage uses: (1) a distinct spice/seasoning recipe and (2) a meat recipe.

Step 1: Select a spice/seasoning mixture for your sausage. See recipes.

Step 2: Meat preparation: Trim it of excess fats if you desire. Cut meat into pieces that will go through the throat of your grinder or food processor. If you're using frozen ground meat, thaw it.

Step 3: Coarse grind meat over a sausage plate ($^3$/16-inch-diameter holes or larger).

Step 4: Mix the recipe's liquid/spice seasoning mixture. The liquid may be water, milk, beer, wine, or brandy.

Step 5: Mix ground meat with the liquid mixture very thoroughly. Then fine grind over the hamburger plate ($^1$/8-inch-diameter holes). This is not necessary for finely pre-ground meat such as previously ground frozen chicken or turkey. Package sausage for the refrigerator or freezer if you don't stuff it or make Sausage Without Casings with it, which continue as Steps 6 through 9.

For Stuffed and Linked Sausages: See Stuffing and Linking in this chapter.

## Charlie K's Summer Sausage Without Casing

Here's your opportunity to prove that you truly have the "pioneer" spirit. You can smoke-cook most Sausages Without Casing using this method. Your smoker must be able to develop 200°F. to 275°F. smoke-cooking temperatures and hold these temperatures for one hour. You'll use heavy smoke for 50 to 60 minutes. Beyond 60 minutes, you dry out this sausage unless you baste it.

## Smoking Sausage Without Casing

Step 6: Refrigerate ground sausage from Step 5 for 2 to 4 hours for better shaping. Shape 4 pounds of mixed sausage meat into three loaves 1½" to 2" diameter by 10" to 12" long. Place sausage loaves on 18-inch-long pieces of plastic wrap or Saran, then roll up tightly. You knead this sausage loaf to eliminate air pockets in this sausage. Prick any air pockets with knife or ice pick, and twist the ends loosely to make a temporary plastic casing for each sausage.

Step 7: Place the wrapped sausage loaves running across the wires on the smoker's grid. This will produce better appearing finished sausage slices. Leave ¼-inch spaces between sausages for smoke and heat to penetrate each sausage loaf. Wet smoke-cook in a water smoker (See Index) or cook in a custom cooker or kettle grill or bake in a kitchen oven. Cook about 45 to 50 minutes at 250°F. Do not exceed 275°F.; you may melt the plastic. Do not set plastic-covered loaves over a hot direct fire. You heat sausages just long enough to "set up" the meat, which occurs around 120°F. to 130°F. internal temperature of the sausage. Now, you're ready to smoke them.

Step 8: Remove loaves from the smoker and cool for 10 to 30 minutes in the plastic. You want the liquids to be reabsorbed by the meat, which gives you a moist sausage. Then, remove the plastic wrap. Remove any liquid and sediment on the sausage's surface with a paper towel so that the sausage can "take" heavy smoke before being overcooked. Set up the smoker for dry smoking (See Index).

Step 9: Then Dry Smoke in a water smoker or use a standard smoking procedure in other smokers or pits for 40 to 60 minutes. Smoke-cook the sausage loaves to 150°F. to 155°F. (please check the center of the sausage from its end with a meat thermometer). Remove immediately when done, then cool and refrigerate it. Don't oversmoke. This can give it a bitter taste.

All sausage turns a light pink when sodium nitrite or salt peter cures are used. Age sausage for 12 hours up to 5 days in the refrigerator for mellowing out before serving. Cover with plastic or foil to keep it moist. You can freeze this sausage up to six months without great loss of flavor by wrapping it in aluminum foil and placing it inside of a plastic bag.

## Cooking Lean Fresh Sausage

Place a small amount of water with the sausage in the skillet and cover with a lid. This helps keep your sausage juicy. Begin cooking over medium heat. In 5 to 7 minutes, you should have the sausage cooked enough to be browned. Remove lid, pour off liquid, then cook down any liquid that remains in the skillet. Turn sausage and brown on both sides. Add sausage liquid back as needed to keep from overbrowning the sausage. Remove sausage patties or links to paper toweling to absorb any surface fats. Do not overcook.

John, you can tell J.J. that eating homemade sausage is not death-provoking with cholesterol and saturated fats like she imagines. She'll be okay if she eats it in moderation. In fact, it could improve her health over her double chocolate cake, high-cholesterol cheeses and fat-laden snacks.

## "Red Eye" Sauce

When you fry any meat, it gives up juices which become a browned meat glaze. This glaze and the browned meat particles remaining in the skillet can be made into a delicious "red eye" sauce. Pour off all rendered fats and replace one to two tablespoons in the skillet. Heat skillet until fat starts to barely smoke. Add ½ teaspoon granulated sugar and brown it as you cook. Add ½ to 1 cup hot water (be careful of steam), depending upon the amount of drippings, browned crumbs, and glaze, etc., in the skillet. Then use a wooden scraper to loosen the glaze and the crumbs on the bottom and sides of the skillet. Bring liquid to a boil as you scrape. Then add 1 to 2 tablespoons of milk. Bring gently to a boil again. Replace sausage in skillet and heat together before serving. This "red-eye" sauce is eaten along with your sausage and as a gravy over hot buttermilk or baking powder biscuits.

Now, John, in a good ole southern and many northern households, your "red eye" sauce is really a low-cal defatted red eye gravy. But John, please call it a "sauce," not a gravy. In today's "food-panicked" world, a nice sauce is okay, but ole-time gravy scares the Blossom types to death. And John, we guarantee you'll relish it. It's tasty, good ole American food made healthy — it's easy to make and you'll actually save money. Finally, you can suggest to Blossom, there's a real world of "new sausage" out there that's safe. And she needs to learn some of the real world's FOOD TRUTHS.

# U.S. TO METRIC CONVERSIONS

U.S. DRY & LIQUID MEASURES: from teaspoons (tsp.), tablespoons (Tbsp.), and cups (c.) to milliliters (ml) and liters (L) nearest equivalent.

| | | |
|---|---|---|
| ⅛ tsp. | = ¹⁄₄₈ oz. | = ½ ml |
| ¼ tsp. | = ¹⁄₂₄ oz. | = 1 ml |
| ½ tsp. | = ¹⁄₁₂ oz. | = 2 ml |
| 1 tsp. | = ⅙ oz. | = 5 ml |
| 1 Tbsp. (3 tsp.) | = ½ oz. | = 15 ml |
| ⅛ c. (2 Tbsp.) | = 1 oz. | = 30 ml |
| ¼ c. | = 2 oz. | = 59 ml |
| ½ c. | = 4 oz. | = 118 ml |
| 1 c. | = 8 oz. | = 240 ml |
| 2 c. (1 pt.) | = 16 oz. | = 475 ml |
| 4 c. (1 qt.) | = 32 oz. | = 950 ml |
| 4 quarts (1 gal.) | = 128 oz. | = 3.8 L |

| U.S. Can No. | Wt. or Fluid Oz. (Check Label) | Approximate Cups | Metric |
|---|---|---|---|
| No. 300 | 14-16 oz. | 1¾ | 415 ml |
| No. 303 | 16-17 oz. | 2 | 475 ml |
| No. 2 | 1 lb. 4 oz. | 2½ | 595 ml |
| | 1 pt. + 2 oz. | | |
| No. 2½ | 1 lb-1 lb. 13 oz. | 3½ | 830 ml |
| No. 3 | 46 oz. (juice) | 5¾ | 1360 ml |
| No. 10 | 6½ to 7 lb. | 12-13 | 3 L |

U.S. WEIGHT MEASURES: ounces (oz.) and pounds (lb.) to grams (g) nearest equivalent.

| | | |
|---|---|---|
| 1 oz. | | = 29 g |
| 4 oz. | = ¼ lb. | = 115 g |
| 8 oz. | = ½ lb. | = 225 g |
| 16 oz. | = 1 lb. | = 450 g |
| 32 oz. | = 2 lb. | = 900 g |
| 36 oz. | = 2¼ lb. | = 1,000 g (1-Kg) |
| 64 oz. | = 4 lb. | = 1,800 g |
| 80 oz. | = 5 lb. | = 2,260 g |
| 160 oz. | = 10 lb. | = 4,536 g |

U.S. MEASURE MULTIPLIERS to Metric Measures in milliliters (ml), liters (L), grams (g), kilograms (Kg), centimeters (cm).

| | | | |
|---|---|---|---|
| 1 tsp. | teaspoon | 4.9 | ml |
| 1 Tbsp. | tablespoon | 15.0 | ml |
| 1 fl. oz. | fluid ounce | 29.7 | ml |
| 1 c. | cup | 0.237 | L |
| 1 pt. | pint | 0.47 | L |
| 1 qt. | quart | 0.95 | L |
| 1 gal. | gallon | 3.781 | L |
| 1 oz. | ounce | 28.3 | g |
| 1 lb. | pound | .45 | Kg |
| 1 in. | inch | 2.54 | cm |

Temperature conversions from °F. to °C. on page 6 of SECRETS'.

# Uniquely Delicious Recipes

## Sausages and Sauces
## to Barbecue and Breads

# Uniquely Delicious Recipes

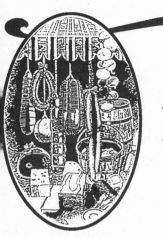

# Easy, Tasty Lean Sausages

Lean Pork Sausage to easy-to-make
Smoked Summer Sausage without casing

## LEAN PORK SAUSAGE

"This recipe has received raves from old time sausage makers. Fat and calories reduced 50% compared with commercial sausage."

5 pounds pork (Boston butt or
    shoulder), trimmed of some fat
1 tablespoon plus 2 teaspoons non-
    iodized (canning) salt
2½ teaspoons black pepper
3 tablespoons ground or rubbed
    sage

1 tablespoon sugar
½ teaspoon thyme
½ teaspoon ground coriander
¹⁄₁₆ teaspoon cayenne
1 cup water

    Mix the dry seasonings, then mix into water. Finally mix with meat. See index: Basic sausage steps 1 through 5.
    Sausage with casing: See index: Stuffing and linking sausage in 31 to 34 mm casings or package for bulk sausage.

## BRATWURST SAUSAGE

Cook in beer or water, then grill. "It's lean, juicy, and tasty."

5 pounds pork (pork butts,
    shoulders, or picnic)
2 teaspoons nutmeg
1 tablespoon plus ½ teaspoon salt
1 tablespoon plus 2 teaspoons
    ground white pepper

1½ teaspoons sugar
½ teaspoon ground ginger
½ teaspoon MSG
1 cup water

    Follow Master Sausage steps 1 through 5. Stuff in 31 to 34 mm pork casings and link into 4 to 6 inch links.
    Simmer bratwurst gently in water, beer, or milk. This prevents bursting when browning. Drain well. Brush each sausage lightly with oil, then grill gently over a medium fire for 3 to 5 minutes on each side. Watch carefully to prevent over-browning. Makes 35 to 40 links.

## BOCK WURST

"This is Charlie's favorite sausage. It's good - real class."

5 pounds coarse ground pork
(Boston butt or shoulder), fat
trimmed
1⅔ tablespoons ground nutmeg
4 teaspoons salt (canning, non-
iodized)
1⅞ teaspoons white pepper
1½ teaspoons sugar

1 teaspoon MSG
1⅞ teaspoons ground thyme
2 eggs
¾ cup milk
2½ inch diameter fresh bunch
parsley
3 large green onions with tops
½ small onion

See index for making standard fresh sausage. After the meat coarse grinding step, grind the parsley, green onions, and onion. Run a little meat afterwards to retrieve all of the green seasonings. Whip the eggs and mix with milk along with the ground onions and parsley. Mix with the coarse ground pork. Grind over hamburger plate. Link in 31 to 34 mm casings. See stuffing and linking.

## SWEET ITALIAN SAUSAGE WITH WINE

"Great for any dish calling for Italian sausage."

5 pounds coarse ground pork
(Boston butt, pork roast, or pork
shoulder), deboned and fat
trimmed
1½ tablespoons non-iodized salt
(canning salt)
4 teaspoons black pepper

2½ tablespoons ground fennel
1½ tsp. ground oregano
1¼ tsp. garlic (powder or granule)
¼ teaspoon sugar
½ teaspoon MSG
1 cup red wine

Mix dry ingredients in the water or wine, then mix thoroughly with coarse ground pork. Grind over a hamburger plate (⅛ inch holes). Package in plastic bags or stuff into 31 to 34 mm pork casing. See stuffing and linking.

## BOUDIN' BLANC

"Brightly flavored white New Orleans style sausage."

2½ pounds coarse ground pork
butt or roast
2½ pounds ground chicken
2½ teaspoons non-iodized salt
2½ tablespoons white pepper
2½ cups sauteed onions
4 tablespoons butter
2½ cups warm milk

1½ cups bread crumbs, soaked in
milk
2 eggs
¼ bunch fresh parsley, chopped
⅜ teaspoon nutmeg
⅛ teaspoon cloves
⅛ teaspoon cinnamon
¼ teaspoon ginger

Melt butter; saute and brown onions. Soak bread crumbs in warm milk. Mix eggs, nutmeg, cloves, cinnamon, and ginger. Mix onions, soaked bread crumbs, and parsley with meats thoroughly. Grind over hamburger plate (⅛ inch holes). Stuff into 31 to 34 mm hog casings. See index: Stuffing and linking.

## PORK SAUSAGE WITH "HEAT"

"Help yourself to the cayenne pepper, but think of your kin folks and friends."

5 pounds coarse ground pork
(Boston butt)
1½ tablespoons salt (canning non-
iodized)
2 tablespoons black pepper
3 tablespoons ground/ rubbed
sage

1 tsp. coriander
½ teaspoon MSG
1 to 6 teaspoons red or cayenne
pepper (to taste)
1 tablespoon ground thyme
1¼ teaspoons sugar
1 cup water

Mix dry ingredients with water, then mix thoroughly with coarse ground pork. Grind over hamburger plate (⅛ inch holes). Package in plastic bags or stuff in 31 to 34 mm pork casings. See index: Stuffing and linking.

## HELLENIC SAUSAGE

"Rated HIGH by our tasting panel. Gives a good Greek flavor."

5 pounds coarse ground pork
¾ cup red wine
1 tablespoon ground oregano
6 green onions or scallions,
chopped finely
1 tablespoon non-iodized salt

1½ teaspoons ground allspice
2 tablespoons lemon pepper
¾ teaspoon MSG
Zest from 3 oranges
¾ cup water

Mix dry ingredients. Mix them with wine and water. Mix meats with liquid mixture throughly. Grind over hamburger plate (⅛ inch holes). Package for patty sausage or stuff in 31 to 34 mm hog casings. See Master Sausage Making steps 1 through 5. See stuffing.

## KIELBASA - POLISH

"A tasty smoked Polish sausage - can smoke without casing."

3½ pounds coarse ground pork
(Boston butt, pork roast, pork
shoulder, picnic)
1½ pounds very lean beef (defatted
arm roast)
4 teaspoons black pepper
2½ teaspoons Morton's Tender-
Quick

1 tablespoon garlic powder
1 tablespoon salt
1¼ teaspoons allspice
4 teaspoons marjoram
1 teaspoon sugar
½ teaspoon MSG
8 ounces water

Mix all spices and seasoning together, then mix in water. Mix meats with seasoning mixture. Grind sausage meats over hamburger plate (⅛ inch holes). Pack and chill.

See Master steps 1 to 9 for Smoking Sausage without casing, page 105, or you can stuff and link it, pages 97-98.

## METTWURST SMOKED SUMMER SAUSAGE

"Original old-fashion mettwurst summer sausage. Can make without casing."

1½ pounds beef chuck (trim
surface and seam fat)
2½ pounds pork (Boston butt,
shoulder; leave nearly all fat)
1 tablespoon non-iodized salt
(canning salt)
1½ tablespoons ground pepper
1 tablespoon and 1 teaspoon
Morton's Tender-Quick (found in
farm stores, mail-order catalogs)

1 teaspoon sugar
3 teaspoons garlic powder
½ teaspoon MSG
¼ teaspoon cayenne pepper (or to
taste)
5 ounces cold water

Mix the spices with the water, then mix this with the 4 pounds of ground meats thoroughly. (Can substitute thawed frozen ground chicken or turkey for pork and beef.) If meat is coarse ground, it should be ground again over a hamburger plate (⅛ inch holes) for a finer textured sausage. Makes 3 sausages.

Smoked sausage without casing: See page 105.
Smoked sausage with casing: See page 96-98.


## VENISON-ELK METTWURST SMOKED SUMMER SAUSAGE

"Even ladies like this deer sausage with moistness, texture and mild flavors."

2½ pounds deer or elk, trimmed of
surface fat and seam fat if you
want to reduce the gamey flavor
1½ pounds pork shoulder or
Boston butt (not trimmed of fat)
1 tablespoon non-iodized salt
(canning salt)
1½ tablespoons ground pepper
1 tablespoon and 1 teaspoon
Morton's Tender-Quick (found in
farm stores, sausage mail-order
catalogs)

1 teaspoon sugar
3 teaspoons garlic powder
½ teaspoon MSG
¼ teaspoon cayenne pepper (or to
taste)
5 ounces cold water
¼ teaspoon garlic powder
1 teaspoon coarse black pepper

Mix the spices with the water, then mix this with the 4 pounds of ground meats thoroughly. Grind again over a hamburger plate (⅛ inch holes) for a finer textured sausage. Makes 3 sausages.

Smoked Sausage without casing: See page 106.
Smoked Sausage with casing: See pages 96 through 98.

## Charlie K's Summer Sausage Without Casing

Here's your opportunity to prove that you truly have the "pioneer" spirit. You can smoke-cook most Sausages Without Casing using this method. Your smoker must be able to develop 200°F. to 275°F. smoke-cooking temperatures and hold these temperatures for one hour. You'll use heavy smoke for 50 to 60 minutes. Beyond 60 minutes, you dry out this sausage unless you baste it. See Master Steps 1 through 5 pages 97-98.

### Smoking Sausage Without Casing

Step 6: Refrigerate ground sausage from Step 5 for 2 to 4 hours for better shaping. Shape 4 pounds of mixed sausage meat into three loaves 1½" to 2" diameter by 10" to 12" long. Place sausage loaves on 18-inch-long pieces of plastic wrap or Saran, then roll up tightly. You knead this sausage loaf to eliminate air pockets in this sausage. Prick any air pockets with knife or ice pick, and twist the ends loosely to make a temporary plastic casing for each sausage.

Step 7: Place the wrapped sausage loaves running across the wires on the smoker's grid. This will produce better appearing finished sausage slices. Leave ¼-inch spaces between sausages for smoke and heat to penetrate each sausage loaf. Wet smoke-cook in a water smoker (See Index) or cook in a custom cooker or kettle grill or bake in a kitchen oven. Cook about 45 to 50 minutes at 250°F. Do not exceed 275°F.; you may melt the plastic. Do not set plastic-covered loaves over a hot direct fire. You heat sausages just long enough to "set up" the meat, which occurs around 120°F. to 130°F. internal temperature of the sausage. Now, you're ready to smoke them.

Step 8: Remove loaves from the smoker and cool for 10 to 30 minutes in the plastic. You want the liquids to be reabsorbed by the meat, which gives you a moist sausage. Then, remove the plastic wrap. Remove any liquid and sediment on the sausage's surface with a paper towel so that the sausage can "take" heavy smoke before being overcooked. Set up the smoker for dry smoking (See Index).

Step 9: Then Dry Smoke in a water smoker or use a standard smoking procedure in other smokers or pits for 40 to 120 minutes. Don't oversmoke. This can give it a bitter taste. Smoke-cook the sausage loaves to 150°F. to 155°F. (please check the center of the sausage from its end with a meat thermometer). Remove immediately when done, then cool and refrigerate it.

All sausage turns a light pink when sodium nitrite or salt peter cures are used. Age sausage for 12 hours up to 5 days in the refrigerator for mellowing out before serving. Cover with plastic or foil to keep it moist. You can freeze this sausage up to six months without great loss of flavor by wrapping it in aluminum foil and placing it inside of a plastic bag. (Complete sausage making directions pages 91-99.)

## SMOKED kNOTE WURST

Nutmeg and marjoram make this sausage speak - you'll like what it says.

4 (1 pound) tubes frozen ground
  chicken, thawed
6 tablespoons onion powder or
  granules
1½ Tbsp. ground marjoram
2½ tablespoons dried parsley
1¼ teaspoons ground nutmeg
1 tablespoons Morton's Tender-
  Quick

½ teaspoon salt (non-iodized,
  canning)
1 teaspoon white pepper
½ teaspoon MSG
1½ tablespoons chicken bouillon
  granules
9 ounces water

Dissolve bouillon in boiling water; cool. Add the remaining spices. Wet hands, then mix spice/water mixture with chicken. Refrigerate for 3 to 4 hours. Makes 3 sausages.

Smoked Sausage without casing: See page 105.
Smoked Sausage with casing: pages 97, 98.

## CAJUN SAUSAGE

"Smoke to make a delicious Andouille - sparkles as a  fresh sausage."

5 pounds coarse ground pork butt,
  roast, or shoulder
1 tablespoon pepper
1½ tablespoons salt
5 tablespoons onion powder or
  granules
1½ teaspoons thyme

½ teaspoon ground bay leaf
⅝ teaspoon allspice
⅝ teaspoon nutmeg
⅝ teaspoon cayenne
¾ teaspoon sugar
¾ teaspoon paprika
1 cup water

Mix spices with water. Mix with coarse ground meat. Grind over a hamburger plate (⅛ inch holes). Stuff in 31 to 34 mm casing for Cajun Sausage.

Andouille Sausage: Smoke without casing or stuffing 38 to 44 mm hog casing or 60 mm collagen casings and smoke. See page 105, 97-98.

# Sensational Smokings

Chicken, turkey, pork, beef
lamb, fish, wild game

## BARBECUED PORK ROAST

"Taste the great flavor of traditional southern barbecue like the pros do it."

1 (4 to 7 pound) pork roast (Boston butt or picnic, skinned and defatted
Pork rub (Zap-II or Hugh's Cajun Rub)

Buy a Boston butt (pork butt, pork shoulder roast, all the same cut). Buy it deboned or debone yourself. Use a sharp knife. Cut the meat next to the bone and pull this cut meat back; this lets you see where to make your next cut, then continue to cut, following the bone's outline.

When smoking Boston butt or pork shoulder, cut nearly into two parts, (butterfly fashion), each about 2 inches thick. Wet smoke and dry smoke for maximum flavor. See index. If these cuts of meat are left whole, you can wet smoke to complete doneness.

Sprinkle meat with a pork rub generously. Rub in. Place meat in a plastic bag and cure at room temperature for 2 hours or in the refrigerator for up to 72 hours. Stop cooking when the pork reaches 160°F.

## DRY SMOKED PORK RIBS

"You'll be the envy of your friends, outstanding ribs; you can challenge the best."

| | |
|---|---|
| 2 or 3 sides spareribs or loin back ribs (baby back ribs)<br>Pork rubs (Zap II, Lela's Brown Sugar Rub, or Hugh's Cajun Rub) | Remove the membrane covering rib bones. Remove diaphram muscle and breast cartridge from the spareribs. Apply pork rub generously to both sides of the ribs; rub in. Marinate in a plastic bag for 2 hours at room temperature or in refrigerator up to 72 hours. |

Smoke cook at 200°F. to 275°F. for 3 to 5 hours or until done. "Doneness" test: Spareribs are "done" when ⅛ to ¼ inch of end bone shows and ribs separate easily. Try eating them without a tomato based barbecue sauce. They're delicious and called "dry ribs."

## SMOKED BREAKFAST SAUSAGE ROLLS

"Smoking adds a unique flavor to breakfast sausage - and you can smoke it easily."

| | |
|---|---|
| 1 pound rolls or tubes whole hog pork sausage (or make your own 2 inch diameter rolls from homemade sausage)<br>Cheesecloth | Cut pieces of cheesecloth large enough to totally wrap up a roll of sausage and have an overlap. Wrap each sausage roll with 2 separate pieces of cheesecloth.<br><br>Cold smoke at 85°F. to 120°F. for 2 to 5 hours, depending on how much smoke flavor you like. Keep smoker's temperature below |

120°F. High temperature melts fat. After smoking, cool. Remove cheesecloths. Slice like standard breakfast sausage and fry, grill, or bake. Keep refrigerated or frozen.

## SMOKED GOURMET HAM

"Sliced thin, it's more elegant - makes an inexpensive party food."

| | |
|---|---|
| Shank end of smoked, cooked cured ham<br>½ gallon apple cider or apple juice<br>1½ cups brown sugar, packed or honey<br>1 teaspoon ground cinnamon<br>1 teaspoon ground allspice<br>2 teaspoons ground cloves<br>½ teaspoon maple flavoring (Mapleine) | 1. Prepare ham by skinning and trimming nearly all fat.<br>2. Squeeze to remove added water.<br>3. Drain and dry in refrigerator.<br>4. Mix all the remaining ingredients together.<br><br>Place ham in plastic bag. Pour marinade over ham to cover over ½ of ham. Store in refrigerator for 5 to 10 days, turning daily.<br><br>Remove from marinade, drain, and dry. Dry smoke at 220°F. to 250°F. for 1 to 2 hours, until colored to your liking and temperature reaches 130°F. Cool. Slice very thin. |

# ALICE'S SUGAR CURED COUNTRY HAM

"Takes time to develop flavor, but it's worth it."

1 (16 to 18 pound) fresh ham
2 cups canning salt
2 tablespoons black pepper
1 tablespoon red pepper
5 tablespoons brown sugar

Mix all dry ingredients together thoroughly. Open up shank end of the ham. Work the sugar cure deeply into the meat around the bone to prevent "bone souring." Dissolve 3 tablespoons cure into 1 cup water. Shoot this liquid around the bone using an animal syringe. Apply curing mixture heavily all over ham. Wrap in brown butcher paper. Wrap in cloth sack. Twist bag tightly and tie. Hang in a cold, safe area with shank end down. This will drip. Cure for 6 to 8 weeks. Soak in water for 12 to 24 hours to remove some salt. Slice and fry.

# SMOKED CHICKEN

"More juicy than smoked turkey. You should receive lots of compliments."

1 (3½ to 4½ pound) whole frying chicken
Poultry rub (Zip II, Hugh's Cajun Rub)

Rinse the abdominal neck cavity and the exterior thoroughly with water. Season cavities and exterior with rub. Sprinkle poultry generously, approximately 1 to 2 tablespoons per chicken. Place in plastic bag and marinate at room temperature up to 2 hours or up to 72 hours in the refrigerator.

Paint smokers grid wires with vegetable oil or Pam to reduce sticking and clean up time. Place chicken on grid, breast side up. Smoke-cook at 200°F. to 275°F. until it reaches good smoke colors. Smoke-cook until done at 165°F. (see doneness chart). Serves 3 to 4.

# SMOKED TURKEY

"This size smokes beautifully and comes out juicy."

1 (12 to 14 pound) frozen turkey, thawed completely
Poultry rubs (Zip II or Hugh's Cajun Rub)

Don't stuff the turkey. See index: Turkey preparation. Rinse abdominal and neck cavities and exterior thoroughly with hot water. Remove excess moisture. Season cavities and exterior with rub. Sprinkle generously, approximately 3 to 4 tablespoons per turkey. Place turkey in a plastic bag and marinate at room temperature for up to 2 hours or up to 72 hours in the refrigerator to develop extra flavor. The dry rub helps protect the bird during the 72 hour "frig" time.

Paint smoker's grid wires with vegetable oil or Pam to reduce sticking and clean up time. Place turkey on grid, breast side up. Smoke-cook at 200°F. to 275°F. until it reaches good smoke color. Smoke-cook until done at 165°F. Serves 12 to 16.

## SMOKED PORK SAUERBRATEN

"Tasty and unusual - maybe not quite the Black Forest."

2 envelopes onion soup mix
⅓ cup brown sugar, packed
¼ teaspoon ground ginger
1 large bay leaf or 2 small
½ teaspoon pepper
1 cup red wine vinegar

1 cup apple juice
½ cup water
1 (4 to 5 pound) pork butt roast,
  deboned and trimmed of excess
  fat

Combine all ingredients. Bring to boil. Simmer for 5 minutes; cool. Place pork in plastic bag; pour marinade over it. Marinate overnight in refrigerator or up to 24 hours. Drain; smoke-cook to 160°F. internal temperature. Remove and keep warm for 10 minutes before carving. Serves 6 to 8.

## SMOKED PORK LOIN

"Save 40%. Serve a steak quality dish."

4 to 7 pounds pork loin
Pork rub (Zap II or
  Hugh's Cajun Rub)

Trim loin's top layer of surface fat down to less than ⅛ inch thick and any deposits of visible fat that you can trim out easily. Sprinkle meat with rub generously. Rub in the rub; place meat in a plastic bag and cure at room temperature for 2 hours or in the refrigerator for up to 72 hours.

Paint smoker's grid wires with vegetable oil or Pam. This reduces sticking and clean up time. Use paper toweling and dry meat. Place loins on grid. Wet smoke for 40 minutes at 200°F. to 275°F. Dry smoke until cooked to 155°F. to 160°F. (Test with meat thermometer.) To get a good smoked color and flavor, you need considerable smoke. See smoking guide for either electric or charcoal smokers. See manufacturer's instructions for gas smokers, kettle, or square grills.

## SMOKING DEER AND ELK

Use roasts 2 inches thick or more. Trim all surface fats. Use general purpose wild game marinade. Marinate for 24 to 72 hours. Smoke-cook tender cuts only. Use Brisket Smoking directions unless the animals are very young. For a young animal, sprinkle a rub over the meat and rub in. Marinate in refrigerator for 48 to 72 hours. Dry meat on refrigerator rack for 2 hours. Rub with canola or other vegetable oil. Smoke-cook to 160°F. Check for tenderness with a fork. If tough, wrap in aluminum foil; add 2 to 3 tablespoons of the vinegar based salad dressing. Bake in the oven for 1 hour at 250°F. Carve deer and elk cross grain in ⅛ inch slices or thinner for maximum tenderness.

# BRINED SMOKED WILD GOOSE

"Old-fashioned way to brine game."

1 (4½ to 5½ pound)
Canadian goose
1 gallon water
1 cup salt
¼ cup sugar
Hugh's Cajun Rub, to
taste

Dissolve salt and sugar in water. Brine goose for 3 to 4 hours. Remove. Flush with water. Dry in refrigerator or with an electric fan. Sprinkle rub in tail and neck cavities generously. Marinate for 2 hours at room temperature or up to 24 hours refrigerated.

Smoke-cook in a water smoker at 220°F.-250°F. Cook until done at 165°F. in the skin pocket between the thigh and the breast, about 2½ to 4 hours.

# SMOKING WILD GEESE

"This is easy to do and reduce fat."

Season heavily with Zap II Rub. Place in plastic bag to marinate for 2 hours at room temperature or up to 72 hours in the refrigerator.

Follow Basic Master Smoking steps. Smoke-cook the wild goose for 2½ to 4 hours, depending on size. Geese are "done" at 165°F. Check temperature by inserting meat thermometer into the thickest breast meat. Check for tenderness with a fork. If tough, wrap in aluminum foil and add 2 to 3 tablespoons of the vinegar based salad dressing. Bake in the oven for 1 hour at 325°F.

# SMOKED PHEASANT

"Great flavor; baste to keep it moist."

2 pheasants
Rub (Zip II or Hugh's
Cajun Rub)

Pheasant has little fat and will be dry. Baste the complete bird lightly with vegetable oil, then apply rub generously in the cavity and over the skin. Marinate for 2 hours at room temperature or up to 24 hours in a refrigerator. After 45 minutes, baste with melted butter. Smoke-cook to 165°F. maximum!

# SMOKED LAMB SHOULDER

1 (5 to 8 pound) lamb
shoulder
Rub (Hugh's Cajun Rub,
Zap II, or El Greco)

Trim shoulder of fat; remove layers of fat and pin back with wooden picks if you want to cut calories. Sprinkle shoulder generously with the rub and rub in. Marinate for 2 hours at room temperature or up to 24 hours in the refrigerator. Smoke to 150°F. to 160°F., internal temperature. Serves 8 to 10.

## SMOKER WATER PAN SAUCES

Start with less liquid in the water pan to save boiling down. Use a total of 1½ quarts instead of 2 quarts liquid for an electric smoker, more for a charcoal smoker for a 4 hour smoking period - the approximate time needed for a 12 pound turkey, or two 4 pound chickens. You might like to add wine, beer, cola, apple cider or apple juice, or some other seasonings for more flavor.

Check the water pan for dryness at 2½ hours. Add extra liquid if needed. When finished, strain this liquid through a wire strainer to remove solids. If you want a clear sauce, strain it again through a paper towel. Use ice cubes to congeal and remove fat. Add smoked wing tips or skin to liquid to increase smoke flavor. Boil down to taste and pour sauce over sliced meat.

## SMOKED CHICKEN LENTIL SOUP

"Gives this soup a special lift."

| | |
|---|---|
| 2 cups dried split lentils (1 pound) | ¼ teaspoon thyme |
| 2 cups coarsely chopped celery | ½ teaspoon salt |
| with tops | ⅛ teaspoon pepper |
| 1 cup coarsely chopped carrots | 1 bay leaf |
| 1 large onion, finely chopped | |

Use the skin, wing tips, and carcasses from two smoked chickens. Cook in 1½ quarts of water. Bring to a boil. Simmer for 1 hour. Cool, then strain and pick pieces of chicken off the bone. Squeeze the skin to give you 2 quarts of season liquid or add water, then add the listed ingredients. Bring to a boil. Cover and simmer for 1 hour, until lentils are soft. Season to taste. Serve hot. Serves 8.

## HOT SMOKED CHICKEN SALAD

| | |
|---|---|
| 2 cups smoked chicken, diced | 1 cup mayonnaise |
| 1½ cups sliced celery | ½ teaspoon salt |
| 1 tablespoon chopped onion | Pepper to taste |
| 1 tablespoon lemon juice | Crushed potato chips |
| ¼ cup slivered, toasted almonds | ½ cup grated Cheddar cheese |

Mix together chicken, celery, onion, lemon juice, and almonds. Mix together mayonnaise, salt, and pepper. Add to chicken mixture and toss gently. Pour into greased shallow pan. Sprinkle top with crushed potato chips and grated cheese. Bake in 425°F. oven for 25 to 30 minutes, until it bubbles. Serves 4 to 6.

## SMOKED CHICKEN ALA KING

6 tablespoons butter or margarine
6 tablespoons flour
1 teaspoon salt
½ teaspoon pepper
2 tablespoons sherry (optional)
1½ cups well seasoned chicken
  broth

1 cup milk
1½ cups diced smoked chicken
¼ cup sliced green bell pepper
¼ c. sliced pimiento or red sweet
  bell pepper

Melt butter in medium saucepan. Add flour; stir until it forms a roux. Stir in salt, pepper, chicken broth, and milk. Continue stirring and cooking until sauce thickens. Stir in chicken, peppers, and sherry. Serve on top of toasted bread cubes, noodles, or rice. Serves 4 to 6.

## DIJON SMOKE CHICKEN FETTUCINI

"Exciting pasta treat."

4 tablespoons butter
3 teaspoons finely chopped garlic
3 teaspoons finely chopped
  shallots or onions
½ pound sliced fresh mushrooms
1½ cups heavy cream
3 tablespoons Dijon mustard
½ teaspoon salt
Freshly ground pepper (to taste)

4 green onions and tops, finely
  chopped
2½ cups smoked chicken or
  smoked turkey, diced
1 cup chopped fresh plum
  tomatoes, seeded
½ cup grated Parmesan cheese
1 pound fettucini

In large skillet, melt butter and lightly saute the garlic, shallots, and mushrooms. On low heat, add the cream, mustard, salt, and pepper; mix well to blend. Remove from heat and set aside.

Cook fettucini in salted water until desired doneness. When fettucini is almost finished, add chicken, green onions, plum tomatoes, and Parmesan cheese to cream sauce. Place over low heat and warm. Drain fettucini.

Serve smoked chicken sauce over fettucini on a warmed platter. Serves 6.

## SMOKED TURKEY-MUSHROOM QUICHE

"Glamorous Leftover Turkey."

1 partially baked pie crust (400°F.
  oven for 10 minutes)
1 cup chopped smoked turkey or
  chicken
½ pound fresh mushrooms,
  sauteed in 1 teaspoon butter

¾ cup shredded American cheese
1 (10¾ ounce) can condensed
  cream of shrimp soup
¼ cup milk
4 eggs, slightly beaten

Arrange turkey and mushrooms in pie crust. Sprinkle with cheeses. In small saucepan, combine soup and milk. Heat just to boiling, stirring constantly. Gradually stir into eggs. Pour soup mixture over cheese. Bake in 325°F. oven for 40 to 45 minutes or until knife inserted off-center comes out clean. Serves 6.

## SMOKED CHICKEN STRATA

"Give this dish extra class for a luncheon."

6 slices bread
2 cups smoked chicken, diced
½ cup chopped onion
½ cup chopped celery
¼ cup chopped green pepper
¾ cup mayonnaise
¾ teaspoon salt

Dash of pepper
2 eggs
1½ cups milk
1 (10½ ounce) can cream of
  mushroom soup
½ cup sharp American cheese

Cube 2 slices of bread and trim crusts from remaining bread (cut up crusts).
Place cubed bread and crusts in bottom of greased 8x8x2 inch pan.
Combine smoked chicken, onion, celery, green pepper, mayonnaise, salt, and pepper. Spoon over bread cubes. Place reserved 4 bread slices on top of chicken mixture. Combine eggs and milk. Pour over all. Cover and chill for 1 hour or overnight. Cover top with cream of mushroom soup. Bake until set. Sprinkle top with cheese last few minutes of baking. Bake in 325°F. oven for 1 hour.

## MIROTON

"Delicious leftover smoked beef (roast or brisket)."

Leftover smoked beef
¼ cup margarine or
  butter
2 large yellow onions
¼ cup flour
2 tablespoons wine
  vinegar
2 cups water
2 cubes or 2 teaspoons
  bouillon
1 to 2 cups dry bread
  crumbs

Slice roast beef and set aside. Slice the onions thinly and cook them in margarine over low heat until golden and soft. Sprinkle with flour to make a light roux. Stir the mixture thoroughly for 2 to 3 minutes. Add vinegar; continue stirring. Dissolve bouillon in water. Add to onion mixture. Simmer for 30 minutes.

Pour a layer of sauce into a shallow baking dish. Arrange meat in overlapping slices and cover with remaining sauce. Cover and bake in 350°F. oven for 1 hour. Remove cover. Sprinkle surface with bread crumbs. Spoon melted butter over bread crumbs. Continue baking for 30 minutes. Sprinkle top with chopped fresh parsley.

# Great Grillings

Steaks, burgers, pork steaks, lamb chops, chicken, turkey, fish, sausages, vegetables

## GRILLED FLAMED BEEF TENDERLOIN

"Your guests and family will oh and ah. You'll be recognized as a genius at the ole' grill.'"

**4 to 7 pounds beef tenderloin, trimmed of fat**
**2 ounces melted bacon drippings (optional canola oil)**
**Worcestershire sauce**
**Lemon pepper**
**Garlic granules or powder**
**Meat thermometer**
**Serving platter, heated to 300°F.**
**Garlic salt**
**Parmesan cheese**
**4 ounces sherry (pale dry or other dry)**
**2 ounces vodka (brandy is optional to sherry and vodka)**

Remove the 1/16 inch tough silver membrane from tenderloin (see beef chapter). Bring to room temperature. Skewer thin end and double over, for same thickness if you do not want some well done steak.

Beef tenderloin's long fiber with little marbled fat is "healthy heart" food. These fibers dry out, harden, and become stringy easily. Use a moderate 350°F. charcoal fire or gas grill with cover open, one side lighted. Baste the tenderloin 2 or more times with Worcestershire sauce and let it soak in before grilling.

Baste meat with bacon drippings liberally. Sprinkle liberally with garlic and lemon pepper. Insert meat thermometer deeply in the center of end of the tenderloin.

Place meat on oiled grid of the grill. Grill for 5 minutes. Turn over and baste tenderloin with bacon drippings. Sprinkle with garlic and lemon pepper. Turn, baste, and season every 4 to 5 minutes, until you have grilled meat and browned all sides. Check meat temperature for doneness; stop grilling at 140°F. for rare.

Mix sherry and vodka; heat gently. Remove tenderloin and carve meat into 1 inch thick slices, cross grain. Place on heated platter. Sprinkle with lemon pepper, garlic salt, and Parmesan cheese. Pour heated sherry/vodka mixture over tenderloin and flame. Serves 8 ladies and gentlemen or 6 hungry kids.

## LEAN AND JUICY "BURGERS"

1½ pounds lean ground
beef (chuck grade)
1 tablespoon cornstarch
3 ounces water
6 tablespoons Blue cheese
(or American process)
1 teaspoon bouillon
granules or 1 cube
1 teaspoon salt
Vegetable oil
1 tablespoon
Worcestershire sauce
3 tablespoons instant
minced onions
Lemon pepper seasoning
(optional)

Dissolve the bouillon in the water, then add salt, Worcestershire, minced onions, and cornstarch. Stir liquid to dissolve and mix. Please use the salt along with the water; it dissolves some of the meat's protein which makes a sticky "paste." (This "paste" holds the ground meat together on the grill without the use of egg for binding.)

Next, mix the liquid mixture with the lean ground beef without packing. Lightly form 12 patties about ¼ inch thick - you "stick" the meat together without pressure. Place one tablespoon of Blue cheese on bottom patties, then cover with the top patties, and seal and smooth out edges completely. Baste the bottom of the burger with oil to help prevent sticking.

Place the pre-formed burgers on the heated, oiled grid and grill for 2 minutes using a medium hot fire. Using a long handled large 2 tined fork, straddle the grid wire underneath the front edge of each burger and lift gently. Lifting eliminates some of the sticking of the ground meat particles to the grids. Sticking causes crumbling of the burgers. Grill the burger for 1 to 2 minutes more, until firmed up, before turning with a long handled pancake turner. The burgers' turned side should be browned with nice grill marks, so you serve this side up. If desired, sprinkle them with lemon pepper seasoning lightly after turning.

Next, you start checking the turned burgers for "doneness" using SECRETS' finger test. Cover your index finger with a thick cloth; gently push on the edge of the burger. The longer you cook the burgers, the more their centers firm up to springy and finally to very firm for over-done. Cook until juices run clear and are not rosy, and center is brown, to be safe from E. coli.

## SHERRY HAMBURGER BASTE

"Helps hamburger stay moist and tasty."

½ cup canola oil or other
vegetable oil
1 cup sherry
1 tablespoon soy sauce
6 tablespoons Worcestershire
sauce

1 teaspoon garlic powder
1½ teaspoons dry mustard
½ teaspoon salt
¼ teaspoon ground pepper

Mix the dry ingredients together; add to the liquids. Shake vigorously to mix. Brush the sherry baste over the surfaces of burgers and steaks or other meat and grill. Grill burgers and baste as you cook. Stores for months in refrigerator. Shake to remix after standing. Makes 2 cups.

# GRILLED LONDON BROIL

"Cooked medium rare, carved thinly cross grain, marinated in all purpose marinade, you'll be more pleased with this flank steak."

| | |
|---|---|
| 1 to 2 pound flank steak, trimmed of fat and membrane<br>All Purpose Marinade (see Index) | Score steak 1/16 inch deep in diamond patterns across grain or fibers. Marinate steak up to 2 hours at room temperature or up to 24 hours in a refrigerator. Remove from marinade and dry. Grill over medium hot fire for 3 to 4 minutes, until grill marked and lightly charred. |

Turn and grill second side for 2 to 3 minutes. Cook to medium rare, 145°F., to protect against E. coli. Don't overcook — you'll toughen it. Check for doneness (see Index). Carve cross grain in 1/8 inch thick slices, holding the knife nearly parallel with the meat to produce wide slices.


# GRILLED STEAK WITH BLUE CHEESE TOPPING

"Nice combination - steak, Blue cheese, garlic."

2 (¾ to 1 inch thick) top sirloin steaks or higher quality

Topping:
¼ pound Blue cheese
1 tablespoon olive oil
¼ teaspoon pepper
¼ teaspoon powdered or granular garlic

Mix ingredients into a stiff paste. Choose a serving side for the steak. Grill over a medium fire. Brush cold vegetable oil on the hot grid of the grill. Grill steak for 2 minutes, then lift to prevent sticking. Turn over when steak is grill marked and brown. Season with salt and pepper.

Spoon Blue Cheese Topping generously over steak. Continue grilling over medium heat until it's a medium rare, 145°F. Serves 6 to 8.

# GRILLED TOP SIRLOIN STEAK

"Delicious way to grill steak."

| | |
|---|---|
| **4 pounds top sirloin steak (1 to 1½ inches thick)** **Worcestershire sauce** **Granular garlic** **Lemon pepper** | Trim surface (rind) fat. Generously coat the meat with Worcestershire sauce. Sprinkle garlic and lemon pepper on meat. Marinate meat at room temperature for up to 2 hours or overnight in the refrigerator. |

Brush heated grill with cold vegetable oil to reduce sticking. Grill over medium hot fire for 3 to 4 minutes to sear and grill mark; turn. Grill for 2 to 3 minutes. Reduce heat; cook to desired doneness. Serves 6 to 8.

# GRILLED STEAK AU POIVRE

"Pepper steak, a distinct, warm, spicy touch."

| | |
|---|---|
| **1 teaspoon granular garlic** **½ teaspoon ground oregano** **½ teaspoon paprika** **½ teaspoon onion powder** **¼ teaspoon ground celery seed** | **⅛ to ½ teaspoon cayenne pepper (to taste)** **Coarse ground pepper** **2 rib-eye, T-bone, or Porter House steaks (1 inch thick)** |

Mix 6 top ingredients together. Sprinkle on steaks and rub in. Let stand for 30 minutes. Sprinkle 2 tablespoons of coarse cracked black pepper evenly over both sides of steaks. Push pepper into steaks. Grill over medium hot fire for 3 to 4 minutes to grill mark and brown. Turn and finish grilling to a medium rare, 145°F. or more. Serves 2 to 4.

# HAMBURGER STEAKS

| | |
|---|---|
| **1 pound lean ground beef (chuck quality)** **4 lengths thick bacon, warmed gently and stretched** **2 tablespoons instant onion** **¼ green pepper, chopped finely** | **1 tablespoon Worcestershire sauce** **1½ tablespoons corn starch** **1 teaspoon beef bouillon** **½ teaspoon salt** **¼ teaspoon pepper** **3 ounces water** |

Dissolve bouillon in water, then mix all other ingredients, except bacon and beef, together thoroughly. Mix this with the beef gently. Divide beef mixture into 4 parts, forming 2 inch balls. Wrap each ball with a strip of bacon. Fasten it with a sucker stick or wooden picks. Push the ground meat gently into the bacon, forming a steak.

Oil the grill's grid (rack) to prevent sticking. Grill for 3 minutes over a medium-hot fire. Lift each steak with a wide tined serving fork to prevent sticking. Turn when steak is browned. Cook until the center of the steak is firm and its juices are clear. Remove and serve.

## STEAK MUSHROOM SAUCE

"Hamburger Steak may sound ordinary to some folks, so you add a nice touch with a quick mushroom sauce."

1 (10¾ ounce) can beef gravy
1 (4 ounce) can mushrooms, sliced
    and drained

1 tablespoon Worcestershire
    sauce, or to taste

Heat and blend. Serve over Hamburger Steaks.

## BASIC HAMBURGER RECIPE FOR GRILLING, BROILING, OR FRYING

1 pound ground beef
1½ ounces water
1 teaspoon bouillon or 1
    cube
¼ teaspoon MSG
¼ teaspoon salt
½ teaspoon sugar
⅛ teaspoon black pepper
1 teaspoon corn starch

Gently mix water, bouillon, MSG, salt, sugar, and pepper with ground beef. Form into 4 patties ¾ inch thick. This burger does not need egg or other "sticking" materials to keep it together. Handle gently on the grill.

Grill over a medium hot fire to grill mark, 3 to 4 minutes, turn and grill to medium, 160°F.

## BOURBON BASTE

"Superb baste for burgers."

1 cup canola oil or other
    vegetable oil
1 cup bourbon
2 tablespoons soy sauce
6 tablespoons
    Worcestershire sauce
3 cloves garlic, crushed

Blend all ingredients in electric blender for easier basting. Brush both sides of burgers generously with the baste. Grill over medium hot fire and continue basting. See Index for Grilling Hamburgers.

## BOURBON BEEF KEBABS

"Good combination of seasonings for beef."

1 cup bourbon
1 cup canola
¾ cup soy sauce
¼ cup Worcestershire
½ cup lemon juice
¼ cup dry mustard
2 teaspoons pepper
½ teaspoon granular garlic
  (powdered)

Bay leaves
2 pounds top sirloin steak, cut in
  1¼ inch cubes
Small potatoes, cut in halves
Medium onions, cut in eighths
Green pepper
Cherry tomatoes

Mix first 8 ingredients together. Pour over beef cubes in a plastic bag. Marinate for 2 hours at room temperature, up to 36 hours refrigerated. Drain. Soak bay leaves in white wine for 6 to 12 hours.

Parboil potatoes and onion pieces (not quite done). Skewer a beef cube, bay leaf, potato, onion, tomato, pepper, then repeat (beef cube, etc.). Grill over medium high heat until cooked to at least medium rare as a proctection against E. coli. Serves 6 to 8 people.

## BEEF SKEWER

8 tablespoons margarine, melted
1 cup olive oil
1 cup cider vinegar
8 tablespoons lime juice
3 tablespoons Worcestershire
  sauce
3 teaspoons salt

1 teaspoon white pepper
½ teaspoon cayenne pepper
1 clove garlic, peeled and chopped
1 teaspoon dried mint
4 pounds boneless top sirloin,
  trimmed and cut into 2 inch
  cubes

Marinate for 4 hours. Thread cubes on skewer. Reserve the marinade. Grill over medium hot fire to medium rare as a protection against E. coli. Baste with marinade; turn 5 minutes.

# GROUND MEAT KEBABS FOR BEEF, PORK, LAMB, CHICKEN, TURKEY, SAUSAGE MEATS

"Delicious and inexpensive; unusual way to serve ground meats."

Important: Ground meatballs fall apart when skewered and lifted until cooked. You turn them by gently rolling. Meatballs must not stick to the grill's grid (rack). Use recipes which hold meats together, use normal amount of salt plus water or eggs. Use rectangular or V-shaped skewers, not round.

Grill vegetables separately. Chill meat after forming balls before skewering. Grill over medium hot fire. Brush hot grid with cold vegetable oil. Brush meatballs with oil lightly. After 1 or 2 minutes of grilling, use a wide 2 tined turning fork and lift meatballs ¹⁄₁₆ inch. Lift directly under each ball. Use pancake turner for meatballs you can't reach. Must break loose all meatballs before trying to roll to turn them over. Roll skewers gently 180° to grill other side. Do not lift meatballs with the skewer until meat has firmed up on all sides and in the center. Baste as you turn.

Grill until meat has brown center with clear juices. Don't overcook any ground meats.

# HULI HULI CHICKEN

3 chickens
¼ cup catsup
¼ cup soy sauce
½ cup white wine or chicken broth

3 tablespoons frozen concentrated pineapple juice
1 teaspoon Worcestershire
1 teaspoon fresh ginger or garlic

Mix ingredients together. Marinate for 2 hours at room temperature or 24 hours in refrigerator. Grill over a low to medium fire, watch out for burning.

# LIME-CHILI GRILLED CHICKEN

"Outstanding way to get a southwest flavor. It's sweet."

8 chicken breast halves
1 (4 ounce can) green chili, diced
½ cup chopped green onions
⅓ cup lime juice

⅓ cup plum sauce
1 teaspoon ground coriander
Salt and pepper to taste

Combine first 5 ingredients. Run sauce over blender. Salt and pepper chicken breasts, then marinate up to 24 hours. Grill over medium fire for 30 to 60 minutes, until brown. Baste with sauce as you turn.

## SECRETS' CHICKEN BURGERS

1 pound thawed, frozen ground
chicken (available at some
supermarkets)
¾ teaspoon salt
1 teaspoon chicken bouillon
2 tablespoons instant onion
1½ teaspoons ground marjoram

2 teaspoons dried parsley
¼ teaspoon nutmeg
3 ounces water
½ cup homemade fine cracker
crumbs
Vegetable oil (canola)

Dissolve chicken bouillon in water. Add onion, spices, and salt to the water; mix. Add this to the thawed chicken along with the cracker crumbs. This meat is very finely ground and the mixture is sticky, so moisten your hands with cold water before you mix.

After mixing thoroughly, shape into 4 inch diameter patties, about ½ to ¾ inch thick. Place patties on an oiled pan or plate, otherwise they'll stick when you move them to the grill. Brush patties and grid with oil. Grill over medium-high fire. Lift with a 2 tined fork as with Lean and Juicy "Burgers."

## COCKTAIL CHICKEN WINGS

"Delicious light oriental flavor. Nice contrast to hot chicken wings."

1½ pounds frozen chicken
wing pieces, thawed
3 tablespoons soy sauce
3 tablespoons lemon juice
¼ teaspoon onion powder
1 teaspoon honey
1 tablespoon catsup
⅛ teaspoon pepper
Canola oil or vegetable oil

Mix soy sauce, lemon juice, and onion. Marinate chicken pieces up to 2 hours at room temperature or 12 hours refrigerated. Drain chicken. Mix honey, catsup, pepper, and 1½ tablespoons of marinade for a baste. Grill wings over medium fire. Use a Grill Topper or equivalent that has been heated and brushed with oil. Turn frequently and baste. Watch for sticking and burning. Grill until the chicken is done (no longer pink where the meat is thickest next to large bone or joint). Grilling time: 25 to 30 minutes. Serves 4 to 6.

## GRILLED HOT CHICKEN WINGS

"Just the right amount of cayenne heat. Your mouth doesn't burn for hours."

Canola oil
2 tablespoons corn starch
1 teaspoon paprika
1 teaspoon cayenne
pepper or to taste
½ teaspoon garlic powder
½ teaspoon salt
⅛ teaspoon MSG
2 pounds frozen chicken
wing pieces, thawed

Dry chicken pieces. Baste lightly with canola oil. Mix all dry ingredients in a bowl. Use a large spoon to crush all lumps and blend well. Place in a large paper grocery sack.

Dust the wing pieces with a light coating of the cayenne mixture. Spread chicken pieces out. Grill on a grill topper (or equivalent) over medium heat. Heat the grill topper, then brush with cold oil. Turn every 5 to 7 minutes. Do not baste with oil unless they dry out. Grill until browned and chicken is done at the thickest bone or joint. Grill time: 25 to 30 minutes. Serves 4 to 6.

# GRILLED MEDITERRANEAN LEMON CHICKEN

"You can nearly taste the sun!"

1 teaspoon garlic (granulated or powdered)
1 teaspoon salt
1 teaspoon dried whole oregano
1 teaspoon ground rosemary
¼ teaspoon pepper

¼ cup lemon juice
Zest from 2 lemons (lemon peel)
4 tablespoons canola oil or vegetable oil
½ teaspoon paprika
1 large frying chicken, cut up

Mix all ingredients together (except chicken). Wash chicken pieces, then dry. Marinate chicken from 30 minutes to 2 hours at room temperature or overnight in refrigerator. Grill over medium low heat. Turn and baste every 5 to 7 minutes. Grill for 30 to 50 minutes. Serves 3 to 4.

# GRILLED CHICKEN FOR A LARGE CROWD

"This baste turns grilled chicken into a crowd pleaser."

1 gallon canola oil or vegetable oil
1 gallon lemon juice
Lemon zest from 12 lemons
2 cups salt
11 tablespoons paprika

5 tablespoons garlic powder
11 tablespoons onion powder
6 tablespoons thyme (whole leaf)
1¼ cups basil (whole leaf)

Mix all ingredients together. Shake chicken pieces to dry. Marinate for 30 minutes to 2 hours in plastic buckets. Drain chicken. Be prepared for flame ups as the baste hits the fire. Grill over charcoal medium fire. Turn and baste every 8 to 10 minutes. Save some marinade that has not been exposed to raw chicken for your final basting when you take the chicken off the grill. Makes enough baste for 125 to 150 chicken pieces.

# KNOTE'S FAVORITE CHICKEN MARINADE

"Our most outstanding chicken marinade."

⅜ cup canola oil or other vegetable oil
½ cup lemon juice
1 tablespoon salt
1 teaspoon paprika
½ teaspoon onion powder
½ teaspoon garlic powder
½ teaspoon thyme (whole leaf)
2 teaspoons basil
1 tablespoon grated lemon peel (zest)
1 (3½ to 4 pound) frying chicken, cut up

Mix dry spices and all liquid together thoroughly. Marinate chicken at room temperature up to 2 hours or in refrigerator overnight. Grill over a slow to medium fire. Brush hot grid with cold vegetable oil to keep chicken from sticking. Shake each piece to remove excess marinade. Place pieces, bone side down.

Arrange leg, thigh, and breast pieces in center of grid to cook with higher heat. Watch for flame ups as you place chicken on the grid. Use intermittent flame ups to produce a light char. Baste and turn chicken every 5 to 7 minutes and as you remove it from the grid to serve it. Grill until browned with juices running clear and meat next to bone is no longer red or pink. Makes over 1 cup.

## LAMB SKEWER

1 cup red wine vinegar
1 cup olive oil
3 tablespoons dried oregano
3 tablespoons chopped parsley
½ teaspoon granular garlic
2 tablespoons dried basil

4 tablespoons chopped fresh mint
2 tablespoons lemon pepper
Salt and pepper to taste
3 pounds boneless leg of lamb, cut into 1½ inch cubes

Mix ingredients and marinate for 4 hours. Thread lamb cubes onto metal or bamboo skewers. Reserve marinade. Grill for 5 to 7 minutes over medium hot fire. Baste and turn, grill to your preferred doneness. Serves 6 to 8.

## BBQ LAMB KEBABS

"Lamb will sparkle."

3 pounds lamb, trimmed of excess fat
½ cup red wine
¼ cup water
¼ cup canola oil or vegetable oil
1 tablespoon Worcestershire sauce
1 Tbsp. lemon juice

1 teaspoon dry mustard
½ teaspoon paprika
½ teaspoon garlic (granular or powder)
2 teaspoons granular onion
12 drops hot sauce

Cube lamb into 1 to 1¼ inch pieces. Mix all remaining ingredients with lamb. Marinate for 2 hours at room temperature or overnight in refrigerator. Drain and reserve marinade. Skewer meat pieces. Grill over medium hot fire. Turn and baste with marinade every 3 to 4 minutes, until done to your own preference. Don't grill past medium done. Serves 8.

## GRILLED RACK OF LAMB

"An elegant presentation that's much less expensive than it looks."

1 (8 rib) rack of lamb, Frenched
¾ bulb of garlic
½ cup olive oil
Juice of 3 to 4 lemons plus zest of 2 lemons
4 tablespoons dry mustard
2 tablespoons Hugh's Cajun Rub, or to taste, see Index
1½ tablespoons ground tarragon

Ask your butcher: Cut through the chine bone for easier carving individual chops. Trim rack of excess fat. Combine all remaining ingredients in a blender and liquefy. Marinate lamb for 1 to 2 days in refrigerator. Turn every 24 hours.

Grill over medium hot fire to sear, meat side down, to grill mark. Turn over in 3 to 5 minutes. Grill, bone side down, over medium fire. Use meat thermometer. Stop grill at 140°F. for rare. Serves 4 to 5.

# GRILLED LAMB CHOPS OR LEG STEAKS

"Lambs' good flavor and unique taste come through with this rub. Don't overcook lamb."

Use 1 inch thick lamb leg steaks, lamb rib chops, or lamb shoulder chops. Choose a serving side. Trim the steaks' outer rind fat as well as any large layered fat deposits between the layers of lean. Lamb has little marbled fat; brush lightly with olive or canola oil. Sprinkle ¼ to ½ teaspoon of El Greco (see Index) to each oiled side and rub in. Marinate lamb for 30 minutes up to 2 hours at room temperature, or overnight in the refrigerator. Score edge every 1½ inches to prevent curling.

Cook over a medium hot fire. Heat food rack for 2 minutes. Brush with cold vegetable oil. Place steaks, serving side down, on grid to sear for 3 to 4 minutes to develop the traditional caramelized browned, slightly charred "outside" flavor with the grid marks. Turn and grill other side for 3 to 5 minutes, depending on the "doneness" you prefer.

Using a sharp knife, cut next to the bone about 1 to 2 minutes before it should be "done" to your liking, then continue grilling to your preferred doneness. Serve it hot, serving side up.

# GRILLED DRESSED WHOLE FISH

"Fresh farm raised catfish have good flavor and no fishy odor. Rainbow trout cook faster."

**4 (8 to 12 ounce) whole dressed catfish or trout, washed**
**4 tablespoons canola oil or vegetable oil**
**4 tablespoons lemon juice**
**1 tablespoon lemon zest**
**2 teaspoons paprika**
**½ teaspoon salt**
**½ teaspoon sugar**
**Lemon pepper**

Mix ingredients except catfish and lemon pepper. Pour over fish and marinate for 30 minutes up to 2 hours at room temperature or up to 24 hours, covered, in refrigerator. Remove from marinade. Sprinkle generously with lemon pepper. Heat Grill Topper or similar device over medium fire. Brush with cold vegetable oil. Grill fish for 2 to 3 minutes. Loosen with turner or spatula. Baste with marinade, turning after 6 to 7 minutes. Grill second side until fish flakes easily at the thickest meat next to the back bone. Baste fish to keep from drying out. Serves 4.

Thirteen minutes for 1½ inch thick trout to flake in back. Turn and baste at 5½ minutes. Whole skinned catfish need to be grilled longer than trout due to the density of the meat.

The grilling rule for fish: A medium hot fire takes 8 to 10 minutes to cook a 1 inch thick fish to the flaking stage.

## EASY GRILLED FISH FILETS

"New BBQ tool solves fish grilling problems."

Fish filets (¼ to ½ inch thick)
1 quart cold water
1 tablespoon salt
1 teaspoon baking soda
Cornstarch
Paprika without lumps
Sugar
Canola oil
Lemon pepper
Grill Topper™

To freshen frozen fish, soak thawed frozen fish filets or steaks in cold water, salt, and soda for 30 minutes. Wash with water to remove salt; drain and dry with paper towels.

Brush lightly with oil. Mix paprika, cornstarch, and a little sugar. Coat fillet, shake off excess powder. Sprinkle generously with lemon-pepper. Heat Grill Topper over medium hot fire for 2 to 4 minutes. Brush with cold vegetable oil. Grill fillets for 1 to 2 minutes. Use a pancake turner to loosen; grill to browning stage. Turn fillets and grill for 1 to 2 mintues until opaque or flaky. Serve browned side up. Total grilling time: 4 to 6 minutes. They overcook easily.

## GRILLED BLACKENED FISH

"Orange roughy's flavor dramatically increased."

6 fillets of any good fish (up to ¾ inch thick; semi frozen), dried
4 ounces butter, melted
¼ cup lemon juice
Zest from 2 lemons
3 tablespoons Hugh's Cajun Rub (see Index)
1 teaspoon sugar

Gas grill on high or charcoal grill with 2 thickness of briquets. Heat cast iron skillet or griddle until the bottom forms a white haze, 25 to 30 minutes. Mix remaining ingredients. Place in shallow wide dish. Dip each fillet into butter mixture. Place in skillet. Fish cooks rapidly. Turn in 1 to 2 minutes. Cook for 3 minutes. Brown remaining butter. Pour over fish. Serve immediately. Serve 2 to 3.

## GRILLED SHRIMP

"Grilled in the shells slows people down - some. Outstanding appetizer."

¼ cup margarine or butter, melted
2 tablespoons lemon juice
½ teaspoon granular garlic (powdered)
1 green onion with top, chopped fine
2 teaspoon onion (powder or granules)

2 teaspoons basil
1 teaspoon ground thyme
1 teaspoon salt
½ teaspoon white pepper
2 pounds raw shrimp

Split tails to remove the mud vane. This allows marinade to penetrate better. Mix all ingredients and run over a blender. Dry shrimp with paper towels. Pour marinade over shrimp and marinate for 30 minutes to 2 hours. Using the Grill Topper or similar device, grill over a medium hot fire for 3 minutes, then turn for 3 minutes. Do not overcook. Serve hot. Serves 10 to 12 people.

# GRILLED SCALLOPS

"You didn't fix enough."

2 pounds sea or bay scallops,
washed and dried
¼ cup canola oil
¾ teaspoon granular garlic
2 green onions (scallions; tops
.included)

1½ teaspoons basil
¾ teaspoon thyme
1 teaspoon salt
½ teaspoon white pepper
⅛ teaspoon Tabasco sauce

Mix all ingredients together. Pour over scallops; marinate for 15 minutes to 2 hours. Grill on Grill Topper for 2 minutes. Turn and grill until done. Baste.

# GRILLED ROCK LOBSTER TAILS

"One time a year elegant splurge."

8 (2 to 3 ounce) frozen
rock lobster tails
Seafood Butter Sauce and
Baste (see Index)

Thaw lobster tails. Using sharp scissors, cut the membrane along both edges of the shell and remove. Crack the hard shell to keep tail from curling. Baste with seafood butter sauce. Grill, meat side down, to brown, then turn and grill until the meat is opaque. Serve with hot Seafood Butter Sauce. Serves 4.

# MUSTARD PORK TENDERLOINS

"They're lower cost and excellent. They dry out easily, keep them basted."

3 tablespoons canola oil
1 tablespoon Dijon
mustard
½ teaspoon salt
½ to ¾ teaspoon pepper
2 pork tenderloins (¾ to 1
pound)
¼ cup white dry wine

Combine oil, mustard, salt, and pepper. Baste tenderloins with mixture. Place in plastic bags. Marinate in refrigerator for 8 to 24 hours.

Mix 1 tablespoon of marinade with white wine and baste the tenderloins every 5 minutes as you grill it. Grill over medium low heat to 155°F. in the center of the thickest portion of the pork tenderloin.

Serve by dim candle light to picky friends and family. They'll love this pork. Serves 4.

# BEER GRILLED ½ INCH THICK PORK CHOPS

"This marinade stays mixed. Browned, tasty, juicy pork chops."

1 (12 ounce) can beer
3 tablespoons vegetable
oil
3 tablespoons dry
mustard
1 tablespoon paprika

Mix in blender for 1 to 2 minutes. Marinate pork chops for 30 minutes up to 2 hours at room temperature, or up to 24 hours in refrigerator. Chill in freezer before grilling. Grill over medium heat. Don't overcook.

## JOHN'S GRILLED GREEK RIBS

"Tasty with a light touch of oregano."

2 slabs (sides) pork ribs,
cartilidge, breast bone, and
diaphram muscle removed
Pepper or lemon pepper

Garlic (granular or powdered)
Lemon juice
Ground oregano

Sprinkle ribs generously with pepper and garlic. Using indirect grilling, cook for 30 minutes, meat side down. Turn; grill for 30 more minutes. Sprinkle oregano and lemon juice generously over both sides of ribs about 15 minutes before the ribs will totally be done.

## BARBECUED RIBS

"Bob's masterpiece."

2-4 pounds pork ribs
¼ cup soy sauce
2 tablespoons honey
2 tablespoons brown sugar
2 tablespoons hoisin sauce

2 tablespoons cider vinegar
2 tablespoons dry sherry
3 to 4 cloves garlic, minced
2 tablespoons chicken stock

Partially slice ribs in sections. Blend all ingredients together. Marinate ribs 2 hours at room temperature. Cook over medium fire and hickory sawdust 40 to 60 minutes or until done.

## LEMONY BARBECUED RIBS

"Unusual, but delicious approach to pork ribs."

4 pounds meaty pork
spareribs, breast bone
and cartilidge removed
1 cup lemon juice
⅜ cup canola oil
¼ cup brown sugar,
packed
1 teaspoon ground
coriander
2 teaspoons salt
1 teaspoon ground ginger

Have ribs cut in 2 to 3 inch wide strips. Combine remaining ingredients. Marinate spareribs for 2 hours at room temperature, up to 24 hours in refrigerator. Drain and reserve marinade. Wrap ribs in aluminum foil. Cook until ⅔ done, about 1 hour over medium fire. Unwrap; grill slowly until brown and done, basting with marinade. Cut ribs into 2 or 3 rib serving sizes or individually for appetizers. Serves 6 to 10 for appetizers.

# GRILLED SHERRIED PORK NUGGETS

"Party food! Your mother-in-law will brag."

**1 pound pork butt or fresh picnic, trimmed of fat and cut into ¾ inch cubes (save trimmings)**
**1 medium onion, chopped coarsely**
**½ pound fresh mushroom slices**
**1 to 1½ tablespoons canola oil or vegetable oil**
**4 slices bread, toasted (no butter)**
**½ cup pale dry sherry or other sherry**
**1 teaspoon to 1 tablespoon Nutmeg Clove Rub (see Index)**

Coat pork nuggets with oil. Sprinkle with Nutmeg Clove Rub. Coat mushrooms and onions with oil lightly, separately. Grill over a medium fire. Heat Grill Topper; coat lightly with oil. Grill pork for 3 minutes. Turn with a pancake turner. Add mushrooms and onions. Grill for 4 to 7 minutes or until done.

When using a skillet on the side of the grill, saute pork trimmings in a skillet. Produce a brown crumbled glaze in the pan. Dispose of fat pieces and drippings. Add sherry; using a wooden scraper, deglaze meat juices and meat particles in pan. Cook sherry for 2 to 3 minutes to concentrate it. Return pork nugget mixture to pan. Warm and blend with the sherry sauce. You can double recipe easily. Serve immediately over toast. Serves 4 to 6.

# LEAN PORK KEBABS

"Fat trimmed, they're low in cholesterol and very tasty."

Use pork picnic (1¼ inch slices), deboned and fat trimmed. Use any one of Secret's Pork Rubs (see Index). Sprinkle one tablespoon of the rub per one pound of cubed pork, then mix thoroughly. Marinate the meat up to 2 hours at room temperature or up to 48 hours in a refrigerator.

Flat metal skewers work best for turning the meat while cooking. Water soaked (30 minutes) bamboo or wooden skewers are O.K. Leave ⅛ inch space between pieces of pork so heat can penetrate and cook the meat evenly. Also, this space will allow you to apply barbecue sauce after you start grilling. Baste the skewered lean pork with vegetable oil before grilling.

Brush grill with cold vegetable oil to keep meat from sticking. Grill kebabs over medium heat. Baste with barbecue sauce shortly after putting kebabs on the grill. Dry to a thin glaze on the meat. Don't overcook pork. You'll dry it out.

## CHARLIE'S GRILLED SWEET CORN

"Revives older sweet corn that's past its prime. Extra good for fresh picked."

6 ears sweet corn,
   shucked and silked
12 tablespoons 2% milk
6 teaspoons butter or
   margarine
6 teaspoons sugar
Salt
Pepper
12 pieces aluminum foil
   (9x10 inch)

Make a boat shape with the first sheet of foil. Lay one ear in boat. Add 2 tablespoons of milk, ½ teaspoon each butter and sugar, then pepper and lightly salt. Wrap foil around ear of corn loosely. Twist ends loosely. Use the second sheet of foil to cover the seam of the first one. Wrap loosely. This prevents leakage as you rotate corn. Grill over medium high heat for 4 to 6 minutes and rotate 90°. Continue grilling and turning for 15 to 20 minutes, until done. It's hot! Handle with tongs. Serves 4 to 6.

## GRILLED HONEY BAKED CORN STICKS

"You'd better make lots of these."

1¼ cups corn meal (yellow or
   white)
¾ cup all-purpose flour
2 teaspoons baking powder
½ teaspoon baking soda
½ teaspoon salt
1 cup buttermilk

¼ c. canola oil
¼ cup honey
1 egg, beaten
2 tablespoons melted bacon
   drippings or butter, margarine,
   or canola oil

Mix dry ingredients. Add milk, honey, egg, and oil. Heat cast iron corn stick mold over medium high fire. Add bacon drippings and wait until the mold starts to smoke. Pour the corn meal mixture into each mold; fill ¾ full. Grill at 400°F. to 450°F. until browned, or about 20 minutes. Remove corn sticks and reheat the mold; pour second batch. Keep first batch warm. Makes 12 to 15 sticks. Test with toothpick for doneness. Gas grill works well.

## FRENCH TOAST BATTER

"Use dried out French bread or Texas toast, any bread that is thick and dry."

2 eggs, beaten
1 cup flour
1 teaspoon baking powder
½ teaspoon salt

1 tablespoon sugar
⅔ cup milk
2 tablespoons melted butter

Make a batter. Coat the bread on both sides. Grill on a hot skillet. It's excellent. Guaranteed, the kids will love it.

# Rubs, Bastes Marinades, Sauces

From "ZIP" and "ZAP" rubs
to BBQ sauces and glazes

## LEMON PEPPER THYME RUB FOR STEAKS AND BURGERS

"Sets a steak off as something extra special."

6 tablespoons lemon pepper
2 tablespoons ground thyme
2 tablespoons paprika
2 teaspoons granular garlic
1 teaspoon sugar

½ teaspoon salt
½ teaspoon MSG
¼ teaspoon ground coriander
⅛ teaspoon ground cumin
⅛ teaspoon cayenne pepper

Mix all ingredients together with a large spoon, removing all lumps. Apply generously to steaks or burgers. Store in covered glass container. Marinate for 30 minutes or up to 2 hours before grilling. Stores for 3 to 6 months. Makes ⅝ cups.

## HUGH'S CAJUN RUB

"Comes straight from New Orleans. It's got zip and real character."

4 tablespoons salt (non-
    iodized)
3 tablespoons granulated
    garlic
3 tablespoons ground
    black pepper
1 tablespoon ground
    cayenne pepper
1 tablespoon Spanish
    paprika

Mix ingredients with a large tablespoon. Crush all lumps. Store in a closed glass container under cool, dry, dark conditions. Makes ⅜ cup.

Apply 1½ tablespoons of rub per pound of pork roast, then "rub" in. Let pork stand at room temperature for 2 hours or refrigerate up to 72 hours, then smoke-cook or grill.

Turkey breast: Brush canola oil over turkey breast. Apply chicken bouillon granules all over the turkey breast. Sprinkle Cajun Rub generously over the turkey breast. Marinate at room temperature for 2 hours or up to 24 hours in refrigerator, then smoke-cook.

## LELA'S BROWN SUGAR RUB

"Great for dry glazed ribs and you can use ½ to make a BBQ sauce."

¼ cup brown sugar, packed (free of lumps)
1 tablespoon chili powder
1 tablespoon ground celery seed
1 teaspoon salt
¼ to ½ teaspoon cayenne pepper to taste
½ teaspoon granular garlic
2 sides spareribs

Mix all ingredients together removing any lumps. Prepare ribs (see Index: Pork Ribs). Apply rub generously and let ribs set for 30 minutes to 2 hours at room temperature, or overnight in refrigerator.

Smoke-cook using low temperature or pre-cook the ribs in hot water, then apply the rub and grill (see Index: Grilling Ribs). After rubbing ribs, save 5 tablespoons of the rub. Mix with 8 ounces of tomato sauce, ¼ cup vinegar, and 2 tablespoons Worcestershire sauce. Apply BBQ sauce to ribs during the last 10 minutes of grilling or 30 minutes of smoking. Dry to a glaze. Serves 3 to 5.

## NUTMEG CLOVE RUB

"Decidedly different! For grilling or smoking pork, beef, lamb, and chicken."

½ cup sugar
5 tablespoons salt (non-iodized)
2 tablespoons paprika
2 teaspoons MSG
1 teaspoon ground nutmeg
1 teaspoon ground rosemary
1 teaspoon ground marjoram
½ teaspoon ground clove

Mix ingredients together, using a large spoon. Crush all lumps. Sprinkle on meats and poultry; rub in. Marinate for 30 minutes up to 2 hours at room temperature, or up to 24 hours in refrigerator. Store in capped glass container in a cool place. Keeps for 3 to 6 months. Makes 1 cup.

## DRY RIB RUB

"It helped win a Memphis in May grand championship."

2 tablespoons black pepper
2 tablespoons paprika
1 tablespoon chili powder
1 tablespoon red pepper
1 tablespoon garlic powder
1¼ teaspoons celery salt
⅝ teaspoon dry mustard

Mix ingredients together thoroughly (eliminating any lumps). Sprinkle on ribs. Refrigerate for 4 to 10 hours before starting to cook. Cook ribs for about 5½ hours over charcoal pit kept at 180°F. to 200°F. Soak wood and smoke for sweet flavor. This rub contains no sugar which can cause burning.

## ZEP RUB

"Seasons fish quickly; produces nice grilled flavor, or smoke-cook."

| | |
|---|---|
| 2 tablespoons salt | ¼ teaspoon garlic powder |
| 1 tablespoon sugar | 2 teaspoons white pepper |
| 1 teaspoon marjoram (ground) | 1 teaspoon paprika |
| 2 teaspoons onion powder | ½ teaspoon MSG |
| 1 teaspoon fine ground, dried | 1 teaspoon ground thyme |
|   lemon peel | |

Mix ingredients with a large tablespoon. Crush all lumps. Store in a closed glass container under cool, dry, dark conditions.

Skin-on <u>dressed Whole Fish</u>: Remove top fin. Score fish along both sides at 1½ inch intervals. Score top of fish. Brush fish with canola or olive oil. Apply to the fish and rub into scored areas. Apply to the abdominal cavity, then grill or smoke. Makes ⅜ cup.

## ZAP II RUB

"Gives pork a sagey sweet flavor."

| | |
|---|---|
| 1 tablespoon white sugar | 1½ teaspoons thyme |
| 1 tablespoon brown sugar | 1½ teaspoons oregano |
| 1½ tablespoons salt | 1½ teaspoons garlic powder |
| 1½ teaspoons paprika | 1½ teaspoons black pepper |
| 1 tablespoon ground sage | ½ teaspoon MSG |

Mix ingredients with a large tablespoon. Crush all lumps. Store in a closed glass container under cool, dry, dark conditions.

Apply 1½ tablespoons of rub per pound of pork roast (cubed) or sliced pork, then "rub" into meat. Let pork stand at room temperature for 2 hours or refrigerate up to 72 hours, then smoke-cook or you can grill the pork with this rub. Makes ¼ cup.

## ZIP II

"Spicy with nutmeg and allspice - different, for smoking pork."

| | |
|---|---|
| 2 tablespoons sugar | ½ teaspoon ground nutmeg |
| 2 tablespoons salt | ½ teaspoon MSG |
| 1½ teaspoons black pepper | 1 teaspoon ground allspice |
| ½ teaspoon red pepper | |
| 2 teaspoons paprika (Spanish, not | |
|   hot) | |

Use a tablespoon to mash out all seasoning and spice lumps. Mix completely and thoroughly. Apply generously to all surfaces of the pork and rub in. Marinate for 2 hours at room temperature or up to 72 hours in a refrigerator in a plastic bag. Makes about ⅜ cup.

## CUMIN BEEF RUB

"Cumin supports and enhances beef and remaining flavors."

| | |
|---|---|
| 1 tablespoon chili powder | 1 teaspoon sugar |
| 1 tablespoon garlic (granular or powder) | 1 teaspoon salt |
| | ¾ teaspoon ground cumin |
| 1½ teaspoons ground oregano | ¼ teaspoon cayenne pepper |

Mix together, using a large spoon to crush all lumps. Apply generously to steaks or burgers 30 minutes or up to 2 hours at room temperature before grilling or smoking. Store in covered glass container. Stores for 3 to 6 months. Makes over 3 tablespoons.

## BOURBON STREET SEASONING

"Low salt New Orleans' seasoning compared to commercial brands - just a light sprinkle adds real character to foods."

| | |
|---|---|
| 4 tablespoons non-iodized salt (canning salt) | 2 teaspoons garlic powder |
| | 1½ teaspoons ground thyme |
| 2 tablespoons onion powder | 1½ teaspoons allspice |
| 1 tablespoon black pepper | 1½ teaspoons sugar |
| 1 tablespoon cayenne pepper | ¾ teaspoon ground nutmeg |
| 1 tablespoon paprika | ¾ teaspoon ground bay leaf |

Use as a rub for beef, pork, lamb, chicken, turkey, fish, sausage, and vegetables. Stores for 3 to 6 months in closed glass container. Makes nearly ¾ cup.

## FENNEL RUB

"Complements grilled lamb and other meats."

| | |
|---|---|
| 2 tablespoons ground rosemary | 1½ teaspoons thyme |
| 1 tablespoon ground marjoram | 1½ teaspoons non-iodized salt |
| 1 tablespoon ground fennel | 1½ teaspoons cayenne, to taste |
| 2 tablespoons pepper | 1½ teaspoons sugar |
| 2 tablespoons paprika | |

Blend ingredients together. Sprinkle gently on lamb and other meats. Let stand for 2 hours at room temperature or 24 hours in refrigerator. Makes ⅝ cup.

## LEMON-PEPPER TARRAGON RUB

"Gives grilled fish, poultry, beef a nice touch."

| | |
|---|---|
| 1 tablespoon lemon pepper | ½ teaspoon cayenne |
| 1 tablespoon paprika | ½ teaspoon salt |
| 1-2 teaspoons tarragon | ½ teaspoon sugar |
| 1 teaspoon garlic powder | |

Blend ingredients together. Sprinkle on meats and rub in gently. Makes nearly ¼ cup.

# B.B.Q. SPICE AND RUB

"Will pep up any sauce."

| | |
|---|---|
| 1 teaspoon cinnamon | 1/2 teaspoon ginger |
| 1/2 teaspoon nutmeg | 1/4 teaspoon cayenne |
| 1/4 teaspoon cloves | 1/4 teaspoon salt or to taste |
| 1/4 teaspoon allspice | |

Blend ingredients together. Use a large spoon to remove all lumps. Mix with sauce to taste or apply directly to meat very gently.

# ITALIAN RUB

"Sweet Italian flavor."

| | |
|---|---|
| 1 tablespoon garlic (granular or powder) | 1 tablespoon oregano |
| 1 tablespoon ground fennel | 1 1/2 teaspoons ground thyme |
| 2 tablespoons black pepper | 1 1/2 teaspoons salt |
| 1 tablespoon paprika | 1 1/2 teaspoons sugar |

Blend ingredients together. Sprinkle gently on meat. Let stand for 2 hours at room temperature or 24 hours in refrigerator. Makes over 3/8 cup.

# BROWNING RUB FOR THIN CHOPS AND STEAKS

"Use on 1/2 inch thick cuts for better browning and juiciness."

2 tablespoons sugar
1 tablespoon salt
2 tablespoons paprika
1 tablespoon MSG
2 teaspoons pepper

Mix and remove lumps. Apply 1/2 teaspoon per chop or more for bigger pieces and rub in. Place chops on a cookie sheet and freeze slightly. This cools the meat's centers. Grill over medium high heat and produce a browned crust without overcooking the centers. Grilling time needs increasing. Makes 1/2 cup. Helps create a delicious full flavored browned "outside" and juicy rare to medium center for thin cuts of meat.

# ALL PURPOSE DRY SEASONING

"This seasoning mixture approximates a national brand in flavor and browning ability. Can use as a rub."

| | |
|---|---|
| 2 tablespoons sugar | 1 teaspoon ground thyme |
| 1 1/2 tablespoons salt (non-iodized, canning salt) | 1/2 teaspoon onion powder |
| 1 1/2 teaspoons ground celery seed | 1/4 teaspoon garlic powder |
| 1 teaspoon white pepper | 1/2 teaspoon ground nutmeg |
| 1 teaspoon paprika | 1/4 teaspoon MSG |

Crush all lumps. Mix together with a large spoon in a bowl. Stores in a dry place for 3 to 6 months. Makes 3/8 cup.

# ITALIAN DRY SEASONING

"Use to make salad dressing or season bread crumbs. Nice Italian combination."

| | |
|---|---|
| 2 tablespoons rosemary | 2 teaspoons oregano |
| 2 tablespoons basil | 1 tablespoon parsley |
| 1 teaspoon garlic | |

Mix all together. Keep in covered jar. Stores for 3 to 5 months. (Use 1 tablespoon - 8 ounces vinegar and oil dressing.)

# ALL PURPOSE MARINADE

"Very good on beef and game."

| | |
|---|---|
| 1 cup salad oil | 1 teaspoon salt |
| ¼ cup soy sauce | 1 tablespoon ground black pepper |
| ½ cup vinegar | 2 teaspoons chopped fresh parsley |
| ⅓ cup lemon juice | ½ teaspoon garlic powder |
| ½ cup Worcestershire sauce | ½ to 1 teaspoon Tabasco sauce |
| 2 tablespoons dry mustard | (optional) |

Mix all ingredients together. Blend in a food blender to puree parsley. Can be used as a baste. Makes 2½ cups.

# BEEF WINE MARINADE

"Nice for lean beef before smoking."

| | |
|---|---|
| 1½ cups red wine | 1 tablespoon ground rosemary |
| ¼ cup canola oil | 1 teaspoon pepper |
| 2 teaspoons granular garlic | ¼ teaspoon red pepper sauce |
| (powdered) | |

Mix together; pour over beef roast. Marinate in plastic bag for 12 hours to 2 days in refrigerator, then smoke. (Turn roast 2 or 3 times while marinating.)

# SWEET AND SOUR ORIENTAL MARINADE

"Gives grilled pork chops a big lift - nearly equal to a good steak."

⅓ cup vinegar
⅓ cup soy sauce
⅓ cup honey

Stir ingredients together and blend for 5 minutes. Enough for 6 pork chops. Cover meats or brush meats with marinade. Keep at room temperature for up to 3 hours. (All three ingredients together control bacteria.) Marinating in the "fridge" causes honey to separate out. Stir to remix. Drain marinated chops for 5 minutes before grilling, particularly if they are less than ¾ inch thick.

Baste meats with marinade during the last 10 minutes of grilling. Use low fire and slow grilling. Honey burns easily. Grill pork chops to a very light pink/white center stage. They dry out easily.

# LAMB MARINADE FOR KEBABS

"Enhances lamb and other meats."

¾ cup white wine
½ cup lemon juice
¼ cup canola oil
2 tablespoons Worcestershire
   sauce
1 teaspoon ground oregano
½ teaspoon ground thyme
½ teaspoon ground basil

1 teaspoon garlic (granulated or
   powdered)
1 tablespoon salt
1 teaspoon pepper
Bay leaves, moistened with water
3 pounds Certified American lamb
   shoulder, trimmed of fat

Cut lamb into 1 to 1¼ inch cubes trimmed of fat. Mix seasoning ingredients. Marinate lamb cubes up to 2 hours at room temperature or overnight refrigerate in plastic bag or non-aluminum container.

Drain and reserve marinade. Thread cubes on skewers alternating with moistened bay leaves. Grill over a medium hot fire, turning and basting with marinade. Grill until (10 to 15 minutes) medium done. Serves 8.

# TERIYAKI MARINADE

"An easy oriental flavor for beef."

½ cup soy sauce
3 tablespoons sugar
2 tablespoons dry sherry

½ teaspoon garlic powder or
   granules
½ teaspoon ginger

Mix together. Marinate meat for 2 hours at room temperature or overnight in refrigerator. Makes over ½ cup.

# CINDY'S MARINADE

"For shish kebabs - beef, pork, chicken."

1 cup soy sauce
½ cup brown sugar,
   packed
½ cup white vinegar
¾ cup pineapple juice
1 teaspoon garlic (powder
   or granular)

Mix all ingredients. Bring to a boil; simmer for 5 minutes. Cool. Marinate meat for up to 2 hours at room temperature or in refrigerator up to 72 hours, turning meats every 24 hours.

Great for hamburger seasoning. Mix ¼ cup with 1 pound of ground beef, then grill.

## BEEF BRISKET MARINADE

"Tenderizes and flavors brisket and game."

5 pounds beef brisket
2½ cups canned pineapple juice
1¼ cups soy sauce
½ cup bourbon or sherry
½ cup vinegar

2 tablespoons Worcestershire
  sauce
1 teaspoon unsalted meat
  tenderizer
3 cloves garlic, finely chopped

Mix all ingredients together except the brisket. Place the brisket in a plastic bag and cover with marinade. Turn over 2 or 3 times while marinating for 12 to 24 hours.

## VINEGAR CAYENNE BASTE

"North Carolina style baste for Pig Pickin."

1 quart white vinegar
1½ cups water
2 tablespoons fine black pepper

1 tablespoon cayenne
1 teaspoon non-iodized (canning)
  salt

Mix ingredients together in a pan. Makes 1¼ quarts. Baste as you cook. Cooking and smoking calms vinegar and peppers. Experience is a great teacher; go gently!

## SPICE VINEGAR RECIPES

"You make most any flavor vinegar you like."

1 quart wine, cider, or
  distilled vinegar
½ ounces (3 to 4
  tablespoons) of the
  spice of your choice

Heat vinegar to almost boiling; pour over spice, then cover tightly with lid. Marinate in a warm room for 10 to 14 days. Shake every other day or so to mix better. Use in marinades and salad dressings.

## FISH AND SEAFOOD BRINE

"Gives fish and seafood the traditional brined taste for smoking."

½ gallon water
¾ cup salt
¼ cup brown sugar
3 tablespoons lemon juice
1 teaspoon garlic powder

1 teaspoon white pepper
2 teaspoons onion powder
1½ teaspoons ground dill weed
¼ teaspoon Tabasco sauce

Mix salt, brown sugar, and lemon juice with water. Mix dry ingredients, garlic, dill, onion, Tabasco sauce, and enough water to make a paste. Add this mixture to the ½ gallon of liquid. Makes ½ gallon.

# RED EYE SAUCE

"Adds juiciness to sausage; it's great on biscuits; very few calories."

When you fry any meat, it produces juices which become a meat glaze. Use this glaze and the browned particles in the skillet for a great "red eye" sauce. Set meat aside, keep warm. Pour off all fat, then replace one tablespoon. Heat skillet until fat starts to barely smoke. Add ½ to 1 cup hot water, depending upon the amount of drippings (be careful of steam). Use a wooden scraper to loosen the glaze and the crumbs in the skillet. Add 1 to 2 tablespoons of milk. Boil again. Reheat sausage in skillet before serving.


## BARBECUE SAUCE WITH MUSTARD

"Great for smoked chicken, turkey, ham, or hot dogs."

| | |
|---|---|
| 1 cup molasses | ¼ tablespoon oregano (ground) |
| ½ cup vinegar | ½ teaspoon thyme (ground) |
| ½ cup sugar | 1 teaspoon salt |
| 1 cup tomato catsup | ½ teaspoon black pepper |
| 1 cup prepared mustard | ⅛ teaspoon red pepper (to taste) |
| 2 tablespoons canola oil | ½ teaspoon cornstarch |

Mix dry ingredients together. Add a little vinegar to make a paste. Mix the liquid ingredients together; add the vinegar paste. Bring all ingredients to boil, stirring continually; simmer for 10 minutes. Let cool. Stores for 3 months in refrigerator. Makes about 4 cups.


## EASY QUICK SMOKY BBQ SAUCE

| | |
|---|---|
| ¼ cup cider vinegar | 1 teaspoon brown sugar |
| ½ cup spicy catsup | 1 teaspoon dry mustard |
| 1 tablespoon water | ½ teaspoon soy sauce |
| 1 tablespoon Worcestershire sauce | 2 tablespoons liquid smoke |
| 1 tablespoon canola oil or vegetable oil | |

Dissolve brown sugar in water and vinegar. Mix remaining ingredients together. Makes about one cup. Blend flavors for 24 hours. Don't heat.


## MARINADE FOR SQUASH, ETC.

| | |
|---|---|
| ⅔ cup soy sauce | ½ cup canola oil |
| 6 cloves garlic, crushed | 1 teaspoon MSG |
| 2 teaspoons ground ginger | 2 tablespoons brown sugar |
| 2 teaspoons dry mustard | 1 tablespoon white or red wine |

Mix very thoroughly in a blender. Marinate vegetables for 1 or 2 hours and stir-fry in Grill Topper wok on grill.

## BEER BBQ SAUCE

"A very good tasting BBQ sauce."

1 cup beer
1 cup catsup
¼ cup white vinegar
¼ cup Worcestershire sauce
1 teaspoon dry mustard
1 tablespoon onion powder

¼ cup brown sugar, packed
1 teaspoon chili powder
½ cup finely chopped onion
Juice of 1 lemon
Zest of 1 lemon

Mix together first 8 ingredients. Bring to a boil; simmer for 5 minutes. Add lemon juice, zest, and onion. Simmer for 2 minutes. Run over a blender to puree onion and lemon zest. Cool. Yield: 2 cups.

## CREOLE BBQ SAUCE

"Creole seasoned. Lots of pep, but not overwhelming."

¾ cup catsup
¼ cup canola oil
¼ c. cider vinegar
3 tablespoons lemon juice

1 tablespoon Worcestershire
2 tablespoons Hugh's Cajun Rub
(see Index)

Mix all ingredients together; let blend for 1 hour before using.

## "DOCTORING" BBQ SAUCES

"Make a more spicy BBQ sauce - quick and easy!!"

1 cup of any BBQ sauce
¼ cup Worcestershire
   sauce
1 teaspoon brown sugar

Mix Worcestershire sauce and brown sugar thoroughly until sugar is dissolved, then mix into BBQ sauce. If you like it hot, add cayenne or red pepper or red pepper sauce to taste.

## JOHN'S HOT STUFF

"For folks who like heat. Use sparingly in sauces."

1 gallon white vinegar
1 pound whole black
   peppercorns, cracked
1 pound chili powder
1 pound cayenne (red)
   pepper

Bring vinegar to a boil. Add all the peppers. Cook under a ventilator fan. Stir to mix completely. Keep lid on container when not stirring. Stir every minute or two. Simmer for 20 minutes. Strain out the pepper. Use to season hot foods.

# MOP SAUCE FOR PORK SHOULDER

"You don't need a rub."

| | |
|---|---|
| 1 (10½ ounce) can beef bouillon | 1 teaspoon MSG |
| 1⅓ cups water | 1 teaspoon dry mustard |
| ¾ cup Worcestershire sauce | 1 teaspoon garlic powder or |
| ½ cup cider vinegar | granules |
| ⅓ c. canola oil or vegetable oil | ½ to 1 teaspoon red pepper |

Mix together. Blend at room temperature. Baste pork shoulders regularly during smoking or in direct grilling.

# HOT TANGY BASTE

"Blends with pork nicely for a flavorful BBQ."

| | |
|---|---|
| 2 tablespoons lemon juice | 2 tablespoons dry mustard |
| Zest from 1 lemon | ½ teaspoon cayenne pepper |
| 1 cup water | 1 tablespoon Worcestershire sauce |
| 1 cup white vinegar | 1 teaspoon black pepper |
| 2 tablespoons canola oil | |

Mix all ingredients. Bring to a boil, simmer 5 minutes. Cool. Baste meats as they are smoked.

# ORANGE BBQ SAUCE

"Nice spicy orangy tomato taste - different!"

| | |
|---|---|
| ¼ cup catsup | ½ teaspoon garlic powder |
| ¼ cup canola oil | 1 teaspoon pepper |
| ¼ cup orange juice | ¾ teaspoon salt |
| 2 tablespoons cider vinegar | |

Mix all ingredients together. Carefully use as a baste for last 10 to 20 minutes of grilling. Makes over ¾ cup.

# WHEE-BBQ SAUCE

"Add cayenne and taste until you say 'Whee'."

| | |
|---|---|
| 1 cup spicy catsup | 1 tablespoon cider vinegar |
| 3 tablespoons brown sugar | 1 teaspoon garlic powder |
| 2 tablespoons Worcestershire sauce | ¼ to 1 teaspoon cayenne pepper (to taste) |

Blend catsup, brown sugar, Worcestershire sauce, and garlic powder, then add cayenne pepper (¼ teaspoon) to taste. If "heat" is OK, bring to boil and simmer for 5 minutes. Cool, then taste. If "heat" is too mild, add more cayenne.

## ENGLISH STYLE MUSTARD

"Use where a sharp pungent mustard flavor is preferred."

Make a paste by mixing dry mustard with water, vinegar, wine, or beer for one of the following: a hot, mild, English, pungent or extremely hot mustard.

## DILLED TARTAR SAUCE

"Adds a nice touch to fried or other kinds of fish."

1 cup mayonnaise                    1 to 2 dill pickles, chopped
¼ cup chopped onion

Mix together. Serve with favorite fish. Makes 1¼ cups.

## SEAFOOD BUTTER SAUCE AND BASTE

"Great baste when grilling seafood; enhances any seafood as a heated table sauce. Use butter on low fat fish."

½ cup butter
½ teaspoon rosemary
½ teaspoon tarragon
¾ teaspoon salt
1 tablespoon lemon juice

Melt butter. Add remaining ingredients. Baste raw seafood before grilling and as it is grilling. As a dipping sauce, serve heated with shrimp, crawfish, crab, or lobster. Makes ½ cup.

## SHRIMP DIPPING SAUCE

"It's peppy, but not overwhelming."

1 cup spicy catsup
1 cup chili sauce
1 to 2 tablespoons Worcestershire
  sauce
1 tablespoon horseradish (or to
  taste)
¼ teaspoon dry mustard

Mix all together. Place sauce in a small bowl in middle of medium platter. Surround with cooked shrimp. Serve cold. Makes over 2 cups.

# Starters And Appetizers

From Steak Tartare to
Stuffed Mushrooms

## HOT SHRIMP GARLIC CHEESE DIP

"Make a double batch."

1 can cream of shrimp soup
1 package garlic cheese or 6
   ounces Velveeta cheese
½ pound shrimp, cooked

½ pound mushrooms
1 tablespoon lemon juice
1 teaspoon powdered garlic

Heat soup. Add cheese and let it melt. Saute mushrooms and add to cheese mixture along with shrimp. Season with lemon juice and garlic powder. Serve in chafing dish with Melba toast.

## CURRY DIP FOR VEGETABLES

"Good curry dip - not heavy."

1 teaspoon tarragon vinegar
1 teaspoon garlic salt
1 teaspoon curry powder

1 teaspoon horseradish
1 teaspoon finely grated onion
1 cup mayonnaise

Mix all ingredients together and place in serving dish. I usually serve this dip with raw carrots, celery, broccoli, and cauliflower.

## BEER CHEESE SPREAD

1 pound sharp Cheddar cheese
1 pound mild Cheddar cheese
1 (6 ounce) tomato paste

1 teaspoon garlic salt
3 teaspoons Worcestershire sauce
1 to 1½ cups beer

Grate the sharp and mild Cheddar cheeses together in a large bowl. Add tomato paste, garlic salt, and Worcestershire sauce. Gradually stir in beer until mixture is of spreading consistency. Chill. Serve with crackers or dark rye bread.

## CHEESE SPREAD

1 pound Velveeta cheese
5½ ounces horseradish
7 drops Tabasco sauce

9 tablespoons mayonnaise
1 teaspoon dry mustard
Garlic salt to taste

Melt cheese in double boiler; remove from heat. Mix remaining ingredients together and add to cheese in mixing bowl. Beat well. Store in a cheese crock. Serve with assorted crackers.

## BRIE APPETIZER ROUND

1 (2½ pound) fully
 ripened Brie
⅔ cup coarsely chopped
 pecans
2 to 3 tablespoons brown
 sugar

Remove rind from top of cheese, cutting to within ¼ inch of outside edges. Place cheese on an ungreased cookie sheet. Arrange pecans over top of cheese. Sprinkle with brown sugar. Broil 8 inches from heat for 3 to 5 minutes or until sugar and cheese are bubbly (watch very carefully; do not burn). Serve with crackers.

## STEAK TARTARE

2 pounds lean beef steak, ground
 very fine
4 egg yolks
½ cup chopped chives
2 tablespoons chopped onion
4 teaspoons chopped parsley

2 teaspoons paprika
1 teaspoon dry mustard
2 teaspoons Worcestershire sauce
Dash of cayenne pepper
2 tablespoons brandy

In a bowl, thoroughly mix chopped steak, egg yolks, chives, onion, seasonings, and brandy. Mold into a ball. Spread on rye bread slices. Garnish with capers, anchovies, and lemon wedges. Be careful of E. coli. Start with round steak and grind your own.

## LIVER PATE

6 to 8 slices of bacon
1 pound chicken livers, chopped
 into small pieces
½ pound pork sausage
2 eggs, slightly beaten

⅔ whole garlic bulb, chopped
Salt and pepper
2 to 3 tablespoons cognac or
 brandy
1 teaspoon dehydrated onion

Line bottom of casserole with slices of bacon. Pour mixture over bacon. Cover with bacon slices. Sprinkle top with thyme and 2 bay leaves. Cover tightly with foil or a lid. Bake for 3 hours at 250°F.

## CRAB CHEESE DIP

1 can crabmeat or 6 ounces frozen
  crabmeat
1 (8 ounce) package cream cheese
1 tablespoon milk

2 tablespoons chopped onion
1/2 teaspoon horseradish
1/4 teaspoon salt
Dash of pepper

Mix all the ingredients together and top with slivered almonds. Bake at 375°F. for 15 to 20 minutes or until bubbly. Serve with crackers.

## CLAM LOAF

2 (8 ounce) packages
  cream cheese
2 cans minced clams
3 to 4 green onions,
  chopped
1 to 2 tablespoons
  chopped parsley
1 loaf shepherd bread
  (unsliced)

Mix cream cheese, clams (including juice), onions, and parsley. Slice top from bread. Remove inside of loaf, leaving a shell. Place cream cheese mixture inside. Replace top of loaf; wrap in heavy duty foil and bake for 3 hours at 250°F. Serve hot. Use pieces of scooped out bread to dip.

## BROILED HAMBURGER

"Quick and easy for a super appetizer."

1 pound ground beef
1 1/2 teaspoons Worcestershire
  sauce
1 1/2 teaspoons horseradish
1/3 cup chili sauce or catsup

1 tablespoon or more chopped
  onions
Salt and pepper
Small hamburger buns

Cut buns in halves and butter. Mix ground beef with everything except buns. Spread meat mixture to the edge of the buns. Broil 10 minutes or more, until brown on top, and juices run clear. Then cut in serving pieces.

## SHRIMP DIP

1 can cream of mushroom soup or
  cream of shrimp soup
1 (8 ounce) package cream cheese

1 tablespoon chopped chives
1 teaspoon lemon juice
2 cups sliced shrimp, cooked

Heat soup and cream cheese for 4 minutes on REHEAT or 7 in the microwave or until cheese is melted and mixture is quite warm. Add chives, lemon juice, and shrimp. Keep warm in a chafing dish. Serve with Melba toast points or crackers.

## SHRIMP MOLD

1 can tomato soup
4 small packages cream cheese (3 ounces)
1½ tablespoons gelatin
1 cup mayonnaise

¾ cup finely chopped celery
¾ cup finely chopped onion
2 cans shrimp or ½ pound fresh cooked shrimp, sliced

Soak gelatin in ¼ cup cold water. Heat soup to boiling. Dissolve gelatin in soup. Add cream cheese (mix with electric mixer). When mixture thickens, add mayonnaise, celery, and onion. Season with salt and pepper. Place in greased mold, layer mixture, layer shrimp, etc.; end with mixture. Refrigerate. Serve with Melba toast or other crackers.

## SPINACH DIP

2 cups sour cream
1 cup mayonnaise
1 package dry leek soup mix
1 (10 ounce) package frozen chopped spinach

½ cup fresh parsley
½ cup chopped green onions
1 teaspoon dry dill weed
1 teaspoon Italian seasoning

Mix all together; serve with vegetables.

## TEX-MEX DIP

3 medium size ripe avocados
2 tablespoons lemon juice
½ teaspoon salt
¼ teaspoon pepper
1 cup (8 ounces) sour cream
½ cup mayonnaise
1 package taco seasoning mix
2 (10½ ounce) cans jalapeno flavored bean dip
1 large bunch green onions with tops, chopped (1 cup)

3 medium size tomatoes, halved, seeded, and coarsely chopped (2 cups)
1 can pitted ripe olives, drained and chopped
1 cup sharp Cheddar cheese, shredded
Tortilla chips or Fritos

Peel, pit, and mash avocados with lemon juice, salt, and pepper; set aside. Combine sour cream, mayonnaise, and taco seasoning.

To assemble: Spread bean dip on a large shallow serving platter. Top with seasoned avocado mixture. Layer with sour cream/taco mixture. Sprinkle with chopped onions, tomatoes, and olives. Cover with Cheddar cheese. Serve chilled or at room temperature with tortilla or Fritos chips.

# HOT ARTICHOKE SPREAD

1 (14 ounce) can artichoke hearts,
  drained and chopped
1 cup mayonnaise

1 cup Parmesan cheese
Garlic powder to taste
Instant dried onions

Mix all ingredients together and put in a 5 cup ramekin. Top with instant dried onions. Heat in 350°F. oven for 20 minutes or until mixture bubbles. Serve with Fritos chips or crackers.

# TOASTED CHEESE TIDBITS

1 large loaf thin sliced
  white bread
4 jars Old English cheese
1 pound margarine,
  softened
1 teaspoon Tabasco
1 teaspoon onion powder
1½ teaspoons dill weed
1 teaspoon Beau Monde
  seasoning

Trim crusts from bread. Mix remaining ingredients together until smooth. Spread mixture on the tops of three slices of bread. Stack one on top of the other - frost the outside of the stack like a cake (do not frost bottom).

Repeat with remaining bread and spread. Freeze on a cookie sheet. Cut each stack in half lengthwise and cut twice crosswise (6 pieces from each stack). Bake in 350°F. oven for 20 minutes. These freeze very well.

# VEGETABLE PIZZA

2 packages crescent rolls
1 cup mayonnaise
2 (8 ounce) packages
  cream cheese
1 package Hidden Valley
  Ranch dressing
½ cup sour cream
Shredded carrots
Chopped broccoli,
  cauliflower, green
  pepper, red pimento
Grated Cheddar cheese

Press crescent rolls into a flat pan to form a crust. Bake in 375°F. oven for 10 to 12 minutes or until lightly browned. Cool.

Mix mayonnaise, cream cheese, Hidden Valley Ranch mix, and sour cream together. Spread on cooled pizza crust. Sprinkle the fresh vegetables on top of the mayonnaise cheese mixture. Sprinkle top with grated Cheddar cheese. Chill. Cut into small squares before serving.

# CHEESE BALL

1 small tub Cracker Barrel
  Cheddar cheese spread
1 (8 ounce) package cream cheese

½ to 1 cup chopped dates
Chopped nuts

Mix the Cheddar and cream cheeses together until well mixed. Fold in chopped dates. Shape into a ball and roll in chopped nuts. Chill. Serve with crackers.

## LITTLE SAUSAGE APPETIZERS

2 packages (8 ounces) or 1 pound
  cocktail sausages
2 packages (5 ounces) little
  smoked sausages
1 (12 ounce) jar chili sauce
½ cup crushed pineapple

½ cup currant jelly
1½ tablespoons brown sugar
1½ tablespoons vinegar
2 dashes of Tabasco sauce
½ tablespoon Worcestershire
  sauce

Heat everything, except the sausages, to simmering. Add the sausages and keep hot in a chafing dish or over a candlewarmer for serving. Makes 10 servings.

## GLAZED SAUSAGE BALLS

⅓ pound bulk pork sausage
¾ pound ground pork or beef
½ teaspoon salt
½ teaspoon dry mustard
½ teaspoon crushed coriander
  seed
¼ teaspoon crushed allspice

1 egg, lightly beaten
¼ cup dry bread crumbs
¼ cup sliced green onions
½ cup apple jelly
½ cup Major Grey's chutney,
  chopped
1 teaspoon lemon juice

Mix sausage, ground meat, salt, dry mustard, coriander seed, allspice, egg, bread crumbs, and green onions until well blended. Shape into 1 inch balls. (At this point, you may refrigerate until next day or freeze.) Place on rimmed cookie sheet. Bake, uncovered, in 500°F. oven for about 8 minutes or until well browned.

In a large frying pan over low heat, stir together apple jelly, chutney, and lemon juice. Cook, stirring, until jelly is melted. Add meatballs. Cover and simmer for 8 to 10 minutes or until glazed. Serve in chafing dish.

## BLUE CHEESE MUSHROOMS

12 to 14 large, fresh
  whole mushrooms
¼ cup chopped green
  onions
¼ cup butter or
  margarine
¼ cup crumbled Blue
  cheese (1 ounce)
⅓ cup fine dry bread
  crumbs

Remove stems from mushrooms; chop stems. Cook stems and onions in butter till tender, but not brown. Add cheese, 2 tablespoons of the crumbs, and salt and pepper to taste. Fill mushroom crowns with mixture; sprinkle with remaining crumbs. Place on baking sheet. Bake in moderate 350°F. oven for 12 minutes for fresh mushrooms. Makes 4 to 6 servings.

# BAKED DEVILED STUFFED MUSHROOMS

1 pound fresh mushrooms
1 (3 ounce) package
cream cheese, softened
1 (14½ ounce) can
deviled ham
2 cups soft bread crumbs,
divided
1 teaspoon onion powder
⅛ teaspoon ground black
pepper
3 tablespoons butter

Rinse and dry mushrooms. Remove stems; set caps aside. Chop enough stems to measure ½ cup; reserve for later use. Combine cheese, deviled ham, ½ cup bread crumbs, reserved chopped stems, onion powder, and black pepper.

Melt butter; brush outside of caps. Mound stuffing into mushroom caps. Sprinkle remaining bread crumbs over stuffed mushrooms. Place in shallow pan. Bake in 350°F. oven for 15 minutes.

# CAVIAR DIP

"Looks odd; you cannot stop with one bite."

2 cups mayonnaise
1 teaspoon dry mustard
2 tablespoons finely chopped onion

2 ounces black caviar
1 tablespoon Worcestershire sauce

Mix together thoroughly and chill for at least 1 hour. Use dippers of choice: Crackers, carrot sticks, cauliflower, broccoli, celery, green pepper, etc.

# CRAB QUESADILLAS

"Mexican style cheese sandwich."

1 (10.5 ounce) tub Neufchatel
cheese with Ranch flavor
1 (7¼ ounce) can crab, drained
1 (4 ounce) can chopped green
chilies

3 green onions, thinly sliced
2 tablespoons chopped ripe olives
12 (7 inch) flour tortillas
2 tablespoons margarine, melted

Mix together cheese, crab, onions, and olives. Divide mixture between 6 tortillas. Spread to within ½ inch of edges. Top with second tortilla. Place quesadillas in single layer on 2 cookie sheets. Brush tops with melted margarine. Bake in 350°F. oven for 10 minutes or until edges are lightly browned and crisp. Cut into quarters. Serve with guacamole and salsa.

# CRABMEAT SPREAD

"Low cal - very tasty."

| | |
|---|---|
| 1 cup crabmeat, shredded | 1 cup cottage cheese |
| 1 onion, chopped | 1 cup bean sprouts |
| ½ green pepper, chopped | ¼ cup chopped fresh parsley |
| 1 stalk and top celery, chopped | ¾ to 1 cup mayonnaise |

Blend all ingredients together. Add just enough mayonnaise to moisten mixture. Yields 3 cups.

Lobster, tuna, salmon, or shrimp may be substituted for crabmeat.

# COOKED CHEESE

"A crowd pleaser."

| | |
|---|---|
| 1 (8 ounce) package Brick cheese | 1 teaspoon butter or margarine |
| 1 small can evaporated milk | Caraway seed (optional) |

In top of a double boiler, cut cheese into small pieces and add milk. Place pan over boiling water. Stir until cheese melts. Do not boil. Beat in butter and caraway seed. Pour into glass jar and cover.

# STUFFED CHERRY TOMATOES

"Colorful tasty tidbits."

1 pint (about 30) cherry
tomatoes
1 (4½ ounce) can deviled
ham
¾ cup finely grated Swiss
cheese
½ cup finely chopped
stuffed olives
1 tablespoon minced
onion

Rinse and dry tomatoes. Thinly slice the tops from tomatoes. Scoop out pulp with a teaspoon or melon baller. Drain shells upside down on paper toweling.

In a small mixing bowl, stir together deviled ham, ½ cup cheese, olives, and onion; spoon into tomato shells. Sprinkle with remaining cheese. Refrigerate until ready to serve. Yields 30 hors d'oeuvres.

# SALSA FRIA

"Cold sauce from the sunbelt."

3 fresh jalapeno chilies, seeded
and chopped very fine
1 large onion, chopped very fine
3 to 4 plum tomatoes, chopped
fine
2 cloves garlic, minced

1 bunch fresh parsley, chopped
fine
¼ cup vegetable oil
¼ cup (or less to taste) red wine
vinegar

Mix all ingredients together. Let stand at room temperature for 1 hour before serving. Serve with tortilla chips as a dip. Yields 2 cups.

This salsa is good with tacos, fajitas, burritos, or with grilled meats.

# FOR A QUICK GUACAMOLE

2 avocados
2 to 3 tablespoons Salsa
 Fria

Peel and mash avocados. Blend in Salsa Fria; chill. Serve as a dip or as an accompaniment to your favorite Mexican dish.

# ANTIPASTO

"Good way to start a party."

1 (8 ounce) can mushroom stems
 and pieces
1 (14 ounce) can artichoke hearts
1 (16 ounce) jar Spanish salad
 olives
1 (9 ounce) can ripe olives, sliced
½ cup bell pepper, chopped
½ cup celery, chopped
¾ cup white wine vinegar
¾ cup olive oil

¼ cup minced onions
2½ teaspoons Italian seasoning
½ teaspoon onion powder
1½ teaspoons salt
1 teaspoon seasoned salt
1 teaspoon garlic salt
1 teaspoon sugar
1 teaspoon cracked pepper
1 teaspoon MSG (Accent;
 optional)

Mix together the first 6 ingredients and place in a large jar. Combine and boil remaining ingredients. Pour over vegetables. Cover tightly with lid. Refrigerate overnight. Shake the jar several times a day to stir up ingredients. Serve as an hors d'oeuvre or as a relish.

# MARINATED MUSHROOMS

"Low-cal nibble food."

2 cans button mushrooms
2 small onions, sliced thinly into
 rings
½ cup salad oil

½ cup vinegar
¾ cup sugar
1 teaspoon salt
½ teaspoon pepper

Drain mushrooms. Add onion rings. Mix remaining ingredients. Pour over mushrooms and onions. Marinate overnight.

## SWISS SAUERKRAUT BALLS

"Takes time, but worth it."

3 tablespoons butter
1 onion
¼ pound bulk pork sausage
¼ pound cooked ham, finely
   ground
¼ pound ground beef
5 tablespoons flour
1 pound sauerkraut, drained and
   chopped

1 cup milk
½ teaspoon dry mustard
½ teaspoon salt
1 tablespoon parsley, chopped
¼ pound Swiss cheese, cubed
Additional flour
2 eggs, well beaten
Dry bread crumbs
Deep fat or oil, heated to 375°F.

In a skillet, saute onion in butter. Add pork sausage, ham, and ground beef. Saute until meat is cooked; drain excess fat. Sprinkle the mixture with 5 tablespoons flour and continue to cook, stirring until it is well blended. Add sauerkraut, 1 cup milk, dry mustard, salt, and chopped parsley. Cook mixture, stirring constantly, over moderate heat until it forms a thick paste (4 minutes). Spread on a cookie sheet and chill for 1 hour.

Shape mixture into 1 inch balls. Punch a hole in the middle and place a cube of Swiss cheese in the center. Reshape ball. Roll balls in flour, then in beaten eggs, then in bread crumbs. Deep fat fry a few at a time. Serve hot on toothpicks. Serve with Thousand Island dressing, Mustard-Mayonnaise Sauce.

## MUSTARD-MAYONNAISE SAUCE

½ cup mustard
½ cup mayonnaise

Mix together.

## GARLIC ROASTED PECANS

"Makes great Christmas presents."

1½ to 2 sticks margarine
10 heaping cups pecans
1 tablespoon plus 1
   teaspoon popcorn salt
2 teaspoons garlic powder

Melt margarine in bottom of roasting pan. Add pecans, salt, and garlic powder. Stir until pecans are well coated with margarine. Cover. Bake in 250°F. oven for 1 hour. Remove cover; stir pecans. Continue baking, stirring pecans every 10 minutes, for another hour. Remove from oven. Add 1 teaspoon garlic powder. Stir thoroughly. Cool.

# Tasty Salads & Dressings

Delicious Tomato Dill Aspic to
Italian Sweet Sour Dressing

## AVOCADO SALAD

"Smooth and creamy."

1 (3 ounce) package
  lemon jello
1 cup boiling water
1 cup mashed avocado (2
  to 3)
1 cup mayonnaise
1 cup sour cream

Place jello in blender. Add boiling water and blend until mixed. Add avocado, blending well. Add mayonnaise and sour cream; blend until just mixed. Chill in a ring mold. Fill center with unpeeled apple slices or banana slices marinated in French dressing, or fill with sliced fresh strawberries. Serve 6 to 8.

## CRANBERRY SALAD

"Thanksgiving Day favorite."

1 can crushed pineapple
1 (No. 2½) can pineapple
  slices
1 large package cherry
  jello
¼ cup sugar
1 teaspoon lemon juice
2 cups ground fresh
  cranberries
1 whole orange, chopped
1 cup chopped celery
½ cup broken California
  walnuts

Drain pineapple; reserve syrup. Add enough water to measure 2 cups. Heat syrup and water. Add jello; stir until jello is dissolved. Add 2 cups cold water. Chill till partially set.

Mix together cranberries, crushed pineapple, lemon juice, orange, celery, walnuts, and sugar. Place pineapple slices in bottom of ring mold. Cover with a small portion of jello mixture. Refrigerate until set.

Fold cranberry mixture into remaining jello. Gently pour on top of molded pineapple slices. Chill until firm. Serves 12.

# NITA'S TOMATO ASPIC

"Easy, tasty aspic."

1 cup dill pickle juice
1 (3 ounce) package lemon jello
1 (16 ounce) can stewed tomatoes,
  chopped (juice and all)

½ cup celery

Heat dill pickle juice. Add jello and stir until dissolved. Add tomatoes and celery. Pour into a 9x9 inch dish. Serve 4 to 6.

# SEVEN LAYER SALAD

"Special picnic salad."

½ bunch fresh spinach
Salt and pepper
1 teaspoon sugar
7 hard-boiled eggs, chopped
1 pound bacon, fried crisp and
  crumbled

1 package frozen peas (uncooked)
½ head iceberg lettuce, chopped
1 tablespoon sugar
2 cups mayonnaise
¾ pound Swiss cheese, grated

1. Place spinach in bottom of 9x14 inch dish. Sprinkle with salt, pepper, and sugar.
2. Layer boiled eggs.
3. Layer bacon.
4. Layer frozen peas.
5. Layer iceberg lettuce; sprinkle with sugar.
6. Spread mayonnaise over the top of the lettuce layer.
7. Sprinkle Swiss cheese over all.
Cover; chill for at least 24 hours before serving. Serves 6 to 8.

# KOREAN SALAD

"Elegant salad your friends will love."

1 bag washed spinach, stems cut
  off
1 can water chestnuts, drained
  and sliced

1 can bean sprouts, drained
2 hard cooked eggs, sliced
5 strips bacon, fried and crumbled

Dressing:
½ cup granulated sugar
¼ cup vinegar
1 cup oil
2 tablespoons Worcestershire
  sauce

⅓ cup catsup
1 small chopped onion
Salt and pepper

Mix dressing in blender. Toss salad lightly.
Tear spinach into medium pieces. Add water chestnuts and bean sprouts; toss lightly with dressing. Top with egg slices and crumbled bacon. Serves 6 to 8.

# SALAD NICOISE

"A French favorite from the Riviera."

1 can green beans
1 can sliced white potatoes
1 can artichokes
1 small red onion, sliced into rings
1 box cherry tomateos

½ cup black olives, sliced
2 cans tuna fish
2 ounces anchovy fillets
3 hard cooked eggs

Dressing:
1 cup olive oil
¼ cup tarragon vinegar
1 clove garlic, crushed

1½ teaspoons dry mustard
Pepper
1 teaspoon salt

Marinate green beans, potatoes, artichokes, and onion rings in half of dressing for 6 hours in refrigerator.

Toss together remaining ingredients with marinating vegetables. Toss all ingredients with salad greens with remaining dressing. Serves 8 to 10.

Dressing: Mix all together.

# DILLED POTATO SALAD

"Hot weather delight and different."

5 to 6 boiled potatoes, diced
3 dill pickles, chopped
1 medium onion, chopped

1 to 2 teaspoons dill weed
2 to 3 tablespoons dill pickle juice
1 cup mayonnaise

Mix gently the potatoes, pickles, onion, and dill weed. Blend dill pickle juice into mayonnaise. Add to potato mixture. Adjust seasoning to taste; chill. Serves 6.

# "B's" POTATO SALAD

"A very different form of potato salad."

4 to 6 potatoes, boiled
Salt and pepper
1 red onion, sliced
2 tomatoes, sliced
3 to 4 tablespoons
    mayonnaise
1 to 1½ cups cottage
    cheese
Olives, sliced

Boil potatoes. Slice into dish underpeeled. Salt and pepper generously while hot. Cover with sliced onions. Cover with sliced tomatoes. Cover with a layer of mayonnaise. Cover with a layer of cottage cheese. Garnish with sliced olives.

Prepare early to give salad time to season.

## PASTA SALAD ALA RUTH

2 cups uncooked elbow macaroni
1 to 2 tablespoons dry Italian
   dressing seasoning
1 to 2 cloves garlic, crushed
4 green onions, chopped
2 cups mixed vegetables (such as
   cooked asparagus, carrots,
   green peppers, zucchini)

¾ cup mayonnaise
2 teaspoons sugar
2 tablespoons red wine vinegar
1 teaspoon dill weed

Cook macaroni in water with 1 tablespoon oil until fork tender. Rinse and cool. Add remaining ingredients and chill. Serve on lettuce leaves. Sprinkle with grating of Asiago or Parmesan cheese. Surround with wedges of cherry tomatoes and hard cooked eggs. Serves 6.

## SHOESTRING TUNA SALAD

"Even men like tuna this way."

1 (6½ to 7 ounce) can tuna,
   drained
1 medium red apple (unpeeled),
   diced
½ medium onion, chopped
1 large carrot, shredded

¾ to 1 cup mayonnaise, diluted (if
   desired) with a small amount of
   milk and stirred until smooth
1 (4 ounce) can shoestring
   potatoes

Combine tuna, apple, onion, and carrot; mix lightly. Add enough mayonnaise to moisten mixture. Just before serving, fold in shoestring potatoes. Serves 6.

## TUNA FISH SALAD

1 (6½ ounce) can tuna fish
¼ pound small shrimp
2 slices ham, diced
½ pound fresh mushrooms
1 hard cooked egg
½ medium green pepper, chopped
4 green onions, sliced

2 stalks celery, chopped
1 clove garlic
1¼ teaspoons lemon juice
½ cup mayonnaise
1 teaspoon Worcestershire sauce
Few drops of Tabasco sauce

Mix together the tuna fish and shrimp. Saute together in a little oil the ham and mushrooms. Add to tuna and shrimp mixture. Add the chopped egg, green pepper, onions, celery, garlic, and lemon juice to tuna mixture. Mix together mayonnaise, Worcestershire sauce, and Tabasco; add to tuna mixture and toss lightly. Pour into shallow baking dish. Refrigerate for 1 hour.

Top with buttered bread crumbs. Sprinkle with Parmesan cheese. Bake in 350°F. oven or until heated through, 25 to 30 minutes. Serves 6 to 8.

# EMERSON SLAW

"Great for picnics - travels well. Stores for a week."

1 large head cabbage, shredded fine
1 large onion, sliced fine

Dressing:
⅞ cup sugar
1 cup cider vinegar
¾ cup salad oil
2 teaspoons salt
1 teaspoon celery seed
1 teaspoon dry mustard

Layer cabbage and onion; end with layer of cabbage.

Dressing: Mix sugar, vinegar, oil, salt, celery seed, and dry mustard together. Heat to boiling point. Pour <u>hot</u> dressing over cabbage; <u>do not stir.</u> Cover. Place in refrigerator overnight. Stir before serving. Will keep for a week. Serves 8 to 10.

# BARBARA'S CRISP-TART COLD SLAW

"Delightful change."

1 large head cabbage, shredded
1 medium onion, chopped
1 green pepper, finely chopped
1 tablespoon salt
1 cup boiling water
1 cup sugar
1 cup white vinegar
½ cup oil
1 tablespoon celery seed
1 teaspoon mustard seed
1 (2 ounce) jar pimiento, chopped

Combine cabbage, onion, and green pepper in large bowl. Sprinkle with salt and pour boiling water over all. Let stand at room temperature for 1 hour. Drain into colander.

Combine sugar, vinegar, oil, celery seed, and mustard seed. Add to cabbage mixture. Stir in chopped pimiento. Cover and refrigerate.

# SWEDISH CUCUMBER SALAD

"Old world style cucumbers."

2 cucumbers
1 small onion
1 tablespoon vinegar
1 teaspoon salt
1 teaspoon sugar
¾ cup mayonnaise
½ cup sour cream
1 tablespoon chopped fresh dill or dried dill weed
1 tablespoon chopped fresh parsley

Slice cucumbers and onion into a medium size bowl. Toss with vinegar, salt, and sugar. Let stand for 30 minutes; drain. Mix mayonnaise, sour cream, dill, and parsley. Add to cucumbers and onion.

## BILL'S ITALIAN TOMATO SALAD

"Super! Prepare a day ahead dish for a cookout."

1 package Good Seasons Zesty
  Italian dressing
1 tablespoon brown sugar
1 tablespoon dry mustard
¼ cup vinegar (cider or wine)
2 tablespoons water

½ cup canola oil or salad oil
1 can anchovy filets
2 large tomatoes, sliced
1 large onion (red, yellow, or
  white), sliced and divided into
  rings

Use a cruet jar. Add vinegar and water. Add brown sugar, dry seasonings, and mustard. Shake vigorously to dissolve and mix thoroughly. Next, add oil and oil from anchovies. Shake again to mix. Layer tomatoes and onion rings in large flat dish. Add some anchovies to each layer. Top with anchovies. Cover with dressing. Marinate in refrigerator for 4 to 8 hours before serving.
Reruns the next day are even more tasty. Serves 4 to 6.

## MEXICAN SALAD

"Good for a hot summer day."

1 head iceberg lettuce
1 large chopped onion
3 tomatoes
2 avocados
2 pounds ground beef

2 cans kidney beans
½ (9 ounce) bag Fritos
1 bottle creamy French dressing
¼ cup picante sauce

Mix together lettuce, onion, tomatoes, and avocados. Refrigerate. Cook ground beef. Add kidney beans and liquid. Cook for 3 minutes. When ready to serve, add hot mixture to salad. Add Fritos, dressing, and picante sauce. Toss lightly. Serves 8 to 10.

## PERFECTION SALAD

"Charlie's favorite and it's low cal."

1 (3 ounce) package lime jello
1 (3 ounce) package lemon jello
2 cups boiling water
1½ cups cold water
2 tablespoons vinegar
1 teaspoon salt
¼ teaspoon pepper
2 cups shredded cabbage

½ cup shredded carrots
¼ cup chopped celery
3 chopped green onions
4 chopped sweet pickles
2 tablespoons chopped green
  pepper
¾ cup sliced green olives

Dissolve jellos in boiling water. Stir until gelatin is dissolved. Add cold water. Chill until slightly set. Fold in vegetables, vinegar, salt, and pepper. Pour into molds. Chill. Top with chopped pimiento stuffed olives. Serves 8.

# POPPY SEED DRESSING

"Pretty dressing for fresh fruit salad. Piquant flavor."

½ cup sugar
1 teaspoon salt
1 teaspoon dry mustard
1 teaspoon fresh grated lemon peel
1 teaspoon finely minced onion

⅓ cup freshly squeezed lemon
  juice
¾ cup salad oil
Few drops of red food coloring
1 tablespoon poppy seed

Combine all ingredients, except food coloring and poppy seeds, in electric blender or covered container. Cover and blend or shake until thoroughly mixed. Tint a delicate pink color with red food coloring. Stir in poppy seeds. Chill before serving with fresh fruits in season. Makes 1½ cups.

# FRENCH DRESSING #1

½ cup vinegar
½ cup sugar
½ cup salad oil
½ cup catsup (¼ cup chili sauce,
  ¼ cup catsup)

½ onion, grated
½ teaspoon salt

Blend well and chill.

# VINEGAR AND OIL DRESSING

"Good basic dressing."

1 tablespoon sugar
1 teaspoon salt
5 tablespoons salad oil
2 tablespoons vinegar

Mix all ingredients together in a jar and shake well. I normally use Heinz cider vinegar. For a different flavor, wine vinegar or tarragon flavored vinegar may be substituted.

# FRUIT SALAD DRESSING

½ cup sugar
1 teaspoon paprika
1 teaspoon dry mustard
1 teaspoon salt

¼ cup grated onion
1 cup salad oil
¼ cup wine garlic vinegar

Mix together in electric blender. Make a salad with lettuce, pears, grapefruit, pineapple, bananas, avocado, and fresh strawberries.

## MAYONNAISE

"This is an old-fashioned boiled dressing."

3 egg yolks
¼ cup vinegar
¼ cup water
¼ teaspoon dry mustard
2 teaspoons flour
2 tablespoons butter or oil
¼ teaspoon salt
Sugar*

Melt butter in saucepan. Add flour, sugar, salt, and mustard; stir until blended. Add water and vinegar. Cook, stirring, until blended and has a glazed appearance. Whip egg yolks. Stir some of the hot mixture into the egg yolks to warm the yolks, then add to the hot mixture. Cook, stirring, until it begins to thicken.

* Use ¼ cup if for fruit, 1 tablespoon for fish or meat, 2 tablespoons for vegetable salad.

## GINGERED LEMON SOUR CREAM DRESSING

"Fresh way for fruit."

1 cup sour cream
1 tablespoon fresh grated lemon
peel

1 tablespoon granulated sugar
½ teaspoon ground ginger

Combine all ingredients thoroughly. Cover and refrigerate for at least 2 hours before serving. Yields 1 cup.

## ITALIAN SWEET-SOUR SALAD DRESSING

½ cup oil
⅓ cup red wine vinegar
2 tablespoons sugar
½ teaspoon salt
½ teaspoon celery salt

½ teaspoon ground black pepper
½ teaspoon dry mustard
½ teaspoon Worcestershire sauce
¼ teaspoon Tabasco sauce
1 clove garlic, minced

Combine all ingredients in a jar. Shake well; refrigerate.

## BLUE CHEESE DRESSING

1 pound Blue cheese
2 cups mayonnaise
1 cup sour cream
Juice of 1 lemon
1 small onion, grated

Combine ingredients and mix until creamy. Makes 1 quart.

Cut recipe in half. Stores well refrigerated.

# Main Events other than BBQ

Southern Smothered Chicken
to Creole Burgers

## ALABAMA CHICKEN

"Light luncheon. Particularly nice for a ladies' lunch."

2 pounds whole chicken, cooked
and cut in pieces (save broth)
1 stick butter
1 cup chopped green pepper
1 cup chopped celery
1 cup chopped onion
4½ ounces green spinach noodles

½ pound Velveeta cheese
1 (3 ounce) jar whole green stuffed
olives
½ cup ripe olives, sliced
1 can mushrooms
1 (10½ ounce) can mushroom
soup

Saute green pepper, celery, and onion in butter. Boil spinach noodles in chicken broth; <u>drain.</u> Combine cheese, olives, mushrooms, and mushroom soup. Add mixture to the sauteed vegetables. Add chicken and noodles. Put in greased casserole. Crush cheese crackers on top. Dot with butter.

Preheat oven to 300°F. Baking time: 45 minutes. Pan size: 9x13 inch. Serves 8 to 10.

## FRIED CHICKEN

"Family favorite."

1 frying size chicken, cut
into serving pieces
1 cup flour
1 teaspoon salt
½ teaspoon pepper

Place flour, salt, and pepper in paper bag. Heat ½ oil and bacon fat in heavy deep skillet.

Wash chicken and shake in seasoned flour in paper bag. Place chicken in hot oil mixture. Fry for about 15 minutes or until chicken is brown on one side. Turn chicken, then turn down heat and continue frying, about 25 to 30 minutes.

## CHICKEN BREASTS CORDON BLEU

"Here's an elegant chicken dish which will impress your dinner guests."

4 chicken breasts, skinned, boned,     4 slices Swiss cheese
halved, and flattened              Salt and pepper to season
4 slices (thin) boiled ham

Place ingredients on chicken breasts and roll. Skewer with toothpicks.Egg mixture: Use 1 egg and 2 or 3 tablespoons water.Crumb mixture: Use ½ cup bread crumbs, ½ cup flour, and Parmesan cheese.

Dip rolled breasts in egg mixture, then crumb mixture. Brown in 2 tablespoons of butter and 2 tablespoons oil. Pour sauce over breasts.Sauce: Add 2 tablespoons flour to pan drippings. Add ¾ cup chicken broth and ¼ cup dry white wine.

Chicken rolls can be assembled earlier and browned just before serving. Serves 4.


## PRESSED CHICKEN

"Elegant luncheon dish."

2 (4 pound) roasters
4 cups water
1 cup sherry
1 carrot, pared and sliced
1 cup sliced celery
1 leek, halved lengthwise
2 bay leaves
¼ teaspoon whole cloves
1 teaspoon dried savory
10 parsley sprigs
1 clove garlic, halved
¾ cup onions, minced
¼ teaspoon whole
peppercorns
1 tablespoon salt
3 tablespoons snipped
parsley
1 large carrot, pared
Watercress

In large kettle, place chickens, water, sherry, sliced carrot, celery, leek, bay leaves, cloves, savory, parsley, garlic, onions, peppercorns, and salt. Simmer, covered, for 2 hours or until chicken is tender. Remove chicken to tray. Cool. Skim fat from cooled broth. Strain broth through fine sieve into large saucepan. Boil, uncovered, until 2 cups liquid remains.

When chicken is cool, remove meat from bones in large size pieces. Add chicken to broth. Simmer, covered, for 10 minutes. Stir in snipped parsley.

In 10x5x2 inch loaf pan, arrange chicken lengthwise in layers. Pour on broth. Weigh down with refrigerator dish or another loaf pan about ¾ filled with cold water. Refrigerate overnight.

Make carrot curls: With vegetable parer, shave lengthwise strips from carrot. Curl each around forefinger. Tuck among ice cubes. Refrigerate.

Just before serving next day: With spatula, loosen sides of pressed chicken from pan, then dip pan part way in and out of warm water. Invert serving dish on top of pan; unmold. Down one side of serving dish, arrange carrot curls with cress here and there. Serve, sliced, with jelly or mayonnaise. Serves 8.

## CHICKEN-MUSHROOM BAKE

"It's tremendous - Ruthie just loves this dish."

1 (3½ pound) chicken, cut into pieces (or 3 whole chicken breasts)
½ cup butter or margarine
½ pound fresh mushrooms or canned
1 can cream of mushroom soup
½ pint sour cream

Dredge chicken in flour which is seasoned with salt and pepper. Melt ¼ cup of butter in 13x9x2 inch glass dish. Place chicken, skin side down. Bake in 350°F. oven for 30 minutes. Remove from oven; turn chicken, skin side up, and cover with mushrooms which have been sauteed in ¼ cup butter. Also, cover with the mushroom soup which has been mixed with the sour cream. Bake for 40 to 45 minutes in 350°F. oven. Serves 4 to 6. Reheats easily.

## CHICKEN SPAGHETTI

"Chicken spaghetti is a favorite birthday dish. Our children love this recipe even cold. It is great for entertaining a crowd."

1 (4 to 5 pound) stewing hen
1 large (2 pound) package spaghetti
1 pound fresh mushrooms
1 large green pepper
2 large onions
2 cups frozen cut corn
1 (No. 303) can ripe olives, chopped
2 cans tomato soup
Salt
Pepper
Paprika
Worcestershire sauce
½ pound grated sharp Cheddar cheese

Preheat oven to 325°F. Baking time: 1 hour. Pan size: 8 to 10 quart casserole. Serves 12 to 16.

Boil chicken with 1 carrot, 1 stalk celery, and 1 onion until tender. Debone and cut into julienne pieces. Save broth; add a bit to cut chicken. Chill until ready to use. Boil spaghetti in remaining broth.

Saute onions, green pepper, and mushrooms in butter. Mix together frozen corn, sliced ripe olives, onion, green pepper, mushrooms, chicken, and drained spaghetti. Add tomato soup, Worcestershire sauce, salt, pepper, and paprika (season to taste). Mix lightly. Place in greased casserole. Bake for 40 minutes, then top with cheese. Continue baking for 20 more minutes.

## HERBED CHICKEN IN FOIL

"This will impress your boss."

8 onion slices (¼ inch thick)
1 package long grain and wild rice
½ pound sliced fresh mushrooms
1 teaspoon margarine
1 (2½ to 3 pound) chicken, cut up in fryer pieces
Kitchen Bouquet
1 can condensed cream of mushroom soup
3 tablespoons chopped parsley
2 teaspoons marjoram
1 teaspoon salt or less
Dash of pepper

Cook long grain and wild rice according to package directions. Saute fresh mushrooms in margarine; add to prepared rice. Cut 4 (12 inch) squares of aluminum foil. On each, place 2 slices of onion. Cover onion with ½ cup of cooked rice mixture. Top with 2 pieces of chicken, skin side up. Brush chicken with Kitchen Bouquet.

Mix remaining ingredients; spoon over chicken. Fold foil over and seal securely. Place packages of chicken on baking sheet. Bake in a 450°F. oven for 40 minutes or until chicken is done. Decorate each plate with some parsley and a packet of chicken.

Caution people to unfold foil carefully to avoid the hot steam. Serves 4.

## SOUTHERN SMOTHERED CHICKEN

"Elegant chicken in gravy."

1 fryer, cut up
½ cup flour
Salt and pepper
8 tablespoons butter
½ pound fresh mushrooms

1 can cream of mushroom soup
1 bay leaf
2 tablespoons lemon juice
1 tablespoon Worcestershire sauce
13x9x2 inch glass dish

Coat chicken with flour, salt, and pepper in a paper sack. Slice mushrooms and saute in 4 tablespoons butter. Place chicken in casserole; dot with 4 tablespoons butter. Add bay leaf, mushrooms, lemon juice, and Worcestershire sauce. Add cream of mushroom soup, diluted with ½ cup water. Cover and bake for 1½ hours in 350°F. oven. Serves 6.

# CHICKEN ENCHILADAS

"Tracy's favorite."

| | |
|---|---|
| 2 cups boiled chicken<br>8 ounces cream cheese<br>¼ cup chopped onion<br>½ teaspoon salt<br>3 to 4 cans green<br>  enchilada sauce<br>Flour tortillas | Mix together chicken, cream cheese, onion, and salt. Spread one can of enchilada sauce in bottom of 9x13 inch pan. Spread additional enchilada sauce on tortilla. Place chicken mixture on ⅓ of tortilla and roll up. Place, seam side down, in pan. Continue with other tortillas. |

Top with remaining enchilada sauce. Cover with foil. Bake at 350°F. for 20 to 25 minutes. Add ¾ cup mixture of Cheddar and Monterey Jack cheeses to top. Return to oven and bake until cheese melts. Serves 6 to 8.

# MEXICAN CHICKEN

"Barbara's prize-winning chicken."

| | |
|---|---|
| 6 chicken breast halves<br>¼ teaspoon salt<br>4 eggs<br>5 tablespoons picante<br>  sauce<br>2 cups Italian bread<br>  crumbs<br>2 teaspoons chili powder<br>2 teaspoons cumin<br>1½ teaspoons garlic salt<br>½ teaspoon oregano | Bone and skin chicken breasts. Mix together salt, eggs, and picante sauce; set aside. Mix Italian bread crumbs, cumin, garlic salt, and oregano. Dip breasts into egg mixture, then roll in Italian bread crumbs. Let set for 15 minutes. Repeat the dipping process one more time. Let set for 10 minutes.<br><br>Place in 9x13 inch pan with ¼ cup melted butter. Bake in 375°F. oven for 35 minutes. Serve on a bed of shredded lettuce. Top with a choice of chopped green onions, chopped |

tomatoes, sour cream, avocado slices, shredded Cheddar cheese, and ripe olives.

# RUTH'S BOEUF BOURGUIGNONNE

"Easy version of French cuisine."

| | |
|---|---|
| 1½ pounds chuck roast, cubed<br>1 can cream of mushroom soup<br>1 package dry onion soup mix<br>¾ cup burgundy wine<br>½ pound fresh mushrooms | ¼ cup margarine<br>1 cup sour cream<br>Parsley flakes<br>3 quart casserole dish |

Mix together the mushroom soup, onion soup mix, and wine, then add meat and pour into casserole dish. Cover and cook for 2½ hours in 325°F. oven. Saute sliced mushrooms in margarine. Five minutes before serving, add mushrooms, sour cream, and parsley to meat. Heat for 5 minutes, then serve over buttered and cooked egg noodles.

## ROULADE

"My dear German friend, Dorle, gave me this recipe."

| | |
|---|---|
| 1 slice round steak, cut into serving pieces<br>Salt<br>Pepper<br>Paprika<br>Prepared mustard<br>Bacon, chopped fine<br>Onion, chopped<br>1 cup sour cream | Tenderize and flatten steak pieces with meat hammer. Sprinkle each piece with salt, pepper, and paprika. Spread pieces of steak with prepared mustard. Place chopped bacon and onion in middle of steak. Roll into rolls; tie with string.<br><br>Brown rolls in hot oil; pour off excess oil. Add small amount of water. Cover and simmer till meat is tender, 1 to 1½ hours. Fry additional |

bacon and onion in pan. Add sour cream to bacon and onion mixture. Heat and pour over roulades.

## BOUEF AU LEGUME CASSEROLE

6 slices bacon
1 pound lean beef chuck (about ½ inch thick)
½ cup flour
1 teaspoon salt
1 cup dry red wine
2 tablespoons parsley
½ clove garlic
½ teaspoon thyme

1 (10½ ounce) can condensed beef broth
6 medium potatoes, peeled and halved
12 small white onions, peeled
3 carrots, sliced lengthwise
1 (4 ounce) can mushroom stems and pieces, finely chopped

Cook bacon until crisp; drain on paper towels. Reserve drippings. Cut beef into cubes. Shake a few cubes at a time in paper bag containing flour and salt.

Brown cubes on all sides in bacon drippings; remove to 2 quart casserole. Pour wine into electric blender. Add parsley, garlic, thyme, and beef broth; blend until solid ingredients are pureed. Pour over meat in casserole. Cover casserole; bake at 350°F. for 1 hour.

Stir potatoes, onions, and carrots into casserole. Replace cover. Bake for 1 hour longer or until vegetables are done. Stir in mushrooms. Crumble bacon; scatter on top with additional chopped parsley. Makes 4 to 5 servings.

# STRAW STACKS

"A bit of Tex Mex flavor."

1 cup chopped onion
1 cup chopped celery
⅔ cup chopped green pepper
2 pounds ground beef
3 teaspoons chili powder
2 teaspoons salt
½ teaspoon thyme
¼ teaspoon pepper
2 (6 ounce) cans tomato paste

½ cup catsup
2 cups water
1 (8 ounce) can sliced ripe olives
2 teaspoons Worcestershire sauce
2 to 3 drops Tabasco sauce
Tortilla or corn chips
2 cups shredded Old English
  American cheese

Saute onion, celery, and pepper in hot fat until tender; do not brown. Add ground beef and brown. Add 10 remaining ingredients. Simmer, uncovered, for 1 hour, stirring occasionally. Serve sauce over chips. Sprinkle top with shredded cheese.


# GROUND BEEF STROGANOFF

1 pound ground beef
¼ cup chopped onions
1 clove garlic, minced
½ pound mushrooms or 2 (3
  ounce) cans
3 tablespoons lemon juice
3 tablespoons sherry

1 can condensed consomme
1 teaspoon salt
¼ teaspoon pepper
¼ lb. fine or medium uncooked
  noodles
1 cup (8 ounces) sour cream

Saute meat, onions, garlic, and mushrooms. Add lemon juice, sherry, consomme, salt, and pepper. Simmer all together for 15 minutes. Add noodles. Cook for 5 minutes or till tender. Add sour cream. Add parsley flakes if desired. Serves 4.

## LASAGNE

"A sure fire crowd pleaser."

| | |
|---|---|
| 1 pound ground beef | 1 (10 ounce) package lasagne |
| 1 clove garlic | noodles |
| 3 tablespoons parsley flakes | 3 cups small curd cottage cheese |
| 1 tablespoon basil | 2 beaten eggs |
| 1½ teaspoons salt | 2 teaspoons salt |
| 2 bay leaves | ½ teaspoon pepper |
| 1 medium onion, chopped | ½ cup grated Parmesan cheese |
| 1 (1 pound) can tomatoes | 1 pound Mozzarella cheese |
| 2 (6 ounce) cans tomato paste | 13x9x2 inch glass dish |

Boil enough noodles for 2 layers. Brown meat in electric skillet. Add 1 tablespoon parsley flakes, basil, salt, bay leaves, onion, and tomatoes. Add tomato paste plus 2 cans of water. Simmer, uncovered, for 30 minutes. Remove bay leaves.

In separate bowl, mix together the cottage cheese, beaten eggs, salt, pepper, Parmesan cheese, and 2 tablespoons parsley flakes. Place 1 layer of lasagne noodles on bottom of dish. Cover with ½ cottage cheese mixture, then ½ Mozzarella, and ½ meat sauce. Cover with 1 layer lasagne noodles. Repeat cottage cheese, Mozzarella, and meat layers. Bake lasagne in 375°F. oven for 30 minutes. Let stand for 10 minutes. Serve. Serves 12.

## SWEDISH MEAT BALLS

"Truthfully, an exciting dish worth the time needed to prepare it."

| | |
|---|---|
| 1 pound ground beef | 2 tablespoons margarine |
| ½ pound ground veal | 1 tablespoon salt |
| ½ pound ground pork | ¼ teaspoon pepper |
| ¾ cup dry bread crumbs | ¼ teaspoon nutmeg |
| 2 cups milk | 3 tablespoons shortening |
| 2 eggs, slightly beaten | Electric skillet or 3 quart pot |
| ½ cup chopped onion | Water |

Combine beef, veal, and pork in large bowl. Mix in bread crumbs and milk. Let mixture soak a few minutes. Add the eggs. Saute the chopped onion in margarine in frying pan and add to meat. Mix the salt, pepper, and nutmeg.

Heat shortening in skillet. Moisten hands and shape meat into small balls (1 inch diameter). Brown meat balls in pan. After browning, add 1 cup water and steam meat balls for 15 to 20 minutes over low heat. Serves 6. Reheats easily.

# SPAGHETTI WITH MEAT BALLS

"Our kids were raised on this one and it's still a family favorite."

Meat Balls:
¾ pound ground beef
¼ pound ground pork
1 cup fine dry bread crumbs
½ cup grated Parmesan cheese
1 tablespoon minced parsley

2 small cloves garlic, cut fine
½ cup milk
2 eggs, beaten
1½ teaspoons salt
⅛ teaspoon pepper

Sauce:
4 tablespoons oil
1 cup minced onion
2 tablespoons flour
5 cups cooked tomatoes
6 tablespoons minced parsley
6 tablespoons green pepper

2½ teaspoons salt
¼ teaspoon pepper
3 teaspoons sugar
2 small bay leaves, crumbled
1 teaspoon Worcestershire sauce

Meat Balls: Mix beef, pork, bread crumbs, Parmesan cheese, 1 tablespoon parsley, garlic, milk, eggs, 1½ teaspoons salt, and ½ teaspoon pepper together in bowl. Form meat mixture into 1½ inch balls.

Sauce: Saute onion in oil and brown meat balls in the oil. Blend in the flour, then add tomatoes, 6 tablespoons parsley, green pepper, 2½ teaspoons salt, ¼ teaspoon pepper, sugar, bay leaves, and Worcestershire sauce. Cover and simmer for 1 hour. Serve hot over drained, boiled spaghetti. Sprinkle with grated Mozzarella cheese. Serves about 6.

# CHARLOTTE'S STUFFED ITALIAN SHELLS

"A crowd pleaser."

1 package jumbo shells
1 pound Italian sausage
48 to 52 ounces spaghetti sauce
2 packages frozen chopped
   spinach, thawed and squeezed
2 eggs, beaten
1 (15 ounce) package Ricotta
   cheese

¾ pound Mozzarella cheese
1 teaspoon onion powder
1 teaspoon salt
1 teaspoon garlic powder
½ teaspoon nutmeg

Cook jumbo shells according to directions on the box; drain. Brown sausage; mix in the spaghetti sauce. Simmer for 10 minutes. Set aside.

Mix spinach, eggs, Ricotta cheese, Mozzarella cheese, onion powder, salt, garlic powder, and nutmeg. Place ½ of sauce mixture in bottom of shallow pan. Stuff jumbo shells with spinach/cheese mixture. Place on top of sauce in pan. Pour remaining sauce over shells. Sprinkle top with Parmesan cheese. Bake in 350°F. oven for 30 to 45 minutes. Serves 10 to 12.

## CREOLE BURGERS

"Children love juicy burgers."

1 pound ground beef
½ cup chopped onion
1 can Campbell's chicken gumbo
 soup

2 tablespoons catsup
2 tablespoons prepared mustard
¼ teaspoon black pepper

Brown ground beef and onion in heavy skillet. Stir to separate meat particles. Stir in soup, catsup, mustard, and black pepper. Simmer for 5 to 10 minutes. Serve on 8 split, toasted buns. Serves 8.

## TRES BON SPAGHETTI

"Company fare."

¼ cup butter
2 tablespoons olive oil
1 cup chopped green onions
4 to 5 cloves garlic, pressed
3 cups peeled, cubed fresh
 tomatoes

2 pounds raw shrimp, shelled
½ pint whipping cream
½ cup Parmesan cheese
1 cup grated Swiss cheese
¼ to ½ cup sherry
¾ pound spaghetti

Saute in butter and olive oil the chopped green onions, pressed garlic, and cubed tomatoes. Add shrimp; cook until shrimp turns pink. Add whipping cream, Parmesan, Swiss cheese, and sherry. Blend well. Add salt and pepper. Cook spaghetti; drain. Mix into shrimp mixture. Serves 6.

## MEAT LOAF

"Plain Jane, but good and hearty."

1 pound ground beef
½ pound ground pork
½ cup cracker crumbs
½ cup onion
½ cup green pepper
Salt and pepper to taste

Dash of thyme
1 (1 pound) can tomatoes (juice
 and all)
13x9x2 inch glass dish
Bacon strips

Mix meats together in bowl. Add cracker crumbs, thyme, tomatoes, and chopped onion and green pepper. Shape meat mixture into loaf and place in dish. Top loaf with bacon strips. Bake in 325°F. oven for 45 minutes to 1 hour on lower shelf. Top with catsup. Bake for additional 15 minutes. Serves 6.

# HAM LOAF

"Church ladies' special."

2 pounds cured ham, ground
2 pounds lean pork, ground
4 eggs, beaten

2 cups milk
2 cups cracker crumbs

Sauce:
½ cup water
½ cup vinegar

1½ cups brown sugar
3 tablespoons dry mustard

Blend together milk and beaten eggs. Add mixture along with crackers to meats and mix well. Shape into a loaf and place in shallow baking pan. Cover with sauce.

Sauce: Mix all ingredients together. Pour over Ham Loaf. Bake in 350°F. oven for 1 hour, basting occasionally with sauce.

# PORK SAUERBRATEN

"Unusual version of German pot roast."

4 to 6 pounds boneless
    pork shoulder blade
    Boston roast, trimmed
    of fat
2 env. onion-mushroom
    dry soup mix
⅓ cup brown sugar
¼ teaspoon ginger
1 large bay leaf
1 cup red wine vinegar
1 cup apple juice
1 cup water
2 tablespoons shortening
⅓ cup golden raisins
¾ cup crushed
    gingersnaps

In a saucepan, combine soup mix, brown sugar, ginger, bay leaf, wine vinegar, apple juice, and water. Bring to a boil and simmer for 10 minutes. Cool.

Place meat in a bowl or plastic bag. Add marinade; turn to coat meat. Cover bowl or tie plastic bag securely. Marinate in refrigerator 18 to 24 hours. Remove meat from marinade to absorbent paper and pat dry. Brown in shortening in Dutch oven. Pour off drippings. Add marinade to meat, cover tightly, and cook slowly for 2½ to 3½ hours or until meat is tender. Remove meat. Keep warm. Remove fat from cooking liquid.

Reserve 3 cups cooking liquid in pan. Add raisins and bring to a boil. Add gingersnap crumbs and cook, stirring constantly, until thickened.

## BUTTERFLIED LEG OF LAMB

"You will win your friends over to lamb with this recipe."

1 (4 pound) lamb leg
  shank half, butterflied
4 tablespoons margarine
Salt
1 large onion, chopped
1 clove garlic, chopped
Dried rosemary, crushed
Dried thyme leaves
Ground black pepper
1 tablespoon olive oil

Melt butter in large skillet. Saute onion, garlic, salt, ¾ teaspoon rosemary, ¾ teaspoon thyme, and ¼ teaspoon pepper until onion is tender. Place lamb flat on work surface; spread onion mixture over lamb. Roll lamb tightly and tie.

Rub lamb with olive oil; rub with ¾ teaspoon rosemary and ¾ teaspoon thyme. Sprinkle with salt and pepper. Place on rack in roasting pan. Roast in 325°F. oven for 2 hours or until thermometer reaches 160°F.

## LINGUINE WITH LAMB

"Surprise way to serve lamb."

2 tablespoons vegetable oil
1 medium onion, chopped
¾ pound ground lean lamb
3 cloves garlic, chopped
¼ teaspoon ground allspice
¼ teaspoon ground cinnamon
1 pound ripe tomatoes, peeled,
  seeded, and chopped or 1 (28
  ounce) can plum tomatoes

Salt
Freshly ground pepper
4 tablespoons tomato paste
1 pound linguine

Heat oil in skillet over medium heat. Add onion; saute for about 5 minutes. Add lamb, garlic, allspice, and cinnamon; saute, stirring often, for about 10 minutes or until meat changes color. Add tomatoes; season to taste with salt and pepper. Cook, covered, for 5 minutes. Stir in tomato paste. Cook, uncovered, for 5 minutes or until sauce is thick.

Cook pasta in salted water over high heat for 8 to 12 minutes. Drain pasta; transfer to heated serving bowl. Add ½ the sauce; toss. Spoon remaining sauce across top of pasta. Serves 4.

## OYSTERS AU GRATIN

"Knote family prize winning favorite."

5 slices buttered bread
½ pound cheese
2 eggs
1 teaspoon salt
1 teaspoon dry mustard
½ teaspoon paprika
½ cup milk
1 pint oysters

Trim crusts from buttered bread and cut each into quarters. Beat eggs. Add seasonings and milk; mix well. Arrange in a greased casserole the bread, oysters, cheese, egg, and milk mixture in alternating layers. Cover with buttered bread. Set casserole in a pan of hot water. Bake in a moderate 375°F. oven for 50 minutes. Serves 6.

## TUNA PUFF SANDWICH

"Ladies appreciate this one."

1 (7 ounce) can tuna, drained and flaked
1½ teaspoons prepared mustard
¼ teaspoon Worcestershire sauce
2 to 3 chopped green onions (tops and all)

2 tablespoons chopped green pepper
3 hamburger buns, split
6 tomato slices
½ cup mayonnaise
¼ cup shredded American cheese

Blend first 6 ingredients. Pile onto bun halves. Top each with a tomato slice. Blend mayonnaise with cheese. Spread over tomato slices. Broil 4 inches from heat until topping browns and puffs. Serves 6.

## HOT HAM AND CHEESE ROLLS

"A toothsome treat."

½ pound ham, cut into ¼ inch cubes
½ pound sharp Cheddar cheese, cut into ¼ inch cubes
⅓ cup sliced green onions

2 hard cooked eggs, sliced
½ cup thinly sliced stuffed olives
3 tablespoons mayonnaise
½ cup chili sauce
12 split frankfurter rolls

Combine ham, cheese, green onions, eggs, and stuffed olives. Blend together mayonnaise and chili sauce. Fold into ham and cheese mixture. Mix well and spread mixture in 12 split frankfurter rolls. Wrap each in aluminum foil, twisting the ends securely. Bake in 400°F. oven for 10 minutes. Serves 12.

May be made up ahead of time and stored in the refrigerator.

## CHEESE STRATA

"Wonderful breakfast treat."

12 slices bread
¼ cup soft butter
2 cups sharp Cheddar cheese, shredded
1½ cups Velveeta, diced
6 eggs, slightly beaten
3½ cups milk
1½ teaspoons salt
1 teaspoon dry mustard

Trim crust from bread; butter and quarter each slice. Alternate layers of bread and cheese in baking dish, ending with cheese on top. Mix remaining ingredients and pour over layers. Cover and chill overnight.

Bake at 325°F. for 1 hour or until firm. Let stand a few minutes and cut into squares. One cup ham may be added to the alternating layers of cheese and bread. Serves 8 to 10.

## BEEF AND VENISON JERKY

"This recipe helps reduce potential fat rancidity."

Use flank steak, if possible, because you will like its longer meat fibers. Use venison with long fibers.

3 pounds venison or beef
1 tablespoon brown sugar
1½ to 3 tablespoons
  canning salt (non-
  iodized)
1 teaspoon onion powder
1 teaspoon garlic powder
1½ teaspoons ground
  rosemary
1 teaspoon ground black
  pepper
¾ cup Worcestershire
  sauce
½ cup water
Tabasco sauce, to taste

Trim all visible fat deposits and any membranes from the meat. Freeze the meat for easier slicing. Cut meat <u>with the grain</u> into ³/16 to ¼ inch thick slices.

In a plastic or stainless steel container, mix all seasonings together. Add meat strips and thoroughly coat. Refrigerate for 8 to 12 hours or overnight. Remove strips and pat dry with paper towel. Place meat strips on an oiled smoker rack to <u>air dry</u> for 2 hours to help form a glaze or pellicle.

Dry smoke-cook at 200°F. to 225°F. for 1½ to 3 hours until the meat is dried out. If you use a water smoker, do not put water in the water pan, because this prevents drying. Your smoker will run hotter without the water. Therefore, you will reduce its temperature by opening its door and setting its dome or lid to one side, if needed. Test and check the meat regularly after ½ hour so that it will not be overcooked and become blackened.

Store your smoked jerky in the refrigerator.

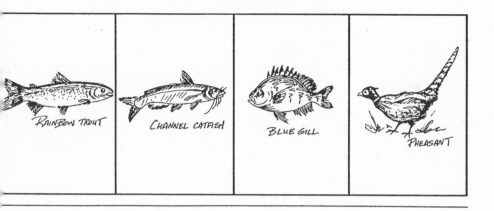

RAINBOW TROUT    CHANNEL CATFISH    BLUE GILL    PHEASANT

# MAIN EVENTS — WILD GAME

## "ROAD KILL"

"It's exciting conversation by macho males told solely for the benefit for squeamish ladies. Road kill needs 4 major steps: (1) collecting, (2) preparing, (3) cooking, and (4) eating — our recommendation for all 4 steps — DON'T BOTHER.

## GAME BIRDS

(1) Game birds contain very little fat. Young birds' claws are sharp. A young pheasant has a pliable spur. Quail breasts can be grilled successfully wrapped in bacon. Young birds can be grilled or broiled using Knote's Chicken Marinade (see index). Split the bird, marinate and baste while grilling. Begin grilling with bone side down over medium fire.

(2) Old birds' claws are blunt from use. Older birds must be moist cooked in a sauce to be tender. If you don't know the age of the bird, moist cook them in wine.

(3) If a bird's intestines have been penetrated by shot, wash with water and soak in vinegar for 5 minutes.

(4) Allow ¾ to 1 pound of dressed bird for each serving.

## SMALL GAME

RABBITS & SQUIRRELS: Grill or cook like chicken (see index) if young. If older, saute with moist heat. Cook until tender in a sauce.

# VENISON, ELK, MOOSE

IF VERY YOUNG: Remove fat to reduce gamy taste. Grill tender cuts like grilling beef — tenderloin, loin chops. Remove the silver sheath or white muscle fiber. If you attempt to grill leg steaks, marinate them in a mixture of 1/3 vinegar-1/3 water-1/3 red wine, salt and pepper, chopped onion, garlic, and bay leaves for 3 days. Dry them. Baste steaks with canola or other vegetable oil before and during grilling. Season steaks with lemon pepper. Grill over medium hot fire. Cook to rare or medium rare.

ROASTS, ETC. FROM VERY YOUNG GAME: Marinate for 2 to 3 days in tenderizing marinade (see index) and smoke-cook holding the temperature at 160°F. for extended cooking time. Moist cook or make sausage or ground meat dishes from other cuts of venison, elk, or moose (see index).

IF OLDER ANIMAL WHERE AGE CANNOT BE DETERMINED, REMOVE FAT TO REDUCE GAMY TASTE. Remove accessible silver sheaths or white muscle fiber. Moist cook to 160°F., adding potatoes, celery, onion, garlic, soy sauce, and vinegar. After cooking, the potatoes and the celery are disposed of. Roasts are then smoke-cooked. Grind thinner cuts of game and make into sausage or use in ground meat dishes (see index: Venison-Elk Sausage) See Deer-Elk Sausage below.

# DEER-ELK METTWURST SUMMER SAUSAGE

"Even ladies like this deer sausage with its moistness, texture and mild flavors."

2½ pounds deer or elk, trimmed of surface fat and seam fat if you want to reduce the gamey flavor
1½ pounds pork shoulder or Boston butt (not trimmed of fat)
1 tablespoon non-iodized salt (canning salt)
1½ tablespoons ground pepper
1 tablespoon and 1 teaspoon Morton's Tender-Quick (found in farm stores, sausage mail-order catalogs)

1 teaspoon sugar
3 teaspoons garlic powder
½ teaspoon MSG
¼ teaspoon cayenne pepper (or to taste)
5 ounces cold water
¼ teaspoon garlic powder
1 teaspoon coarse black pepper

Mix the spices with the water, then mix this with the 4 pounds of ground meats thoroughly. Grind again over a hamburger plate (1/8 inch holes) for a finer textured sausage. Makes 3 sausages.

Smoked Sausage without casing: see page 105.

Smoked Sausage with casing: See pages 97-98, then see Stuffing and Smoking.

# SMOKING DEER AND ELK

Use roasts 2 inches thick or more. Trim all surface fats. Use general purpose wild game marinade. Marinate for 24 to 72 hours. Smoke-cook tender cuts only. Use Brisket Smoking directions unless the animals are very young. For a young animal, sprinkle a rub over the meat and rub in. Marinate in refrigerator for 48 to 72 hours. Dry meat on refrigerator rack for 2 hours. Rub with canola or other vegetable oil. Smoke-cook to 160°F. Check for tenderness with a fork. If tough, wrap in aluminum foil; add 2 to 3 tablespoons of the vinegar based salad dressing. Bake in the oven for 1 hour at 250°F. Carve deer and elk cross grain in ⅛ inch slices or thinner for maximum tenderness.

# WILD RABBIT (HASENPFEFFER)

"Delicious way to cook wild rabbit."

| | |
|---|---|
| ¼ cup oil | 4 cups water |
| ½ cup salt | 1 tablespoon molasses |
| 1 teaspoon pepper | 1 stalk celery, cut up |
| 1 medium onion, chopped | Seasoned flour |
| 2 tablespoons flour | 1 wild rabbit, hair and shot holes |
| 1 to 2 bay leaves | removed; cut up. |
| 2 tablespoons vinegar | |

Soak the wild rabbit in salt water for 1 hour. Remove, dry, coat with seasoned flour. Add oil to a large heavy skillet; brown rabbit, remove from skillet. Saute onion in remaining oil until golden. Add flour, stir for a few minutes. Add bay leaf, vinegar, celery and water, stir until the mixture begins to thicken. Return rabbit to pan. Cover; bake on medium grill or in a 350°F. oven for 1 hour or until tender. Serves 4.

# GROUND VENISON STROGANOFF

"Elegant enough to serve for a wild game dinner, can be doubled."

| | |
|---|---|
| 2 pounds find ground venison (defat before grinding) | 6 tablespoons lemon juice |
| ½ cup canola oil, margarine or butter | 6 tablespoons sherry |
| ½ cup chopped onions | 2 (10½ ounces) cans beef consomme |
| 1 teaspoon granular garlic (powdered) | 2 teaspoons salt |
| 1 pound mushrooms, sliced, or 4 (3-ounce) cans sliced | 1 teaspoon pepper |
| | ½ pound uncooked fine noodles |
| | 2 cups low cal sour cream |
| | Parsley flakes (optional) |

Place oil or margarine in pan; saute venison, onion, garlic, and mushrooms until browned. Add lemon juice, sherry, consomme, salt, and pepper. Simmer together for 15 minutes; add noodles, cook until tender. Add sour cream and dried parsley flakes just before serving; blend together. Serves 8 to 10.

## BAKED PHEASANT IN WINE

"Easy but a special treatment that pheasant deserves."

2 whole pheasants, dressed
1 (10¾-ounce) can chicken soup
½ cup dry vermouth or white wine
1½ teaspoons basil
½ teaspoon thyme
½ teaspoon pepper

Salt to taste
Paprika
4 small potatoes, halved
4 small whole onions or 1 large
  onion, quartered
2 carrots cut up

Clean pheasant of hair and pin feathers and wash. Set aside. Mix next five ingredients together in a large casserole. Place pheasants breast side up in liquid and baste thoroughly. Sprinkle with paprika, cover. Bake at 350°F. for one hour. Then add vegetables. Bake at 350°F. for the second hour. Remove pheasants; make a wine sauce. Serve sauce over carved pheasants and vegetables. Serves 4.

## BAKED WILD DUCK IN SHERRY

"This gives wild duck a tasty flavor."

2 wild ducks, quartered
Seasoned flour
3 tablespoons melted margarine
1 medium onion, chopped and
  sauteed in 1 tablespoon
  margarine

1 (10½-ounce) can beef consomme
½ cup dry sherry
1½ teaspoons thyme
2 teaspoons marjoram
½ cup red wine
4 to 5 stalks celery and leaves

Coat ducks thoroughly in seasoned flour. Brown completely in margarine in a large casserole.Mix sherry, consomme, sauteed onions and herbs and pour over ducks. Place celery leaves and stalks over ducks. Cover casserole and bake at 450°F. for 15 minutes. Reduce temperature to 300°F. Bake until tender, about 2½ hours. Pour red wine over ducks after cooking for 1½ hours. Discard celery when done. Serve ducks and sauce with rice. Serves 4.

## BRINED SMOKED WILD GOOSE

"Old-fashioned way to brine game."

1 (4½ to 5½ pound)
  Canadian goose
1 gallon water
1 cup salt

¼ cup sugar
Hugh's Cajun Rub

Dissolve salt and sugar in water. Brine goose for 3 to 4 hours. Remove. Flush with water. Dry in refrigerator or with an electric fan. Sprinkle rub in tail and neck cavities generously. Marinate for 2 hours at room temperature or up to 24 hours refrigerated.

Smoke-cook in a water smoker at 220°F.-250°F. Cook until done at 165°F. in the skin pocket between the thigh and the breast, about 2½ to 4 hours.

# SMOKING WILD GEESE

"This is easy to do and reduce fat."

Season heavily with Zap II Rub. Place in plastic bag to marinate for 2 hours at room temperature or up to 72 hours in the refrigerator.

Follow Basic Master Smoking steps. Smoke-cook the wild goose for 2½ to 4 hours, depending on size. Geese are "done" at 165°F. Check temperature by inserting meat thermometer into the thickest breast meat. Check for tenderness with a fork. If tough, wrap in aluminum foil and add 2 to 3 tablespoons of the vinegar based salad dressing. Bake in the oven for 1 hour at 325°F.

# SMOKED PHEASANT

"Great flavor; baste to keep it moist."

2 pheasants
Rub (Zip II or Hugh's
    Cajun Rub)

Pheasant has little fat and will be dry. Baste the complete bird lightly with vegetable oil, then apply rub generously in the cavity and over the skin. Marinate for 2 hours at room temperature or up to 24 hours in a refrigerator. After 45 minutes, baste with melted butter. Smoke-cook to 165°F. maximum!

# QUAIL IN VERMOUTH

"Women like quail fixed this way."

6 quail, free of pin
    feathers and hair
Seasoned flour
4 ounces (1 stick)
    margarine, melted
¾ cup chopped onions
¾ cup chopped celery
⅛ teaspoon granular
    garlic or powder
½ cup hot water
1½ cups dry vermouth or
    white wine

Coat birds thoroughly with seasoned flour. Saute birds in margarine in a large metal casserole over medium high grill fire or stove until browned all over. Add onions, celery and garlic along with the bird so they brown somewhat. Cook vegetables until limp; then add hot water. Cover and simmer for 30 minutes; then add 1 cup of wine and cook for 30 additional minutes, covered. Uncover, cook for 15 minutes or until tender. Add more wine to make a thin sauce, adjust seasoning. Serve over wild rice. Serves 3 to 4.

## EASY GRILLED FISH FILETS

"New BBQ tool solves fish grilling problems."

Fish filets (¼ to ½ inch thick)
1 quart cold water
1 tablespoon salt
1 teaspoon baking soda
Cornstarch
Paprika without lumps
Sugar
Canola oil
Lemon pepper
Grill Topper™

To freshen frozen fish, soak thawed frozen fish filets or steaks in cold water, salt, and soda for 30 minutes. Wash with water to remove salt; drain and dry with paper towels.

Brush lightly with oil. Mix paprika, cornstarch, and a little sugar. Coat fillet, shake off excess powder. Sprinkle generously with lemon-pepper. Heat Grill Topper over medium hot fire for 2 to 4 minutes. Brush with cold vegetable oil. Grill fillets for 1 to 2 minutes. Use a pancake turner to loosen; grill to browning stage. Turn fillets and grill for 1 to 2 mintues until opaque or flaky. Serve browned side up. Total grilling time: 4 to 6 minutes. They overcook easily.

## GENERAL PURPOSE MARINADE FOR GAME

"Tames gamy flavor."

2 large onions, sliced
1 large carrot, sliced
3 whole cloves
4 to 5 whole peppercorns, cracked
1 bay leaf
2 sprigs parsley

6 juniper berries
⅓ cup brown sugar
2 cups red wine
¼ cup olive oil
¼ cup vinegar

Combine all ingredients in a non-metal container. Marinate for 2 to 3 days in a refrigerator, turning occasionally, Yields about 3 cups.

# Eat-Along Vegetables & Soups

Mexican Potatoes to
Ruth's Special Baked Beans

## ASPARAGUS CASSEROLE

"Elegant, but simple."

1 can or 1 bunch fresh asparagus
2 hard cooked eggs
½ stick butter
½ cup milk

½ cup asparagus liquid
20 salty Ritz crackers
¼ pound grated cheese

Make alternating layers of asparagus, eggs, and salty crackers in buttered casserole, dotting each layer with butter. Pour liquid and milk on top. Cover with grated cheese. Bake in 350°F. oven for 20 to 30 minutes. Serves 6.

## RUTH'S SPECIAL BAKED BEANS

"Special beans for political picnics."

2 cans pork and beans
1 green pepper, chopped
1 medium onion
Dry mustard
Worcestershire sauce
6 to 8 slices bacon,
  chopped
Maple syrup or maple
  syrup flavoring

Place ½ of chopped bacon in bottom of casserole. Pour ⅔ can of pork and beans into casserole. Add ⅓ of green pepper and onion. Sprinkle with dry mustard and Worcestershire. Continue layers of beans and seasonings. Top with remaining bacon and pour maple syrup over all. Bake at 350°F. for 1 hour. Serves 8.

## SPECIAL BAKED BEANS

"Good one dish meal."

| | |
|---|---|
| 1 teaspoon margarine | 1 tablespoon brown sugar |
| 1 clove garlic | 2 teaspoons Worcestershire sauce |
| 1 medium onion, chopped | 1 dash of hot sauce |
| ½ pound ground beef | 2 (1 pound) cans pork and beans |
| 3 tablespoons catsup | Salt and pepper to taste |
| 1 teaspoon dry mustard | 2 strips bacon |

Saute garlic and onion in margarine for a few minutes. Add ground beef and cook until browned. Add remaining ingredients and pour into a 3 quart baking dish. Place bacon on top. Bake at 450°F. for 25 to 30 minutes. Serves 8.

## CALICO BEANS

"Great picnic dish."

| | |
|---|---|
| 1 can pork and beans | 2 cloves garlic |
| 1 can kidney beans | ½ cup brown sugar |
| 1 can butter beans | ½ cup catsup |
| 1 can green beans | ⅓ teaspoon salt |
| 1 pound ground beef | Dash of Tabasco sauce |
| 1 medium onion, chopped | 2 teaspoons Worcestershire sauce |
| 1 teaspoon margarine | ½ pound bacon, chopped |

Partially drain beans. Brown bacon; set aside. Pour off grease. Saute onion and garlic in margarine until soft; brown ground beef. Combine beans with meat mixture and put in baking dish. Combine sugar, catsup, salt, Worcestershire sauce, and Tabasco sauce. Pour over bean mixture. Add more liquid if it looks too dry. Top with bacon. Bake in 350°F. oven for 1 hour. Serves 8 to 10.

## BARBECUED GREEN BEANS

"Try these on your next cook-out."

| | |
|---|---|
| 4 slices bacon, finely cut | 1 tablespoon Worcestershire sauce |
| ¼ cup onion, chopped | 2 cans French style green beans, |
| ½ cup catsup | drained |
| ¼ cup brown sugar | |

Brown bacon and onion. Add catsup, brown sugar, and Worcestershire sauce. Simmer for 2 minutes. Put beans in casserole bowl. Pour bacon mixture over beans, but do not stir! Bake at 350°F. for 20 minutes. Serves 6.

# SWISS GREEN BEANS

"Family favorite from Judy."

| | |
|---|---|
| 3 cans French green beans | 1 teaspoon salt |
| 2 tablespoons butter | Pepper |
| 2 tablespoons flour | 1 teaspoon sugar |
| 1 cup sour cream | Paprika |
| ½ onion, grated | Swiss cheese |

Blend butter, flour, and sour cream. Add salt, sugar, and onion. Mix in ungreased casserole with beans. Cover with cheese slices and sprinkle with paprika. Bake until cheese bubbles at 375°F. for 15 to 20 minutes. Serves 8 to 10.

# BROCCOLI

"Broccoli dressed up."

| | |
|---|---|
| 2 packages frozen broccoli | 1 can stewed tomatoes |
| 2 to 3 eggs | 1 can Cheddar cheese soup |

Cook broccoli. Add well beaten eggs and stewed tomatoes. Top with Cheddar cheese soup. Season with oregano and chives. Bake at 350°F. for 20 to 30 minutes. Serves 6.

# BAKED CARROTS

"Simple, but delicious."

| | |
|---|---|
| 3 cups sliced carrots | Boil carrots in salt water. Drain and place in |
| ½ cup chopped onion | 1 quart baking dish. Saute onion and green |
| ½ cup chopped green | pepper in butter, then brown bread crumbs in |
| pepper | butter. Sprinkle onion, green pepper, and |
| ¼ cup butter | bread crumbs over carrots. Pour cream over |
| 1 cup dry bread crumbs | carrots. Bake in 350°F. oven for 20 to 25 min- |
| ¼ to ½ cup half & half | utes. Serves 6. |

# MARY'S CORN SOUFFLE

"A tasty corn dish that goes along with cook-outs. Great for indoors, too."

| | |
|---|---|
| 1 (16 ounce) can whole kernel corn, drained | 1 (8 ounce) carton sour cream |
| | 2 beaten eggs |
| 1 (16 ounce) can cream style corn | 1 green pepper, chopped |
| 1 (8½ ounce) package corn muffin mix | 4 or 5 green onions, chopped |
| | 2 tablespoons margarine |
| ½ cup corn oil | |

Saute pepper and onions in butter. Set aside. Mix corn, corn oil, sour cream, and beaten eggs. Add corn muffin mix and sauteed vegetables. Stir only enough to mix thoroughly. Pour into greased baking dish and bake at 350°F. for 45 minutes. Serves 8.

Can be baked on a covered grill with medium low heat.

## BAKED SHOESTRING POTATOES

"A change for your menu."

Aluminum foil
4 medium baking potatoes, pared
3 tablespoons butter or margarine
1½ teaspoons salt

Dash of pepper
½ cup grated American cheese
2 tablespoons chopped parsley
½ cup light or heavy cream

Cut 48 inch length of foil and fold in half. Cut potatoes in thin lengthwise strips as for French fries and place just off center on foil. Dot with butter; sprinkle with salt, pepper, cheese, and parsley. Pull edges of foil upward, then pour cream over potatoes. Fold foil securely. Place on shallow pan and bake in very hot oven (450°F.) for 1 hour or until done. Fold back foil and sprinkle more chopped parsley on top.

May be adapted for baking on a gas or charcoal grill using a medium high heat.

## MASHED POTATOES

"A must with fried chicken."

5 medium potatoes
1 tablespoon butter
1 teaspoon salt
½ to 1 cup warm milk

Peel and cut potatoes in eighths. Place in medium pan. Cover with water. Bring to a boil; turn heat to simmer. Cook until potatoes are tender; drain. Pour potatoes in mixing bowl of electric mixer. Add butter and salt. While whipping potatoes, add ½ to 1 cup warm milk. Whip until light and fluffy.

Place in ovenproof dish. Add 1½ tablespoon size pat of butter on top. Place under broiler until potatoes are browned. Serves 4 to 6.

## POTATO CASSEROLE

"A husband and children pleaser."

1 (2 pound) bag frozen hash brown
   potatoes
1 can cream of chicken soup
1 pint sour cream
1 (10 ounce) package sharp
   Cheddar cheese, grated

¼ cup chopped onion
¼ teaspoon pepper
1 teaspoon salt

Mix all ingredients together and pour into 9x15 inch casserole dish. Melt ½ cup butter or margarine; drizzle over top. Sprinkle 2 cups crushed corn flakes over top. Bake at 350°F. for 45 minutes. Serves 12.

# MEXICAN POTATOES

"Tasty treat; great with BBQ."

4 to 5 medium potatoes
¼ cup finely chopped onions
½ cup half & half
¼ cup chopped pimentos
¼ cup chopped green peppers

1 cup mayonnaise
1 teaspoon salt
½ teaspoon black pepper
½ cup grated American cheese

Topping:
½ to ¾ cup grated American
    cheese

½ cup chopped green and black
    olives

Boil potatoes; peel, cool, and slice medium thick. Combine onions, pimentos, green peppers, half & half, mayonnaise, salt, pepper, and cheese. Pour over potatoes; mix thoroughly. Butter bottom and sides of a shallow 9x13 inch baking dish. Place potato mixture in dish.

Sprinkle top with cheese and olives. Bake in 375°F. oven for 20 to 25 minutes. Serves 6.

# SCALLOPED POTATOES

"A new twist for an old favorite."

4 baking potatoes, peeled and
    sliced thin
Salt and pepper
Sage

Swiss cheese, grated
½ cup white wine
1 cup heavy cream
Gruyere cheese, grated

Layer potatoes and Swiss cheese in a shallow baking dish. Sprinkle each layer with salt, pepper, and sage. Mix together the wine and cream; pour over the potatoes. Top with more Swiss and Gruyere cheese. Bake in 400°F. oven for 1 hour. Serves 6.

# SPINACH SOUFFLE

"Spinach at its best."

2 boxes frozen chopped spinach
2 pounds small curd cottage
    cheese
6 tablespoons flour

6 eggs, beaten
½ to 1 stick margarine
½ pound Velveeta cheese

Cook spinach and drain. Mix all together. Pour into 9x13 inch greased pan. Bake for 1 hour in 350°F. oven. Let stand for 5 minutes before serving. Serves 8.

## SPINACH AND ARTICHOKES

"Sophisticated spinach."

4 (10 ounce) packages
frozen chopped spinach
11 ounces cream cheese
(one 3 ounce and one 8
ounce)
5 tablespoons melted
butter
Juice of 1 lemon
Salt and pepper
Several dashes ground
nutmeg (preferable
fresh)
2 large cans artichoke
hearts, well drained

Cook spinach until just thawed and heated through. Drain and dry as much as possible. Have cheese at room temperature and blend it with the melted butter and lemon juice. Add seasonings and spinach; blend well and adjust to taste.

Cut artichokes in halves and drain again. Place them, cut side up, in a buttered casserole (large). Cover with spinach mixture. Cover with foil. Punch holes in the foil and bake at 350°F. for 30 minutes.

This dish travels well. When making this ahead, the dish should be removed from the refrigerator 1 hour before baking. Serves 12.

## SPINACH QUICHE LORRAINE

"Ladies' Luncheon Star."

1 cup shredded Swiss cheese
¼ cup thinly sliced onion
½ pound fresh mushrooms
1 package frozen chopped
spinach, thawed and queezed

4 eggs, slightly beaten
2 c. half & half
¾ teaspoon salt
¼ teaspoon pepper
Dash of nutmeg

Partially bake 10 inch pie crust (10 minutes in 400°F. oven). Saute onion and mushrooms in 1 tablespoon butter. Place cheese, onions, mushrooms, and spinach in pie shell.

Mix egg and milk with salt, pepper, and nutmeg. Pour on top of cheese mixture in pie crust. Bake in 400°F. oven for 10 minutes. Turn down temperature to 350°F.; continue baking for 40 minutes.

# SQUASH CASSEROLE

"Ruthie Jr.'s treat."

1½ pounds squash
1 large onion, chopped
1 (2 ounce) jar pimentos, drained
1 can cream of chicken soup
1 (8 ounce) carton sour cream
2 cups buttery-flavor crisp crackers, crushed
½ cup margarine, melted
Salt and pepper to taste

Cook squash and half the chopped onion in small amount of salted water; drain. Dot with margarine; let it melt. Stir in pimentos, soup, and remaining onion. Season with salt and pepper. Stir in sour cream. Pour into buttered 1½ quart casserole. Mix melted margarine and cracker crumbs. Place on top of casserole. Bake at 350°F. until hot and bubbly, 25 to 30 minutes. Serves 6.

One-half cup slivered almonds may be added to squash.

# BROILED TOMATOES

"Summer time delight."

6 ripe medium tomatoes
Melted butter
Sugar
Dry basil

Cut ½ inch slice from top of tomato. Make crisscross cut through top of tomato. Pour melted butter over the top of the tomatoes. Sprinkle with sugar and basil. Bake in 350°F. oven for 15 to 20 minutes. Sprinkle Parmesan cheese on top. Return to oven. Broil until cheese melts.

# ZUCCHINI RIPIENI

"Impressive presentation of zucchini."

6 large zucchini
½ pound bulk pork sausage
1 small onion, minced
½ cup fine dry bread crumbs
¼ cup catsup

1 egg, slightly beaten
¼ teaspoon salt
¼ teaspoon thyme
⅓ cup grated Parmesan cheese

Cook whole, unpeeled zucchini in boiling water for 10 minutes or until barely tender; drain. Cut in halves lengthwise and scoop out centers, leaving walls ¼ inch thick. Chop centers.

Fry sausage and onion until done. Pour off fat. Add chopped zucchini, crumbs, catsup, salt, thyme, and egg. Place mixture in shells. Place in a flat baking dish. Sprinkle with cheese. Bake in 350°F. oven for 20 minutes. Serves 6 to 8.

# NOODLE PUDDING

"Unusual; very tasty with chicken."

| | |
|---|---|
| 1 pound noodles, cooked until soft | Handful of raisins |
| 4 eggs | Butter |
| 4 tablespoons sugar | Cinnamon |
| 1 teaspoon vanilla | Sugar |
| ½ pint sour cream | Apples |
| 1½ cups milk | |

Put cooked noodles in strainer; pour cold water over. When drained, add remaining ingredients. Turn into greased casserole, tablespoon of butter here and there. Top with cinnamon and sugar. Bake for 1 hour or more at medium oven temperature until nice and brown. Can add thin sliced apple to this. Delicious as side dish with chicken or roast beef. Serves 8.

# RICE PILAF

"Tasty accompaniment for meat."

| | |
|---|---|
| 1 cup margarine | ½ cup chopped parsley |
| 2½ cups raw rice | 2 cans chicken broth, heated |
| 1 cup chopped onion | ½ teaspoon thyme |
| 1 cup chopped celery | 1 teaspoon salt |
| ½ pound mushrooms | Dash of pepper |

Melt butter in 6 quart Dutch oven. Add rice; stir just to coat rice with margarine. Add onion, celery, and mushrooms, stirring for 5 minutes. Heat broth, thyme, salt, and pepper to boiling. Stir into rice. Reduce heat and simmer, covered, for 30 minutes or until rice is tender. Toss with parsley. Serves 12.

# SYRIAN RICE

"Exotic Mid Eastern flavor."

| | |
|---|---|
| 2 cups dried apricots | Boil apricots and raisins until tender in water. |
| 1 cup white raisins | Add to rice; use broth if rice seems dry. In skil- |
| 2 cups cooked rice | let, melt butter and saute onion, green pepper, |
| ½ cup butter | and curry. Add almonds to the cooked rice |
| 1 cup minced onion | mixture. Correct seasoning and place in |
| ½ green pepper | greased 1 quart baking dish. Bake for 30 min- |
| ½ teaspoon curry | utes at 375°F. Serves 6. |
| 1 cup toasted almonds | |

# CHEESE GRITS PUDDING

"Great with BBQ."

| | |
|---|---|
| 1 cup grits | 6 ounces Velveeta cheese |
| 2 whipped eggs and enough milk to measure 1 cup | 2 to 3 cloves garlic, crushed |
| | 1 stick butter |

Cook grits according to package directions. Melt cheese and butter into hot grits. Add egg and milk mixture and garlic to grits. Pour into 8x9 inch pan. Bake in 325°F. oven for 45 minutes. Serves 6.

# BROCCOLI SOUP

"Good for ladies luncheon."

2 tablespoons chopped onion
2 tablespoons melted butter
3 tablespoons flour
½ teaspoon salt
¼ teaspoon pepper
2 cups milk
1 cup grated American cheese
2 cubes chicken bouillon
1 cup water
1 bunch chopped broccoli*

Saute onion in butter. When onion is transparent, blend in flour, salt, and pepper. Stir and cook for a minute. Add milk. Cook and stir mixture until it begins to thicken. Stir in grated cheese. Cook and stir until it thickens. Remove from heat and set aside.

In another pan, dissolve bouillon in boiling water. Add chopped broccoli. Cover pan and cook until tender. Add broccoli and cooking liquid to cheese mixture. Heat to serving temperature. Yields 5 cups.

* Sometimes I substitute fresh cauliflower and carrots for half of the broccoli. I usually double this recipe.

## CRAB-SHRIMP GUMBO

"Elegant whole meal soup."

6 tablespoons bacon grease
6 tablespoons flour
2 to 3 cloves garlic
1 cup chopped onion
1 cup chopped celery
1 cup chopped green pepper
2 (8 ounce) cans tomato sauce
1 pound okra, sliced (2 packages
   10 ounce frozen)

7 cups water
Salt and pepper
½ to 1 teaspoon cayenne
1 bay leaf
1 pound shrimp (fresh), shelled
1 pound crab meat

In skillet, melt bacon grease. Add flour; cook and stir until the roux turns a dark brown. Add onion, celery, and green pepper. Cook until vegetables are limp. Add tomato sauce, okra, and water. Season with salt, pepper, and cayenne. Simmer for 1 to 2 hours. Add shrimp and crab. Cook only until shrimp turn pink. Serve over rice. Chopped green onions and fresh parsley may be served on top.

File powder may be placed on the table for individuals to add to their own serving (¼ to ½ teaspoon).


## CREAM OF TOMATO SOUP

"Wonderful way to use tomatoes fresh from your garden."

2 cups chopped fresh tomatoes
½ cup chopped celery and leaves
¼ cup chopped carrot
¼ cup chopped onion
1 teaspoon sugar
4 fresh basil leaves
1 sprig fresh parsley
1 sprig fresh marjoram
1 bay leaf

3 tablespoons butter, divided
½ cup chicken stock
2 tablespoons flour
2 cups half & half cream
¼ teaspoon paprika
2 tablespoons chicken bouillon
¼ teaspoon white pepper
¼ cup sour cream
Diced ripe tomato and parsley

Cook first 9 ingredients in 1 tablespoon butter, covered, till vegetables are soft. Discard herbs. Force through food mill with chicken stock.

Make a roux with butter and flour. Stirring gradually, add half & half. Stir constantly till smooth and slightly thickened. Add vegetable puree chicken stock, paprika, and pepper, stirring occasionally. Simmer for 20 minutes. Blend in sour cream; heat while blending. Do not boil. (It will curdle.) Garnish with chopped tomato and parsley.

# SHRIMP AND SPINACH SOUP

"Elegant first course."

6 cups homemade chicken broth
¼ cup finely chopped onion
2 tablespoons dry sherry
1 teaspoon grated fresh ginger
    root

½ teaspoon salt
½ cup small shell macaroni
½ pound cleaned and shelled fresh
    shrimp (raw)
4 cups fresh spinach leaves

In large saucepan, combine chicken broth, chopped onion, sherry, ginger root, and salt. Bring to a boil. Add shell macaroni and boil for 5 to 6 minutes. Add shrimp; boil for 2 minutes or until shrimp turns pink. Add spinach leaves. Serves 6 to 8.

# RUTHIE'S CHILI

"It's different and tasty."

2 pounds coarse ground or
    chopped lean beef
2½ pounds coarse ground or
    chopped lean pork, fat removed
    before grinding or chopping
4 cups chicken broth or 4 cups
    water with 4 teaspoons chicken
    bouillon granules, dissolved
7 cloves garlic, chopped
1½ cups chopped onion
1 (31 ounce) can tomatoes in
    tomato puree or tomato juice
1 (6 ounce) can tomato paste

1 (12 ounce) beer or 12 ounces
    water
1 large chopped green pepper
¾ cup chopped celery
2 (4 ounce) cans green chilies
1½ teaspoons oregano
1½ teaspoons cumin
1½ teaspoons black pepper
3½ tablespoons chili pepper
½ teaspoon thyme
2 teaspoons sugar
2 (16 ounce) cans red beans

Brown meats in 2 tablespoons vegetable oil (brown ⅓ at a time). Drain on paper towels. Add meats to chicken broth in an 8 quart kettle. Saute garlic and onion until limp in remaining meat drippings, then add to the meat and broth mixture. Add remaining ingredients and simmer for 2 to 3 hours. Chill in refrigerator for 24 hours to blend flavors.

Remove any solid surface fat before reheating for a "lite" low cholesterol, low cal chili. Place the pasta, cheese, or onions in bowls on the table. Each person "seasons" the chili to taste.

# Tasty Breads, Rolls, Biscuits

Grandma's Potato Hot Rolls to
Jalapeno Corn Bread

## SWEET CARAMEL ROLLS

Grandma's Roll Dough
2 teaspoons cinnamon
1 cup sugar
20 tablespoons margarine
  or butter
1⅓ cups brown sugar
1½ cups Karo syrup
1 cup pecan halves
1 cup raisins
1 (13x9 inch) cake pan
Raisins

Take 1 batch of Grandma's Roll Dough after second rise and roll to ¼ inch thickness. Melt 8 tablespoons of margarine; spread on dough. Mix cinnamon with sugar; sprinkle over dough. Also sprinkle pecan halves and raisins over dough. Roll into jelly roll and cut into 1½ inch discs.

In bottom of cake pan, place margarine, brown sugar, and Karo syrup. Place the sweet rolls in the pan (it usually takes two 13x9 inch pans). Let the dough rise for 50 minutes, then bake for 30 minutes in a 350°F. oven. Invert rolls onto a cookie sheet after baking and serve.

Can make the roll dough and uncooked sweet rolls the night before and refrigerate overnight. The following morning, let the rolls rise the final time and bake. Makes 1½ dozen rolls.

## RING-A-LINGS

"Christmas morning breakfast treat."

2 packages dry yeast
¼ cup lukewarm water
⅓ cup margarine
¾ cup hot scalded milk
⅓ cup sugar
2 teaspoons salt
2 teaspoons grated
  orange rind
2 unbeaten eggs
4 to 4½ cups flour

Nut Filling:
⅓ cup margarine
1 cup sifted powdered
  sugar
1 cup pecans, ground or
  chopped very fine

Glaze:
¼ cup orange juice
3 tablespoons sugar

Soften the dry yeast in the lukewarm water; set aside. Combine milk and margarine in saucepan. Heat until margarine melts. Cool to lukewarm. Add sugar, salt, and orange rind, then add eggs and yeast mixture. Gradually add flour to form a stiff dough. Cover and let stand for 30 minutes.

In the meantime, cream the margarine and add the powdered sugar. Mix thoroughly. Stir in the pecans. After the dough has risen 30 minutes, roll it into a 22x12 inch rectangle on a floured board. Spread filling over half the dough along the 22 inch side. Fold uncovered dough over filling. Cut into 1 inch strips (crosswise). (Should be 22 strips.) Twist each strip 4 to 5 times. Hold 1 end down on greased baking sheet for center of roll; curl strip around center, tucking other end under. Cover with wax paper or towel. Let rise in warm place (85°F. to 90°F.) until light and doubled in size, 45 to 60 minutes.

Bake in moderate oven (375°F.) for 15 minutes, until light golden brown. Meanwhile, combine orange juice and sugar for glaze. Brush tops of rolls and bake for 5 minutes longer, until deep golden brown. Remove from pan immediately.

## BLUEBERRY BUCKLE

"Lizbe's favorite."

1¼ cups sugar
¼ cup soft shortening
  (Crisco)
1 egg
½ cup milk
2½ cups flour
2 teaspoons baking
  powder
½ teaspoon salt
2 cups well drained
  blueberries
½ teaspoon cinnamon
¼ cup soft butter

Mix ¾ cup sugar, the shortening, and egg together thoroughly with mixer. Stir in the milk. Sift together 2 cups flour, the baking powder, and salt. Add to batter and stir in well.

Sprinkle some flour over the blueberries to coat them. Stir in blueberries with a spoon. Spread batter into a greased and floured 9 inch square pan. Mix together ⅓ cup flour, ½ cup sugar, the cinnamon, and the butter. Sprinkle on top of the batter. Bake in 375°F. oven for 45 to 50 minutes, until wooden toothpick thrust into center of cake comes out clean. Serve warm, fresh from the oven.

## SOUR CREAM COFFEE CAKE

1 cup sugar
1 stick oleo
1 teaspoon vanilla
2 eggs
2 cups flour
1 teaspoon baking powder

1 teaspoon soda
1 cup sour cream
1 cup brown sugar
½ cup chopped nuts
1 teaspoon cinnamon
1 teaspoon vanilla

Cream together first 3 ingredients. Add eggs. Sift flour with baking powder and soda. Add alternately with sour cream. Mix brown sugar, nuts, cinnamon, and vanilla. Place 1 layer batter and ½ of brown sugar mixture, another layer of batter, and other ½ of brown sugar mixture in a greased tube pan. Bake for 45 minutes at 350°F.

## BLUEBERRY MUFFINS

2 cups flour
½ teaspoon salt
4 teaspoons baking powder
¼ cup sugar
1 teaspoon cinnamon

¼ cup butter or margarine
1 egg, beaten
1 cup milk
1½ cups blueberries

Sift flour, salt, baking powder, sugar, and cinnamon into bowl. Cut in butter with pastry blender. Mix in the egg and milk until flour mixture is moist. Fold in the blueberries gently. Ladle into well greased heated muffin tins. Bake for 25 minutes in 450°F. oven. Serve with butter.

## BRAN MUFFINS

1 cup bran flakes
1 cup boiling water
½ cup Crisco
1 cup sugar
2 eggs
½ teaspoon salt

2 cups buttermilk or 2 cups sweet
   milk plus 2 tablespoons lemon
   juice
2½ cups flour
2½ teaspoons soda
2 cups All-Bran

Mix bran flakes and boiling water; cool. Cream Crisco and sugar together. Add remaining ingredients. Fill greased muffin pan (cups) ½ full. Bake for 15 minutes in 400°F. oven or 20 minutes if out of refrigerator.

This batter can be kept <u>covered</u> in refrigerator for 2 months. Nuts and/or raisins may be added.

## OATMEAL MUFFINS

"Cold morning favorite."

1 cup oats (uncooked)
1 cup buttermilk
1 egg
⅓ cup brown sugar
⅓ cup cooking oil

½ teaspoon baking soda
½ teaspoon salt
1 teaspoon baking powder
1 cup sifted flour

Combine oats and buttermilk. Add egg and mix well. Add oil. Sift together flour, salt, baking powder, and soda. Add to oats mixture. Stir only enough to dampen flour. Fill greased muffin pans. Bake in preheated 400°F. oven for 15 to 20 minutes. Makes 12 medium size muffins.

## SURPRISE MUFFINS

2 cups sifted flour
¼ cup sugar
3 teaspoons baking
   powder
½ teaspoon salt
¼ cup soft shortening
1 egg
1 cup milk
Jelly

Sift flour, sugar, baking powder, and salt together into a mixing bowl. Add shortening, egg, and milk. Mix together with pastry blender, then stir just until ingredients are blended. Fill greased muffin cups half full of batter. Drop scant teaspoon of jelly on center of batter. Add more batter to fill cup ⅔ full. During baking, the jelly sinks into center of muffin and gives the "surprise." Bake in 400°F. oven for 20 to 25 minutes.

## CHEESY BISCUITS

"Quick and easy company treat."

1 stick margarine
¼ to ½ cup crumbled
   Blue cheese
2 cans canned biscuits

Melt margarine in shallow baking dish. Mix in Blue cheese; spread evenly in dish. Cut biscuits into quarters. Add to margarine and cheese mixture. Stir until biscuits are well coated. Bake in 375°F. oven for 15 minutes. Serves 6.

## BUTTERMILK BISCUITS

"Jonathan can eat 6 and will look around for more."

2 cups flour
½ teaspoon salt
4 teaspoons baking
   powder
½ teaspoons baking soda
5 tablespoons Crisco
1 cup buttermilk

Place flour, salt, baking powder, and baking soda into sifter. Sift into bowl. Add Crisco and mix with pastry blender until the shortening forms small crumbs. Add buttermilk and mix together. Turn dough onto floured surface. Pat out dough to ½ inch thickness. Cut out with floured biscuit cutter. Bake on ungreased cookie sheet for 12 minutes in a 450°F. oven.

# AMISH FRIENDSHIP BREAD STARTER

"A nice way to remember your friends and neighbors."

1 package active dry
  yeast
1/2 cup warm water
  (110°F.)
1 cup all-purpose flour
1 cup sugar
1 cup warm milk (110°F.)
2/3 cup oil
2 cups flour
1 cup sugar
1 teaspoon cinnamon
1 teaspoon vanilla
1/2 teaspoon salt
1 1/4 teaspoons baking
  powder
1/2 teaspoon baking soda
3 eggs

In a small bowl, soften yeast in water for about 10 minutes. Stir well. In a 2 quart glass, plastic, or ceramic container, combine 1 cup flour and 1 cup sugar. Mix thoroughly or the flour will lump when the milk is added. Slowly stir in milk and yeast mixture. Cover loosely and let stand at room temperature until bubbly. (Consider this day 1 of the 10 day cycle.)

Days 2 to 4, stir with a wooden spoon. Day 5: Blend 1 cup flour and 1 cup sugar. Slowly add 1 cup milk; stir mixture into starter. Days 6 to 9: Stir. Day 10 (which becomes day 1 for the next series): Feed again.

Remove three 1 cup portions. Save one for yourself and give one to a friend. To remaining batter, add last 9 ingredients. Mix all together. Add 1 cup chopped nuts and 2 cups mixed dried fruit bits (or any fruit of your choice), or chocolate chips. Pour into 2 well greased loaf pans. Sometimes I sprinkle a cinnamon and sugar mixture on the sides and bottom of pans. Bake in 350°F. oven for 55 to 60 minutes. Let cool for 10 minutes before removing from pan.

# RUSSIAN RYE BREAD

2 packages yeast
1/2 cup warm water
1 1/4 cups boiling water
2 tablespoons caraway
  seed
2 tablespoons salt
1 1/2 cups buttermilk
2/3 cup dark molasses
1 tablespoon cocoa
6 cups unsifted rye flour
3 to 4 cups whole wheat
  flour
1 cup flour (for kneading)

Add yeast to warm water. Let stand a few minutes. Stir to dissolve. Pour boiling water over caraway seeds and salt. Cool slightly. Slowly add buttermilk, molasses, and cocoa. Cool to lukewarm. Add 3 cups rye flour. Beat until smooth. Stir in yeast mixture. Slowly blend in remaining rye and whole wheat flour until dough leaves sides of bowl.

Turn dough onto floured surface which has been sprinkled with 1 cup white flour. Knead until blisters appear on surface. Cover with wax paper, then a towel. Let rest for 20 minutes. Knead for 1 minute, then divide dough into 4 equal portions. Shape into round loaves. Place on greased cookie sheet. Brush with shortening. Cover and let rise until double in bulk, about 1 hour. Bake at 375°F. for 40 to 45 minutes. Place on rack; brush with shortening.

## WHITE BREAD

"Warm from the oven, it's the staff of life."

2 cups warm milk
3 tablespoons sugar
1 tablespoon salt
2 tablespoons dry yeast
½ cup warm water
  (110°F.)
2 tablespoons soft
  shortening
7 to 7½ cups bread flour

Soften yeast in ½ cup warm water. In large bowl, place sugar, salt, shortening, and warm milk. Stir in yeast mixture. Stir in about 3 to 3½ cups flour to form a sponge. Cover with plastic wrap. Place in a warm place for 30 minutes. Add 2 to 2½ cups flour. Turn out on a floured board with remaining flour. Knead until smooth and elastic, about 5 to 7 minutes.

Grease bowl; place dough in bowl. Turn to grease. Cover with plastic wrap. Return to warm place for 1 hour (should double in bulk). Turn out on floured board. Divide into 2 sections. Cover with cloth and let dough rest for 10 minutes. Shape into 2 loaves. Place in greased loaf pans. Let rise for 50 to 60 minutes. Bake in 425°F. oven for 25 minutes.

## GRANDMA'S POTATO ROLLS

"No holiday or birthday dinner is complete without Grandma's Rolls."

1 cup mashed potatoes
  (warm)
½ cup butter or Crisco
1 cup potato water
1 cup milk
½ cup sugar
1 teaspoon salt
2 well beaten eggs
1 cake yeast
5 to 6 cups enriched flour

Preheat oven to 375°F. Baking time: 15 to 20 minutes.

Dissolve butter in warm mashed potatoes. Dissolve yeast in warm potato water and warm milk. Add to potato mixture the sugar, salt, and eggs. Add enough flour to make a light dough. Knead and let rise until almost double, 1½ to 2 hours.

Punch down and knead. Let rise until almost double, 45 minutes. Knead one more time. Store in a sealed plastic container such as Tupperware until ready to use - in refrigerator. Knead 3 times total. Shape into pocket rolls or pan rolls. Let rise an hour. Bake until brown.

This is a good way to use leftover mashed potatoes. Heat the cold mashed potatoes in 1 cup water, then proceed as directed in the recipe.

## JALAPENO CORN BREAD

"Guaranteed to add spiciness to your meal."

1½ cups white or yellow corn meal
   (Southerners prefer white)
1 tablespoon flour
2 teaspoons salt
½ teaspoon sugar
½ teaspoon baking soda
1 teaspoon baking powder
1 cup buttermilk
⅔ cup bacon drippings or salad oil
2 eggs, beaten

1 small can (1 cup) cream style
   corn
2½ large or 3 small jalapeno
   peppers (without seeds),
   chopped
¼ cup green or red (or both) bell
   peppers, chopped
5 green onions, chopped
¾ cup grated cheese

Mix first 6 dry ingredients. Add buttermilk, oil, eggs, and corn; mix thoroughly. Stir in pepper, onions, and grated cheese. Add bacon drippings or oil to a No. 8 size cast iron skillet or a 9 inch square heavy duty baking pan. It will bake in a preheated 400°F. oven. Therefore, preheat the cast iron skillet with 1 tablespoon bacon grease. Place the skillet on the burner and heat until the bacon grease begins to smoke, then add batter. Bake for 25 minutes or until done. Remove from oven and slice. It's great warmed over for lunch. Serves 8.

# Common Kitchen Pans To Use As Casseroles

**Spring Form Pan**

**Layer Cake or Pie Pan**

**Ring Mold**

**Baking or Square Pan**

**Loaf Pan**

**Brioche Pan**

**Angle Cake Pan**

**Bundt Tube**

## Equivalent Dishes

**4-CUP BAKING DISH**
= 9" pie plate
= 8" x 1 1/4" layer cake pan
= 7 3/8" x 3 5/8" x 2 1/4" loaf pan

**6-CUP BAKING DISH**
= 8 "or 9" x 11 1/2" layer cake pan
= 10" pie pan
= 8 1/2" x 3 5/8" x 2 5/8" loaf pan

**8-CUP BAKING DISH**
= 8" x 8" x 2" square pan
= 11" x 7" x 1 1/2" baking pan
= 9" x 5" x 3" loaf pan

**10-CUP BAKING DISH**
= 9" x 9" x 2" square pan
= 11 3/4" x 7 1/2" x 1 3/4" baking pan
= 15" x 10" x 1" flat jelly roll sheet

**12-CUP BAKING DISH OR MORE**
= 13 1/2" x 8 1/2" x 2" glass baking dish
= 13" x 9" x 2" metal baking pan
= 14"x10 1/2"x2 1/2" turkey roasting pan

## Total Volume of Pans

**TUBE PANS**

| | |
|---|---|
| 7 1/2" x 3" Bundt tube | 6 cups |
| 9" x 3 1/2" fancy or Bundt tube | 9 cups |
| 9" x 3 1/2" angle cake pan | 12 cups |
| 10" x 3 3/4" Bundt tube | 12 cups |
| 10" x 4" fancy tube mold | 16 cups |
| 10" x 4" angle cake pan | 18 cups |

**SPRING FORM PANS**

| | |
|---|---|
| 8" x 3" pan | 12 cups |
| 9" x 3" pan | 16 cups |

**RING MOLDS**

| | |
|---|---|
| 8 1/2" x 2 1/4" mold | 4 1/2 cups |
| 9 1/4" x 2 3/4" mold | 8 cups |

**BRIOCHE PAN**

| | |
|---|---|
| 9 1/2" x 3 1/4" pan | 8 cups |

# Super Cakes & Desserts

THE Cake, Bourbon Derby Pie
and much, much more!

### "THE" Chocolate Fudge Cake

"Richard, Ruthie Jr., and Andrew's favorite and maybe Laura's."

3 squares unsweetened chocolate
2¼ cups sifted cake flour
2 teaspoons baking soda
½ teaspoon salt
½ cup butter

2½ cups packed brown sugar
3 eggs
1 cup sour cream
1 cup boiling water
1 teaspoon vanilla

Frosting:
1 stick butter
4 squares chocolate
1 pound sifted powdered sugar

½ cup milk
2 teaspoons vanilla

Melt chocolate over hot water. Cool. Sift dry ingredients together. Beat butter until soft. Add sugar and eggs; beat together at high speed for 5 minutes. Beat in vanilla and cooled chocolate. Fold in dry ingredients alternately with sour cream. Stir in boiling water. Batter will be thin. Make 2 large 9 inch layers. Bake at 350°F. for 35 minutes (until tests done) in pans that have been greased and floured.

Frosting: Melt chocolate and butter together. Combine remaining ingredients; add to chocolate mixture. Beat in bowl (place bowl in large container of ice water) until spreading consistency.

## CHOCOLATE ANGEL FOOD

"Julie's favorite."

1½ cups egg whites
1½ cups sugar
⅔ cup sifted cake flour
1 teaspoon vanilla
1 teaspoon cream of
   tartar
¼ teaspoon salt
½ cup cocoa

Sift cocoa with the flour. Sift the sugar. Beat egg whites. Add cream of tartar and salt; beat until stiff, but not dry. Add the sugar gradually, beating all the time. Add the vanilla. Fold in flour and cocoa mixture. Pour into an angel cake pan. Bake for 35 minutes at 375°F. Invert pan to cool cake.

## SUE'S CHOCOLATE CHEESE CAKE

"Very rich-luscious chocolate delight."

Crust:
2½ cups graham cracker crumbs

½ cup butter
½ cup sugar

Filling:
1 cup sugar
3 (8 ounce) packages cream
   cheese
2 eggs
6 ounces semi-sweet chocolate
   chips, melted
2 tablespoons whipping cream

1 cup sour cream
¼ cup strong coffee (fresh brewed,
   not instant)
½ cup raspberry liqueur
   (Chambord)
1 teaspoon vanilla

Crust: Mix together and press into bottom and sides of springform pan.

Filling: Stir sugar into cream cheese. Beat eggs and add to cheese mixture. Melt chocolate and whipping cream. Add coffee. Add chocolate mixture to cream cheese mixture. Add sour cream, liqueur, and vanilla. Pour over crust in springform pan. Bake in preheated 350°F. oven for 45 minutes to 1 hour. Serves 12 to 14.

# DOUBLE CHOCOLATE CAKE

"I wooed Charlie with this cake."

1¾ cups sifted flour
1½ cups sugar
1¼ teaspoons double action
  baking powder
½ teaspoon soda
1 teaspoon salt
½ cup shortening

1 cup milk
1 teaspoon vanilla
½ to ⅔ cup unbeaten eggs (2
  large)
2 squares unsweetened chocolate,
  melted
½ teaspoon red food coloring

Chocolate Icing Deluxe:
1 large unbeaten egg
2 cups sifted confectioners sugar
¼ teaspoon salt

⅓ cup soft shortening
2 squares unsweetened chocolate,
  melted

Sift together flour, sugar, baking powder, soda, and salt. Add shortening, milk, and vanilla; beat for 2 minutes. Add eggs, melted chocolate, and food coloring; beat for 2 minutes. Pour into prepared pans. Bake in 375°F. oven for 30 to 35 minutes.

Chocolate Icing Deluxe: Mix all ingredients together. Beat with electric mixer until fluffy. Frost tops and sides of layers.

# NEW POPULAR DEVILS FOOD CAKE

"Rich moist chocolatey cake."

2 (9 inch) layer pans or 13x9 inch
  oblong pan
2⅜ cups sifted Softasilk or 2¼
  cups sifted Gold Medal flour
1⅞ cups sugar
1 teaspoon soda

1 teaspoon salt
⅔ cup soft shortening
1¼ cups buttermilk
3 eggs (½ to ⅔ cup)
2½ squares chocolate (2½
  ounces), melted

Caramel Butter Frosting:
¼ cup butter or margarine
1 cup brown sugar (packed)
⅓ to ½ cup cream

1 teaspoon vanilla
3¼ to 3½ cup powdered sugar

Sift together flour, sugar, soda, and salt. Add shortening and a little over half of buttermilk; beat for 2 minutes. Add remaining milk, eggs, and chocolate. Beat for 2 minutes. Pour into prepared pans. Bake in a 350°F. oven for 30 to 35 minutes for layers and 40 to 45 minutes for the oblong pan. Bake until cake tests done. Cool. Finish with Chocolate Butter Icing or Caramel Butter Frosting.

Caramel Butter Frosting: Melt butter, add brown sugar and cream. Bring to a boil stirring constantly. Boil about 1 minute. Remove from fire, add powdered sugar and vanilla, beat until smooth and of spreading consistency. Makes enough to frost side and top of 8 inch layers.

## CHOCOLATE BROWNIES

"Fudgy squares everyone loves them."

2 squares unsweetened
  chocolate (2 ounces)
⅓ cup margarine
1 cup sugar
2 eggs
¾ cup sifted flour
½ teaspoon baking
  powder
½ teaspoon salt
½ cup broken nuts

Melt together over hot water the chocolate and margarine. Beat in sugar and eggs. Sift together the flour, baking powder, and salt; stir into chocolate mixture. Bake in 350°F. oven for 30 to 35 minutes. Cool slightly and spread with Chocolate Icing. Cut into squares. Makes 16 (2 inch) squares.

Chocolate Icing: Melt over hot water 1 tablespoon butter and 1 square unsweetened chocolate (1 ounce). Blend in 1½ tablespoons warm water. Stir and beat in 1 cup sifted confectioners sugar (until icing will spread easily).

## CHOCOLATELY CHOCOLATE PIE

"It's elegant; so beautiful to serve."

3 squares unsweetened
  chocolate
3 cups milk
1 cup plus 2 tablespoons
  sugar
3 tablespoons cornstarch
¼ cup plus 2 tablespoons
  flour
¾ teaspoon salt
3 egg yolks
1½ tablespoons butter
1½ tablespoons vanilla
9½ inch baked pie shell

Meringue:
3 to 4 egg whites
6 to 8 tablespoons sugar
  (2 tablespoons sugar
  per egg white)

Melt chocolate in top part of double boiler, then add milk. Mix together and continue heating. In a bowl, mix sugar, flour, cornstarch, and salt. Mix a small amount of the hot milk/chocolate mixture into the dry ingredients. Pour this mixture into the remaining hot milk/chocolate mixture and continue to cook while stirring, until thickened. Turn heat down to simmer. Continue cooking for 15 minutes longer, stirring occasionally.

Lightly beat the egg yolks in a separate bowl. Blend a small amount of the thickened mixture into the egg yolks. Pour this egg yolk mixture into the remaining chocolate mixture; mix. Cook until the egg yolks are thickened. Remove from burner. Add butter and vanilla, then mix. Pour into baked pie shell.

To make meringue: Whip egg whites in mixer until they hold soft peaks. Very gradually add the sugar (6 to 8 tablespoons). Again, whip until it forms stiff peaks. Spread on top of pie. Be sure to seal edges. Bake in 300°F. oven for 10 to 15 minutes.

Serves 8, depending on the size of the pieces.

# BLACK BOTTOM PIE

"Superb - very impressive flavor."

Baked pie shell

Custard Filling (2 cups
custard):
½ cup sugar
1 tablespoon corn starch
2 cups milk
4 egg yolks

Chocolate Filling:
1 (6 ounce) package semi-
sweet chocolate chips
1 teaspoon vanilla

White Filling:
1 envelope granulated
gelatine
4 egg whites
¼ cup cold water
½ cup sugar

Custard Filling: Mix together sugar and corn starch. Scald milk. Beat egg yolks and mix a small amount of milk to egg yolks, then add mixture to milk. Slowly stir sugar and corn starch mixture into milk and egg mixture. Cook until custard coats spoon.

Chocolate Filling: To 1 cup of Custard Filling, add chocolate chips and vanilla. Stir until completely melted. Pour into pie shell and chill until set.

White Filling: Soften gelatine in water. Add to remaining custard; chill till slightly set. Whip egg whites until slightly stiff. Gradually add sugar and whip until very stiff. Fold gelatine and custard mixture into egg whites. Pour onto chocolate layer. Chill till set.

Garnish with ½ cup whipped cream. Sweeten with sugar and vanilla; top with bits of decorative chocolate (rum flavoring may be substituted for vanilla).

This is very easy to double for 2 pies.

# CHOCOLATE THUMBPRINT COOKIES

"Not just another chocolate cookie."

1½ cups sifted flour
½ cup butter
½ cup brown sugar,
packed firmly
1 teaspoon vanilla
2 tablespoons milk
¼ cup Nestle's chocolate
chips, chopped

Filling:
¾ cup Nestle's chocolate
chips
1 tablespoon shortening
2 tablespoons corn syrup
1 tablespoon water
1 teaspoon vanilla

Mix all ingredients together. Form in 1 inch balls, place on ungreased baking sheet. Flatten balls with thumb, make depressions in centers. Bake at 375°F. for 10 to 12 minutes. Roll in confectioners' sugar several times while still warm, then cool.

Filling: Melt chocolate over hot water. Add other ingredients and stir until smooth. Cool 5 minutes. Fill depressions in the center of the cookies. Makes about 60 cookies.

## DREAMY CHOCOLATE COOKIES

"Your kids will love them."

2 tablespoons margarine
1½ cups chocolate chips
1 (15 ounce) can Eagle
  Brand milk
1 cup sifted flour
1 cup chopped nuts
1 teaspoon vanilla

Melt margarine and chocolate chips over water. Add Eagle Brand milk, stir well. Add flour, nuts, and vanilla. Mix again thoroughly. Drop by teaspoonfuls on greased baking sheet. Bake at 325°F. for 10 minutes. Don't overbake. Makes 9 dozen.

## PATTI'S CHOCOLATE DELIGHTS

"A great combination of chocolate and peanut butter."

3 cubes almond bark
12 ounces chocolate chips
Ritz or other crackers
Crunchy peanut butter

Melt almond bark and chocolate chips. Spread peanut butter on crackers. Dip in chocolate mixture. Cool on waxed paper.

## CHOCOLATE BONBONS

"Good enough to give to your best friend."

1½ bars German's sweet
  chocolate
12 ounces butterscotch
  chips
2 cups toasted, slivered
  almonds*
Pecans

Melt chocolate and butterscotch chips. Add almonds. Spoon into candy paper liners. Makes over 40 small candy paper cups.

\* Fine candy making coconut may be substituted for almonds.

# SUPER CAKES AND DESSERTS

## RICH GOLDEN CAKE

2 (9 inch) layer pans or 13x9 inch
  oblong pan
2¼ cups sifted Softasilk or 2⅛
  cups sifted Gold Medal flour
1½ cups sugar
3 teaspoons baking powder
1 teaspoon salt
⅔ cup shortening
1 cup milk
1½ teaspoons vanilla
3 eggs (½ to ⅔ cup)

Grease and flour pans. Sift together flour, sugar, baking powder, and salt. Add shortening, ½ of the milk, and vanilla. Beat for 2 minutes. Add remaining milk with eggs. Beat for 2 minutes. Pour into prepared pans. Bake in a 350°F. oven for 30 to 35 minutes for layers or 40 to 45 minutes for oblong pan. Bake until cake tests done. Cool. Finish with desired filling and frosting.

## MARBLE CAKE

1 (1 ounce) square
  chocolate, melted
⅛ teaspoon soda
2 tablespoons milk

Follow recipe for Rich Golden Cake. Reserve 1 cup of batter from Rich Golden Cake. Blend together chocolate, soda, and milk into reserved batter. Drop by spoonfuls in 4 spots on cake batter. Gently pull a knife through batter to make a marbled design.

## SILVER WHITE CAKE

"Wedding cake favorite. This one tastes extra good."

2 (9 inch) layer pans or 13x9 inch
  oblong pan
2⅞ cups sifted Softasilk or 2⅔
  cups sifted Gold Medal flour
1⅞ cups sugar
4½ teaspoons baking powder
1 teaspoon salt
⅔ c. soft shortening
1¼ cups milk
2 teaspoons vanilla
5 egg whites (⅔ cup; unbeaten)

Sift together flour, sugar, baking powder, and salt. Add shortening and a little over half of the milk. Beat for 2 minutes. Add vanilla and egg whites. Beat for 2 minutes. Pour into prepared pans. Bake in a 350°F. oven for 30 to 35 minutes for layers and 35 to 45 minutes for oblong. Bake until cake tests done. Cool. Finish with desired filling and frosting.

## BUTTERKUCKEN (BUTTER CAKE)

"My dear German friends, Cocoa and Antje, gave this recipe to me."

1 cup whipping cream
2 cups flour
1 cup sugar
3 eggs
3½ tesapoons baking
  powder
½ teaspoon salt

Mix together the cream, flour, sugar, eggs, baking powder, and salt. Pour into a jelly roll pan which has been buttered and floured. Bake in preheated 425°F. oven for 10 minutes.

Melt 2 sticks of butter. Add 1 cup sugar and stir in 3 cups of sliced almonds. Add ¼ to ½ cup whipping cream, enough to make the topping spreadable. Pour on top of hot cake. Return to oven and bake for 10 more minutes.

This is a very rich, melt in your mouth, cake. Serves 10 to 12.

## TERESA'S CREAM CHEESE POUND CAKE

"Very moist cake; wonderful with fresh fruits."

½ pound butter
½ pound cream cheese (8 ounces)
2 cups sugar
6 eggs

2 cups flour
1½ teaspoons baking powder
2 teaspoons vanilla

Cream together the butter and cream cheese. Add sugar and eggs alternately with the flour, baking powder, and vanilla. Pour into greased tube pan. Bake at 350°F. for 55 to 60 minutes. Cool for 30 minutes before removing from pan.

## COCONUT POUND CAKE

"Wonderful dessert served with fruits in season."

3 cups plain flour
1 teaspoon baking powder
½ teaspoon salt
1 cup milk
1½ cups vegetable shortening

2½ cups sugar
5 eggs
1 cup coconut
1 teaspoon coconut flavoring
1 teaspoon butter flavoring

Sift flour, baking powder, and salt together twice. Cream shortening and sugar for 10 minutes. Add eggs, one at a time, beating after each addition. Add flour mixture alternately with milk. Stir in coconut and flavorings. Place in a <u>cold</u> oven at 325°F. for 1½ hours. Use large tubular pan.

# BLONDE BROWNIES

"Patti's favorite."

| | |
|---|---|
| 1 cup sifted flour | 1 cup brown sugar |
| 1 teaspoon baking powder | 1 slightly beaten egg |
| 1/2 teaspoon soda | 1 teaspoon vanilla |
| 1 teaspoon salt | 1 cup nuts |
| 1/3 cup butter | 1 cup chocolate chips |

Sift dry ingredients together. Melt butter; add egg, vanilla, and sugar. Add dry ingredients, mixing well. Add nuts. Place mixture in a greased 9 inch square pan; sprinkle with chocolate chips. Bake at 350°F. for 20 to 25 minutes.

# PAINT BRUSH COOKIES

"This is the family Christmas cookie. It also makes cute Valentine and St. Patrick's cookies."

1 1/2 cups sugar
1 cup butter
3 eggs (one at a time)
1 teaspoon vanilla
1/2 teaspoon almond
    flavoring
4 cups flour
1 teaspoon soda
1/2 teaspoon salt

Cream sugar and butter together. Add eggs, one at a time, beating well after each addition. Add flavorings. Sift together dry ingredients; blend in 2 cups at a time. Chill for 1 hour. Roll 1/8 inch thick. Cut with various animal cutters. Bake in 350°F. oven for 10 to 12 minutes on ungreased pans. The icing may be applied with an artists brush.

# PEPPERMINT COOKIES

"This cookie requires patience, but it is worth all the work it requires."

| | |
|---|---|
| 1 cup soft butter | 2 1/2 cups sifted flour |
| 1/2 cup sifted powdered sugar | 1/2 cup walnuts or other nuts |
| 1 teaspoon vanilla | |

Peppermint Fudge Filling:

| | |
|---|---|
| 1/2 cup crushed peppermint candy | 1/2 cup powdered sugar |
| 1/2 cup powdered sugar | 3 tablespoons peppermint and |
| 2 tablespoons cream cheese |     sugar mixture |
| 1 teaspoon milk | Color with 1 drop food coloring |

Cream butter, sugar, and vanilla. Gradually add flour and nuts. Chill dough and shape into balls. Make deep hole in center. Fill with filling. Bake in a 350°F. oven for 12 to 15 minutes or until set. Roll in peppermint candy and sugar mixture.

Crush peppermint candy. Mix with powdered sugar and set aside. Cream together cream cheese and milk. Gradually add powdered sugar and peppermint candy and sugar mixture. Spoon out 1/8 teaspoon of fudge filling onto a piece of wax paper. Place in freezer until well chilled.

# RUM BALLS

1 cup finely crushed
  vanilla wafers
1 cup confectioners sugar
1½ cups chopped nuts
2 tablespoons cocoa
2 tablespoons light corn
  syrup
¼ cup rum
½ cup fine granulated
  sugar
Red candied cherry
  halves

Combine crumbs, confectioners sugar, 1 cup nuts, and cocoa. Add corn syrup and rum; mix well. Shape into 1 inch balls. Roll half in granulated sugar and remainder in the ½ cup nuts. Moisten cut sides of cherry halves with corn syrup, and press one on each sugar-coated rum ball. Store in airtight container. Will ship if airtight.

Note: If preferred, ¼ cup heavy cream and 1 teaspoon rum extract can be substituted for the rum.

# SNICKERDOODLES

"Benjamin's favorite."

1 cup soft shortening
1½ cups sugar
2 eggs
2¾ cups sifted flour
2 teaspoons cream of
  tartar
1 teaspoon soda
½ teaspoon salt

Mix together thoroughly the shortening, sugar, and eggs. Sift dry ingredients together and stir into shortening mixture. Chill dough. Roll into balls the size of small walnuts. Roll in mixture of 2 tablespoons sugar and 2 teaspoons cinnamon. Place about 2 inches apart on ungreased baking sheet. Bake until lightly browned, but still soft. (These cookies puff up at first, then flatten out with crinkled tops.) Bake in a 400°F. oven for 8 to 10 minutes.

This recipe makes about 5 dozen 2 inch cookies.

# SOUR CREAM RAISIN DROPS

½ cup margarine
¾ cup sugar
1 egg
½ teaspoon vanilla
1½ cups flour

½ teaspoon baking soda
¼ salt
½ cup sour cream
1 cup raisins

Orange Frosting:
¼ cup margarine
1 teaspoon grated orange rind

2 cups sifted powdered sugar
4 teaspoons milk

Beat margarine and sugar until light and fluffy. Blend in egg and vanilla. Add combined dry ingredients alternately with sour cream, mixing well after each addition. Stir in raisins. Drop by teaspoon onto ungreased cookie sheet. Bake at 375°F. for 8 to 10 minutes or until set. Cool; frost with Orange Frosting.

Orange Frosting: Beat margarine. Blend in rind. Add sugar alternately with milk, beating until light and fluffy. Makes approximately 5 dozen.

# OATMEAL COOKIES

"Crisp-crunchie cookie."

1 cup brown sugar, packed
1 cup white sugar
1 cup butter or margarine
2 eggs
2 cups flour
1 teaspoon soda

1 teaspoon baking powder
1 teaspoon salt
2 cups oatmeal
2 cups Rice Krispies
2 cups coconut
1 cup nuts

Cream together brown and white sugar with butter. Add eggs; mix well. Sift together the dry ingredients. Mix into creamed sugar and butter mixture. Stir in oatmeal, Rice Krispies, coconut, and nuts. Drop by teaspoon onto greased cookie sheet. Bake in 350°F. oven for 12 to 15 minutes. Yields 10 dozen.

# NEW ORLEANS BREAD PUDDING

"Elegant version of a humble dessert."

4 cups French bread, crumbled
2 cups milk
1 cup sugar
2 tablespoons butter, melted
2 eggs

1 tablespoon vanilla
½ cup raisins
½ cup coconut
½ cup pecans
½ teaspoon nutmeg

Whiskey Sauce:
½ cup butter
1½ cups powdered sugar
1 egg yolk or whole egg

½ cup bourbon or 1 teaspoon rum
  flavoring

Combine all ingredients. Pour into buttered baking dish. Place in unheated oven. Bake at 350°F. for about 1 hour and 15 minutes.

Cream butter and sugar over medium heat until butter is absorbed. Remove from heat; blend in egg yolk. Pour in bourbon gradually to your own taste, stirring constantly. Sauce will thicken as it cools. Serve warm over warm bread pudding.

## PATE A CREPES

"A bit of French magic."

1 cup cold milk
1 cup cold water
4 eggs
1/2 teaspoon salt
2 cups sifted all-purpose
    flour
4 tablespoons melted
    butter

Put the milk, water, eggs, and salt into blender jar. Add flour, then butter. Blend for 1 minute. Scrape sides of blender. Blend for 2 more seconds. Cover and refrigerate for at least 2 hours or overnight.

Brush the inside of small skillet or crepe pan lightly with oil. Heat until pan is just beginning to smoke. Ladle a scant 1/4 cup of batter in pan. Quickly tilt pan in all directions to run the batter all over the bottom of the pan. Heat for about 60 to 80 seconds, until crepe appears dry. Turn; brown lightly. Lift from pan.

Make stacks of cooked crepes. Separate with sheets of wax paper. Makes about 12 crepes. Serve with ice cream tucked inside and either Strawberry Glaze or Praline Sauce on top.

## STRAWBERRY GLAZE

1 quart strawberries
1 1/2 cups sugar
2 tablespoons corn starch

2/3 cup water
Few drops of red food coloring

Crush 2 cups strawberries. Add sugar, corn starch, and water. Cook, stirring constantly, until thickened. Add red food coloring and remaining 2 cups strawberries.

## PRALINE SAUCE

1/2 cup margarine
1/2 cup powdered sugar
2 tablespoons maple syrup

1/4 cup water
1/2 cup finely chopped pecans

Heat butter until light brown. Cool slightly. Gradually add sugar. Stir in syrup and water. Bring to a boil; simmer for 1 minute. Add nuts. Serve warm over the ice cream filled crepes.

## FLAKY PIE CRUST

1 1/2 cups flour
1/2 teaspoon salt
3/4 cup shortening
1/2 cup cold water

Mix flour and salt in bowl. Cut shortening into flour with pastry blender or 2 knives. Blend together 1/4 cup of this mixture with cold water. Add to remainder of flour mixture; mix with fork lightly until dough holds together.

# APRICOT PIE

"This is truly a party pie."

**Pastry:**
1 cup sifted flour
¼ cup sugar
⅓ cup butter or
  margarine
Grated rind of ½ lemon
1 egg yolk

Pastry: Sift flour and sugar into bowl. Cut in butter with pastry blender until mixture looks mealy. Add lemon rind and egg yolk. Work lightly until it holds together. Press evenly over bottom and sides of 9 inch pie plate. Bake in 425°F. oven for 10 minutes or until golden brown. Cool.

**Filling:**
1 cup dried apricots
1 cup heavy cream
¼ cup sugar
1 teaspoon vanilla

Filling: Add enough water to cover apricots. Cook to boiling point; reduce heat and simmer for 10 minutes or until tender. Drain; cool, then chop coarsely.

Whip cream until it holds a shape. Gently mix in sugar. Add vanilla and apricots. Spoon into cooled pie shell and chill. Serves 8.

# PUMPKIN PIE

"Bourbon adds a teetotaling grandmother's touch."

2 eggs, slightly beaten
2 cups pumpkin (16 ounces)
¾ cup sugar
½ teaspoon salt
1 teaspoon cinnamon

½ teaspoon ginger
1 (13½ ounce) can evaporated
  milk
2 tablespoons bourbon
1 (9 inch) unbaked pie shell

Combine eggs, pumpkin, sugar, salt, cinnamon, ginger, evaporated milk, and bourbon in mixing bowl. Stir with rotary beater. Pour into pie shell. Bake in 425°F. oven for 15 minutes. Turn down heat to 350°F. and bake an additional 45 minutes. Test with a knife. Makes 1 (9 inch) pie. Serves 8.

# BOURBON PECAN PIE

"Easy, but elegant."

1 cup sugar
½ cup flour
2 eggs, slightly beaten
¼ pound butter or margarine,
  melted and cooled
1 cup broken pecans

6 ounces semi-sweet chocolate
  chips
1 teaspoon vanilla
2 tablespoons bourbon
1 (9 inch) baked pie shell

Mix sugar and flour. Add eggs, butter, pecans, chocolate chips (unmelted), and vanilla. Pour into pie shell and bake for 1 hour at 350°F.

# FROSTY FRUIT PIE

"Cool and refreshing."

**Filling:**
**1¼ cups crushed
    pineapple**
**1 package lemon flavored
    gelatin**
**¾ cup sugar**
**2 cups whipped topping**

Bake 10 inch pie crust.

Bring crushed pineapple to a boil. Add lemon gelatin; stir until dissolved. Mix in sugar. Cool until almost stiff. Fold whipped topping into pineapple mixture. Pour into baked pie shell. Chill for at least 1 hour. Garnish with additional pineapple or raspberries or strawberries.

# LEMON FLUFF PIE

"Light and tasty."

**1 package cook and serve
    lemon pudding**
**½ cup sugar**
**2¼ cups water**
**2 egg yolks**
**2 egg whites**
**¼ cup sugar**

**Graham Cracker Crust:**
**20 graham crackers**
**¼ cup sugar**
**½ stick margarine,
    melted**

Crush graham crackers. Add sugar and margarine; toss lightly with fork. Press on bottom and sides of 9 inch pie plate. Save a few crumbs.

In medium saucepan, mix and stir pudding mix with sugar, ¼ cup of water, and egg yolks. Stir in 2 cups of water. Cook and stir over medium heat until mixture thickens and comes to a boil, then set aside.

Beat 2 egg whites until foamy. Gradually beat in ¼ cup of sugar until stiff. Gently fold lemon pudding into beaten egg whites. Pour into graham cracker crust. Sprinkle top with seasoned crumbs. Chill. Serves 8.

# TANGY HAWAIIAN PIE

"Sophisticated lemon pie."

**1 cup sugar**
**½ cup sifted flour**
**¼ teaspoon salt**
**2 to 3 teaspoons grated
    lemon peel**
**1¼ cups water**
**¼ to ⅓ cup lemon juice**
**1 cup (9 ounce can)
    crushed pineapple**
**3 egg yolks, slightly
    beaten**
**1 tablespoon butter**

Combine sugar, flour, salt, and lemon peel in a saucepan. Add water, lemon juice, and pineapple; blend well. Bring to a boil, stirring constantly. Cook over medium heat until thick. Blend a little of the hot mixture into egg yolks. Add to hot mixture in saucepan and cook for 2 minutes longer, stirring constantly. Stir in butter. Cover and cool. Pour into a baked pie shell; spread with meringue. Bake in 350°F. for 12 to 15 minutes.

Meringue: Beat 3 egg whites with ¼ teaspoon cream of tartar until slight mounds form. Gradually add 6 tablespoons sugar, beating well after each addition. Continue beating until meringue stands in stiff glossy peaks.

# ORANGE PIE

"California treat."

Crust:
1¼ cups flour
¾ cup soft butter

¼ cup powdered sugar
1 tablespoon grated orange peel

Filling:
1½ cups fresh orange juice
6 tablespoons cornstarch
½ cup sugar
⅔ cup orange marmalade
1 teaspoon vanilla

½ teaspoon nutmeg
½ teaspoon cinnamon
6 large naval oranges, peeled and
   sectioned (no membrane or
   seeds)

Crust: Combine all ingredients. Press in bottom of pan and sides of 10 inch pie pan. Bake in 375°F. oven for 15 to 18 minutes. Cool.

Filling: Dissolve cornstarch in ⅓ cup juice. Add the remainder of juice, sugar, marmalade, vanilla, nutmeg, and cinnamon. Cook, stirring constantly, until thick and clear. Add orange slices; mix gently. Pour into cooled pie crust. Chill for 3 to 4 hours. Serve at room temperature with whipped cream.

# STRAWBERRY PIE

"Springtime favorite."

1 baked pie shell
8 ounces cream cheese
2 tablespoons milk
1 quart fresh strawberries
¾ cup sugar
2 tablespoons cornstarch
½ cup water
A few drops of red food
   coloring

Blend together cream cheese and milk. Whip until fluffy. Spread mixture on bottom of pie shell. Top with ½ the berries. Cut remaining berries and mix with sugar, cornstarch, and water. Cook until thickened, stirring constantly. Add red food coloring; mix well. Pour over strawberries into pie shell. Chill.

# PINEAPPLE SOUR CREAM PIE

"This is a very pretty and easy dessert."

1 baked pie shell
1 (5½ ounce) package instant
   vanilla pudding
1 (8 ounce) can crushed pineapple
   (undrained)

2 cups sour cream
1 tablespoon sugar

Mix together sour cream, crushed pineapple, and sugar in large bowl. Gradually beat in instant pudding. Pour into baked pie shell. Top with whipped cream and garnish with fresh strawberries or raspberries. Chill.

## FRESH PEACH PIE

"Nancy's favorite."

Pastry for 2-crust pie

Filling:
1 cup sugar
4 tablespoons flour
Dash of nutmeg
5 cups fresh peaches
2 tablespoons butter

Line 9 inch pie pan with pastry; reserve some of the pastry for a lattice top.

Filling: Peel and slice peaches. Mix together sugar and flour. Gently mix with peaches; set aside for a few minutes. Pour into pie crust. Dot with butter and nutmeg. Place a lattice top of crust on top of fruit. Bake in 450°F. oven for 10 minutes. Turn heat to 350°F. and bake until crust is nicely browned and juice begins to bubble. Serve with ice cream.

## COCONUT PIE

"A Knote family favorite."

1 tablespoon granulated
  gelatine
½ cup cold water
4 eggs
1 cup sugar
1 cup heavy cream
Pinch of salt
1½ cups shredded
  coconut
1 teaspoon vanilla or
  sherry flavoring

Soak gelatine in cold water for 5 minutes. Separate eggs and beat yolks, adding ½ cup sugar, salt, and ½ cup cream. Cook in double boiler until thick and add the soaked gelatine. Beat egg white stiff, gradually adding ½ cup of sugar. When the custard mixture has cooled, fold in the whites, 1 cup coconut, and flavoring. Pour into pie shell and chill.

Just before serving, spread ½ cup of cream, that has been whipped and sweetened, over top of pie. Sprinkle with remaining ½ cup coconut (which has been lightly toasted).

Pie Crust: Crush 20 to 25 special chocolate cookies (or any chocolate wafer cookie) until very fine. Add ¼ cup melted margarine. Pat into 9 inch pie pan and chill.

## ANGEL PIE

"Heavenly delight."

4 egg whites
½ cup sugar
1 teaspoon vanilla

Beat egg whites until stiff and dry. Gradually add sugar and vanilla. Turn into Graham Cracker Crust. Bake in 250°F. oven for ½ hour.

Graham Cracker Crust: Crush 16 to 20 graham crackers. Add ¼ cup sugar. Mix in ¼ cup melted butter.

Top pie with sweetened whipped cream and chopped nuts.

# CARAMELS

"A wonderful Christmas candy - good anytime."

4 cups sugar
1 pint white Karo syrup
1 quart whipping cream
1 quart chopped nuts
1 tablespoon vanilla

Mix sugar, syrup, and ½ the cream together in a deep pan. Cook, stirring constantly, until it forms a very soft ball or reaches 238°F. Remove from fire and when every bubble disappears, add the remaining cream and cook, stirring constantly, until the thermometer reaches 242°F. Remove from fire. Add vanilla and do not stir. Pour over nuts in a buttered pan. Let stand several hours or overnight. Cut into ½ inch squares and wrap in wax paper. Makes 2 large cookie sheets.

# PEANUT BUTTER CANDIES

"Can't eat just one."

2⅔ cups graham cracker
  crumbs
3 sticks margarine,
  melted
1½ cups peanut butter
1¼ boxes powdered sugar
12 ounces chocolate chips

Combine cracker crumbs, margarine, peanut butter, and sugar in large bowl. Spread mixture on a jelly roll pan. Press evenly. Melt chocolate chips in double boiler. Spread on top of peanut butter mixture. When cool, cut into squares and serve. Makes two 9x13 inch pans. Makes about 100 squares.

# STRAWBERRY PRESERVES

"Makes jewels out of strawberries."

2 cups sugar
1 cup water
1 quart strawberries

Cook sugar and water until it forms a hard ball in cold water. Add 2 cups strawberries; cook for 5 minutes. Add 2 cups sugar and 2 cups strawberries. Cook for 10 minutes. Let stand and plump overnight.

## JELLIED EASTER EGGS

"Fun Pre-Easter project for children."

**12 eggs, candled**
**3 cups hot water**
**2 (3 ounce) packages**
**gelatin (lemon and**
**lime, orange or apple,**
**or flavor of choice)**

Prepare fruit-flavored gelatin using only 1½ cups water per package. Chill until just starting to thicken. Meanwhile, with skewer or fork tine, puncture small holes in narrow ends of eggs. Puncture wider holes in broader ends of eggs. Hold eggs over bowl; put lips to smaller holes. Blow egg out of shell into bowl. Wash shell with cold water and blow all water out of shells.

Hold a candle flame over smaller hole, so melting paraffin drips over them to seal holes. Set aside to harden. When gelatin is chilled, pour into empty shell, using small funnel or spoon. Set eggs upright in carton and place in refrigerator 3 hours or longer, till gelatin is well set.

To remove, crack shells by rolling on table. Peel gently, wetting hands to handle gelatin easily. Refrigerate jellied eggs till serving time. Serve on nest of shredded raw carrots.


## POPCORN BALLS

"Halloween special."

**8 to 10 cups popped corn**
**1 cup brown sugar**
**⅓ cup water**
**¼ cup margarine**

**⅓ cup white syrup**
**¾ teaspoon salt**
**¾ teaspoon vanilla**

Combine all ingredients except popped corn. Cook to 250°F. or until a few drops form a hard ball. Remove from heat; add vanilla. Add popped corn and form into balls.

# Introduction To Meats

Simplified know-how about meats,
poultry, fish & store-bought sausages

# Introduction to Meats

# BUYING MEATS MORE EFFICIENTLY

Some years ago, meat markets used 1,000 different names for meat cuts. This greatly confused U.S. consumers. The National Livestock Meat Board established Uniform Retail Meat Identification Standards (URMIS) — standardized retail names for cuts of red meats, beef, pork, lamb, and veal. These uniform names replaced the 1,000 names with about 350. Now any U.S. supermarket can cut these meats according to URMIS specifications. These cuts can be labeled with standardized names. However, U.S. meat markets are not required to use them. Differences in the retail cuts will continue for the same cut of meat in sections of the U.S. for some time due to the processing customs.

Meat processors divide each meat into major sections called PRIMAL CUTS or wholesale cuts.

BEEF'S PRIMAL WHOLESALE CUTS: Meat processors divide a whole processed beef weighing from 500 pounds to 750 pounds into two "sides." Each side is further divided into 8 major primal cuts. Starting from the front of the beef and moving back along the top of the animal, beef's primal cuts are: (1) chuck, (2) rib, (3) short loin, (4) sirloin, (5) round, (6) flank, (7) short plate, (8) brisket, and (9) shank. These major sections or Primal Cuts are further divided into much smaller retail cuts. See diagram in Beef Chapter. See page 222 for Beef and E. coli.

VEAL'S PRIMAL WHOLESALE CUTS: Veal is processed into nearly the same primal cuts as beef.

PORK'S PRIMAL WHOLESALE CUTS: Meat processors divide a whole hog into two sides from which four major sections or primal cuts are made. Starting from the front of the pork carcass and moving along the back: (1) shoulder (which contains Boston butt) and the picnic shoulder, (2) pork loin, (3) leg or ham, and (4) side which contains the spare ribs and bacon (belly). These major sections are subdivided into retail cuts. See diagram in Pork Chapter.

LAMB'S PRIMAL WHOLESALE CUTS: A lamb yields five primal cuts starting from the front of the animal: (1) shoulder, (2) rib, (3) loin, (4) leg, and (5) foreshank and breast. These are subdivided into retail cuts. See diagram, Lamb Chapter.

URMIS STEAK EXAMPLE: Steak Name: Beef Loin Flat Bone Sirloin Steak — the name for one sirloin steak from the sirloin primal cut. This cut still has the tenderloin and bone attached.

URMIS BEEF ROAST EXAMPLE: "Beef Chuck Blade Roast" comes from the Chuck primal cut of beef and contains the blade bone.

BLADE
CHUCK
ROAST

We urge you to ask your meat market to use these standardized names when labeling its meats. You'll be able to buy more efficiently. To learn URMIS cut names for beef, pork, lamb, and veal and see their cuts' colored pictures, get a copy of "Identifying Meat Cuts" published by the National Livestock and Meat Board, 444 N. Michigan Avenue, Chicago, Illinois 60611. The grades of meat from *Prime* to *Select* are discussed in the following beef chapter. Pork, lamb, chicken, turkey, and fish all have somewhat different grades than beef and are discussed in "SECRETS" last five chapters.

# THE FACTS:  BEEF & E. coli 0167:H7

One old food germ (bacteria), E. coli 0167:H7, showed its "ugly head" in 1993 in Washington state. It produces a poisonous toxin which killed three people and made many very ill. They ate <u>undercooked</u> hamburgers at a restaurant. At the same time, no one became ill from eating T-bone or other beef steaks in Washington state. Why only hamburgers?

Hamburgers are made from ground beef. This E. coli germ can be present on and in only one animal in a herd of cattle. When this animal is processed, the germs can get mixed into the ground beef. The good news is E. coli and its toxin are killed when heated to 145°F. during cooking. However, to be safe, the USDA recommends that hamburgers be cooked to 160°F. — their centers are brown/gray — not pink. Their juices are clear colored — not rosy.

The USDA tells us that beef steaks (not ground beef) are safe when grilled to a medium rare 145°F. centers. Their exteriors are very safe beause grilling's heat of 375°F. to 500°F. kills bacteria, including E. coli, which may be present on their surfaces. This 145°F. medium rare temperature is 10° to 15°F. higher than very rare steaks with red, cold centers which some people like to eat.

However, medium rare steaks cooked to 145°F. can't be all bad, even for these people. These higher temperatures change more of the steak's collagen (tough, connective tissues) into tender gelatin for more tender steaks. Plus, they'll have higher flavor because the longer and higher heat creates more intense, browned (caramelized) tasty surfaces.

If you have further questions, call the USDA Meat and Poultry hot line 1 (800) 535-4555.

# CUT FAT 50% TO 75%, MEATS STAY JUICY, TENDER

## "New-LEAN" Do-It-Yourself Ground Meat System

Meat processors have known for years how to make hamburgers and sausages with extremely lean ground meats. Their problem: When cooked, lean burgers and sausages become hard and dry as old toast. When you take fats out of sausage and ground meats, you lose the smooth, juicy mouth feel and some of meat's flavors. _SECRETS'_ discovery: A new do-it-yourself low-cost <u>home</u> system that lets you put the tenderness, juiciness, and mouth feel back into 90% to 95% fat-free ground meats. You reduce fat calories in your burgers, sausages, meat loaves, and meat balls by 50% to 75%, yet they will still be juicy and taste delicious. We've named this major new do-it-yourself discovery. The "New-LEAN" System — and you receive it <u>FREE</u> in this chapter.

We've all seen and heard about lean hamburgers advertised on TV. Maybe we've seen high quality very lean ground beef or chicken featured at the supermarket with increased prices. The "New-LEAN" System answers this higher price for ground meat users who want tasty, juicy, low-fat meat. "New-LEAN's" meats will help: (1) parents who want to keep hungry kids fed with fewer fat calories; (2) parents who want their children's eating habits to improve; (3) high cholesterol and saturated fat watchers return to eating tasty meat; (4) people who like the taste of real hamburgers and sausages eat them without feeling guilty; and (5) people eat healthier meats that cost less.

"New-LEAN's" two amazing advantages: When you grill, broil, or bake its ground meats, you'll receive a the good mouth feel and the same juiciness, tenderness that ground meats with 20% fats have. It does not add any of its own flavor like many soy products do. "This sounds too good to be true," you say. "It's got to cost big money." The answer to these points is — NO!

"New-LEAN's" System takes a little time and work. Its "secret" ingredients are: (1) <u>extra</u> lean meat, (2) water, (3) a meat broth or standard bouillon, and (4) instant rice flour.

## Key Ingredient:  Instant Rice Flour

The instant rice flour is the key ingredient that makes the "New-LEAN" System function. It has a bland, practically neutral taste. It accepts the flavor of the meat it's mixed with easily. It accepts and holds moisture, keeping the meats juicier. It's made from low-cost ordinary supermarket whole grain Minute or instant rice — nothing very "secret" nor expensive about this "New-LEAN" ingredient.

This instant rice must be ground before using it. You can grind it fine enough in a blender or food processor. If you have access to a food mill, use it. The rice flour needs to be fairly fine, but not like cake flour. One pound of instant rice makes enough flour to make 32 pounds of "New-LEAN" ground meats. You mix this instant rice flour with cold water or cold meat. DO NOT mix it with hot or even warm water — it gels nearly instantly and completely, that's why you use it.

## Three Other Basic Ingredients

MEAT BROTH OR BOUILLON: Meat broths are ideal for maximum, true meat flavor. However, chicken and beef bouillon are usually faster and more convenient. They add some salty taste to the other ingredients. Chicken bouillon works well with ground chicken, turkey, or pork. Use beef bouillon with beef, lamb, venison, and other game.

WATER: Use cold tap water.

SEASONINGS: Use your pepper, spices, and herbs you'd use with each standard ground meat recipe, adjust salt slightly down.

You must start with **EXTRA** lean meats — pork, beef, lamb, chicken, or turkey. The "New-LEAN" System keeps them juicy with a good meat flavor.

YOUR CHOICE OF LEANNESS: BEEF: You can make 95% fat-free ground beef using a beef round roast or make 90% fat-free beef using a chuck arm roast. PORK: You start with fresh hams for 95% fat-free sausage or fresh pork shoulder picnics for 90% fat-free sausage. LAMB: Use shoulder for 90% fat-free meat.

CHICKEN: You start with chicken breasts without skin for 95% fat-free ground chicken; use thighs without skin for 90% fat-free ground chicken. TURKEY: Use turkey breast for the 96% lean or turkey thighs for 90% fat-free ground turkey.

Regardless of the basic meat you choose, you must trim out all of its surface (rind) fat, seam fat, plus the skin on poultry. You remove fat deposits between layers of lean and larger visible fat deposits. The important point: you reduce the basic meat's fat content down to about 6% for 95% fat-free ground meat and 12% for 90% fat-free ground meat.

## Basic Recipe for 5 Pounds of any "New-LEAN" Ground Meats©

**4 lb. 1 oz. extra lean <u>coarse</u> ground pork, beef, lamb, chicken or turkey**
**12.5 fluid oz. water**
**1½ Tbsp. chicken or beef bouillon (your choice) (12½ oz. broth may be substituted for the water and bouillon. See recipe.)**
**2½ oz. by weight (about 6⅔ Tbsp.) finely ground <u>instant</u> rice flour (<u>not</u> standard rice flour)**
**Salt and pepper and other seasonings which you normally add to meats.**

DIRECTIONS: Dissolve bouillon in boiling water. Cool this mixture. Add instant rice flour to bouillon or cool meat broth and mix thoroughly. Then add seasonings to this mixture. Next, mix this bouillon-spice-rice flour mixture thoroughly with the coarse ground meats. Fine grind this meat mixture over the hamburger (⅛" diameter holes) grinder plate. This fine grinding is an essential step for thorough blending of all ingredients for best results. These added ingredients lighten the color of cherry red meats a little but have no effect on their cooking and other qualities. (See Index: Grinding, Mixing, and Making Sausage.)

"New-LEAN" mixed meats can be frozen, then thawed, seasoned and grilled, broiled, smoked, or baked. The "New-LEAN" System adds cooked volume to your grilled and cooked meats. A grilled burger made from 4 ounces of 90% "New-LEAN" beef looks like one made from 4 ounces of 20% fat ground chuck. The "New-LEAN" burger tastes like and is as juicy as one containing 20% fat. It is more tender and, more importantly, you've removed over 90 fat calories from this burger when made with 90% fat-free "New-LEAN" beef.

You can make "New-LEAN" pork sausage easily using fresh pork picnics. Two sausage patties made from 3 ounces "New-LEAN" pork save 140 calories when using "New-LEAN's" 90% fat-free pork compared with two patties made from 3 ounces commercially made whole hog sausage which contains 33% fat.

## "New-LEAN" GROUND BEEF©

"You make your own 95% or 90% fat-free ground beef."

**4 pounds plus 1 ounce coarse ground extra lean beef from beef round roasts for 95% fat-free, or from chuck arm roasts for 90% fat-free beef. Buy extra for deboning and fat-trimming loss.**
**12.5 ounces water**
**1½ tablespoons beef bouillon or substitute 12.5 ounces of concentrated defatted beef broth for bouillon and water**
**2½ ounces (by weight) or 6⅔ tablespoons instant rice flour (See Index)**

Trim all surface (rind) and seam fat from beef. Grind over a sausage plate (3/16" holes). Weigh coarsely ground beef accurately. SET ASIDE. Heat water and dissolve bouillon, cool. Mix thoroughly with instant rice flour. Mix rice flour, bouillon mixture with the coarse ground beef. Regrind over a hamburger plate (1/8" holes). Package in 1- to 2-pound packages, refrigerate or freeze. Will freeze for 3 months. Use to make hamburgers, meat loaves, meatballs, and meat sauces. Reduce recipe's salt level to taste. Lightens color of ground beef. Save 50% to 75% of the beef's fat calories compared to 20% fat commercial ground chuck.

## "New-LEAN" BEEF BURGERS©

"You cut fat calories by 45%. Make juicy tender burgers."

**1 pound "New-LEAN" ground beef**
**1 tablespoon Worcestershire sauce**
**1 teaspoon salt**
**½ teaspoon pepper**
**2 tablespoons granular onion**
**1 teaspoon beef broth, red wine, or water**

Mix all ingredients together thoroughly. Make into ½-inch to ¾-inch thick patties. Grill or broil over medium high heat for 3 minutes or until grill-marked. Turn and reduce temperature to medium. Cook to 160°F., juices run clear, not pink. The center of the burger is brown, not pink.

## "New-LEAN" GROUND PORK©

"Make your own 95% or 90% fat-free ground pork. You'll save more than 140 fat calories from each 3 ounces. Now you can use pork again."

**4 pounds plus 1 ounce extra lean pork from fresh ham for 95% fat-free pork or from a pork picnic for 90% fat-free pork. Buy extra pork (about 8 pounds total) for deboning and fat-trimming loss.**
**12.5 ounces water**
**1½ tablespoons chicken bouillon, or substitute 12.5 ounces concentrated defatted chicken or pork broth for water and bouillon**
**2½ ounces (by weight) or 6⅔ tablespoons <u>instant</u> rice flour (See Index)**

Skin, debone, trim all rind (surface) fats and seam fats completely. Coarse grind meat over sausage plate (³/₁₆" holes). Weigh coarsely ground pork accurately, set aside.

Heat water and dissolve bouillon. <u>Cool</u>. Mix with instant rice flour. Mix rice flour/bouillon mixture with coarse ground pork thoroughly. Regrind over hamburger plate (⅛" holes). Package in 1- or 2-pound packages. Will freeze for 3 months. Use to make sausages, pork burgers, meat loaves, and meatballs and sauces. Saves 60% to 80% of pork's fat calories compared with ground Boston butt. Makes 5 pounds.

## "New-LEAN" PORK SAUSAGE©

"Save 140 fat calories from each 3 ounces compared with whole hog sausage. Now, you can eat juicy, tasty pork sausage again."

**4 pounds plus 1 ounce extra lean pork (buy about 8 pounds of fresh pork picnics or other pork to make up for the skinning, deboning and fat trimming loss)**
**12.5 ounces cold water**
**1½ tablespoons chicken bouillon, or substitute 12.5 ounces of concentrated defatted chicken or pork broth for water and bouillon**
**2½ ounces (by weight) or 6⅔ tablespoons instant rice flour (See Index)**
**1 tablespoon salt (non-iodized or canning)**
**1½ tablespoons black pepper**
**3 tablespoons ground sage**
**¾ teaspoon ground coriander**
**½ teaspoon MSG (Accent)**
**¼ teaspoon ground red pepper (optional)**

Skin, debone, and fat trim picnics completely. Coarse grind very lean pork over sausage plate (³/₁₆" holes). Heat water and dissolve bouillon, <u>cool completely.</u> Mix with instant rice flour. Add remaining ingredients to bouillon/rice flour mixture and mix. Then mix with the coarse ground pork thoroughly. Regrind over hamburger plate (⅛" holes). Package in plastic bags for sausage patties or stuff into 31 to 34 mm hog casings for linking. (See Index.) Makes 5 pounds.

## "New-LEAN" BRATWURST SAUSAGE©

Excellent flavor. Easy-to-make low-cal sausage for grilling. It freezes."

**pounds plus 1 ounce extra lean pork (buy about 8 pounds fresh picnics or other pork to make up for the skinning, deboning and fat-trimming loss)**
**2.5 ounces cold water**
**½ tablespoons chicken bouillon; or substitute 12.5 ounces of concentrated defatted chicken broth for bouillon and water**
**½ ounces (by weight) or 6⅔ tablespoons instant rice flour (See Index)**
**1½ teaspoons salt**
**tablespoon white pepper**
**1½ teaspoon nutmeg**
**¼ tablespoon ground ginger**
**½ teaspoon sugar**
**½ teaspoon MSG (Accent)**

Skin, debone, and fat-trim pork picnics completely. Grind extra lean pork over sausage plate (³⁄₁₆" holes). Weigh meat accurately; set aside. Heat water and dissolve bouillon; cool completely. Mix with instant rice flour. Add remaining seasonings to bouillon and mix. Then mix rice flour/bouillon spice mixture with meat thoroughly. Grind over hamburger plate (⅛" holes). Stuff into 31 to 34 mm hog casings. (See Index.) Simmer in water, beer, or milk plus water before grilling. Grill over a medium fire. Do not overcook. Remove when browned and juices run clear. Makes 5 pounds. Can freeze for 3 months.

## "New-LEAN" GROUND LAMB©

"Make your own 90% fat-free ground lamb."

**pounds plus 1 ounce extra lean ground lamb, from leg shanks and shoulder roasts. Buy extra for deboning and fat trimming loss**
**12.5 ounces water**
**1½ tablespoons beef bouillon; or substitute 12.5 ounces concentrated defatted lamb broth for bouillon and water**
**2½ ounces (by weight) or 6⅔ tablespoons instant rice flour (See Index)**

Debone, trim all surface (rind) and seam fats completely. Coarse grind meat over sausage plate (³⁄₁₆" holes). Weigh out coarsely ground lamb accurately; set aside.

Heat water and dissolve bouillon; cool. Mix with instant rice flour. Mix rice flour/bouillon mixture with coarse ground lamb thoroughly. Regrind over hamburger plate (⅛" holes). Package in 1- or 2-pound packages. Will freeze for 3 months. Use to make lamb burgers, meatballs, sauces, and lamb linguine. (See Index.) Makes 5 pounds.

## "New-LEAN" LAMB SAUSAGE©

"Delicious lamb sausage patties or stuffed into casings and grilled."

**4 pounds and 1 ounce <u>extra</u> lean lamb. Buy enough extra lamb shanks for deboning and fat trimming loss.**
**12.5 ounces water**
**1½ tablespoons beef bouillon; or substitute 12.5 ounces of concentrated defatted beef broth for bouillon and water**
**2½ ounces (by weight) or 6⅔ tablespoons <u>instant</u> rice flour (See Index)**
**1¼ teaspoons salt**
**1½ teaspoons pepper**
**1 tablespoon ground thyme**
**1 tablespoon ground rosemary**
**⅛ teaspoon red pepper**
**⅛ teaspoon MSG (Accent)**

Debone, trim rind (surface) fat and seam fats completely. Coarse grind lean lamb over sausage plate (³⁄₁₆" holes). Heat water and dissolve bouillon; <u>cool completely</u>. Mix with instant rice flour. Add remaining ingredients and mix. Mix the mixture with the coarse ground meats very thoroughly. Regrind over hamburger plate (⅛" holes). Package in plastic bags for patties or stuff into 31 to 34 mm hog casings for linking. (See Index.)

## "New-LEAN" CHICKEN©

"Make your own lower-cost 91.5% fat-free ground chicken. Cut fat calories 55% compared with commerically ground chicken."

**4 pounds plus 1 ounce extra lean chicken, dark meat. Buy extra chicken thighs for skinning, deboning, and fat trimming loss.**
**12.5 ounces water**
**1½ tablespoons chicken bouillon; or substitute 12.5 ounces of concentrated defatted chicken broth for bouillon and water**
**2½ ounces (by weight) or 6⅔ tablespoons <u>instant</u> rice flour (See Index)**

Remove skin and fat deposits completely. Debone, coarse grind chicken over sausage plate (³⁄₁₆" holes). Weigh accurately; set aside. Heat water and dissolve bouillon. <u>Cool completely</u>. Mix with instant rice flour. Mix rice flour/bouillon mixture with coarse ground chicken thoroughly. Regrind over a hamburger plate (⅛" holes). Package in 1- or 2-pound packages. Will freeze for 3 months. Use to make chicken burgers, meat sauces, and other food when ground chicken can be used. Makes 5 pounds.

## "New-LEAN" GROUND TURKEY©

"Make your own 92% fat-free ground turkey, dark meat. Cut fat calories 40% compared with commercially ground turkey."

**4 pounds plus 1 ounce extra lean ground turkey. Buy extra turkey thighs for skinning, deboning, and fat trimming loss.**
**12.5 ounces water**
**1½ tablespoons chicken bouillon; or substitute 12.5 ounces of concentrated defatted chicken broth for bouillon and water**
**2½ ounces (by weight) or 6⅔ tablespoons <u>instant</u> rice flour (See Index)**

Remove skin and fat deposits completely. Debone coarse grind meat over sausage plate (3/16" holes). Weigh coarsely ground turkey accurately; set aside. Heat water and dissolve bouillon. <u>Cool completely</u>. Mix with instant rice flour. Mix rice flour/bouillon mixture with coarse ground meat very thoroughly. Regrind over hamburger plate (1/8" holes). Package in 1- or 2-pound packages. Will freeze for 3 months. Use to make turkey burgers, meat sauces, and other foods where ground turkey can be used. Makes 5 pounds.

# Quality of Tenderness For Various Cuts Of Steaks

The tenderness of each steak depends upon the quality of animal each specific steak comes from. However, with electrical stimulation, USDA Select Grade beef **CAN BE** as tender as USDA Choice. The difference: less flavor and juiciness with the Select grade.

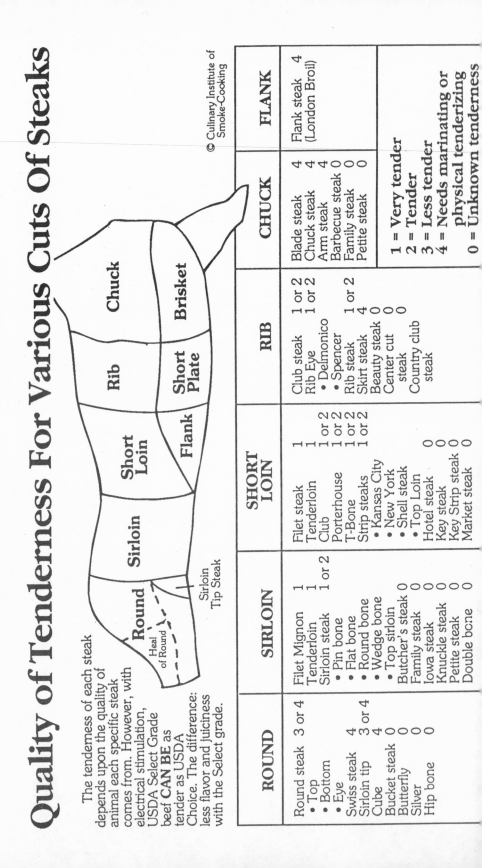

Diagram cuts: Round, Sirloin, Short Loin, Rib, Chuck, Flank, Short Plate, Brisket, Heal of Round, Sirloin Tip Steak

© Culinary Institute of Smoke-Cooking

1 = Very tender
2 = Tender
3 = Less tender
4 = Needs marinating or physical tenderizing
0 = Unknown tenderness

| ROUND | | SIRLOIN | | SHORT LOIN | | RIB | | CHUCK | | FLANK | |
|---|---|---|---|---|---|---|---|---|---|---|---|
| Round steak | 3 or 4 | Filet Mignon | 1 | Filet steak | 1 | Club steak | 1 or 2 | Blade steak | 4 | Flank steak | 4 |
| • Top | | Tenderloin | 1 | Tenderloin | 1 | Rib Eye | 1 or 2 | Chuck steak | 4 | (London Broil) | |
| • Bottom | | Sirloin steak | 1 or 2 | Club | 1 or 2 | • Delmonico | | Arm steak | 4 | | |
| • Eye | | • Pin bone | | Porterhouse | 1 or 2 | • Spencer | | Barbecue steak | 0 | | |
| Swiss steak | 4 | • Flat bone | | T-Bone | 1 or 2 | Rib steak | 1 or 2 | Family steak | 0 | | |
| Sirloin tip | 3 or 4 | • Round bone | | Strip steaks | 1 or 2 | Skirt steak | 4 | Petite steak | 0 | | |
| Cube | 4 | • Wedge bone | | • Kansas City | | Beauty steak | 0 | | | | |
| Bucket steak | 0 | • Top sirloin | | • New York | | Center cut steak | 0 | | | | |
| Butterfly | 0 | Butcher's steak | 0 | • Shell steak | | Country club steak | 0 | | | | |
| Silver | 0 | Family steak | 0 | • Top Loin | | | | | | | |
| Hip bone | 0 | Iowa steak | 0 | Hotel steak | 0 | | | | | | |
| | | Knuckle steak | 0 | Key steak | 0 | | | | | | |
| | | Petite steak | 0 | Key Strip steak | 0 | | | | | | |
| | | Double bone | 0 | Market steak | 0 | | | | | | |

# Don't "Beef" at Beef

Delicious beef —
Still ok to eat it!

"Let's grill steaks tonight," gets everyone's attention immediately! Maybe the family pocketbook is a little thin, because Laura and Andy both need new shoes. Then it's, "Let's grill burgers tonight." That's no big disappointment . . . they'll be classic hamburgers with all the fixins'. Both of these "Let's grill tonights" are first class American foods and they come from first quality <u>American beef</u>, the most reasonably priced quality beef in the world. But lately, much of what you hear about eating beef — "it's really bad stuff."

J.J., John's continuously "food-panicked" wife, started at the supper table, "Blossom Do-Rite and I talked yesterday and she told me that she heard this health speaker. He said 'Beef is not good for you because it contains all saturated fats, loads of cholesterol, and calories.' And many of Blossom's friends said they eat beef only one time per month and never eat hamburger. John, you know I just love steak and a good hamburger, but I'm trying to keep my cholesterol reading about 170 and my weight at 110 pounds. I'm scared if I eat any beef, my cholesterol will go sky high — way over 200 and I'll gain 10 pounds."

Now folks, you could actually see John take a very deep, long breath and look disgusted, but he took J.J.'s food panic comments seriously. She's the mother of his two girls. He knew that they would be "food-fad-fat-freaks" if he didn't get their mother's food gossip straightened out. John had spent a little time lately studying fats and cholesterol. He knew that J.J.'s 170 cholesterol and 110-pound weight wouldn't be grossly affected by some steak nor some lean burgers.

## Six Ounces Per Day

John learned that J.J. could eat 4 ounces of fat-trimmed steaks <u>more</u> than once a month. The American Heart Association recommends 6 ounces of cooked meat per day. And for hamburgers — eating 3 ounces made from a ratio of 80% lean and 20% fat ground beef grilled or broiled would only yield 4 grams of saturated fats. Also, J.J., at 110 pounds, could eat about 14 grams of saturated fat each day.

Food fads and food gossip, and not knowing nor understanding food facts, really affects how millions of Americans eat. Most every knowledgeable person would agree: a fast-food double burger with cheese and French fries cooked in beef tallow is not a healthy diet meal-after-meal day in and day out. Our bodies need a balance of meats, vegetables, fruits, grains, and dairy products to remain healthy.

Beef's high quality protein matches our body's protein needs nearly perfectly There's nothing wrong with 3 to 4 ounces of lean broiled steak, or beef barbecue or grilled lean ground beef pattie without cheese, one or two times per week Particularly if you balance it out with other low-fat foods such as fruits, vegetables and grains.

## All-Or-Nothing Approach

John, you can tell J.J. her "all-or-nothing" food approach of not eating any ground beef should force her to stop eating her great health food — yogurt! Why? Laboratory rats were fed a diet of 100% plain yogurt for a period of time. They grew and reproduced nicely, but 100% of them had cataracts. With her "all-or nothing" food approach, J.J. should never eat one teaspoon of yogurt. So let's eat beef in moderation. It's good for our bodies and it tastes great.

Next, J.J. could ask just how safe, wholesome, and clean is U.S. beef? Every U.S. beef animal is inspected by USDA's trained and certified meat inspectors The USDA Meat Inspection Division (MID) inspects U.S. processing plants and processes. They must meet its high standards for safety, cleanliness, and handling of meat and poultry products.

Finally, the USDA and FDA scientists show that there is no harmful residue from growth hormones (estrogen) fed to cattle to increase their feed's efficiency Much of the continuing hue and cry about the U.S. beef's growth hormone problems comes from European countries' farmers who cannot compete with U.S beef producers' efficiency.

## Buying Beef Better

You want to buy tender, juicy flavorful beef. To be sure it's tender and juicy, the first thing to know: "Where does the cut come from on the beef."

PRIMAL WHOLESALE CUTS OF BEEF: Meat processors divide a whole beef weighing from 600 pounds to 750 pounds into two "sides." Each side is further divided into 9 major sections called "primal cuts" (wholesale cuts). Starting from the front of the beef carcass moving back along the top of the animal, beef primal cuts are: (1) chuck, (2) rib, (3) short loin, (4) sirloin, (5) round, (6) flank (7) brisket, (8) brisket, and (9) shank.

## Quick Guide For Buying Beef

USDA graders know that beef cuts from some animals can be exceptionally good — and other animals produce less tender and drier meats. The graders are on the U.S. consumer's side. (See Index: Playing Steer.)

Graders use the USDA's grading system for beef. It has six grades. Only two grades are normally sold in our supermarkets — *Choice* and *Select*. You'll see the third grade, *Prime* beef, in gourmet meat markets. It is served by upscale hotels and restaurants. Only 6% of the beef grown in the U.S. grades *Prime*. *Choice*-graded beef takes about 68% of U.S. supermarket sales. *Choice* has less fat than *Prime*, but is usually tender and juicy. *Select* grade beef is leaner, less juicy than *Choice*. It can be sold as the "X,Y,Z" Supermarket's "Lean," or "Low Fat," or "Generic" beef, or as USDA *Select*. With the new electrical stimulation method, USDA *Select* grade becomes as tender as *Choice* beef.

The USDA's grading system places a harmless purple stamp on beef's primal cuts. Rarely will you see this purple stamp. Your meat cutter will have trimmed it from nearly all retail cuts when he removes the outside rind or surface fat. Meat processors pay for grading each animal.

## Detailed Beef Grading System

One of our local ladies talked about her aging husband and said, "He's just like an old bull." One of her three older friends gossiped later, "He's just ill tempered." Another said, "He's stubborn." One three-time widow grinned, smiled big and whispered, "He's still got a lot of fire left in his furnace." The wife's truth about her husband: He's just tough like an old bull because he still works hard physically, and he's got tough muscles.

Steers, heifers, bulls, and cows all become less tender the older they get. Their muscles get larger and coarser and their tough connective tissues (collagen) grow thicker and increase in number. How old a beef animal is, makes a big difference in its tenderness.

The USDA grading system tells you much about the age of the beef you buy. (1) Any carcasses coming from a beef under 30 months old may be graded USDA *Prime, Choice, Select,* or *Standard.* (2) Any carcass coming from an animal over 42 months old is automatically graded *"Commercial"* or *"Utility"* and is not sold for steaks by good meat dealers.

## Less Than 30 Months

How can USDA graders tell if a beef came from a 30-month-old or younger animal? They don't know precisely to the day, but they can accurately estimate the age with their "Button System." During processing a beef, the USDA grader inspects the sides for cartilage buttons (transparent tissue) on the ends of the vertebrae bones in the beef's back. As any beef animal ages, these cartilage buttons change to hard bony areas. This change moves from the rump up to the animal's head as it ages. If these buttons are still cartilage in the back area which carries the heart and lungs, this beef is under 30 months old.

## Rib Eye Grading For Quality

Each processed beef is partially cut between the 12th and 13th rib, exposing a cross section of the animal's rib eye muscle. High quality beef contains bright cherry red lean meat with fine-textured fibers and a moderately firm feel. Meat like this comes from a younger animal.

Next, the grader examines the rib eye's size and the amount of marbling in his muscle. Marbling can be specks, flecks, long "strings," or wide "strings" of fat intermingled within the lean. Heavy marbling makes beef juicier and more tender. The amount of marbling in this rib eye muscle carries into the remainder of the meat of the animal. Normally, the heavier the marbling, the higher the USDA grade.

The USDA has seven practical amounts of marbling in beef — from "slightly abundant" in USDA *Prime* grade for 24-to-30-month-old cattle down to "practically devoid" for USDA *Standard* grade 8- to 12-month-old animals. This marbling term of "slightly abundant" is meaningless unless you compare two grades of beef. *Prime* cuts have about 10% to 15% fat specks and streaks of fat in the lean. A USDA grade *Select* has a "slight" rating for its marbling with only 1% to 2% specks and very few streaks of fat in the lean.

## USDA Beef Grades

USDA *PRIME*: Marbling: the amount of marbling must increase from "slightly abundant" in younger beef, to "moderately abundant" for 30-month-old beef. *Prime* is the most expensive grade of beef.

USDA *CHOICE*: Marbling ranges from "moderate" down to "modest," and finally to "small" in young beef. This grade will be juicy, tender beef which produces high quality cuts of steak.

USDA *SELECT*: (old USDA grade *"GOOD"*) Marbling: as low as "slight" in young animals up to "small" in 30-month-old animals. This grade is becoming more popular with the consumer. It is leaner and less juicy with a higher lean to fat ratio — it may be meat-market labeled "lean," "generic," "low fat," or *"Select"*.

USDA *STANDARD*: You'll rarely find this grade in U.S. supermarkets.

USDA *"COMMERCIAL"* AND *"UTILITY"*: Normally used for making ground beef.

NON-GRADED BEEF: Millions of pounds of non-graded U.S. beef are sold to institutions which feed hundreds of people each day. This beef can be *Select* and sometimes even *Choice* or the meat market's private label.

NATURAL BEEF: Grass-fed beef sold at a premium by some U.S. supermarkets and natural food stores. It is usually not USDA graded. Sold to "food-panicked" people who have read the producer's advertisements.

## Real Beef World

The "Real World" of Supermarket Beef: The USDA's basic quality grades give you some guidelines for choosing beef cuts. However, there can be a lot of room between a top *Choice* grade of beef and the bottom *Choice* grade of beef in tenderness and juiciness. At your market, you look at the meat through the clear plastic. Then you try to figure out what to buy.

HIGH QUALITY BEEF: Regardless of the cholesterol/fat content good-tasting juicy tender grilled beef needs some fat marbling. The lean must be bright cherry red colored, velvety, and moist looking. Tender beef's fibers are fine textured and firm. When you press raw meat with your finger, younger meat returns to shape fairly quickly when the pressure is removed. Outer coating of fat should be creamy white and moderately firm, ¼" down to ⅛" thick. The cut ends of the bones will have a red pinkish color and appear to be slightly porous and honeycomb if it's freshly cut younger high quality beef.

## Buying Beef For Steaks

Many cookbooks, magazine, or newspaper writers, or TV cook show hosts start out with, "Buy a good piece of meat." Usually their "good meat" means a *Prime* or *Choice* grade porterhouse, T-bone, or strip steaks.

*Prime* will yield less lean meat because of its higher fat content. Trying to grill a Chuck Arm Steak from *Prime* beef is probably not wise. It will not be as juicy and tender as a club steak from a *Choice* beef.

There are lots of other cuts besides steak from every beef animal! For example: A 1,000 pound live beef animal "dresses out" into 454 pounds of meat, including the bones. This 454-pound *Choice* beef will yield only 125 pounds of tender steaks that can be grilled or broiled. Much of the remainder of the beef's 229 pounds benefits from moist cooking or becomes ground beef.

## Know Steak Names

Meat cutters have created and used at least 43 different steak names for steaks coming from three primal sections of a beef. The Rib, Short Loin, and Sirloin sections produce high quality steak. Their names have ranged from

Beauty" through T-bone to "Butcher" steaks. However, the National Livestock and Meat Board recognizes only 23 steak cuts as having good potential to be juicy and tender when grilled. See beef drawing at the beginning of this chapter.

Our grilling experience: only thirteen steak cuts have been tender and juicy when grilled <u>without</u> tenderizing help — at least sometimes. These steaks also come from only these three primal sections of the beef's back: the rib, the short loin, and the sirloin.

## Thirteen Major Steak Names

THE *RIB* PRIMAL SECTION: next to the shoulder (chuck) produces: (1) rib steaks containing the rib bone and the smaller eye muscle next to the shoulder, and a larger eye muscle next to the *short loin*; (2) rib eye steaks (delmonico) have the rib bone removed.

THE *SHORT LOIN* PRIMAL SECTION: comes from the middle section of the steer's back and produces: (3) the porterhouse steak which has a bone shaped like a T, as well as the larger piece of tenderloin and a large piece of top loin; (4) the T-bone steak which contains the T-bone itself and a tiny to smaller tenderloin, as well as a large piece of top loin; (5) the club steak which has part of the T-bone and only the top loin (sometimes rib steaks are sold as club steaks). The meat cutter takes the T-bone steaks and removes the whole tenderloin from one side of the bone and debones the top loin side of the *short loin* primal section to make (6) a Kansas City Strip steak; and (7) a New York Strip — they are the same steak with different names in different parts of the U.S.

*SIRLOIN PRIMAL* SECTION: (8) The pin bone sirloin steak: with its two large bones, and large tenderloin and some top sirloin; (9) flat bone sirloin steak — large flat bone, plus a medium to large tenderloin and top sirloin; (10) round bone sirloin steak, small round bone, plus a small tenderloin and large top sirloin; (11) wedge bone sirloin steak — a small bone, large top sirloin; (12) boneless top sirloin steaks — bone and tenderloin removed from the complete sirloin primal cut and cut into steaks, (13) whole tenderloin — removed from the sirloin, porterhouse, and T-bone steaks. This whole tenderloin can be divided into (a) chateaubriand, (b) filet mignon steaks, and (c) tournedos.

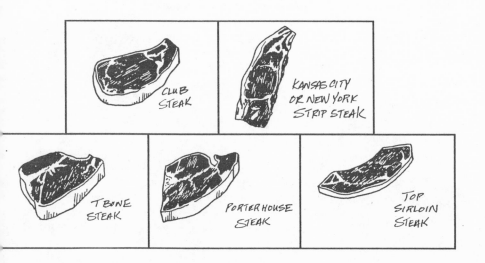

## Real Steak World

Most beef processors now produce "boxed beef" or vacuum-packed beef. They remove all bones and package large sub-primal sections in vacuum-sealed bags.

The reasonably affordable tender juicy real-steak-world starts normally with *Choice* beef. The best buy is usually the boneless top sirloin steak. A portion of these steaks lies close to the porterhouse steak on every carcass.

BONELESS TOP SIRLOIN STEAKS: Most processors remove the bone and the complete tenderloin, leaving a complete top sirloin. Sirloin steaks can be cut with an ordinary butcher knife if you buy the whole top sirloin. If the meat cutter slices your sirloin steak from this primal cut, ask for it to be cut from the portion close to the porterhouse end.

Top sirloin is normally lower priced 25% up to 33% below T-bone or porterhouse steaks, all of which have large bones. The porterhouse is a better buy than a T-bone steak if there is only a few cents difference per pound because of its bigger tenderloin.

WHOLE BEEF TENDERLOINS: When you buy this complete cut on sale, as meat-in-a-bag, it can be a good steak buy — when you compare the actual lean meat you receive. It has no bone and little fat waste to be trimmed away if you choose a good one. Each untrimmed tenderloin has a tough top silver sheath (membrane) cover (about 1/32" thick) which needs to be trimmed away.

Any vacuum-packed tenderloin-in-a-bag will appear dark, but out of the bag and trimmed, tenderloin brightens to a cherry red when exposed to air. You will need to baste with some fat and seasoning to enhance the flavor because a tenderloin is nearly 100% lean. Do not grill filets or a tenderloin well done. They can be very dry and stringy unless you baste.

## Less Tender, Lower Cost Steaks

The chuck, round, and flank primal sections of a beef can be cut into steaks. Meat cutters have used 35 different names for these steaks from a "silver steak" to "California steak." Many people recommend using lower cost steaks for grilling. You marinate and tenderize 3/4" to 1 1/2" thick, (1) top round (nearly all lean), (2) chuck blade bone, (3) flank, or (4) skirt steaks. Then you'll grill them to medium rare and slice them cross grain into thin slices to be tender and juicy. They must come from *prime*, *choice*, and some *select* beef to be tender.

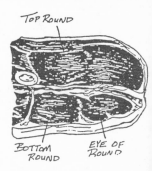
TOP ROUND

BOTTOM ROUND

EYE OF ROUND

TOP ROUND STEAK: Recommended for grilling by some people. It contains little marbling and needs marinating in an acid/oil-based marinade to be tender. Baste with fat while grilling.

SKIRT STEAK: A thin steak coming from the inside chest cavity of the beef. Tenderize and cook to medium rare.

FLANK STEAK

FLANK STEAK: 3/4" to 1" thick, 4" to 6" wide, 12" to 14" long, very little fat. All very long, coarse fibers running lengthwise. Remove the thin membrane covering it if one is present. Score fibers 1/8" deep in a 1-inch criss-cross pattern and marinate with an acid/oil marinade. Grill to medium-rare pink, and carve cross grain ⅛" thick. *Choice* or *Prime* grades will be tasty, and reasonably tender steaks.

SIRLOIN TIP STEAK: Part of the round, very lean and less tender. This cut is sometimes recommended for kabobs. Top sirloin is a more tender cut.

THE "EYE-OF-THE-ROUND": A 12-inch long, 3- to 4-inch diameter piece of meat which looks like a beef tenderloin. It has very coarse long fibers. When grilled like a tenderloin, it can be tough. Moist cook or marinade with an oil/acid marinade and tenderize for best results.

THE CHUCK BLADE STEAK OR ROAST: Comes from the chuck next to the rib primal section. You will need to tenderize it.

BEEF SHORT RIBS: Large bones, make delicious soup or smoked.

CUBE STEAKS: Can be any part of the beef carcass which is lean beef. These are manufactured by putting pieces of beef together and processing them through a cubing machine which cuts the tough muscle fibers. They're better floured and fried. They'll be dry when grilled.

SWISS AND ROUND STEAKS: Are good when moist cooked to a medium done and held at 160°F. for a period of time to tenderize.

HAMBURGER STEAK (chopped beef steak): Ground beef patty ¾" to 1" thick wrapped with bacon which is fastened to the ground beef. (See Index: Hamburger Steak.)

BRISKET: Two different kinds: one half comes with lots of fat, much of it is trimmed off after cooking. This cut requires long cooking. It is a favorite beef entry in barbecue cook-offs. (See Index: Brisket.)

## Beef Roasts

STANDING RIB ROAST: Restaurants and meat dealers call it "Prime Rib" even though it's "Choice" or "Select" grade. It's normally tender. The complete rib contains 7 to 8 ribs. "First ribs" are the best cut because they contain the 11th and 12th ribs. These "firsts" are also called "Small End Rib Roasts." The large end rib roast contains the 6th and 7th ribs which are next to the tougher chuck primal section.

Rib bones are cut in two lengths: a 10-inch-long rib bone, and a 7-inch-short one. The 7-inch roast should be more expensive. Or if you wish, you can buy a deboned rolled and tied rib roast (the most expensive).

Buy the 7-inch rib roast. Have your meat cutter cut the eye loose from the rib bones, or you can do it yourself. Season the bones, the eye, and trim off some fats to make it leaner. Tie the eye back to the ribs and smoke-cook, grill, or roast.

STEAMBOAT ROUND: Meat cutters' or restaurants' name for a 15-pound-and-up piece of round — *Choice* grade. Slowly roast or smoke at 250°F. for 7 to 12 hours depending upon size, to an internal temperature of 145°F. If carved thinly cross grain, most every time will be tender, tasty, and juicy.

STANDING RIB ROAST 10" RIBS

STANDING RIB ROAST 7" RIBS

BRISKET

## Pot Roasts (Moist Cookery)

Retail cuts of meat from the beef chuck and round primal sections of beef (including *Prime* and *Choice* grades) contain less tender meat. It'll be tender when braised or pot roasted. This type of cooking changes collagen into a tender gelatin. A pot roast is tasty but will not have the flavor of a roast that is smoke-cooked with dry heat. There are nine different URMIS (see index) uniform retail-recognized chuck roast cuts and eight different URMIS-recognized round roast cuts. These all probably need moist heat cookery or tenderizing marinades.

## Long Term Beef Aging (Ripening)

Meat scientists find that aging up to 14 days tenderizes meats. Beyond this, meat's flavor increases, but not tenderness. Meats can spend 8 to 10 days traveling through standard marketing channels. Aging beef darkens it to a deeper red color. A few processors age beef by storing it at 34°F. - 36°F. with 85% to 90% humidity for three to six weeks.

## Money Saving "Meat-In-A-Bag"

Use "meat-in-a-bag" (vacuum packaged meats) to save money when buying beef, pork, and lamb. Every meat dealer can order it if he doesn't carry it.

"Beef-in-a-bag" comes in 3-pound to 25-pound pieces of meat called sub-primal and sometimes primal (wholesale) cuts. Ninety-five percent of this meat is boneless. The meat processor places bigger pieces of meat into a plastic bag, then sucks a vacuum. The bag shrinks very close to the beef, which encloses it in an oxygen-free atmosphere. It will be darker in color because it's not exposed to oxygen which gives meat its cherry red color. Vacuum-packed beef lightens up to a standard cherry red when exposed to air. The meat and its dark juices in the bag may be unappetizing in the display case. But it contains safe wholesome USDA inspected meat.

The advantages of meat-in-a-bag are: (1) The real price of edible meat should be lower because the meat market does no processing. It should have minimum waste because it's normally boneless. One pound of this meat may yield up to two to four additional servings compared to bone-in cuts. (2) Because of this unique oxygen-free system, meat can be stored in a refrigerator for 14 to 21 days at 40°F. or for much longer at 30°F. without spoiling. Its tenderness may improve somewhat.

Additional advantages of this system: The meat is aged 8 to 10 days without surface molding or drying out the skin and trimming loss; you trim the fat, making it as lean as you want; you slice the meat with a good butcher knife as thick or thin as you want; you grind meat trimmings for ground meat — as lean as you like.

Disadvantages of meat-in-a-bag: It will be difficult to tell how well marbled the meat is through its plastic cover; however, 80% or more of the sub-primal beef cuts sold in a bag will grade USDA *Choice*. Each package should have a USDA grade and date label.

Available sub-primal cuts of "beef-in-a-bag": Boneless Rib Eyes — weighing 12 to 16 pounds — whole beef tenderloin, 4 to 8 pounds — beef top round, 25 pounds — beef top loin, 12 to 14 pounds — beef top sirloin, 8 to 10 pounds — and beef brisket, 5 to 14 pounds.

When cutting your own steaks for grilling, cut them 1 inch to 1½ inches thick. Then cut each steak into serving pieces after grilling. Any steak cut less than ¾ nches thick should be frozen, thawed slightly, then grilled or pan-grilled for more flavor and juiciness. When you cut roasts, leave a thin fat coating for some flavor and juiciness. If you smoke-cook a roast in a water smoker, you can fat trim it closer for leaner beef. You'll have juicy meat if you cook it no more than rare to medium rare.

## How Much Beef To Buy/How Lean?

(Based upon 3 ounces of cooked meat per serving)

| Steaks | Servings/lb. uncooked meat | Fat-Free Content: contains marbling with separatable fat removed |
|---|---|---|
| Flank steak | 3-4 | 90% |
| Porterhouse steak | 2 | 85% |
| Rib steak | 2 | 83% |
| Rib eye (Delmonico) | 3 | 80% |
| Sirloin with bone | 2½ | 89% |
| Top sirloin | 3-4 | 91.5% |
| T-Bone | 2 | 84% |
| Tenderloin (filet) | 3 | 87% |
| Top loin (New York, | 3 | 90% |
| Kansas City Strips) | 3 | 90% |
| Top round | 3-4 | 93% |
| Whole round steak | 3-4 | 91.5% |
| **Ground Beef** | | |
| Meat market ground beef | 3-6 | 90% down to 70% |
| Ground chuck | 4-5 | 80% - 82% |
| Ground round | 4-5 | 88% |
| **Roasts** | | |
| Brisket fat trimmed | 4-5 | 87% |
| Chuck, arm/blade bone | 2 | 83% |
| Rump, boneless | 3 | 89% |
| Standing rib | 2 | 79% |

BIG BEEF SALES: Big ads for "untrimmed" beef can loose 33% or more compared to already-trimmed beef. The ad may say, "naturally aged." All meat is "aged" from 4 to 5 up to 10 days. "Baby beef" comes from 400- to 600-pound animals and will not be full flavored.

All whole cuts need some fat to be tender and juicy when cooked. Be a good assertive meat shopper; do not remain silent — tell your meat cutter, "My, that was a good cut of beef." Or, "That last beef was not so hot, it was tough." After all, he did not butcher the beef, but he had it available for you to buy. And he needs you to buy it again and again to stay in business.

## Ground Beef/Hamburger

VERY IMPORTANT BUYING HINT: Grinding any grade of beef from *Prime* to *Utility* grade tenderizes it! Grinding cuts tough muscles and connective fibers into ⅛" diameter by ¼" long lengths. It produces about 35,000 tiny pieces per pound. Therefore, whether you start with *Prime* or *Utility* grade beef, you get tender ground beef after it's ground. Both <u>can</u> contain the same amount of fat. Ground beef made from a *Utility* grade animal may have yellow-colored or rancid-tasting fat. Lean ground beef made by a reliablemeat market should be juicy and tender, whether it's from sirloin, round, chuck, or lean trimmings of meat.

Some supermarkets label their ground beef "chuck style," which means that they trim it to give you about the same percentage of fat as "chuck." You'll save money over the years if you'll settle for 80% lean/20% fat ground beef or chuck style or grade. Chuck and beef trimmings, when ground, taste as good as ground round, or sirloin and will be just as tender.

Buy your ground beef from a meat or supermarket which is very picky about cleanliness. Because of E. coli see page 222. You'll be safer cooking any ground beef to 160°F.

## Higher Quality Ground Beef

The real key to buying ground beef is the fat content. It varies from 3.5% up to a 30%, the legal fat limit — or from 70% to 96.5% fat free. New commercially made ground beef mixtures will contain only 3.5% up to 10% fat. The processor starts with extra lean cuts of beef which are trimmed of all fats then ground. This ground beef is blended with beef broth, or bouillon, and a gum or gel, such as a carrageenan or ground oat bran, or others. These ground beef mixtures are safe and leaner to eat.

Standard ground beef needs 18% to 20% fat for flavor and to make a juicy hamburger. One very dependable cookbook writer said about 20% fat ground chuck hamburger, "When I eat a hamburger, I want it to be good and juicy, and I expect to compensate for my cholesterol/fat in another way."

High quality ground beef will have a bright cherry red color and moist appearance without bloody spots. If the ground beef is not labeled with a lean percentage, ask your supermarket for the lean/fat ratio for their ground beef. He should tell you. If he can't or won't, find another market which will.

A meat market's fresh ground beef should keep its flavor and freshness for at least two days after you buy and refrigerate it. When stored for several days, the interior part of the ground beef may develop a darkened red/brown color. It returns to its normal cherry red beef color (called "bloom") when exposed to the air's oxygen.

"CHUBS" OR ROLLS: Fresh ground beef is vacuum packed into one-, two-, or three-pound plastic rolls with a use-by date. Lean/fat ratio should be printed on the package.

One pound of lean ground beef serves 4 to 5 people: One pound of fat-ground beef serves only 3 to 4 people, and contains excess fat which you may want to avoid. However, in USDA tests, 75% lean grade was judged more juicy and flavorful than 85% lean. They both had about the same cooking weight loss.

The "lean" burgers sold by the fast food drive-ins contain lean beef, water, beef-flavored bouillon, and carrageenan. The carrageenan absorbs water and holds it throughout cooking. Trained taste-testers state that these lean burgers have about the same mouth feel and taste as a standard hamburger from the drive-in. The beef is labeled 93% fat-free.

When you freeze ground beef, you should keep the air away from the frozen beef by wrapping it tightly without air pockets. Use a vapor type wrapper, such as Saran® or aluminum foil or equivalent, to eliminate freezer burn.

## Veal

U.S. veal comes from young bull calves, rarely heifers. They are saved to become cows. Therefore, the supply is reduced 50% automatically. The popular large black and white spotted Holstein dairy cows produce lots of profitable lower-fat milk. Their bull calves weigh 150 to 200 pounds at birth. They grow efficiently into an 800- to 1000-pound steer by eating low-cost grass. They can be put into a feed lot for a short time and then marketed at 1,200 to 1,500 pounds. Their meat is lean and the fat is white. Institutions and supermarkets buy them as *"Select"* grade beef or non-graded. There is a scarcity of young Holstein vealer-sized bull calves. Veal will be expensive because the U.S. has a small supply of vealer calves.

Back some years ago veal was marketed as a 6-week-old 150-pound milk-fed calf. Now, it's a 3-month-old calf weighing 350 pounds. This so-called veal from these larger and older calves has darker reddish pink-colored meat. It is not white like milk-fed veal. Veal needs little or no fat trimming to become a lean meat. One disadvantage of veal — its cholesterol content ranks somewhat higher than pork or beef. Veal's USDA grades are *Prime, Choice,* and *Select* (old USDA *Good*).

HIGH QUALITY VEAL: Veal, a very bland-tasting meat, needs tasty French-style sauces. Veal comes from 8- to 12-week old calves weighing up to 350 pounds. They have nursed their mothers for 3 to 4 days and then are fed a milk replacer. True young veal contains little visible fat, no marbling. Veal is lean pale creamy pink to a reddish pink, sometimes a whitish color; it's firm, velvety-fine texture, and moist looking. It'll have small bones, with red cut surfaces, if fresh cut. Its fat will be whiter than its lean. However, some veal with a yellowish outside fat comes from small breeds of dairy cattle. This is good veal.

RETAIL VEAL CUTS: Veal's Primal wholesale sections are the same as beef with 8 divisions. Therefore, you can expect the same name and kinds of cuts as beef with one exception: veal cutlets. These are very thin slices cut from the round (hind leg) of the animal.

VERY IMPORTANT VEAL COOKING TIPS: Use moist heat cookery for most veal and calf cuts because: (1) You should only pan grill veal loin chops, no grilling, unless tenderized; (2) Veal contains two times the amount of connective tissue (collagen) compared to a 12-month-old beef.

# Pork Cuts

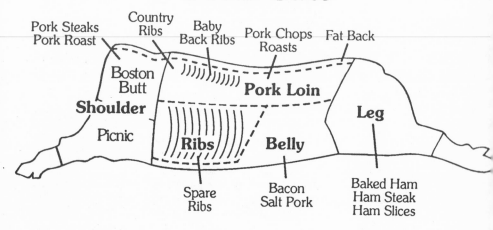

Pork Steaks
Pork Roast

Country Ribs

Baby Back Ribs

Pork Chops Roasts

Fat Back

Boston Butt

**Pork Loin**

**Shoulder**

**Leg**

Picnic

**Ribs**

**Belly**

Spare Ribs

Bacon Salt Pork

Baked Ham
Ham Steak
Ham Slices

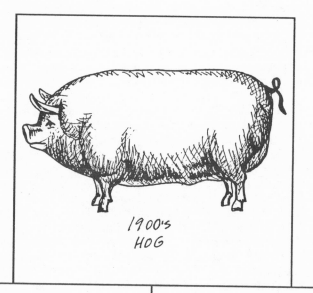

1900's HOG

1940's HOG

1990's HOG

# Let's Not Forget Pork

## It's much leaner and safer than most people think

### Possibly the 1990's Major Food Rebirth

Some people recommend that the lowly pig be crowned Sir PIG when eating it. It's more honored as pork meat than when it's alive. When he gave his famous Iron Curtain speech in 1947 at Fulton, Missouri, Sir Winston Churchill ate Missouri country ham. He said, "The pig has reached the highest state of evolution in this ham."

However, the poor pig has been degraded thousands of times. People compare us humans' less-than-desirable traits with those of the pig: "He eats like a pig" and "He is as fat as a pig." In defense of THE PIG, experts say they are smarter than most dogs, lots smarter than cats, and can be trained to use the sandbox easily.

Before you get the wrong impression, we're <u>not</u> on the payroll of the National or Missouri Pork Producers. (Unfortunately, they have not sent us a check and we don't think it's in the mail.) However, Charlie the author grew up on a hog farm eating pork with gusto, and thinks you'll feel better about eating pork when you learn about its truths. You'll like it even better with <u>SECRETS'</u> low-fat approach.

### The Short Ham

Ruthie, a young bride, stood in the kitchen next to Lucy, her mother, and watched. Lucy was sawing the shank of a small Easter ham — finally a 3-inch-long piece of the shank dropped off. Then Lucy put the ham in her big roaster. It was nearly "lost," but she baked it there anyway.

Ruthie was trying to learn about cooking, so she asked Lucy, "Momma, does cutting off the shank end improve the ham's flavor? Or does it help bake the ham better?" Lucy responded, "I don't know — but I do know your grandmother cut off the shank for years — and she always served the most delicious, juicy ham."

Later that day, Ruthie asked her grandma why she cut off the shank. "Back in those days, I had a very short roasting pan. I had to cut off the shank to make the ham fit in my roaster," she said. Ruthie nodded; she had just witnessed humanity in action, "I saw or heard it done that way 20 years ago, therefore it's done today." Pork's bad reputation clings like a coat-of-paint, but you can fat-trim and it's delicious when cooked.

Then, there's J.J., good ole John's continuously "food-panicked" wife. She walked through their kitchen door, set down her groceries — and started non stop, "John, Blossom Do-Rite told me today that her doctor told her, "Don't eat pork because it's very high in cholesterol and calories. And it's nearly all saturated fats. You must cook it absolutely white done to 185°F. to be safe from trichinosis — and John, she said she hadn't touched pork in two years."

John just listened — he knew Blossom's doc's reputation — a big prescriber of cholesterol pills for people too old to really matter. It gave some of them diarrhea and constipated others. John liked pork's taste. He knew that it was one of the best buys for tender cuts of meat for grilling and barbecuing. He was tired of eating J.J.'s insipid chicken. She cooked with very little seasoning for the last three days straight. He had heard something good about pork recently and he tried to mentally dig-it-up.

## False Cholesterol Reputation

John, to enlighten your dear J.J., here are pork's cholesterol facts. The U.S. government's market basket survey compared three different meats for cholesterol — all three-ounce servings: pork had 66 mg., chicken breast meat without skin had 73 mg., chicken dark meat, with skin 78 mg., and beef tenderloin 71 mg. You can tell J.J. that a healthy diet allows up to 300 mg. of cholesterol daily.

When you smoke a sirloin pork roast you can easily trim its surface layered fat for 93% fat-free pork. Now, let's compare its flavor and delicious taste with commercially prepared water-filled, sliced-paper-thin 95% to 97% fat-free turkey breast. Most everyone would choose "real food," the smoked sirloin pork roast for flavor, juiciness, and lean meat.

Let's look at all fats including vegetable oil fats. They all contain some saturated fat, as well as poly-unsaturated, and mono-unsaturated fats. Canola oil has the least saturated fat with only 6.0% and chicken with 31%. Pork fat (lard) has only 41% saturated fats . . . not the 100% that J.J. believes.

Registered Dieticians tell us that we need to eat about 30% fats to be healthy and that 10% of the calories we consume can safely be saturated fats. Pork fat has a high percentage of mono-unsaturated fats which lowers the cholesterol. Pork's lean (pork loin) is safe with only 7.0% fat . . . Pork is not a fast food cheeseburger with French fries cooked in animal fat like the media has implied. America's pork now comes from leaner breeds of pigs. It contains 50% less fat than just 20 years ago. You can cut around fat and leave it on your plate.

## False Trichinosis Reputation

Pork never deserved the 185°F. cooked-white-done-trichinosis-reputation. Pork has no trichinosis problem if we know one FOOD TRUTH. "We kill all trichinosis in pork at 137°F. internal cooked temperature," say the USDA's meat scientists. The 137°F. is about the done temperature for a rare T-bone steak or rare lamb which people eat everyday in the U.S. Today, cooks stop cooking pork at 160°F. for a more juicy better doneness temperature. You'll find it's delicious. You'll be rated as a great outdoor cook because it will be juicy and tasty. Freezing pork to 5.0°F., for only 20 days, kills trichinosis also.

## Good Ole American Barbecue

The famous old-time French chef, Escoffier, "knocked" pork severely in his nternationally recognized cookbook <u>Guide Culinaire</u>. He wrote "However deservedly pork may be praised, it could never have been included in the preparation of first class cookery (except as a subsidiary) had it not been for the culinary value of ham!"

This Frenchman never had the privilege of eating our good ole American Pork Barbecue — he could start with country style ribs, spare ribs, or pork loin, pork shoulder, all smoke-cooked, juicy and tender . . . barbecued U.S. style. Americans made barbecue into great eatin', and the world has adopted it from us. Pork barbecue is one of the great traditions of most southern folks. It's featured in the big "feeds" in much of the Southern U.S. For example: A BBQed whole hog is laid out on the cook-out table. Forks are stuck into the hog from head to toe. Guests walk by with their plate, take a fork and pick off pieces of BBQed pork meat. It's called a "pig pickin'." Even transplanted Northerners get excited about barbecue after tasting the real thing.

Some U.S. doctors, cookbook and media writers should begin to look at pork through more scientific eyes. It's not fair that Americans miss the opportunity of eating good ole American Pork Barbecue. Yes, it contains some saturated fats, but so do solid margarines, solid vegetable shortenings, and most cheeses.

BASIC PORK TRUTHS: (1) An estimated 400 million hogs continue to be raised for food throughout the world every year; (2) The pig was the second wild animal to be tamed for mankind's food; and (3) In the U.S., pork is <u>the chosen meat</u> for the Memphis in May celebration, an International Professional Barbecue Contest. This famous contest has three distinct pork-cooking categories: pork ribs, pork shoulder, and whole hog.

The world-famous American Royal BBQ contest is held each fall. It is part of the American Royal Livestock exposition and show. Pork ribs and one other pork entry are two of the meat categories in this six-meat cook-off.

## USDA Pork Quality Grading

Our U.S. dressed-pork grading needs improvement to compare with the USDA beef grading system. At this time USDA graders grade a pork carcass as either *acceptable* or *unacceptable*. The USDA minimum *acceptable* carcass is defined.: "The loin eye muscle (the large lean meat portion of pork chops) has (1) at least slight firmness, (2) a slight amount of marbling in the lean, (3) the lean's color ranges from grayish pink to darker red color."

The USDA does have four quality grades for pork; a carcass is cut up into wholesale (primal) cuts. The weight of the <u>lean</u> primal cuts — hams, loins, picnics, and Boston butts compared with the total carcass weight determines the carcass grade: U.S. No. 1 grade, over 60.4% lean cuts; U.S. No. 2 grade, 57.4% to 60.3% lean cuts; U.S. No. 3 grade, 54.4% to 57.3% lean cuts; and U.S. No. 4 grade, less than 54.4% lean cuts.

## Few Buy on USDA Grade

Today a few U.S. processors are buying hogs using their own grading system, but not the USDA system. If you examine the USDA system, a U.S. No. 4 pork carcass contains more than 45% *non-lean* cuts of meat. This means that this No. 4 carcass probably had 1½-inch-or-more-thick fat coating on the pork loin compared to a 1-inch coating for a No. 1 carcass. You'll never see either the 1½" nor the 1" back fat coatings. They will both be trimmed off! However, the remainder of the No. 4 carcass will contain lots of extra fat.

All four USDA grades are graded *acceptable*, regardless of their fat content if all other quality factors are satisfactory. You can buy fat pork coming from fatter hogs easily if your meat cutter is "not-on-the-ball" or purposely sells lower grades.

## BBQ Consulting

Our personal BBQ consulting experience tells lots about buying pork shoulders for a barbecue business from three different major sources of supply. Our clients wanted to serve lean pork to their customers. Therefore, we tried to start with lean raw pork to smoke-cook and barbecue. So, we weighed each shoulder before skinning, deboning, and severely fat-trimming. Our total weight loss of bone, skin, and fat was only 39% on a very good lean shoulder, compared with 54% weight loss on fat shoulders.

## High Quality Fresh Pork

Younger porkers yield more tender meat. Their lean meat will be a grayish pink tinged with red color, not deep red colored; it is fine grained, firm with some marbling in the lean of the loin, ham and shoulder. Press the lean meat with your finger; it should return to its original position fairly fast if the cut is from a young animal.

High quality pork's exterior fat layer should be a creamy white color and firm when chilled. This layer should not be over ⅛-inch to ¼-inch thick (you can trim off 90% or more). The cut end of the bone should be red if you're buying a cut of pork from a young, recently processed animal.

This first quality porker starts with a lean-breed hog. It has not been exercised and run on the pasture for months for its food like a steer. It's processed at a much younger age of 5 to 6 months compared with 14 to 18 months for high quality beef. Lean hogs can be processed into cured hams with an exterior fat coating plus the skin of no more than ½-inch thickness at the thickest fat/skin area.

## Buying Pork Cuts

Don't pay big prices for layers of fat between lean meat as well as thick surface fat. This thick fat cover carries over into the lean. Try to examine pork for thickness of fat cover between the visible meat and the area hidden by the packaging. Check Boston butts, whole shoulders and cured ham. A 250-pound hog will yield a carcass weighing 175 pounds, with retail cuts of pork weighing 125 pounds.

## Pork Cuts For Smoking, Barbecuing, and Cooking

SPARE RIBS: Come in "sides" or "slabs" from meat dealers. Better quality spare ribs come from younger hogs. They will weigh 3½ pounds per slab and down. Slabs weighing 4 pounds and over probably come from old sows. Their rib bones are much larger and the ends are flattened ovals compared with round ends of ribs coming from younger hogs. Ribs contain about 40% bone. All larger slabs from older hogs probably will

SPARE RIBS

need longer cooking. The meat of many ribs has been scraped down to the bones by the processing. Avoid buying these.

Some meat cutters cut sides of spare ribs into "St. Louis," "Chinese," "cocktail" ribs, etc. These are two- to three-inch-wide strips of spare ribs. After you smoke or barbecue them, cut them into 1 or 2 rib serving pieces for hors d'oeuvres or Oriental ribs. Have your meat cutter cut a standard "side" of spare ribs down to 3-inch-wide strips and save money.

BABY BACK and LOIN RIBS: Usually, these ribs are meatier and more expensive than spare ribs. Sides weighing 2½ pounds and down come from 250-pound and smaller hogs. Many Pro barbecuers prefer this cut of rib in barbecue cook-offs.

COUNTRY STYLE RIBS: The shoulder end of a bone-in pork loin. This cut divided into 2 joined "butterfly" portions. These ribs are normally cut into ¾-ich to 1½-inch-wide serving pieces. If not cut, have your meat cutter saw them or you for much easier serving after smoking. Don't overcook country style ribs eyond 155°F; they dry out easily because they contain more lean meat.

PORK SHOULDER: Whole front leg of the hog less the foot.
houlders contain a good fat/lean ratio for making pork sausage
nd other sausages. You trim their surface and visible fat if you want
lean sausage (18% fat). However, all sausages need some fat to
e juicy. For low-fat smoked or barbecued pork shoulders, they'll
ed closer fat trimming than for sausage. Whole fresh shoulders
eighing from 12 to 16 pounds are the best size for barbecuing.
upermarkets sell whole shoulders as two cuts: (1) the top portion equals a Bos-
n butt (pork shoulder roast); and (2) the bottom shank portion equals a fresh
cnic or "callie."

BOSTON BUTT/PORK SHOULDER ROAST: The Boston butt portions will
eld about 70% to 76% ready-to-cook meat after deboning and heavily trimming
e surface fat. Pork steaks come from this cut. Boston butts are usually the least
xpensive and easiest pork cut to debone and prepare for barbecuing, or smoke-
ooking. One large area of surface fat on the skinned side consists of two layers
 fat with a small, thin layer of "false" lean between them. These three layers can
 trimmed away without great loss of lean meat for smoking or barbecuing. If
u do not trim their fat, Boston butts are excellent cuts for mixing with the lean
 a totally defatted venison or other wild game meats for making wild game
usage. (See Index: Venison and Elk Sausage.)

PICNIC or "CALLIES": Picnic portions will yield 60% to 65% ready-to-cook
eat when skinned, deboned and heavily trimmed of surface fat. There's more
an meat on a trimmed picnic than on a trimmed Boston butt. However, debon-
g and skinning the picnic takes much more time.

FRESH HAM: Hind leg of the hog. When injected and cured with a brine
vater, salt, sugar, sodium nitrite, and a harmless phosphate) and then smoked,
 injected with liquid smoke, processors produce a standard cured ham for super-
arkets. A lean fresh (green) ham is too lean for sausage. You'll need to add
me fatter pork (a Boston butt) to make good sausage. You can smoke-cook a
esh ham for excellent barbecue. You'll need to skin it and trim the surface fat
efore smoking. *SMOKING RESEARCH (SR): In a taste test comparing deboned,
osely fat-trimmed, seasoned, and smoke-cooked fresh ham with a smoke-
ooked fat-trimmed seasoned fresh shoulder, the shoulder won; also it had a
wer price per pound of usable meat.*

PORK LOINS WITH BONE-IN: Lowest cost way to buy low cholesterol/low
 t very elegant meat to smoke-cook, barbecue or roast. You trim off much of the
p layer of fat before smoking or cooking. The pork loin's tenderness and elegant
vor compares with a beef tenderloin. However, the trimmed pork loin will cost
out 40% of the price of the trimmed beef tenderloin. Smoke-cooked in a water
noker (See Index) to 155°F., you'll serve juicy, tender elegant, delicious meat.

Don't overcook it to the white 185°F. doneness stage. It'll be dry because it
nearly all lean with little marbled fat. Pork chops come from this major cut of pork.
A complete pork loin contains two meats: the loin itself and the tenderloin.

## Your Meat Cutter

If you buy a whole bone-in pork loin, and are afraid to debone it, ask you
meat cutter to help you. Have him/her cut center-cut pork chops ¾-inches thic
for grilling or stuffing, and the rib end portion into country style ribs for smokin
and barbecuing; then, the sirloin end for smoking or roasting.

BONELESS PORK LOIN: One complete piece of loin without bone weighin
5 to 8 pounds. It may appear to be two pieces. Buy the 5- to 6-pound size. It wi
usually come from a younger hog. Smoke-cooked fat-trimmed pork loin is 93%
fat free.

SIRLOIN PORK ROAST: The ham end of the pork loin has a large piece o
tenderloin; in addition to the loin itself. Usually it's a good buy for lean tende
pork. (Trim off surface fat. Our loss was only 15.0%.) It contains considerabl
bone, but is 93% fat-free.

CENTER CUT PORK CHOPS: The most expensive chops. Avoid chops with
deep red-colored lean; they can be tougher because they may come from olde
hogs or may come from hogs that have been stressed. For a better buy, have you
meat dealer cut two ¾-inch-thick chops from the "good" end of a sirloin pork
roast. This roast is normally much cheaper per pound than center cut pork chops
Use the remainder of the roast to smoke or roast for sandwiches.

PORK TENDERLOIN: Very lean tender pieces of meat 1" to 1½" diameter
about 6 inches long are located in the same position as a beef tenderloin. The
have little fat and dry out easily unless marinated with some vegetable oil o
wrapped in bacon and smoked to a safe-to-eat light pink color of 155°F.

FRESH PORK SAUSAGE (called breakfast and farm sausage): Commercia
processors are permitted to make this sausage containing up to 50% fat. One o
our locals said, "With that fat sausage, I think folks are sold a-pig-in-a-poke." I
you buy 1-pound plastic tubes of pork sausage, buy those which are labeled whole
hog sausage which contains about 35% fat or less. It may cost more, but will be
leaner.

## Smoked Pork Products

WHOLE BONE-IN SUPERMARKET HAM: It's ready-to-eat, cured and
smoked, and weighs from 18 pounds down to 12 pounds. Most processors fast-
cure hams today by injecting the curing liquid into the meat, using mechanical
needles. These hams will contain the USDA-allowed 10% curing liquid. After
curing and smoking, this brings the ham back to about its original moisture content.

The salt content will be about 2%, equal to most of today's commercially
produced luncheon meats and bologna. It's other added ingredients are safe to

eat, if you're not "food-panicked." USDA and FDA Food scientists have studied them for years. They state that <u>these ingredients perform necessary curing functions for a tender, juicy, safe ham, after cooking.</u> These ingredients are not a cancer threat unless you eat nearly 100 pounds of ham each day for thirty years (this is an exaggeration, but much closer to the truth than some anti-meat reports are telling you).

PORK RIB
CHOP

CENTER CUT
LOIN CHOP

Supermarkets remove a ham's center slices which are sold separately. Your best buy: a complete ham if you have the space to store it. Have the meat cutter slice these choice center slices for you. You can use the shank and butt ends for baking later. Ham freezes well for six months. Ham will have a fat content from 16% to 22%. When roasted, it will yield 61% up to 65% lean meat with about 3.0% fat; the rest is skin and bone.

BONELESS SMOKED HAM: Four to 8 pounds, contains 10% added water and curing ingredients. Check brands for the amount of smoked processing rind or "skin" which is tough and may need to be removed before cooking. This ham is a better buy than another product called, "Boneless Ham and water Product" which may be displayed in the same meat case.

BONELESS HAM and WATER PRODUCT (honest, that's one of the correct names and many others are not so revealing) weighing 4 to 6 pounds, containing 30% to 33% water. This is not a very good buy; it gives a false value. Its price must be increased 20% or more per pound to make it equal to a boneless smoked ham above. The labels on this and similar "watered" products may say, "95% fat-free." This type of product illustrates Charlie's kNOTE-WORTHY 1990s Food-Panicked "LAW": "EAT WATER — It's 100% Fat-FREE."IMPORTANT: Fully-cooked standard ready-to-eat supermarket hams or picnics should be heated up to 130°F. or only 140°F. They dry out. You will like the more intense flavors.

DO-IT-YOURSELF GOURMET HAM: *"Here's an opportunity to turn a sow's ear into a silk purse,"* as one of our locals said. Start with a supermarket ham and create a tasty, low-salt flavorful lean cut of meat, using either the shank or the butt portion. (See Index: Gourmet Ham recipe.)

DRY CURED COUNTRY HAM: Each processor has his own special system for dry-cured country hams, such as Smithfield, Virginia, Georgia, Tennessee, Kentucky, or Missouri hams. After dry curing with salt, sugar, and seasoning for weeks, they are smoked for days. Most are aged and lose about 20% to 30% of their original weight.

Country hams contain about 4% salt which prevents spoilage. Therefore, you need to soak most dry-cured hams in water for hours. This reduces the salt level and adds moisture back to the meat before cooking it. Country hams have not been cooked, therefore, they must be cooked (baked or fried) to 150°F. to develop flavor. Follow the individual processor's directions for cooking times and temperatures.

These hams have robust flavor. After cooking, they can be served hot or chilled and sliced very thin. They may have a harmless surface mold when you buy them wrapped in paper. Light surface mold does not hurt the ham; you scrub it off with a brush and water. Country ham, plus other meats, are used to make the famous southern red eye gravy.

PROSCIUTTO HAM or Parma ham originally come from Italy. Some U.S. processors are curing Prosciutto-type hams. They are sliced very thin and served raw with fruit or to flavor cooked dishes. U.S. processors use "certified" fresh hams which are frozen to minus 10°F. for 10 days to kill the trichinosis before curing.

CURED SMOKED PICNIC or "CALLIE": Can be ready-to-eat or not (read labels). Picnics start with the shank portion of a pork shoulder. When sliced ⅛-inch thick, smoked picnics give you bacon's flavor with lots of lean and about half of bacon's fat content and normally costs less.

BACON: The cured and smoked "side" meat (called "bellies") of the hog which covers the hog's ribs. Old-fashioned dry-cured bacon can take two weeks or more to cure and then smoke. Much of today's bacon is fast cured in 12 hours by pumping a brine through hollow needles. Some processors add liquid smoke flavoring to the brine, others actually smoke it.

CANADIAN BACON: Produced in the U.S., Canada, and Denmark. It comes from a pork loin. Trimmed carefully of fat, cured, and smoked like a ham; it tastes like ham, is ready to eat, but needs to be cooked to 130°F. to 140°F. to develop good flavor.

## Deboning Fresh Pork Shoulder or Ham

First, please don't be afraid to try. You'll probably make mistakes, but don't tell anyone. Actually, 99.9% will never know it when you smoke-cook, then slice the meat. Meat trimmings can be useful for flavoring vegetables, etc.

Keep meat extra cold to reduce slickness prior to deboning. Use a knife with a very sharp 4½-inch to 6-inch-long blade for skinning and deboning. Remove all blood spots. Skinning: Start skinning by cutting the skin into two parts at the shank end's narrowest skin area. Push knife between the skin and the meat and peel the skin back by cutting it loose. Then pull up the skin and cut through the fat layer between the meat and the skin. And continue until the meat is skinned. After skinning, trim the surface fat.

DEBONING: Start removing the bone by laying the meat flat on the table toward your cutting hand with the shank or butt end toward you. You want to uncover the leg bone by splitting the meat butterfly fashion. Make your first cut toward the bone from the meatier side parallel with the table, one-half way down on the shoulder. Pull the meat up and away; look and feel for the bone and continue to cut to the bone. When the bone is uncovered, "outline-it" by cutting down each side, around and underneath it; then continue to cut, pull up, look, cut and scrape the meat scraps from the bone. Some meat may still cling to the bone, but you haven't wasted much. The next shoulder or ham you debone will go easier.

## Smoking Deboned Pork

When you barbecue or smoke-cook a Boston butt, shoulder, or fresh ham, the object is to produce the maximum browned crusty "outside" meat; this has maximum flavor. Slice the meat nearly in half from the side. Leave connecting meat, like butterflied pork chops. You can apply a rub on all exposed meat surfaces easier. You'll smoke-cook it better while producing more outside barbecued meat.

Now, John, you can see why pork might be "re-born" in the 1990s. Pork is nutritious, juicy, delicious, and excellent when barbecued. J.J. claimed pork has lots of "problems" . . . well, they nearly all disappear when you know pork's true facts and you use good judgment when fat trimming and cooking.

# "Chic" Chicken

You'll appreciate chicken
even more!

'Food safety continues to be a growing concern of American consumers. In 1989, one out of every twelve Americans was buying and eating less poultry, or no poultry. They have growing concerns about poultry's contamination with various diseases," reports the Institute of Food Technologists' Muscle Foods Division. Before you "turn-off" chicken, please read the scientific facts about salmonella. Many "food-panicked" Americans prefer to believe food rumors, food half-truths, instead of scientific food facts.

## Chicken and Salmonella Truths

J.J., John's continuously "food-panicked" wife, hates one word with a passion — "germs," particularly salmonella in chicken. You could feel sorry for her if she's trying to learn the truth about germs. Not J.J. — she just plows right in by going all-out. She even inspects John's barbecue grill. You'd think that he was going to perform heart by-pass surgery inside the grill the way she inspects it.

When John starts to grill she nearly always says, "John, now you clean that grill with that wire brush, then scrub it with soap and water, and John I want you to soak the grill's rack in full-strength chlorine bleach for 10 minutes before you cook on it. You know it's too easy to get sick with that salmonella disease from chicken. You remember, John, you grilled chicken last weekend, and I heard Blossom Do-Rite say that chicken causes millions of cases of salmonella each year in humans."

Please, John, take heart, ole man. You've got to give dear J.J. some salmonella facts. She probably won't believe you. She probably has her mind made up — but you know she might listen to the facts, and you've gotta try.

First, let's not let the word salmonella scare us to death. Salmonella is a human disease of the stomach and intestinal tract, and many folks call it the "24-hour stomach flu." In plain words, it's diarrhea and it's really harmful to tiny babies and older sick people. However, it causes few deaths in the U.S. But it's scary, painful, very interruptive, disruptive, draining, and inconvenient. There's a new, more potent form now reported which the U.S. Public Health Service (USPHS) is watching.

In one recent year, nearly 50,000 cases (not deaths) of salmonella were reported to the USPHS. Properly cooked and handled chicken did not cause these or any salmonella problems. However, poor handling and inadequate cooking of raw chicken and raw eggs, along with poor handling of cooking utensils and cooking surfaces cause salmonella.

## Chicken Not A Problem

Chicken is not a salmonella problem if you follow four steps: (1) You stop salmonella from reproducing by keeping raw chicken cold at 40°F. or less and cooking it within 48 hours or freezing it immediately when you bring it home. (2) You kill salmonella when you wash the utensils, working surfaces, and your hands, that have touched the chicken or its juices, thoroughly with soap and warm water. (3) You can be 1,000% safe by swabbing the counter top with clothes bleach (5.25% sodium hypochlorite). Use is at 2 tablespoons per quart of water, then rinse with plain water. (4) You kill salmonella when you cook the chicken to 165°F. internal temperature. Never partially cook chicken to 120°F. and let it "rest" for 6 hours at room temperature. It can get you. Salmonella can multiply 10,000 times when stored for 6 days at 40°F., which is cold for the average home refrigerator. Normally, they run at 45°F. and up. You may want to check yours.

When chicken is cooked to a minimum approved interior temperature of 165°F., the chicken's exterior skin temperature will be over 225°F. in a smoker (300°F.) or more on a grill. This kills germs on the skin surfaces and in the neck and tail cavities of whole chickens.

Even then, there are always some "nervous Nellies and Neds" who'll try to scare you with, "Poultry's got those salmonella germs," like poultry's got a terrible social disease. But consider that each person in the U.S. now averages eating 84 pounds of chicken a year. Two ounces of chicken can harbor over 100 million salmonella germs — enough to cause the "big diarrhea."

If salmonella caused by chickens is as bad as some of the media writers picture it, J.J.'s rumored millions of cases would be true and people would fall in the street with it. Americans would need to build thousands of new public restrooms just to handle "the big diarrhea" problem. Fortunately, this wild rumor, like many other negative food rumors, is only the result of some uninformed people's wild imaginations.

Please don't get us wrong! Salmonella poisoning is no fun and hurts babies and old ill people. Now, for the real world of delicious healthy chicken, read on.

## Chicken the Cholesterol/Fat-Fighter

"Hurray, here's XYZ's new cereal, your big new improved cholesterol/fat fighter," shout the big ads for the BRANS — oat, rice, and wheat.

One of our local "boys" said, "The claims they make for that oat bran, it ought to solve any problems for a senior in his golden years. And you know, some of that oat bran tastes like sugar-coated, baked dried hay — but it's good for ya, they say!" Yes, it's a good healthy food, but it's not a cure-all for mankind. Let's have another look at other foods.

We have this good ole American food — chicken! And it's recognized as a cholesterol/fat-fighter too. You can cook it 30 different ways. It's full of juiciness, great flavors, and delicious taste when barbecued, grilled, or smoke-cooked. It doesn't cost as much per pound as that fancy box of bran cereal and it's lots more exciting and fun to eat.

These cereal folks aren't the only far-out ones: You can get poor advice from cookbook writers. One said, "Eat only the chicken breast. Throw away the legs and thighs; they're too fat and unhealthy." The truths from USDA data: Chicken

)asted, 3½ ounces cooked portion: (1) white breast meat 7.7 grams of fat; (2) ark meat 13.4 grams of fat. The American Heart Association says that our daily iet can safely contain 30% fat, a mixture of all three fats — saturated, mono-nsaturated, and poly-unsaturated fats — to stay healthy. This is about 40 to 60 rams of fat per day for the average woman, depending upon how much physical /ork she does.

## Why Chicken Costs Less

Producing chickens is one of the modern miracles of efficient American agri-ulture. With automatic feeders and waterers, and other labor-saving and poultry-nanagement practices, two people now care for 250,000 growing chickens com-ared to only 10,000 twenty-five years ago. Chickens eat less than 2 pounds of ed per pound of weight gain compared to 8 pounds per pound of gain for cattle, nd 4 pounds for porkers. Professional chicken farmers produce high-quality lressed fryers weighing about 3½ to 4 pounds in 6 to 7 weeks.

Compare this chicken growth with one steer taking one year to grow to 1,000 ounds and netting only 450 pounds of edible meat and bone. However, please ive beef cattle credit. Remember, they use very cheap, unusable grasses for most f their food for most of their lives. (Otherwise we could be stuck with goats to asture the land, and that's lots of goat meat to eat — not good ole American eef.)

## Compare Calories and Dollar Values

Dressed frying chickens average having 60% meat and 40% bone and skin. 1) When shopping, you have a choice of a 3.2-pound or 3.54-pound frying hicken. Choose the bigger chicken. It gives you proportionally 30% more breast neat. Small chickens are not a great meat buy, except for commercial restaurants. 2) When comparing protein content, a 3½-pound chicken at $1 per pound quals fairly lean ground beef costing $1.33 per pound. (3) Three-and-one-half unces of chicken white meat without skin, grilled or smoke-cooked, equals 173 alories; and (4) Three-and-one-half ounces of dark chicken meat with skin, fried quals 285 calories.

Chicken leg and thigh muscles are somewhat tougher because the chicken ses them 24 hours per day. Chickens squat on their legs even when they sleep, nd the legs may need to be cooked somewhat longer to be tender. Legs and highs have a higher flavor, are juicier than breast meat in many people's opinions.

## How to Buy High-Quality Chicken

*"Some folks would have you believe a skinny rooster is the best one. That's rue, only when he's chasing hens," according to a local man of the cloth, "not vhen you plan to eat him."*

HIGH-QUALITY FRESH CHICKEN: May or may not be labeled USDA rade "A" (the processor pays for this grading) — yellowish or white colored, right, smooth-textured, moist skin. Well-developed layer of fat in the skin.

WHOLE CHICKENS: The breast: round, plump look, filled in with meat xtending to the crest of the breast bone. This meat is deep and thick and carries long the complete length of a long breast bone. The breast bone does not stick p sharply above the breast meat. The chicken has short legs, no broken bones, s free from pin feathers and hair, and has no bruises or discoloration. The breast nd legs are complete without missing skin, cuts, or tears. A very yellow-colored hicken is probably no fatter than the white one the same age and size.

When you unwrap high-quality chicken, you may have a momentary odor which quickly goes away. Discard any juice and wash chicken with clear water. It may have frost inside from the carbon dioxide ($CO_2$) used in packing it at the processing plant and still not be a frozen chicken. Store at 40°F. or below for no longer than 2 days before cooking, or if longer, freeze the chicken.

HIGH-QUALITY FROZEN CHICKEN: Use the same standards as for fresh high-quality chickens. Plus, it must be practically free from defects caused by freezing or storing. Torn packages, freezer burn on the flesh, "snow" (condensed moisture "sucked" from the chicken when frozen too long) accumulated in the packages are low-quality signs. You may see slight darkening over the chicken's back and drumsticks — but it still has a bright appearance and is okay when thawed. White "pockmarks" caused by the freezer dehydrating the inner layer of the skin are okay if the circles are not over $1/8$" in diameter. Only a few small areas of a thin layer of clear or pinkish-colored ice should be present. Flash frozen, vacuum packed chicken will keep for six months without growing rancid.

## Supermarket Chicken Sizes

SECRETS has divided U.S. supermarket chickens into six different groups, primarily by weight and fitness for smoking and grilling.

SMALL FRYER OR "BROILER": Two pounds to 3 pounds dressed (3 to 5 weeks old). Breast meat thin, pointed breast bone usually — too small for good smoking and grilling. "Too little cooked meat, too much cooked bone and skin," one good cook-out cook said. These are great for fast food chicken restaurants with their breading or batter to make the pieces look bigger and weigh more. If you need to use "broilers" for barbecuing or grilling, turn and baste frequently with marinade containing some vegetable oil, margarine, or butter. Large chicken leg quarters and breasts are better for grilling and certainly for smoking.

LARGE FRYING OR BROILER CHICKEN: Three-and-one-half to $4^1/2$ pounds dressed. The best size for smoking and grilling, and normally the better quality chickens at the supermarket. They usually have a good price and the most flavor when grilled or smoked.

With a 4-pound chicken, you get a tender, plump, broad-breasted bird, with meat which nearly fills the cavity to the top of the breast bone. It has some fat in the skin on the breast, legs, and thighs. To prepare a whole chicken for smoking, remove the heavy fat deposit inside the entrance of the abdominal cavity unless removed by the processor. You remove it easily by pulling it loose with your fingers.

When you cut up your own chicken, you can cut away many visible deposits of fat easily. A three-and-one-half to 4-pound chicken serves 3 to 6 people, depending upon how "lite" the people feed themselves.

"RANGE" CHICKENS: Ninety-nine percent of today's chicken is grain-fed from birth in confinement and not exercised on a "range." The new "in" thing for some cookbook writers and cooks is "range" chicken. They say they taste better — some writers also recommend buying 2-pound broilers which are not too much bigger than pigeon squabs. "Range" chickens are easily and cheaply "created" by large, efficient poultry raisers. Many merely open the doors of each chicken house, which holds up to 10,000 birds, each morning. This allows these chickens to "range" outside into a fenced field.

Gullible consumers do not know that the chickens' feed and water generally stay inside the chicken houses. Result: very few chickens go "ranging" very far on their "range." That night, all the chickens return to the house and the doors are closed. These special, ranch-exercised chickens can cost double the price per pound of standard supermarket chicken.

ROASTING CHICKEN: Dressed, 7 to 8 weeks old, 4½ pounds to 6½ pounds. The 4½ pound roasters are good for smoking, but normally more expensive than chickens labeled "frying chicken" of the same 4½-pound size. Breast meat usually is thicker and excellent. Legs on a large 6 to 6½-pound roaster may be somewhat tougher than the 4-pound to 4½-pound frying chicken. If you smoke-cook a larger roaster and the legs are tough, cut them off and cook a little longer in the microwave or oven after smoking.

CAPON: Four-day-old, castrated male chicks live a very tranquil life. One of our local wags, referring to his friend who was henpecked beyond belief said, "No capon ever ruled the chicken roost." Capons weigh 6 to 8 pounds. They are not exercised but are grain fed from birth, are very tender, and smoke beautifully. You may need to special-order a capon from your local meat market, or it may be available frozen in some larger U.S. supermarkets.

ROCK CORNISH GAME HEN: Normally frozen, small 1 pound to 1¾ pounds dressed, special breed of poultry, which contains all white meat. They smoke beautifully and make an impressive lovely party food — it takes "work" to eat one. "They" (Miss Manners, etc.) should allow you to pick it up and eat with fingers, using many napkins, or you'll waste lots of tasty meat — and that's a shame.

STEWING HEN/STEWING CHICKEN: Five- to 8-pound dressed hens, 10 to 12 months old and no longer lays eggs profitably or may have been raised specially for this market. They normally have high fat content. Moist cook, stew, or braise to be tender. Then use the meat for pasta, casserole, chicken and dumplings, and chicken soup. You'll be better off buying a big fryer for smoking; it'll be tender.

CHICKEN PARTS: Chicken breasts, thighs, legs, and wings are sold in packages of individual pieces. This is a convenient way to buy legs for a child who only eats legs or breast meat and for people who must have white meat only. Packages of parts are good buys during "special sales." These parts are more expensive than buying whole chickens on sale and cutting them up yourself. This is a fast-disappearing talent and is not difficult to learn. Breasts have the most meat in relation to the bone.

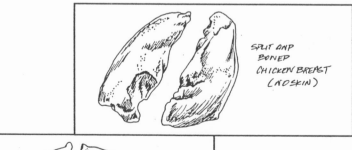

SPLIT AND BONED CHICKEN BREAST (NO SKIN)

SPLIT CHICKEN BREAST

CHICKEN LEG

FRESH GROUND CHICKEN MEAT: Can contain 10% fat or 90% lean. Most comes from ground chicken thighs without skin.

FROZEN GROUND CHICKEN: One-pound plastic tubes of very finely ground, soft chicken meat. Flavor and taste is excellent, but not like ground beef or pork. Use it for grilling chicken burgers, or for fresh chicken sausage. It contains 17% to 18% fat. (See Index: Chicken Burgers, Boudin Blanc Sausage.)

John, now you've got very good scientific facts on chicken and salmonella. If J.J. handles her chicken with reasonable care, neither she nor your kids will suffer from salmonella. Also, just a suggestion, John. Please ask her to read this chapter on chicken. She'll learn some facts on how to buy chicken — you know she really wants to know the facts rather than believe Blossom's rumors.

# Trusty Turkey

## One of America's Outstanding Meats

f J.J., John's continuously "food-panicked" wife, and the "food-panicked" portion of the press ever get started on turkey — wow! Look out! Turkey has early the same salmonella potential as chicken. Thank goodness they haven't arted. There's not need for them to, because turkey is safe when handled orrectly. The same good sanitation rules apply to turkey as they do for chicken.

Some 50 years ago, turkey was served in only the most affluent households - and then only at Thanksgiving or Christmas. In recent years, turkey can be a everyday food for nearly everybody. At the supermarket, you'll find "turkey-verything" today. From sliced turkey breast meat, 97% fat free, through the hole dressed turkeys weighing from 7 pounds up to 30 pounds. Even turkey otdogs are here! Finally, you'll descend down to "turkey ham" containing nearly 2% added water along with a few other added ingredients. It's labeled 95% fat ee.

With this watered turkey ham and other watered foods, please remember HARLIE'S kNOTE-WORTHY 1990s Food Law: "EAT WATER . . . it's 100% at Free," but expensive — $1 or more per glass purchased as "watered" meats, herwise water's free. Turkey is an exciting, low-cholesterol/low-fat dietary meat. urkey gives you a low-cost source of protein — and cooked correctly, a delicious od.

### The Big Turkey Cooking Problem

The breast of a turkey starts out with approximately 16% fat with 75% of is fat in the skin. Therefore, turkey breast meat contains only 4.0% fat. This east meat needs to be protected from drying out when grilled. If you're smoking a water smoker, it will not dry out too badly! However, use a meat thermometer d stop smoking when the bird reaches 165°F. in the breast/thigh skin pocket.

BUYING FACTS: (1) Whole dressed turkeys average yielding 69% cooked eat and 31% bone and skin. (2) Hen turkeys are processed to weigh 8 pounds 14 pounds, and toms 16 pounds to 24 pounds. In the 14-pound to 16-pound oup, you'll find a mixture of large hens and small toms. Buy the hen every time; ey'll have short, stubby legs and very full breasts. (3) Normally you'll need ¾ 1 pound of ready-to-cook bone-in whole turkey to feed one person adequately.

## Kinds of Turkeys

Live turkeys are divided into two general groups 99% come from the large broad-breasted breeds The large-breed toms weigh 16 up to 40 pounds and the hens up to 16 pounds. Most U.S. breeders produce white turkeys because they don't leave black pin feathers and hair in a dressed turkey.

## Frozen or Fresh Turkey?

WHICH SHOULD YOU BUY? Only at holidays will you find fresh-dressed turkeys at a reasonable price in many U.S. supermarkets. And even these may be thawed, frozen turkeys. Frozen whole turkeys are available year-round at more reasonable prices than fresh. You'll find frozen turkey breasts, thighs, legs, wings, and prepackaged frozen ground turkey meat year-round. Most frozen whole turkeys have been injected with 3% to 5½% turkey broth, sugar, phosphates, salt, hydrolyzed vegetable protein (a safe soybean product) and vegetable oil. This helps keep the turkey breast meat moist while smoking or roasting.

FROZEN TURKEYS: Most whole dressed turkeys are vacuum packaged, then flash frozen, in a heavy, white plastic bag. This bag is sealed to keep out moisture and oxygen. This means the turkey can be held frozen for up to a year. If shipped correctly to the supermarket a minus 10°F. to minus 20°F., never thawed, and sold within 6 months after processing, a flash-frozen turkey nearly equals fresh-dressed turkey. Use a frozen turkey within 6 months of purchase to keep it from growing rancid. The turkey may have been stored for 6 months before you purchased it. Turkeys' fat contains lots of poly-unsaturated fats which become rancid quickly.

If the plastic bag is broken, the turkey will "freezer burn." How do you buy what you can't see? Highly advertised, national-brand frozen turkeys are not always the best buys. Look for the USDA "A" Grade seal. You'll get a good bird.

To buy maximum quality, you'll need to examine the frozen whole turkey for the broadness of the breast. This means no sharp breast bone because you want it nearly covered with meat. Also, a sharp breast bone probably means a small, immature turkey. SECRETS does not recommend that you buy a frozen, stuffed turkey to smoke-cook. In one test, the cooked turkey meat's temperature was 200°F. (way overdone) and the stuffing, a very unsafe 90°F.

## High-Quality Frozen Turkey

When your frozen turkey is thawed, examine it for: (1) a full, plump, broad breast, with its breast meat filled nearly even with the breast bone; (2) any signs of having been thawed and refrozen (thigh and wing back areas may have collected lots of very bloody-colored ice); (3) no black and blue bruises; (4) no pin feathers and hair. Smell the abdominal cavity opening for spoilage and rancidity of the fat. You may have purchased an old turkey carried over from the previous holiday season and the fat is rancid. Frozen high-quality turkey may look blue under the skin on the back, but after thawing it has a white skin. However, if your turkey does not measure up, return it immediately to the meat dealer for a refund or exchange. If you do not plan to cook your turkey within 96 hours, save your receipt for later when you do your quality-check.

## Whole Turkey Sizes

Fryers up to 7 pounds: May be only 2 months old. They're not full-flavored when cooked. You'll be more pleased with buying parts, such as thighs or breasts. to 14 pound size: You can be quite positive it will be a hen. The processor has injected this turkey with liquids. However, doing your own injection of legs and thighs plus more to the breast will produce a juicier turkey. 14 to 16 pounds: May e full-grown hen or an immature tom. Look for broad breast and short, stubby egs and it will be a hen. 16- to 20-pound-and-up turkey: will be a tom 4 to 5 months old. It will have been injected. But, inject the thigh and leg and the breast you want to cook it beyond 165°F. up to 185°F. doneness. Check for broadness nd deepness of the breast meat.

## Turkey Parts

FROZEN BONE-IN TURKEY BREAST: Four-and-one-half pounds to 8 ounds, white meat only. It contains 10% injected turkey broth, etc. It will have onsiderable rib bones beyond the breast bone, which are waste. Buy the heavier irkey breast, more meat with less bone. You may have your meat dealer cut the irkey breast into ¾"- to 1"-thick steaks and cut across the breast bone for grilling. 3ecause of its low fat, you must baste or marinate these steaks with some oil. This ounds like a good idea, but the skin, bone, and fat loss is high.

FRESH BONE-IN TURKEY BREAST: Four pounds to 8 pounds, probably njected with 10% liquid (not labeled so you can tell). Turkey breast has 79% neat and 21% bone along with the skin.

TURKEY THIGHS: Contain 70% meat and 30% bone and skin.

TURKEY LEGS: Must be extremely low priced to compensate for the bone nd hard tendons, which are a loss. Legs are a tasty meat, however.

FROZEN BONELESS TURKEY ROLL: Three to four pounds, completely leboned white and dark meat with skin with 15% added liquids. The meat proba- ly comes from a small turkey (convenient, expensive, use in an emergency). A rozen bone-in turkey breast probably is a better buy.

FROZEN GROUND TURKEY: One-pound frozen plastic tubes used for re- placement of ground beef or other meats. (See Index: Turkey Sausage.)

## Preparing Whole Turkeys

DO-IT-YOURSELF TURKEY INJECTION: Turkey processors inject turkey roth, salt, phosphates, and hydrolyzed vegetable protein (a soybean product) nd vegetable oils into the breast of most turkeys. These injected solutions are afe to eat. They help keep the turkey's breast moist during cooking.

If you can buy a turkey without the processor-injected liquids, make your wn turkey broth by stewing the giblets in a little water to make a concentrated roth. Then inject 4 to 6 ounces with an animal syringe (large animal needle) in 3 to 10 different places under the skin of breast, thigh, and legs. In place of broth, ou can inject the turkey with melted margarine or butter. Any one of these will ncrease the juiciness of your turkey and greatly improve the leftovers, but in- reases the fat calories.

## Thawing Frozen Turkey

When thawing a 12- to 20-pound frozen turkey, there are 3 problems: (1) getting the frozen neck out of the abdominal cavity, (2) getting the frozen sack of iblets out of the neck cavity or the abdominal cavity, depending on the size of the turkey, and (3) keeping the turkey's skin temperature cold enough to control bacterial growth.

Each turkey starts out at minus 10°F. up to 0°F. from the freezer. You must warm the meat to the 60°F. before the turkey starts reproducing large numbers of bacteria in hours. The U.S. Public Health Service (USPHS) recommends thawing frozen poultry in a refrigerator. SECRETS' experience: It takes three or more full days to thaw a 20-pound frozen turkey in a refrigerator. If you have enough home refrigerator space to store a frozen turkey for 3 days or more, use it. It's the safest and the best way. Today's serious home cook is a very busy woman/man who must fit cooking into her/his tight schedule. Three days to thaw a turkey just doesn't "cut it" for many home cooks. The USPHS and the USDA recommend running cold tap water over the frozen turkey for several hours for faster thawing. This cold water thawing still takes hours and uses lots of water.

If you have a microwave oven, and a small turkey (under 12 pounds), and 30% power level for defrosting, start here. The metal leg-holding clip in many frozen turkeys is extremely hard to remove. Microwave experts tell us it is not a problem for the newer ones unless it touches the oven's side walls.

Do not thaw the turkey in the sink or in a pan on the kitchen table at room temperature all day. Do not cook a turkey without thawing it. You'll overcook thawed meat while cooking the frozen area "done" and safe.

PAPER BAG THAWING METHOD: This is not an approved method. However, it's better than thawing in the sink. The approved running water thawing method allows the turkey's skin to climb to 55°F. to 65°F., the temperature of the tap water method.

One other method recommended by a recognized cookbook writer: Place plastic-sealed turkey inside a doubled brown paper bag. Then keep the bag at room temperature. These bags act as an insulator and create a "cool refrigerator" inside. SECRETS tried a three-brown-bag. The temperature of the turkey's skin in the bags during thawing was close to the 55°F. produced with the water thawing method.

## Preparing the Turkey for Smoking

You will gain maximum smoke flavor of the turkey in the neck cavity if you will cut the neck skin down to a one-inch "overhang" of the wishbone. Then trim the abdominal cavity skin, leaving a ½-inch "overhang." Smoke will penetrate these areas.

WISHBONE REMOVAL: To make longer slices of turkey, remove the wishbone before cooking. Locate the wishbone's two forked bones with your finger. Use a sharp knife and cut along and around each side of each forked bone. Lift the two bones about ⅛", then cut them off with poultry shears or a knife at the shoulder bone. Next, bend the wishbone up and twist or cut it off at the breast bone. You will be pleased with how nice the breast meat carves with the wishbone removed.

Happy turkey smoking, turkey grilling, and turkey eating. Please remember, don't overcook — you will dry it out.

# Under-rated Lamb

### Trying lamb is like kissing —
### Try it. You'll like it.

J.J., John's continuously "food-panicked" wife, said on Friday night after supper: "John, I'd like to get more adventuresome with our foods. I hate to just eat salad, chicken, turkey, fish, just a tiny bit of beef and pork. I'd like to eat something that's delicate and makes me feel like I've moved up in the world. John honey, I want to feel like a princess one more time in my life — my first time was that special brunch on our honeymoon. I know you remember!

"And, I've heard about lamb ever since I was a little girl. It always sounded so exotic — I know it's supposed to be expensive and all those scary 'chop' things, like lamb sirloin chops, sorta bother me. And I hear that it's got some saturated fats. I know I'm picky, but I'll even accept a little cholesterol this time to be adventuresome. I'd like you to grill lamb just one time for us. You're very adventuresome — you were when you married me."

John sucked in his belly quickly, and started off, "J.J., I'm a very tolerant guy, but have you ever smelled lamb cooking? My daddy served in the South Pacific in World War II and ate that Australian mutton to where he just quit eating at the army mess. He said mutton stinks up the complete house and it had that muttony, goaty' taste."

J.J. came right back with, "John, when have you ever eaten lamb? Not since I've known you. — Boy, aren't you intolerant of any new food ideas. You talk about my food prejudices, and you've got no sense of adventure. Well, fella, I think you'd better look in the mirror. Why can't we just try lamb? I'd like to be part of these adventuresome people who will even try it. Some say, "Eating lamb's like kissin'; if you really try it just one time, you'll like it'."

## Muttony Taste Disappears

J.J., you're right. John needs to "smell the coffee"! American lamb has changed greatly since World War II. . .and for the better. Besides, it's not mutton, it's Certified Fresh American lamb. Expert cooks have researched it and found answers to the "muttony" taste. They certainly don't recommend that you fry it and make milk gravy with the fat that's left.

Let's get rid of the one big old problem — the "muttony" off-flavor and odor. American GI's were fed Australian mutton during World War II, and it did have a muttony flavor. Even now, lambs from Australia and New Zealand are bred to produce wool, and are processed at 70 to 80 pounds. The Aussies and Nev Zealanders like their lamb with a stronger muttony flavor.

Good American lamb has a different but more unique flavor than beef, bu it does not taste rancid or "goaty." Our lamb now comes from meat-breed sheep which are grain fed for 4 to 8 weeks and weigh 125 to 140 pounds before pro cessing. This eliminates nearly all of lamb's "muttony" taste and odor. These larg lambs give us Certified Fresh American lamb, a new leaner lamb. This certified grading is performed by a USDA grader.

When you mention lamb to nearly anyone, their immediate reaction i "Lamb? Gosh, it's so expensive." Lamb has an expensive image, if they've gone to the "best" white tableclothed trendy restaurant. . .and ordered the "Sell d'A gueau Leait" (boned rack of baby lamb) at $50 for the entree with everything else extra, including your glass of ice water.

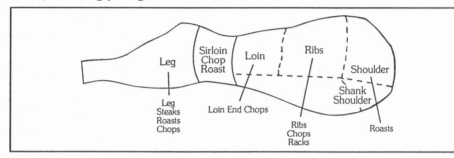

## Low Cost Lamb Steaks

You'll be surprised at the money-saving qualities of lamb, especially if you barbecue lamb leg steaks. Buy a whole leg of certified lamb about 7 to 9 pounds Have your meat cutter cut off the sirloin chops (sirloin steaks) and enough uppe leg steaks (not shank) one-inch thick to grill. Then freeze the rest for a small leg of lamb roast or for smoking later. Or he'll cut one or two lamb leg steaks for you which will be more expensive. If you buy a whole leg and cut lamb steaks, the will cost about the same as beef round steak. . .but they'll be naturally tender; you can grill them.

Or you can buy low-cost Certified Fresh American Lamb shoulder chops which compare in tenderness and juiciness with T-bone steak at only 50% to 60% of the cost of the steak. They are naturally tender, and don't need a tenderizer. However, you'll need to cut out the layered fat. This will lose about 20%, bu they'll still be reasonably priced, juicy, tender, and unique.

Many processors now package all of their primal cuts of lamb in vacuum packages. This allows you to age it for 10 to 14 days if you want to while it wholesomeness is protected. When you unwrap this aged meat, it may have a slight odor as does any vacuum-packed meat. But the odor goes away quickly.

LAMB'S HEALTH FACTS: Lamb contains 58% saturated fats and little fa marbling. You can trim off all surface fats and much of the inner layered fats easily. Three ounces of cooked lamb contains (1) About 78 mg. of cholesterol — no rea difference compared with roasted chicken dark meat with its skin off, beef, or pork. (2) And these three ounces contain about 176 calories, which is about equal with beef, pork, and chicken. Its balanced protein contains all 8 amino acids in proper ratios for easy absorption by humans. It has a reputation for being easy to digest.

## Compare Lamb and Mutton

If you want tender meat to grill, buy lamb! USDA's lamb-grading system divides lamb and sheep into (1) Lamb: under one year old which can be called *genuine lamb*" or *"lamb"* and even *"spring"* lamb. All Certified Fresh American lamb is as tender as any *"spring"* lamb available at Easter time in big U.S. cities. (2) USDA grade yearling mutton comes from one- to two-year-old sheep. (3) USDA mutton is any sheep over two years old.

Some British people are fond of mutton. We'll rarely find mutton in the U.S. supermarkets, only at large city ethnic markets. However, some is served at Western Kentucky barbecue restaurants and large political rallies.

The USDA graders tell whether it's lamb or mutton through visual inspections of the animal carcasses: (1) They check for the presence of a special bone joint just above the ankle on the front leg called the "break" joint on all lambs and sheep. During processing, this joint is exposed, and its four red, moist knobs tell them that it is lamb about 6 months old. If these knobs are white and dry — it's about 12 months old. If they have grown together to a solid bone, it is older than 12 months. (2) Round red rib bones mean younger lambs. Whiter flat rib bones means older animals. (3) Rarely will you see these grading points, but the USDA grader uses them every day to protect you, the consumer.

The USDA inspector grades each carcass: *Prime*, the top grade, is wasteful to buy because it carries too much extra fat. About 90% of the lamb marketed in the U.S. grades *Choice* or *Prime*.

## Certified Fresh American Lamb

This new grade was created in 1990 by U.S. lamb growers to meet consumers' desires for lamb with less fat. Certified Fresh American lamb must be USDA *Prime* or *Choice* with a fat cover of no less than 1/10" and no more than 1/4" thick over a lamb's loin section. The USDA grader checks for this and will stamp a blue "Certified" stamp on the primal cuts of approved lamb. This level of fat carries to the other cuts of the carcass which means more tender younger lamb without excessive fat. When you buy Certified lamb, you'll very rarely receive a cut which has a "muttony" flavor. Always fat-trim any cuts of lamb — this reduces the calories and the potential for "muttony" flavor.

## High Quality Lamb

The obvious choice is to buy Certified Fresh American lamb. If it is not available, buy USDA *Choice* grade. You will lose less fat in trimming and it's still tender. Many major *Primal* cuts — leg of lamb, shoulder, 8-rib rack, and loin — may be vacuum packed for safe storage up to 21 days when refrigerated at 40°F. or less.

High-quality lamb comes from live animals weighing from 90 to 150 pounds. The leg of lamb, complete with bone, weighs about 6 to 7 pounds if it comes from a 60- to 100-pound live lamb, and 9 to 10 pounds if it comes from 130- to 140-pound lamb. Other cuts from these lambs are sized in proportion to the size of the lamb.

The color of high-quality lamb ranges from pink red for the young 90-pound lamb, to a dull brick red in the 130-pound lamb. "Feed-lot" lamb has nearly the same bright red color as high-quality beef. High-quality lean will be firm, velvety, fine textured, and moist. FAT COVER: white, firm, waxy; BONES: center will be red, moist, and porous in a young lamb; MARBLING: lamb will have little or none. Even high-quality fresh lamb may have a slight "lamby" odor. You'll get lamb's unique flavor and no "lamby" odor after it's grilled or cooked.

## Imported Frozen Lamb

Frozen imported lamb takes 10% of the U.S. lamb market. New Zealand and Australia are the biggest exporters to the U.S. Their frozen lamb is darker in color and has a higher "muttony" flavor and odor. Their legs of lamb and other cuts are smaller than our American lamb because they raise smaller sheep for more efficient wool production. Like all frozen meats, examine the package for loose frost or "snow," freezer burn or broken packages, and thawed edges of the cuts.

## Lamb Cuts or "Chops"

In addition to lamb's reputation for off-odor and taste, lamb's cut names are different. Its cut names ("blade" and "loin chops," etc.) and prestige cuts of "racks," "saddles," and "crown roasts" keep some people from even asking their meat cutter about lamb.

Please don't be confused by lamb's "fancy cut" names. They were created by 16th century butchers who imitiated the emerging medical doctors' lead with their fancy new medical terms . . . only the butchers stopped with only 3 or 4 names because sheep couldn't talk back and admire their new technical language. AND as one of our local wags is fond of saying, "Old names never die . . . so it's lamb chops, and more chops."

The best way to understand lamb's chop terms and cuts: relate a lamb carcass to a beef carcass. Both have nearly the same bone and muscle structure. Today, a 130-pound lamb is a "miniature" beef and compares with a 1,300-pound steer. The lamb term of "chop" is confusing — but it came from the old-time butchers who were able to "chop" lamb's fine small bones with a meat cleaver. This saved them lots of time. Now, our meat cutters use meat saws.

LAMB CHOP COMPARISON: (1) A "lamb leg sirloin chop" is called a "beef flat bone sirloin steak." (2) A "lamb chop" is a short name for "lamb rib chop", which equals a rib pork chop from a hog or a rib steak from a beef. (3) A "lamb leg chop" may be called a "lamb leg steak" which equals a beef round steak. Lamb is simple; you relate it to beef.

RACK ROAST

SQUARE CUT
SHOULDER ROAST

LEG OF LAMB

## Rack and Crown Roasts

One fancy lamb name you'll hear is a "rack of lamb." This is one side of the rib section of the lamb carcass without the backbone. It contains 8 rib bones and the "eye" or muscle, just as a beef standing rib roast contains the "eye" or muscle and rib bones. Restaurants divide one full-sized 8-rib lamb rack into two 4-rib racks and charge megabucks for the two "racks." Or they divide it into one 2-rib rack and two 3-rib racks.

Meat markets cut this 8-rib rack into 8 single or 4 double lamb rib chops. Sometimes, they'll decorate these rib chops by "frenching" the tips of the rib bone — they cut the meat back from the ends of the rib bones about 1 inch, down to the lean eye meat of the chops. They may decorate this exposed bone with a "paper hat." Most crown roasts or rib chops are normally "frenched" by upscale restaurants. You can do it yourself. Some meat cutters "french" a whole leg of lamb by cutting the meat back on the shank; this provides a handle for the carver and makes an elegant presentation.

The most elegant restaurant presentation of lamb is a "lamb crown roast." Here the chef uses butcher's twine to tie two complete 8-rib racks together into a circle. The inside of the circle may contain a dressing.

### Saddle of Lamb

Whole dressed lambs are small, weighing 40 up to 75 pounds total each. To handle them efficiently, they are cut into two major divisions — the "fore saddle" and "hind saddle." You may hear someone talk about eating a saddle of lamb. This really consists of both loins — all bones still intact — you better bring really big money if you plan to eat it at a classy restaurant. Remember, you can "do-it-yourself" and that evening, light a couple of dinner candles; you'll be so impressive! Please don't forget to carve the saddle of lamb.

Then there's the lamb term "fell" — this is a thin membrane covering the complete exterior of the carcass after the skin is removed. Normally the "fell" is removed from chops — at least scored (cut through the fell and the fat) every 1½ inches to keep the lamb chop from curling while grilling. If you trim surface fat on the roast, you will automatically remove it.

SHOULDER BLADE BONE CHOP     LAMB RIB CHOPS     FRENCH RIB CHOPS     LOIN CHOP

### Grilling and Smoking Lamb

Use a cut ¾" to 2" thick. LAMB RIB CHOPS: Same cut as pork rib chop (pork chop); look for a large lean "eye" and little fat. Ask for the rib chops cut next to the loin; they'll have a larger eye. Grilled: Fat content 10.5%. LAMB LOIN CHOPS: Same as beef porterhouse steak and T-bone steaks. Contain the top loin muscle eye and a very small tenderloin muscle. They cost 30% more than the rib chops. Grilled: Fat content 7.5%. LAMB LEG STEAKS: Or "leg chops" — very little bone, nearly all lean. Grilled: fat content 7.75%. LAMB SHOULDER BLADE CHOPS: Contains blade bone of shoulder (same cut as pork steak). Buy a whole shoulder cut into 1-inch-thick chops. You can remove the fat layers easily. Fat content 10.0%. Don't Be Fooled: Neck slices are not loin chops nor blade chops, but look much like them in a meat case. Neck slices must be moist cooked, not grilled.

LAMB KABOBS: Cubes of lean tender lamb cut into squares 1¼" to 1 ½". Use thick slices from the shoulder or upper leg.

LAMB CUTS FOR SMOKE-COOKING OR GRILLING: Leg of lamb, shoul der, and rolled roasts smoke and roast well.

BONELESS ROLLED BREAST: Lamb breast is deboned, rolled, and tie with twine. Moist cook, then smoke for flavor. This is the toughest meat on lamt

DENVER RIBS: Breast bone,  rib tip bones, about 3" wide and 6" lonç trimmed of surface fat and connective tissue. These need long smoking to becom tender to cook out the fat.

LAMB STEW MEAT: Any lean piece of lamb cut from nearly any portion c the lamb carcass. Lamb shanks make especially flavorful stew meat.

GROUND LAMB: Available in large city supermarkets or ethnic stores. Mak your own by grinding a shoulder. Keep some surface fat for making many unusuá dishes, including Lamb Linguine. See Index.

## Don't Overcook Lamb

When cooked "well done" to 170°F. to 185°F., lamb dries out and lose flavor — it has little or no marbling. For the best flavor, juiciness, and tenderness cook lamb to the "pink done" stage which is about 145°F. to 150°F., or red rar 140°F. You grill it over high heat (500°F.) to sear, then cook to your likeness However, many people like lamb cooked to a non-pink done stage. Don't over cook past 165°F.

To keep your home free of lamb odor when cooking it, the American Lam Council recommends that you do not exceed 325°F. when roasting or sautein lamb. When you grill outside, you use 500°F. or a medium high fire and you ge only a delicious aroma when you sit down at the table or start to dine on thi feast.

## Surprise: Lamb's Comparative Low Cost

You can treat your family and guests to elegant lamb. . .and not spend half c next month's paycheck. We grilled Certified Fresh American lamb blade shoulde chops, and leg chops without marinading or tenderizing them. They're juicy an tender, great flavor without the "muttony" taste and odor. These lamb chops cos about the same price per pound as their comparable beef cuts — chuck steak an round steak. And you'll marinate and tenderize these beef steaks and still cros your fingers sometimes when you grill them.

Now lamb is no longer a mystery. It's just a delicious meat that's had a "ba rap" and it's greatly improved in recent years. Please don't "sell-it-short." (Se Index: Lamb Recipes.)

# Simply Delightful Fish

### Important inside information
### on delicious fish

J.J., John's continuously "food-panicked" wife, had a big mission in her life! She was determined to teach John all about the healthy goodness of eating fish.

She practically preached, "John, fish is nearly free of cholesterol, and low in fat, low in calories, and very high in protein. I'd rank it one notch above turkey on my approved food list. And, John, don't forget, eating fish gives you omega 3 fish oil, which is highly advertised as being lower in cholesterol. Yes, I know it has some P.C.B.'s from our gulfs, lakes, rivers, bays, and oceans. But Blossom Do-Rite told me that these problems did not really affect fish sold by the stores in the United States."

Then, she stopped and asked John one thoughtful question, "John, that 'fresh-fish' I bought at the supermarket yesterday, well, I didn't think it tasted like it was really fresh fish. I wonder how they get those ocean fish overnight so they can advertise, 'fresh fish' every day. We're 500 miles from the gulf, and 1,000 miles from the ocean. I've heard that Maine lobster gets here in 24 to 48 hours, but I also heard the air freight costs a pretty penny — and my fish wasn't all that expensive, nor was it really good tasting."

Well, John, with that thought you can say J.J. isn't dumb, and not "off-the-wall," all the time — when she asked about fresh fish every day at inland or even at many coastal supermarkets.

Some cookbook writers say, "Buy absolutely fresh fish from a fish monger." In much of the U.S., that's a tough order unless you become your own fish monger and catch 'em yourself, or live along the coast or next to one of the great lakes. Only a small percentage of the fish raised on fish farms (aqua culture) is sold fresh at local markets.

### Fresh Fish

Fresh fish means any fish which has not been cooked or processed, which changes its meat which can be described as "cooked." Roll mops are pieces of raw herring pickled in vinegar and become "cooked" fish, even though they are still raw. only an estimated 1% of the fish sold in the U.S. is fresh-from-the-water fish, available 24 to 48 hours after being caught.

America's fresh fish come from two sources. One major source is supermarket-thawed frozen fish. Cod, haddock, scrod, whiting, and halibut are caught in the North Atlantic. These fish are frozen in 15.4-pound boxes and larger, but consumers want to buy one 1 or 2 pounds. So a block of fish is thawed by the store. Other species come from Alaskan waters and are frozen and shipped to the supermarket, which thaws them. These fish have not been cooked; consequently, they can still be called "fresh."

The second major source of fresh fish comes from very large fishing ships which fish-on-location for two weeks in either the Atlantic or Pacific oceans. Then they travel to a U.S. port. These fish are stored in refrigerated sea water during this long wait. They are still fresh fish when shipped by truck or air to inland cities. Both kinds of fresh fish can be wholesome and tasty. However, some may be rated only "acceptable" because they are the best fresh fish of that species you can buy that time of year.

Some kinds of fish vary greatly from month to month during the year. For example, the fat content of herring varies from 8% up to 20% during the 12 months of the year. Only 11 out of 30 popular kinds of fish are available fresh every month of the year. There are 19 kinds of fish which have been frozen and thawed if you eat "fresh fish" during their off months.

## Fish Buying Problems

Buying fish can be complicated because there are more than 20,000 known species in the world. Over 100 of these are available in the U.S., having an estimated 300 different marketing names. Sometimes, the same fish species has three different names, even in the same city.

Fish's biggest quality problems occur when processed and shipped after they come out of the water. This handling may occur at several places and over a period of time before you cook them. This means that you can eat either top quality fish or some that are only "acceptable" for flavor, but generally are wholesome.

Fish naturally contain some spoilage bacteria when pulled from the water. These bacteria are adapted to cold water temperatures. Therefore, fish need icy cold temperatures of 31°F. to 32°F. (this compares to 34°F. to 36°F. for meats) to keep these bacteria in check during handling and shipping. Any spoilage started by bacteria releases the fish's natural enzymes, which causes much more rapid spoilage and fishy off-odors and flavors. Fish contain lots of unsaturated fats (omega 3) and that's why they're "heart healthy." These fats become rancid quickly, causing off-odors and flavors.

## Your Seafood Market

SECRETS gives you some guidelines for buying much higher quality fish than just "acceptable." Become aware of "fishy" odors and you'll buy higher quality. Spend some time training your nose to sniff out poor-quality fish so that you don't buy them. You sniff "fishy" dead old odors: (a) as you walk into the store, (b) at the store's fish counter, and (c) the fish itself.

Pay careful attention to the market where you buy fish! Good seafood markets should have a sweet, briny, fish odor, not an old, dead "fishy" odor at the fish counter. Fishy odors are usually heavier in the summertime. Good stores clean up thoroughly daily and handle lots of good quality fish. Many leave the heads on the fish they sell, then fillet them in front of you. Fish already filleted go downhill faster.

Supermarket Storage of Fresh or Thawed Fish and Seafood: The supermarket should store fish in plastic bags or on metal trays sitting on ice in the counter. When displaying fillets and steaks, the tray should contain little juice. If they display whole fish, their heads should be tilted "uphill" with the cavities draining.

When you go to the supermarket, be willing to accept a fish which may be your second choice. When you buy the second choice fish, you may receive better quality that day.

Look for fish which carries the PUFI seal (Packed Under Federal Inspection) from the U.S. Department of Commerce and is labeled U.S. Grade A. Only about 11% of the fish brought to port are inspected. Only about 1/3 of these will be Grade A; these are mostly frozen fish. This voluntary grading is paid for by the fish processor. Nearly all of the remaining 89% of the fish are wholesome and healthy. Imported fresh or frozen fish are not graded.

Buy from an established fish market. Roadside truck dealers may be dealing with seafood from contaminated waters. Buy individually "flash" frozen fish that are still frozen, if you can store them and use them efficiently. You'll save one to two days extra freshness, compared to the same thawed frozen fish in the store. Fresh or thawed fish and seafood stored on ice in a market have a short shelf life. Some good fish cooks feel that they get better-quality frozen ocean fish that are still frozen then "fresh ocean fish" which have been frozen and are now thawed.

## Fish Buying Terms

When talking with the supermarket, know these fish terms: (1) <u>Whole fish or "round":</u> These are fish as they come from the water, guts and all, and will yield about 45% of edible meat; the rest is waste; (2) <u>Drawn:</u> eviscerated or gutted, yields 50% edible meat; (3) <u>dressed fish (pan dressed):</u> eviscerated or gutted, scaled, head and fins removed, yields 67% edible meat; (4) <u>Steaks:</u> skin on and bone in, cross-sectional cuts of larger fish, 84% yield; (5) <u>Fillets:</u> strips of fish cut lengthwise parallel with the backbone, 100% yield; (6) <u>nuggets and chunks:</u> pieces of fish, 100% yield.

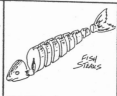

ROUND FISH     DRESSED FISH     FILLETS     FISH STEAKS

## High-Quality Fresh Fish

Use smaller-sized whole fish for better flavor, rather than fillets of steaks.

BUYING GUIDELINES: EYES: crystal clear, bright, full bulging black pupils; GILLS: bright red or pinkish red, containing a clear thin mucous, free of slime, have no off-odor; SKIN: bright, shiny, metallic skin, glistening scales stick tightly to the skin; FLESH: firm, elastic when pressed gently with your finger, flesh fills back in fairly fast; flesh is translucent, moist-looking when cut; flesh sticks to the bones, does not separate, not dark, cloudy, or cottony; AROMA: fresh, mild, very faint fishy sea breeze odor; and BODY CAVITY: clean, no blood or viscera, smells clean, no old, off-odor.

## High-Quality Fillets and Steaks

BUYING GUIDELINES; FILLETS: strips of fish ¼" to ¾" thick cut lengthwise parallel with the fish's backbone with or without skin; does not separate into segments or start to flake. More different kinds (species) of fish are filleted than cut into steaks. STEAKS: ¾" to 1" thick cross-sectional slices of larger 3-pound to 6-pound or larger fish including the backbone. The cut flesh should be translucent, clear, firm, elastic, bright, glistening, and moist on both sides of the cuts with cleanly-cut edges. FINGER TEST: your finger dent fills back in fairly quickly when pressed gently. When you run your finger over the fish, it is moist, but free of slime; and AROMA: smells fresh with a mild fresh sea breeze odor.

## Basic Fish Groups

Fresh and salt water fish are divided into two basic groups. These two groups are further divided into high fat and low fat by species or kind. Fish's fat concentrates in the liver. When fish are eviscerated, the livers are removed and the fat level drops below 5% in many kinds of fish.

## Salt Water Fish

### SALT WATER — LOW FAT UNDER 5%

Cod (Scrod: cod under 3 pounds)
Cusk
Drum
Flounder (sole family)
Grouper
Haddock (Finnan Hadie)
Halibut
Hoki (Whiting)
Monk
Mahi Mahi (dolphin fish)
Ocean Perch
Pollack

Pout
Rock
Salmon-pink, chunk
Sea Bass
Sea Trout
Snapper (red)
Sole
Swordfish
Turbot (European)
Whiting (hoki)
Wolf

### MEDIUM FAT — 5% TO 10%

Butter
Herring
Mackerel (Spanish)
Orange Roughy
Pompano
Salmon (Atlantic, Coho, Sockeye)
White

### HIGH FAT — over 10%

Eel
Herring
Mackerel
Mullet
Sable
Salmon (Chinock)
Shad
Turbot (Greenland)

DOVER SOLE

GREENLAND TURBOT

RED SNAPPER

HADDOCK

WHITING

FLOUNDER

ATLANTIC COD

## Fresh Water Fish

OW FAT UNDER 5%

ass
uegill
eam
atfish (channel)
rappie
erch
ke
alleye

IGH FAT — OVER 10%

el

MEDIUM FAT — 5% TO 10%

Buffalo Carp
Carp
Coho Salmon
Herring
Lake Trout
Rainbow Trout (steelhead)
Salmon
Smelt
Sturgeon
Whitefish

RAINBOW TROUT

CHANNEL CATFISH

BLUE GILL

SILVER SALMON

If you're traveling with fish, wrap in plastic wrap and layers of newspaper for xtra insulation. Place in a thick efficient cooler. For longer than 72 hours, if the roduct is not frozen, <u>don't ice, but freeze seafood.</u>

Fresh caught, eviscerated, and degilled fish will travel well in a refrigerated uck buried in ice. However, when buying absolutely fresh fish, look for those nat are produced locally, such as trout or catfish produced on local aqua culture ish) farms.

HOME STORAGE OF FISH: Keep fish at 32°F. or below in your refrigerator ) have high-quality fish. Place them in a plastic bag on ice on the bottom shelf f a 45°F. or lower home refrigerator for overnight storage. Use as quickly as ossible. If you can't use fresh fish quickly, you'd better freeze it. If these are fish ou have caught, handle them quickly, and get them on ice. If you can't use them ו 2 days, you'd better freeze them. Refreezing fish reduces its quality.

## Frozen Fish and Seafood

Ocean-going fishing ships now flash freeze fish and other seafoods. They reeze them soon after them come out of the ocean. The processors use two nethods: (1) Individually Quick Frozen (IQF). Each piece is glazed with a water pray, then exposed to sprays of liquid nitrogen. This completely freezes small ieces in 4 minutes. (2) Block frozen fish and seafood, which takes longer to reeze. IQF seafood preserves more of the seafood's original quality than other reezing methods.

Commercially frozen fish should be handled carefully — all the way from the ea to the market's display freezer and finally to your home to be first quality. ⁄lake sure the packaging has no tears or holes. This fish should be solidly frozen, ven to the edges — no discoloration or browning, or dry looking or papery dges; no freezer burn or signs of dryness; no white cottony patches on the fish, ⁄r dry, dull icy look on the fish's surface or loose white snow in the package. All hese indicate fish which have been frozen for a long time.

Individually frozen fish, when repacked by the supermarket, should be balanced in the center of the package, with no formed ice in the package. The packaging should be tightly wrapped around the fish. If rosy colored or white ice forms in the plastic display tray, the fish may have been thawed and refrozen when repackaged. Look for supermarket expiration dates on the package.

## Frozen Fish

Take frozen fish home quickly with no side trips. If you are <u>not</u> going to cook it, leave it in its original wrapping and place it in the freezer immediately. When frozen fish is thawed, it should look firm and glossy without a dull, shredded surface.

When fish is slowly frozen in a home freezer, bigger ice crystals are formed. Always freeze fish against the sides of the freezer. To thaw frozen fish, place in plastic bag, then submerge the bag in a pan of cold water. Or you can thaw in a microwave, following oven manufacturer's instructions. Then cook the fish immediately.

Some good fish cooks rejuvenate thawed frozen fish, or seafood, by soaking them in salt/baking soda water for 30 minutes (½ gallon cold water, ½ cup salt, 3 tablespoons baking soda). Then rinse fish thoroughly. This soaking takes out freezer odor and freshens the fish.

## Fresh Caught Fish

Fish have fast working and brutally efficient digestive juices to digest their food. After a caught fish stops living, these powerful juices digest the fish's own stomach walls in a matter of a few hours. Consequently, their stomach and intestinal contents can <u>be carried into the flesh of the fish itself</u> if it's not gutted. If you don't gut them, you'll have spoiled, off-flavor fish, which are not very safe to eat.

The opaque flaking done stage of some cooked fish is only 135°F. This temperature is not high enough to kill some of the common food-borne bacteria. Therefore, as soon as fish die, they should be eviscerated to eliminate this potential contamination. Trailing caught fish alongside the boat lowers its quality very quickly. Hit the fish on the head and gut it.

MUDDY FRESH FISH: Eviscerate them within 1 to 2 hours after removal from the water, if possible. Fillet the fish and soak in heavy salt water — ½ cup salt per quart, plus 2 ounces vinegar for 1 to 2 hours. Refrigerate during the soaking time. After soaking, flush with tap water to remove salt.

## Home Freezing and Cooking Fish

Place fish in milk cartons and cover with ice water and freeze them. Fish that re two pounds or less in size can be frozen whole. If they are five pounds or 1ore, cut them into steaks or fillets. Make certain that the freezer runs at 0°F. or )wer. Store fatty fish for 3 months and lean fish for 6 months.

## Cooking Fish

Many people say, "I'm afraid to try to cook fish." They have this fear because 1ey do not have basic information. *Fish have no tough connective muscle fibers ke other meat animals. Many raw fish change from a water-translucent appear-nce to an opaque done at about 135°F. Always check the thickest portion of neat next to the backbone. When the flesh becomes opaque, stop cooking.*

People use a porcelainized metal plate with ¼" holes and turn grilled fish asily. It's worth the small cost. One brand is called the "Grill Topper." Other peo-le use a wire-framed fish holder.

# DELICIOUS SEAFOOD

Seafood is more perishable than fish and should be handled more carefully. It may have fed in contaminated waters. When purchasing from an established market, generally these factors have been taken care of for you. HOW TO TELL IF SEAFOOD IS FRESH: To be safe, buy only live lobsters which close their tails when you pick them up. Live crabs and crayfish actively wave their legs and claws. Live oysters, clams, and mussels, etc., close their shells tight. Shrimp tails feel firm and smell sweet, not soft, old, and fishy.

## Shrimp (Low-Fat)

Scampi is the "fancy" name given to shrimp by pricey trendy restaurants. They sell large shrimp for scampi at megabuck prices. Shrimp are different animals than scampi. There are few true scampi. If the Chinese restaurant menu lists "brushwood" shrimp, it obviously will be an exotic way to eat shrimp. Say, "No thank you," unless you like to eat cooked grasshoppers.

SHRIMP

Shrimp tails with the shells on are graded and priced by size. Extra large shrimp cost more. The best word descriptions for shrimp: Colossals: are less than 10 per pound. (Some people call these prawns, but technically they are not. Prawns are from fresh water, and shrimps are from salt water.) Jumbos — come 10 to 15 per pound, Large — 16 to 20 per pound, Medium — 21 to 30 per pound, Small — are 31 to 35 per pound. You'll find smaller ones even up to 60 per pound. Tiny ocean salad shrimp will have about 150 per pound and are the lowest price. There are 300 species world wide. The U.S. imports more than 50% of its shrimp. Over 90% of the imported shrimp are frozen.

"FRESH SHRIMP": Unless you live close to the gulf, or southeast U.S. coast, raw ("green") shrimp tails are probably thawed from frozen shrimp by your seafood market. Buy tails that are fully filled, firm, have a springy feeling and are clean smelling. Raw shrimp tails' natural colors range from greenish gray to brownish red. Their color depends upon what part of the world they come from. All shrimp change color to a bright pink when cooked. You'll lose 50% in weight when you take off the shells and devein the shrimp. Cooked shrimp can be refrigerated for five days. You can store thawed green shrimp at 32°F. for two to three days. Do not buy tails which have black or dark gray rings next to where the shell segments join each other. These have been held too long before freezing.

FROZEN SHRIMP: If you have freezer space, buy 2- or 5-pound boxes of frozen shrimp and thaw your own. Check for the black rings. If you plan to keep them frozen for weeks, and if there is no ice cover, add ice water to the top of the box. When it freezes, it will help retain their original quality.

COOKING SHRIMP: Shrimp are very easy to overcook to a "tough" stage. After 2 minutes of cooking time in boiling water, start checking the tails with a toothpick. When they are solid, firm, and pink remove from the hot water and cool in cold water to stop further cooking. If grilling, cook about 3 to 6 minutes on a medium hot fire. Check for doneness using the toothpick method.

## Crabs (Low Fat)

An American statesman, John Hay, said, "There are two species of creatures, and when they're seen coming — they're going." He included women and crabs. We don't think that old John Hay could stay with the pace of American women today! And about crabs, well, he's correct, they travel backwards. Next to shrimp, crabs are the most popular seafood in the U.S. There are 4,400 species in the world and are all edible.

HARD SHELL BLUE CRABS: These come from the East Coast and Gulf of Mexico. They have a fresh sweet smell — no off-odors. Remove their legs, if you are buying live crabs.

SOFT SHELL CRABS: The hard-shelled blue crab molts (sheds) its hardshell to grow. At this stage, you clean it, cook it in a little butter, and eat the meat and soft unformed shell and all. Some people rave about them.

*CRAB*

DUNGENESS CRABS: One of the largest crabs which comes from the West Coast. They are one of the finest, most delicious crabs and can be shipped cooked. They weigh 1¼ pounds up to 3½ pounds.

ALASKAN KING CRABS: Frozen cooked legs, claws, and clusters. Remove part of the shell and reheat gently; don't cook very long, they'll toughen easily. They have finer firmer flesh than other crabs. Buy precooked ones to grill. Baste with butter after removing part of the shell.

SNOW CRABS: About ½ the size of king crabs. These come from the Atlantic and Pacific Oceans. Some people feel they have a superior flavor and texture. They are sold cooked and frozen.

SOUTHERN STONE CRABS: Primarily from Florida — delicious — only the claws are eaten.

PASTEURIZED CRAB MEAT: Available in some larger city markets. It has nearly a fresh crab taste and texture. Processors heat raw crab meat in a sealed can to a high enough temperature to pasteurize it. This kills the bad bacteria, but it is not heated high enough to give it a canned flavor. Must be refrigerated and eaten within 4 to 5 days.

## Lobsters (Low Fat)

WHOLE LOBSTERS: Live lobsters in supermarket tanks start to lose flavor as soon as they are removed from the ocean. Any lobster kept in a tank over 5 days will be of much poorer quality. Seafood experts say that lobsters packed in seaweed have a better flavor because they are inactivated and still kept alive. Lobsters should be alive until they're cooked. Live lobsters curl their tails under their body when picked up.

Lobsters are normally the most expensive seafood in the U.S. Live lobsters come from the Northeast Coast, down to New Jersey. The U.S. imports millions of pounds from Canada. Suppliers sell them by size: "chicken lobsters" — one pound each; "quarters" — 1¼ pound each; "large" are 1½ to 2 pounds each and "jumbos" are over 2 pounds.

You need to buy lobsters with a hard shell. Soft shelled and watery lobster are poor quality. The tail and the two large claws contain the most meat. You'll receive about 33% edible meat from a whole lobster. When buying cooked lobster meat, it should be snow white with a red tint. Whole fresh lobsters can be shipped by air. Don't overcook them because you'll make them tough. If you grill a whole lobster, it should be killed and split. Place the lobster on a flat surface and quickly insert a knife where the tail joins the body to kill it, then split the tail to grill.

LOBSTER TAILS (low fat): These come from the African rock lobster family which are not technically lobsters, but are close relatives of crawfish. Normally the frozen tails are 1 ounce to 8 ounces in size. The U.S. imports most of them, but produces some off the shores of Florida. This same lobster tail is produced on the West Coast and called the spiny lobster. They have no claws like a standard lobster and grill nicely. You must thaw them completely a short time before cooking to keep them tender. Use low temperatures and a short cooking time. All lobsters turn brigh red when cooked. They're done when the flesh turns opaque.

MINIATURE LOBSTERS: These are sold as "rock shrimp." They look like medium-sized shrimp, but have a lobster taste. They are harder to clean than shrimp, but lower in price. They are found in seafood markets next to the seashores in the U.S. They may also be found frozen in some large city markets.

## Oysters (Low Fat)

Pre-Columbian Indians on both the Atlantic and Pacific Oceans made oyster stew — native Americans taught the New England settlers how to make it.

Only live oysters are safe to eat. They keep their shell closed tightly when live. Eastern oysters come from the Gulf of Mexico up the coast to Massachusetts. They're bigger than the Olympian (Western) oysters, which come from the Puget Sound areas. Oysters may be eaten the year around in the U.S., not just in the "R" months, as it is normally thought. The "R" months produce bigger, more solid oysters. The summer months produce thinner, watery ones.

Oysters have names such as Blue Point, Long Island, etc., which indicate the area where they were grown. Refrigerate live oysters with their deep cup shell down so their juice cannot leak out. Cover them with a damp cloth. Oyster meats should be plump, have a creamy color, a good aroma, and be sure they are surrounded by clear liquids. One quart of shucked oysters equals 36 medium-sized oysters. Shucked oysters are graded by size. Be certain to buy oysters from a good seafood market. Eating them raw may be somewhat chancy because of the virus which they can carry.

## Clams

Clams can live from 1 to 10 years. They develop growth ridges on their shells. Their heart beat ranges from 2 to 20 beats per minute. Consequently, they don't move even as fast as the turtle. So Mother Nature must bring their food to them. They bury themselves in sand or mud. If you eat them raw, be on guard about the markets where you buy them. Clams can carry virus diseases. Steaming one minute or more to open them does not kill the viruses down in the meat.

*CLAMS*

There are two major kinds of clams on the East Coast: (1) round "hard-shell", and (2) long necked "soft-shell" clams. Clams go by market sizes: "little neck" for the smallest; "cherrystone," up to 3 inches in diameter, and "chowder" size over 3 inches in diameter. The largest are used to make clam chowder because they are tougher and obviously older. Quahog ("ko-hog") is the American Indian name for clams. It is used on the East Coast. Cherrystone and little neck are market names for Quahogs. Geoduck ("gooey-duck") is the West Coast clam and is much larger, weighing up to 5 pounds including the shell. "Steamers" are long necked soft-shell clams. They have thin, long shells, and their necks extend beyond the shell.

BEST QUALITY CLAMS: Fine-textured, concrete gray-colored shells. Coarse-textured, light-yellowish striped shells mean a softer meat with less flavor. Broken or slightly open shells indicate that the clams are dead.

## Scallops

There are three kinds: (1) "sea scallops," big 1½-inch to 2-inch in diameter (2) "bay scallops," ½-inch to ¾-inch in diameter. They are fewer, have a shorter season and are more expensive; and (3) "calico scallops" from Florida, ½-inch in diameter. The meat should be firm and have a sweet smell. Usually they have white meat, but tan, orange, or blue-tinted meat is satisfactory. Don't overcook. Use larger scallops for kebabs or grilling.

## Crawfish (Low Fat)

Crawfish has other names — crayfish and crawdads. This is one of the major undiscovered seafoods in the U.S. This brown 4-inch to 6-inch creature's tail and large claw taste like lobster. In fact, they are lobsters' kinfolk. Louisiana and other southern states and California now have crawfish farms. They alternate with rice giving the farmer two crops per year.

When buying live crawfish, make sure they wiggle their claws to be safe to eat because they spoil quickly. Stun them in ice cold water for 30 seconds, then cook the tails quickly in boiling water. They'll toughen if overcooked. Frozen tail meat is available as well as whole, frozen cooked crawfish and certainly as fresh ones in season in certain areas of the U.S.

## Mussels (Low Fat)

Mussels are one of the safer shellfish because people cook them as compared to oysters. They are a neglected, overlooked seafood. They're delicious and tastier than oysters. They come from the East and West Coasts. They must be alive before being cooked. You can tell if they're alive by holding the shell between the thumb and forefinger. Then try to slide the top shell across the bottom one. Throw away any that slide too easily because they're sick.

Mussels have a "beard" which looks like seaweed which attaches to rocks. must be removed as well as any sand before cooking to have good mussels. may take work to harvest them out in the wild. It takes work to remove the "beard" and prepare them ready to be eaten, but they're tasty when steamed or grilled very gently. Available shucked, cooked, pickled, and frozen. When the shell open, they are cooked. Don't overcook; you'll toughen them.

CRAWFISH

# NEW UNIQUE BARBECUE CORRESPONDENCE COURSE

## The Culinary Institute of Smoke-Cooking's

## Master Cook-Out Cook Correspondence Course

Be recognized as a MASTER COOK-OUT COOK!

Eliminate cook-out's many uncertainties and embarrassments.

Invest in a lifetime of more flavorful foods and pleasure for your entire family and friends.

Dare to dabble in the profitable business of BBQ.

Discover 100's of new BBQ secrets through hands-on training with your own BBQ equipment. The cookbook, *BARBECUE & SAUSAGE-MAKING SECRETS*, serves as your comprehensive textbook.

# "A good job of conveying accurate information…"

Dr. Max Judge, Meat Scientist of Purdue University

**D**r. Charles E. Knote, author of *BARBECUEING & SAUSAGE-MAKING SECRETS*, and gourmet cook, Ruth Knote, have prepared this exciting, informative course for everyone who enjoys cooking outdoors.

With the assistance of registered dietician, Patti Knote, this correspondence course will tremendously increase your knowledge of barbecuing and sausage-making. You'll learn many secrets you won't learn elsewhere.

Enroll today for a fee of $100 which may be tax deductable depending on your eligibility. Or make an initial deposit of $30 followed by four monthly payments of $20 each.

This correspondence course must be completed within one year of enrollment to qualify for official certification by the Culinary Institute of Smoke-Cooking.

**TAX DEDUCATIONS FOR EDUCATIONAL EXPENSES**

---

# WORKS CONSULTED

1) American Heart Association, The American Heart Association Cookbook. Ballantine Books, NY, 1984.

2) Apicius, Cooking and Dining in Imperial Rome, Dover, NY, 1977.

3) Beard, James, The Theory and Practice of Cooking Good Food, Alfred Knopf, NY, 1977.

4) Bowers, Jane, "Meat Consumption Patterns and Influences," Muscle Foods Division, Institute of Food Technology, Volume 17, No. 1, Chicago, IL, 1991.

5) Childs, Julia, The Way to Cook, Alfred Knopf, NY, 1989.

6) Escoffier, Auguste, Escoffier Cookbook, Crown Publishing Company, NY, 1969.

7) Farrell, Kenneth, Spices, Condiments and Seasonings, Second Edition, Van Nordstrand Reinhold, NY, 1990.

8) Fletcher, Anne, Eat Fish, Live Better, Harper & Row, NY, 1989.

9) Gisslen, Wayne, Professional Cooking, John Wiley and Sons, NY, 1989.

10) Harris, Marion, The Sacred Cow and the Abominable Pig, Simon & Schuster, NY, 1985.

11) Judge, Max, et al, Principles of Meat Science, Kendall/Hunt Publishing Company, Dubuque, IA, 1989.

12) McGee, Harold, On Food and Cooking, MacMillan Publishing Company, NY, 1984.

13) Missouri Beef Council, "Check Off News," Jefferson City, MO, (Winter 1991).

14) National Livestock and Meat Board, "Identifying Meat Cuts" Chicago, IL.

15) Ockerman, Herbert, Sausage & Processing Meat Formulations, Van Norstrand Reinhold, NY, 1989.

16) Pearson, Albert, et al, Processed Meats, Van Norstrand Reinhold, NY, 1984.

17) Poretz, Mel, et al, The First Really Important Survey of American Habits, Price, Sterns, Sloan, LA, 1989.

18) Reitz, Carl A., A Guide to the Selection, Combination and Cooking of Foods, The Avi Publishing Company, Westport, CT, 1961.

19) Romans, John, et al, The Meat We Eat, Inter State Publisher Printers, Danville, IL, 1966.

20) "Salt," St. Louis Post Dispatch, November 24, 1990.

21) Sleight, Jack, et al, Home Book of Smoke-Cooking, Stack Pole Books, Harrisburg, PA, 1971.

22) Smith, Jeff, The Frugal Gourmet Cooks American, Morrow Company, NY 1986.

23) Wells, Carolyn, Barbecue Greats, Memphis Style, Pig Out Publications, Kansas City, MO, 1989.

## Supplier of Sausage Material

The Sausage Maker, 177 Military Road, Buffalo, NY 14207
Supplies a complete line of casings, etc., for making sausage by mail. Ask for free mail order catalog.

# Notes

# Notes

# INDEX

Dear Charlie & Ruthie,
 thoroughly enjoy your new cookbook, *BARBECUING & SAUSAGE-MAKING SECRETS*. It's very useful. I would like to see the following stores carry it:

Name _____ Phone _____

Address _____

City/State/Zip _____

Name _____

Address _____

City/State/Zip _____

Comments _____

_____

_____

_____

Signature _____

✂ -----------------------------------------------------------------

Dear Charlie & Ruthie,
 thoroughly enjoy your new cookbook, *BARBECUING & SAUSAGE-MAKING SECRETS*. It's very useful. I would like to see the following stores carry it:

Name _____ Phone _____

Address _____

City/State/Zip _____

Name _____

Address _____

City/State/Zip _____

Comments _____

_____

_____

_____

Signature _____

## Culinary Institute of Smoke-Cooking
### 2323 Brookwood Drive
### Box 163
### Cape Girardeau, MO 63702-0163

❑ Please send me _____ copies of Charlie and Ruthie Knote's *BARBECUING & SAUSAGE-MAKING SECRETS* at the price $14.95 each plus $2.50 shipping and handling.
*(Missouri residents add 6.125% sales tax)*

❑ I have enclosed my check/money order for $ _____
Mail *SECRETS* to the following address:

Name _____

Address _____

City _____

State/Zip _____

*Please allow 3 to 4 weeks for processing and delivery*

✂ - - - - - - - - - - - - - - - - - - - - - - - - - - - - - - - - - - - - -

## Culinary Institute of Smoke-Cooking
### 2323 Brookwood Drive
### Box 163
### Cape Girardeau, MO 63702-0163

❑ Please send me _____ copies of Charlie and Ruthie Knote's *BARBECUING & SAUSAGE-MAKING SECRETS* at the price $14.95 each plus $2.50 shipping and handling.
*(Missouri residents add 6.125% sales tax)*

❑ I have enclosed my check/money order for $ _____
Mail *SECRETS* to the following address:

Name _____

Address _____

City _____

State/Zip _____

*Please allow 3 to 4 weeks for processing and delivery*